THE ADVENT OF THE FATIMIDS

The Institute of Ismaili Studies
Ismaili Texts and Translations Series, 1

The Advent of the Fatimids

A Contemporary Shi'i Witness

An Edition and English Translation of
Ibn al-Haytham's

Kitāb al-Munāẓarāt

by

WILFERD MADELUNG AND PAUL E. WALKER

I.B.Tauris
LONDON • NEW YORK
in association with
The Institute of Ismaili Studies
London

Published in 2000 by I.B.Tauris & Co Ltd
Victoria House, Bloomsbury Square, London WC1B 4DZ
175 Fifth Avenue, New York NY 10010
website: http://www.ibtauris.com

in association with The Institute of Ismaili Studies
42–44 Grosvenor Gardens, London SW1W 0EB

In the United States of America and in Canada distributed by
St Martins Press, 175 Fifth Avenue, New York NY 10010

ISBN 1 86064 551 8

A full CIP record for this book is available from the British Library
A full CIP record for this book is available from the Library of Congress

Library of Congress catalog card: available

Typeset in ITC New Baskerville by Hepton Books, Oxford
Printed and bound in Great Britain by WBC Ltd, Bridgend

The Institute of Ismaili Studies

The Institute of Ismaili Studies was established in 1977 with the object of promoting scholarship and learning on Islam, in the historical as well as contemporary contexts, and a better understanding of its relationship with other societies and faiths.

The Institute's programmes encourage a perspective which is not confined to the theological and religious heritage of Islam, but seek to explore the relationship of religious ideas to broader dimensions of society and culture. They thus encourage an interdisciplinary approach to the materials of Islamic history and thought. Particular attention is also given to issues of modernity that arise as Muslims seek to relate their heritage to the contemporary situation.

Within the Islamic tradition, the Institute's programmes seek to promote research on those areas which have, to date, received relatively little attention from scholars. These include the intellectual and literary expressions of Shiʿism in general, and Ismailism in particular.

In the context of Islamic societies, the Institute's programmes are informed by the full range and diversity of cultures in which Islam is practised today, from the Middle East, South and Central Asia and Africa to the industrialized societies of the West, thus taking into consideration the variety of contexts which shape the ideals, beliefs and practices of the faith.

The above objectives are realised through concrete programmes and activities organised and implemented by various departments of the Institute. The Institute also collaborates periodically, on a programme-specific basis, with other institutions of learning in the United Kingdom and abroad.

The Institute's academic publications fall into several distinct and interrelated categories:

1. Occasional papers or essays addressing broad themes of the relationship between religion and society in the historical as well as modern contexts, with special reference to Islam.
2. Monographs exploring specific aspects of Islamic faith and culture, or the contributions of individual Muslim figures or writers.
3. Editions or translations of significant primary or secondary texts.
4. Translations of poetic or literary texts which illustrate the rich heritage of spiritual, devotional and symbolic expressions in Muslim history.
5. Works on Ismaili history and thought, and the relationship of the Ismailis to other traditions, communitics and schools of thought in Islam.
6. Proceedings of conferences and seminars sponsored by the Institute.
7. Bibliographical works and catalogues which document manuscripts, printed texts and other source materials.

This book falls under category three listed above.

In facilitating these and other publications, the Institute's sole aim is to encourage original research and analysis of relevant issues. While every effort is made to ensure that the publications are of a high academic standard, there is naturally bound to be a diversity of views, ideas and interpretations. As such, the opinions expressed in these publications must be understood as belonging to their authors alone.

Contents

Preface

The purpose of this volume is to present to the modern world a new source for the history of the rise of the Fatimid caliphate in North Africa. The work is a personal memoir composed by a scholar from Qayrawan named Abū ʿAbdallāh Jaʿfar b. Aḥmad b. Muḥammad b. al-Aswad b. al-Haytham. He called it the *Kitāb al-Munāẓarāt* ('The Book of Discussions') and included in it a record of his own conversations as a young recruit with the leaders of the Ismaʿili mission in Qayrawan in its crucial first few months there. As a document of this kind for a period so remote, it is unique; and, as will be seen, not only does it belong among the most valuable sources for the history of medieval North Africa, but also deserves a special place in the literature of Islamic revolutionary movements.

Despite the obscure origins of the Ismaʿili movement and the provincial remoteness of the Maghrib where these events took place, what we know about the advent of the Fatimids comes to us from an unusual array of sources, owing in part to the religious character of what transpired and the inherent hostility of the parties to each other. In the Maghrib itself, which later fell almost exclusively under the control of Mālikī Sunnism, the Fatimid caliphate came to be remembered for religious heresy and repression. Nevertheless, in local histories and chronicles, Mālikī writers preserved information about the appearance of the new dynasty and, in the literature of the classes of scholars (*ṭabaqāt*), they related many relevant details in the individual biographies of those who suffered through it. Fatimid sources remembered the same events, although from a decidedly sympathetic point of view. For the Isma'ili writers the advent of the Imam as caliph represented a major defining moment in history. It was the restoration of true religion, the end of Sunni repression, the triumph of good over evil, a victory of righteousness, an arising of God's friends to a position of power and the suppression of those who had unjustly usurped their proper God-given place.

The final steps of the Fatimid revolution, which saw the collapse of the former Aghlabid governorate and the rise of a Shi'i caliphate in its place, occurred, from the perspective of the predominantly Sunni inhabitants of Qayrawan, relatively quickly. For a brief time they suspended their natural hostility to the Isma'ili *da'wa* that was behind the new ruling power while they waited to see what might happen and how they and their personal religious loyalties would fare under the new regime. An answer was not long in coming and within months the Sunnis of North Africa reasserted their old enmity toward the Shi'is who, in turn, undertook to suppress this opposition. Still, despite lingering resistance, the Ismailis had won and, some ten months later, their Imam appeared to proclaim his rule in Raqqāda, the administrative city-suburb of Qayrawan, in the year 297/910, and to establish a dynasty that was to last for two and a half centuries.

Up to now Isma'ili libraries have produced at least two highly informative accounts of the Fatimid revolution. One, the work of Qāḍī al-Nu'mān, is a general history of the coming of the movement from the east to the Maghrib and its progress there until it finally achieved the victory that subsequently allowed it to establish a state. The other is more personal; it features the story of the Imam's travels from Syria to Egypt, to the distant Maghribi town of Sijilmāsa, and ultimately to Raqqāda, as told by the manservant Ja'far who accompanied him.

All along, however, there existed among the records preserved by the Fatimids and their Ṭayyibī successors in the Yemen yet a third major source. This personal memoir by the North African scholar and *dāʿī*, Ibn al-Haytham, which he had called with deceptive simplicity the 'Book of Discussions' (*Kitāb al-Munāẓarāt*), contains a fascinating reconstruction of his own personal encounters with the leaders of the revolution just after its initial victory. Although apparently not mentioned by works written during the later Fatimid period, it survived nonetheless and was copied verbatim into a sixteenth century compilation of texts assembled under the title of *Kitāb al-Azhār* by Ḥasan b. Nūḥ al-Bharūchī, a distinguished Ṭayyibī author of Indian extraction.

Although its importance becomes obvious upon a careful reading of this unusual text, Ibn al-Haytham's *al-Munāẓarāt* has, until now, not been consulted for the information it supplies about the rise of the Fatimids, and has only been available as a manuscript, and that as one relatively small part of al-Bharūchī's massive collection of other Isma'ili works. It is, however, replete with information about details of events and conversations that took place during the first months of Isma'ili rule – the period from the victory of the *dāʿī* Abū 'Abdallāh in Rajab 296/March 909 until the arrival of the Imam al-Mahdī in Rabīʿ II 297/January 910. Moreover, it supplies us directly with an insider's view of the thoughts and attitudes of the major players, what they said to each other and how they explained what they did, particularly for the two brothers, Abū 'Abdallāh, who was the architect of the Fatimid triumph, and Abu'l-'Abbās, who was to govern North Africa for almost seven months, from June 909 until the Imam finally arrived to claim his caliphate.

Detailed information about that particular period has been scarce. With the discovery of these memoirs of Ibn al-Haytham, however, the situation changes dramatically. It is precisely this early phase that he covers in his record of intimate conversations with these leaders and rulers. He thus recounts for us both major events and the words of those who were a part of them. Moreover, he often explains the background to them. A native of Qayrawan and a Shi'i scholar in his own right, he was an eager convert to the Fatimid cause and the Isma'ili *daʿwa.*

Thus, his was an uncommon perspective. Having come to the movement from within the previous scholarly milieu, he could offer a uniquely detailed view of how the scholars of Qayrawan reacted to the new power and its religious policies. Ibn al-Haytham's work thus provides precious information about his native city and, in general, presents in its various discussions a rare intellectual portrait of a time and place: Qayrawan, the provincial capital of the Maghrib at the end of the third Islamic century. Most revealing are his impressions of each of the two brothers who were to control his life for most of that revolutionary year in 296–7/909. Once the brothers and several of their chief supporters had been accused of treason and executed, later Fatimid tradition was not always well disposed to them. In fact it laid heavy blame on Abu'l-'Abbās, and therefore, one of the most fascinating features of Ibn al-Haytham's account is its entirely laudatory depiction of the brothers, both of whom impressed and deeply influenced the author, though each for slightly different traits and virtues. And, as a record of the Isma'ili *da'wa* and its *dā'īs* in action, it is unparalleled. Here is a personal account of a Shi'i sympathizer's recruitment, conversion, oath of allegiance, and training as a new *dā'ī*. There are in it, as well, a few highly significant hints and allusions about the author's own subsequent career in that same *da'wa*. All in all, this text adds enormously to our understanding of the Fatimid takeover in North Africa and to the exact role in it of many of its key figures.

Because this text has been, until now, unknown in modern scholarship, we have assumed the burden of presenting it and the information in it in as complete a form as possible. It is, thus, necessary first of all to provide here a critical edition of the Arabic text of Ibn al-Haytham's *Kitāb al-Munāẓarāt*. We have added to that a comprehensive translation with full notes and an extensive introduction in order not only to explain the technical terms and references in the text, of which there are a great many, but also to link the work to its historical background and the previously known sources about events and individuals mentioned in it.

Acknowledgements

Several years ago I read an interesting conference paper by Professor Sumaiya Hamdani, a younger colleague in the field of Isma'ili studies, about a series of Sunni–Isma'ili debates that had taken place in the Maghrib during the first few months of Fatimid rule there. Her account reminded me that, among the undigested materials that I had then collected, there was a text of obvious relevance to the same subject – one that I had once examined rather cursorily and put aside without a further look. Spurred on by a renewed interest partly stimulated by this unexpected coincidence, I returned to that manuscript. It was Ibn al-Haytham's *Kitāb al-Munāẓarāt,* and I discovered that it was not the ordinary doctrinal treatise I had once thought it to be. Instead it proved astoundingly rich in information about a host of issues connected with the advent of the Fatimids, a fact that became more and more evident as I worked through it in the precise and careful detail necessary in order fully to apprehend and appreciate all that it has to offer.

Now convinced of its exceptional value, I proceeded to transcribe it and look for additional manuscripts from which to form an edition of the Arabic text. Luckily, Professor Abbas Hamdani, an old friend and mentor in matters of this kind, was willing to supply a copy of the one he owns personally, and I must register my sincerest thanks for his generous help on this occasion as so many times in the past. Another two were in the possession of The Institute of Ismaili Studies in London and, with the kind assistance of Dr Farhad Daftary, Mr Alnoor Merchant, and other friends there, I obtained photocopies of those as well.

With all three in hand I produced a preliminary version of the text and began to analyse the great variety of names of persons, of incidents, and items of either religious or philosophical doctrine in it, and to compare all this information with material in the other previously published sources for North African history at the time of the Fatimid revolution.

As this project grew more complex, I frequently found myself consulting Professor W. Madelung (as I had done with many other previous investigations, but especially most recently in the effort that resulted in our joint collaboration in bringing the *Ismaili Heresiography* of Abū Tammām to print). Again it soon seemed natural that we pool our resources and knowledge and that we continue this project as another joint effort.

Our primary task was to establish a critical edition of the Arabic text prior to undertaking a translation of it and adding an introduction and commentary. In this case, although the manuscripts are not themselves badly corrupted, many names and details in the work have been lost in the transmission of the text. All of the copies available to us are quite recent. To amend the text properly, we used a number of different resources as well as the advice and expert knowledge of several colleagues, among them Professors Emilie Savage-Smith, Wadad Kadi, Muhammad Ali Khalidi, and Heinz Halm. Dr. F. W. Zimmermann at one point read carefully the philosophical discussion that begins part two of the work and he suggested a number of emendations as well as providing important references to secondary materials. Likewise Professor Everett Rowson examined an early draft of both the Arabic text and the translation of the second part and offered many useful suggestions for its improvement. At a final stage in the preparation of the English portion of this study, Bruce Craig read the text and caught a number of errors.

Paul E. Walker

Introduction

1. THE HISTORICAL BACKGROUND

The Fatimid Revolution

As the defeated Aghlabid state collapsed, its last ruler fled ignominiously in the direction of Egypt. Behind him a Kutāma Berber army swarmed towards the administrative city of Raqqāda. The victors in a long struggle for revolutionary change in the Maghrib, the army was led and directed by its 'lord' and chief, the Isma'ili missionary-*dā'ī* Abū 'Abdallāh called locally the 'Shi'i'. The end of Abū 'Abdallāh's struggle had come swiftly, so swiftly that his troops were not even close to Raqqāda when the Aghlabid Ziyādatallāh, seized by fear and wanting to carry away as much of his gold and other movable possessions as possible, loaded a caravan of pack animals and left. The populace in the vicinity, and from as far away as Qayrawan, a distance of some 9 kilometres, rushed out ahead of the advancing army to plunder and loot the palaces of the recently departed prince. For several days, no one interfered with their rampage. Finally, however, the first troop of calvary – the advance guard of the new power – reached Raqqāda and immediately brought order and calm. Not long afterwards, Abū 'Abdallāh arrived to take up residence in one of the old Aghlabid palaces where he launched a new government, and with it a new era. A largely conservatively Sunni province of the once unified 'Abbasid caliphate almost overnight became Shi'i and would no longer pay allegiance in any form to the supreme ruler in Baghdad.[1]

The events just recalled occurred in early Rajab 296/late March 909. The victory which had brought Abū 'Abdallāh and his Berber army to power gave him instant dominion over the whole of Aghlabid territory, including the areas of modern Tunisia, Algeria, portions of Libya, and Sicily. In realizing this achievement, however, he was not acting for himself but on behalf of an Imam who was at that triumphant moment still under house arrest, two months' march away, in the distant Maghribi town of Sijilmāsa. The revolution wrought by the *dā'ī*, though at last in possession of a vast political domain with its attendant resources, was thus incomplete. Without its Imam it lacked the real reason for its existence; the appeal, the *da'wa*, on which it was based, and for which it was created, depended on the safe arrival of the Imam and the eventual proclamation of his caliphate and the right of his Fatimid ancestors and descendants to rule the Islamic world. But that was not to happen for almost another ten months. Only in late Rabī' II 297/January of 910, did the Imam finally reach Raqqāda where he was proclaimed caliph with the messianic regnal name of al-Mahdī.[2] The intervening months were, however, critically important for the new government. Abū 'Abdallāh, though long accustomed

1. For the broad general background to the Fatimid victory, see in particular Mohamed Talbi, *L'Emirat Aghlabide (184–296/800–909)* (Paris, 1966); Farhat Dachraoui, *Le Califat Fatimide au Maghreb, 296–362/909–973: histoire, politique et institutions* (Tunis, 1981), and most especially Heinz Halm, *Das Reich des Mahdi: Der Aufstieg der Fatimiden (875–973)* (Munich, 1991), Eng. trans. M. Bonner, *The Empire of the Mahdi: The Rise of the Fatimids* (Leiden, 1996).

2. The most recent general study of the beginning of the Ismaili movement and its relationship to the advent of al-Mahdī as imam-caliph is Halm's *Reich des Mahdi,* but see also the important article by W. Madelung, 'Das Imamat in der frühen ismailitischen Lehre,' *Der Islam,* 37 (1961): 43–135, and Farhad Daftary, *The Ismā'īlīs: Their History and Doctrines* (Cambridge, 1990), especially 91–143.

to lead, was without experience in the requirements for ruling cities and large territories. His previous career as a *dāʿī* was in the main limited to the Kutāma Berber tribes which had formed his immediate following and supplied his army. Now he had to create a government for an empire. But his most urgent task– a task he would entrust to no one else – was to assemble an expeditionary force to rescue the Imam.

Yet while he was absent from Raqqāda in pursuit of his mission, he needed to delegate the government of North Africa to a completely reliable person from among those loyal both to him and to the *daʿwa* for which he worked. Fortunately for Abū ʿAbdallāh and for his revolution, such a figure was available in the person of his own brother who, at the moment of Fatimid victory, was awaiting news of the outcome of Abū ʿAbdallāh's struggle in Tripoli, to the east of Raqqāda. When Abu'l-ʿAbbās, whom he had not seen for almost eighteen years, during which the brothers had pursued separate careers in the *daʿwa*, at last joined him, Abū ʿAbdallāh appointed him to rule in tandem with the Kutāma leader Abū Zākī and set out for Sijilmāsa. Until the return of Abū ʿAbdallāh in the retinue of the liberated Imam al-Mahdī, Abu'l-ʿAbbās was to all intents and purposes the ruler of the former Aghlabid, now Fatimid, state.

In contrast to the remoter regions, where Abū ʿAbdallāh found an enthusiastic Berber following, the religious proclivities of the Arab elite of the North African cities were at the time dominated by scholars belonging to either the Mālikī or Ḥanafī legal schools, both of which were quite hostile to Shiʿism (the Ḥanafīs by and large less so than the Mālikīs). There were, nonetheless, some learned and moderately influential Shiʿis in the major urban centre of Qayrawan who had in the past been forced to conceal their beliefs.

In the period before the Fatimid army launched its final drive toward Qayrawan and Raqqāda, the local *fuqahā'* were more concerned with their own, often quite intense, internal rivalries. The Ḥanafīs were generally pro-ʿAbbasid, while the Mālikīs were pro-Umayyad. Perhaps in accordance with these tendencies, the Aghlabid court, following the policies of the caliphate on behalf of which it governed, tended to favour the Ḥanafīs, while the Arab populace favoured the Mālikīs. The advent of the Fatimids and the onset of a Shi'i revolution in their midst obviously caused a severe dislocation and unsettling trauma for the Sunnis of North Africa.

Before the collapse of the Aghlabid state, friction aroused by the old conflict between the Mālikīs and the Ḥanafīs was often aggravated by theological disputes between Mu'tazilī and Murji'ī Ḥanafīs and traditionalist Mālikīs. Despite evidence of a certain degree of respect and accord between various individual scholars of both sides, enmity and harsh disagreements could, and frequently did occur. In this situation, the *madhhab* of the qadi of Qayrawan became a crucial matter. The appointment of a Ḥanafī judge could signal a period of revenge against the other side, and certain of the Mālikīs who specialized in disputation were noted for their antagonism toward and deliberate baiting of the Ḥanafīs.

The task of the new rulers, even in the period before the arrival of the Imam, was thus complex and difficult, and neither Abū 'Abdallāh, nor Abu'l-'Abbās, nor most certainly any of the Kutāma leaders in their retinue were quite prepared for it. The measures they took and the events of the months between the military victory and the arrival of the Imam, nevertheless, form a key chapter in the story of the establishment of the Fatimid caliphate. Many aspects of how the new regime was to organize and present itself were determined during that period. When the Imam al-Mahdī who, like the brothers, had never governed a territorial state, nor ruled over subjects who were not already his sworn adherents, assumed full power, he tended to confirm the appointments and the policies they had initiated, although they were by then no longer themselves in charge.

Barely two days after his assumption of power, on Monday, 3 Rajab 296/27 March 909, Abū 'Abdallāh received a congratulatory visit from Ibn al-Haytham, a visit which was to bring this young scholar into the *da'wa* and membership of the movement behind the rise of the Fatimid caliphate. That moment was for

Abū 'Abdallāh important enough, but for Ibn al-Haytham it was obviously unforgettable and many years later he could still recall it in remarkable detail. This event marked the beginning of his own career with the Fatimids and it is also the starting point of his personal memoir of what happened to him over the next ten months.

The Career and Mission of Abū 'Abdallāh

Although to a casual observer the career of Abū 'Abdallāh may seem spectacularly successful and his rise to power swift and stunning, the process had in reality been slow and difficult.[3] When he received Ibn al-Haytham on the second night of his triumph and his residence in the old Aghlabid palace, Abū 'Abdallāh could complain of having spent almost eighteen years in the field. Over these long years he had patiently propagated his message and that of the *da'wa* among the Berbers of the Algerian hinterland. Indeed, two of his companions on that same night, the men who introduced Ibn al-Haytham to Abū 'Abdallāh, were the Kutāma chieftains Abū Mūsā b. Yūnus al-Azāyī of the Masālta and Abū Zākī Tammām b. Mu'ārik of the Ijjāna,[4] whose association with the *da'wa* had begun far back with the arrival on Kutāma territory of the *dā'ī* on Thursday,

3. The main source for the career of Abū 'Abdallāh is Qāḍī al-Nu'mān's *Iftitāḥ al-da'wa wa ibtidā' al-dawla*, ed. by Wadad Kadi (Beirut, 1970), and by Farhat Dachraoui (Tunis, 1975). For convenience in what follows references will be given only to Dachraoui's edition. Compare also Halm's reconstruction of these events in his *Reich des Mahdi*.

4. Abū Mūsā was known as the 'shaykh of shaykhs' (*shaykh al-mashā'ikh*) and obviously played an important part in the mission of Abū 'Abdallāh. The account of Ibn al-Haytham confirms this judgement. Nonetheless, there is remarkably little information about him in the other sources, perhaps because of his later treason and execution. See Qāḍī al-Nu'mān, *Iftitāḥ*, Dachraoui's introduction, p. 52 n. 2, 70–1, 132; paras 46, 109–10, 282; Idrīs 'Imād al-Dīn, *'Uyūn al-akhbār*, ed. M. al-Ya'lāwī as *Tā'rīkh al-khulafā' al-Faṭimiyyīn bi'l-Maghrib: al-qism al-khāṣṣ min kitāb 'Uyūn al-akhbār* (Beirut, 1985), 89, 183–4; Abu'l-'Abbās Aḥmad b. Muḥammad al-Marrākushī Ibn 'Idhārī, *al-Bayān al-mughrib fī akhbār al-Andalus wa'l-*

15 Rajab I 280/June 893.

Upon meeting the young Ibn al-Haytham, Abū 'Abdallāh, as was clearly his long-standing habit, proceeded without hesitation to engage him in an elaborate interrogation about his religious views and attitudes. The *dā'ī* obviously realized the importance of winning the local Shi'is to the Fatimid cause and of expanding in this way the *da'wa* among the Arabs in the newly conquered urban populace.[5]

Abū 'Abdallāh's own recruitment and affiliation had begun long before in his native town of Kufa in the Arab east. There, in about 278/891, Abū 'Abdallāh, whose full name was al-Ḥusayn b. Aḥmad b. Muḥammad b. Zakariyyā', was brought into the *da'wa* with his older brother, Abu'l-'Abbās Muḥammad,[6] by a *dā'ī* called Abū 'Alī in Fatimid sources, but known in Iraqi and 'Abbasid records as Ḥamdān Qarmaṭ, names which may both be assumed to have cloaked his secret and highly dangerous activities. This Abū 'Alī/Ḥamdān Qarmaṭ was then head of the *da'wa* in 'Iraq.[7] Fairly soon after their conver-

Maghrib. Vol. 1, ed. G. S. Colin and É. Lévi-Provençal (Beirut, 1948), 160; Abū Bakr al-Mālikī, *Kitāb Riyāḍ al-nufūs fī ṭabaqāt 'ulamā' al-Qayrawān wa-Ifrīqiya*, ed. Bashīr al-Bakkūsh (Beirut, 1981–83), II, 62–3; Halm, *Reich*, 152, 153f, 218, trans., 163, 165–7, 242. For Abū Zākī, the case is similar, even though he was nominally in charge of the government during Abū 'Abdallāh's absence. See Qāḍī al-Nu'mān, *Iftitāḥ*, 33, 53, 70, 92, 121, 125, 133, 134, 273–5, 312 (para. no. 286, on his execution); Idrīs, *'Uyūn*, 89, 110–11, 124, 156, 165–9, 184–6; Ibn 'Idhārī, *al-Bayān*, I, 126, 152, 163; Halm, *Reich*, 122, 133f, 136, 153–5, 161, trans., 130, 141, 145, 165–6, 174. His uncle Abū Yūsuf Māknūn b. Ḍubāra was head of the Ijjāna tribe of the Kutāma and as such occupied a major place in the campaigns of the Fatimid army. Much later he was governor of Tripoli, at which time he was forced to execute his own nephew.

5. It is noteworthy, however, that he had apparently made no effort to do so prior to the final conquest.

6. For complete references to Abu'l-'Abbās in the sources, see below n. 72.

7. For the identity and career of this *dā'ī*, see Wilferd Madelung's recent study 'Ḥamdān Qarmaṭ and the Dā'ī Abū 'Alī,' *Proceedings of the 17th Congress of the UEAI* [Union Européenne des Arabisants et Islamisants], (St. Petersburg, 1997), 115–24.

sion, he dispatched the two brothers to Egypt. In Egypt Abū 'Abdallāh joined the annual pilgrimage caravan to Mecca. From there he moved on again, accompanying Yemeni pilgrims returning to the Yemen where he joined the local *da'wa* of the famous Manṣūr al-Yaman, Ibn Ḥawshab, in early 279/April 892.[8] The Isma'ili *da'wa* was by that time spreading rapidly in numerous far flung directions, but of these the mission of Ibn Ḥawshab, begun in 267/881, was the most successful in terms of the acquisition of territory and power.[9] Not quite a full year later, the *da'wa* ordered Abū 'Abdallāh once again to join the Yemeni pilgrimage caravan and return to Mecca. For this assignment he was paired with another *dā'ī*, a certain 'Abdallāh b. Abi'l-Malāḥif, who was, in fact, subsequently to accompany him all the way to his eventual destination in Kutāma territory. Such joint missions were the preferred method for spreading the *da'wa.* In this case it caused extreme hardship for Ibn Abi'l-Malāḥif's daughter, who is reported to have lost her mind when her father disappeared. Out of pity and sympathy for her plight, Ibn Ḥawshab eventually sent a replacement so that Ibn Abi'l-Malāḥif could return to her.[10] That second *dā'ī* was Ibrāhīm b. Isḥāq al-Zabīdī, known in the Maghrib as the 'lesser lord' (*al-sayyid al-ṣaghīr*) because he was junior in rank to Abū 'Abdallāh who was called simply the 'lord' (*al-sayyid*).[11] This second *dā'ī* was still with Abū 'Abdallāh many years later in 296/909 when Ibn al-Haytham met him.

The point of noticing these details is the indication they provide of the careful planning and preparation that went into Abū 'Abdallāh's mission. The official account of it emphasises his astute exploitation of an incidental opportunity to win over some Kutāma pilgrims who he happened to meet in Mecca

8. On Ibn Ḥawshab in general see W. Madelung, 'Manṣūr al-Yamān,' in the *EI2*, and for his early activities also Halm, *Reich*, 38–44, 55–7, trans., 31–9, 51–3.

9. On the spread of the Ismaili *da'wa* in this period, see Halm's *Reich des Mahdī*, as well as Daftary's *The Ismā'īlīs.*

10. Qāḍī al-Nu'mān, *Iftitāḥ*, par. 31 (pp. 31–2).

11. Ibid., par. 32 (p. 23).

and cleverly prompted to urge him to follow them back to their homeland. But the *da'wa* surely knew what it wanted him to accomplish and had some notion of how to go about it. Among the original party of Kutāma pilgrims, at least two were already Shi'i. There are, moreover, valid reasons to consider other instances of Shi'ism in the Maghrib prior to Abū 'Abdallāh's arrival there, particularly in regard to the mission of the obscure al-Ḥulwānī, mentioned in several places. Ibn al-Haytham refers to this person, who in Isma'ili sources is said to have been sent to North Africa by the Imam Ja'far al-Ṣādiq to spread Shi'ism there. However, these various accounts all name men who were converted by al-Ḥulwānī and yet who also met and supported Abū 'Abdallāh, which is chronologically impossible. Nevertheless, the Isma'ili *da'wa* is likely to have known a great deal about the situation and may have planned from the beginning to use it to its advantage.

Abū 'Abdallāh and his party, in any case, travelled back through Egypt where his brother had remained and where Abu'l-'Abbās would continue to work as an operative and courier in direct contact with the headquarters of the *da'wa* as a whole in Salamiya in north-central Syria, the residence of the movement's supreme leader. Abū 'Abdallāh himself reached the Kutāma controlled region of eastern Algeria in the mountains of the Lesser Kabylia in Rabī' 280/June 893. Thereafter he established an 'abode of refuge' (*dār al-hijra*) in a barely inhabited rural area known as Īkjān[12] and began to proselytize by teaching and instructing any of the Berbers who would listen and accept him. Among his very first recruits were Abū Zākī and Abū Mūsā, the latter already a powerful clan chieftain, and the former the young nephew of another.

Despite some success in the recruitment of important adherents, the mission of Abū 'Abdallāh was not always and

12. The exact location of Īkjān is known only approximately, in part because no direct physical evidence has survived to our day from this one relatively brief period. However, it was east of, and perhaps fairly near, Setif and certainly west-northwest of Constantine in what is modern Algeria. See Halm, *Reich*, 47, n. 92, trans., 41.

everywhere accepted. But, because he pursued his activities in the mountains and away from major cities, at first the Aghlabids ignored him. Odd and dissident religious movements among the unsettled Berber tribes were common and the central state government could ill-afford to send an army to put down each of them. Furthermore, it preferred to expend its military energy in the lucrative war against the Christians of Sicily and the Italian mainland which produced a steady supply of gold, loot, and slaves. Internal opposition to Abū 'Abdallāh's mission among the Berber groups soon developed, however. Not all were Shi'i, since many tribes were then, and continued to remain, Kharijite and thus implacably opposed to the Isma'ili appeal. Abū 'Abdallāh also ran foul of clan rivalries and at one point had to move his whole operation from Īkjān to Tāzrūt.[13]

Not until some time after Rajab 289/June 902 – shortly after the coincidental departure of the Aghlabid ruler Ibrāhīm II for the holy war in Sicily – did Abū 'Abdallāh risk an attack on a significant town, in this case Mīla.[14] His occupation of this town provoked the first overt reaction on the part of the central government. An ill-timed military expedition was sent against him which became bogged down in winter snows and thus proved ineffective. The Isma'ili cause was therefore not permanently harmed or suppressed; but Abū 'Abdallāh still moved slowly and with great caution. His next major victory did not occur until the autumn of 292/905 when he defeated an Aghlabid army and reaped a large reward of booty.[15] In the following March, Aghlabid troops, who were being assembled to move against him, revolted instead under their commander Mudlij b. Zakariyyā' and briefly occupied Qayrawan.[16]

13. These events have been recounted by Talbi, Halm, and others in greater detail, based primarily on Qāḍī al-Nu'mān's *Iftitāḥ*.

14. Mīla was a town in central-west Algeria, about a third of the way west from Constantine to Setif and thus in the middle of Kutāma territory.

15. He forwarded a portion of the booty to the Imam who was by then residing in Sijilmāsa. On this see below.

16. During this revolt they freed the inhabitants of the local prison – an event of special importance since one of the prisoners was Abu'l-

With the Aghlabid state showing signs of weakness and an inability to muster a strong resistance, the rebels began bolder operations. Ṭubna fell next in Dhu'l-ḥijja 293/Sept.–Oct. 906, followed by Bilizma. Bāghāya was taken in Sha'bān of 294/May-June of 907. These were important cities arrayed like steps on the route to Qayrawan and Raqqāda. But, despite such progress, the end was not in sight until a final confrontation took place at al-Urbus in the Spring of 296/909. When that last city fell to Abū 'Abdallāh on Sunday, 23 Jumādā II/19 March, Ziyādatallāh waited no longer but left Raqqāda himself on the same day. On Monday the looting of his palaces began and on Tuesday the only remaining Aghlabid general who might have opposed the Kutāma fled from his last refuge in Qayrawan. Upon learning of what had happened, Abū 'Abdallāh immediately dispatched Gazwiyya, one of his Berber commanders, with a detachment of 1,000 horses to scatter the looters and restore order as quickly as possible. Abū 'Abdallāh himself entered Raqqāda on Saturday, 1 Rajab 296/25 March 909.

The Coming of the Imam to North Africa

After the two brothers had been sent out on the respective missions assigned them, the supreme head of the Isma'ili movement died and was succ eeded by the man who was eventually to take the throne name al-Mahdī. In contrast to the policy of his predecessors, around 286/899 this new leader began to suggest in his official correspondence that he would soon publicly announce his claim to be the Imam.[17] His declaration

'Abbās, Abū 'Abdallāh's own brother. This event occurred in Jumādā II 293 (March 906). On the revolt of Mudlij, see Ibn 'Idhārī, *al-Bayān*, I, 139. The information about Abu'l-'Abbās's escape comes from Qāḍī al-Nu'mān's *Sharḥ al-akhbār fī faḍā'il al-a'imma al-aṭhār*, ed. Muḥammad al-Ḥusaynī al-Jalālī (Beirut, 1994), III, 430, and Qāḍī al-Nu'mān, *Iftitāḥ*, 260. See also Halm, *Reich*, 105, trans., 109, and 118, trans., 118; and Talbi, *Aghlabide*, 657ff.

17. On this development and its background see Madelung, 'Das

caused considerable consternation in many sections of the *da'wa*, particularly but not exclusively in the east, especially 'Iraq. Previous Isma'ili doctrine clearly held that the Imam was Muḥammad b. Ismā'īl b. Ja'far al-Ṣādiq who was then, according to the accepted teaching, in occultation and about to reappear as either Imam or Mahdi. What difference there might have been between this public expression of doctrine and a private, secret understanding on the part of the high ranking *dā'īs* is impossible to determine with any confidence. Nevertheless, there are obvious indications of a rejection of the new pronouncement on the part of some of them. What followed is fraught with confusion. *Dā'īs* such as the famous 'Abdān and his brother-in-law Ḥamdān Qarmaṭ (Abū 'Alī) at first denied the Imam's claim and broke off their activities on his behalf. Others, however, ostensibly remained loyal to him. Shortly afterwards 'Abdān was murdered by the loyalists and Ḥamdān disappeared, soon to re-emerge in Egypt using the name Abū 'Alī and once again firmly on the side of the new Imam.[18]

One result of the confusion, however, was the premature revolt in Syria of the *dā'ī* Zakarūya and his two sons, who were known in history as the Man with the She-camel (*ṣāḥib al-nāqa*) and the Man with the Mole (*ṣāḥib al-shāma*). The story of this revolt need not be repeated here.[19] Its importance in this context is that it constituted a dire threat to the position of the Imam in Salamiya and exposed him to 'Abbasid counter measures and potential arrest. Rather than chance a favourable outcome of the extremely risky venture of these *dā'īs*, whom he most certainly felt he could not trust, the Imam fled south just ahead of them to the Palestinian city of Ramla, there to await the result of their dubious adventure.

The climate within the *da'wa* as a whole, however, must have been one of turmoil, this revolt being but one sign of it. While

Imamat in der frühen ismailitischen Lehre.' The details of this particular schism are summarized in Daftary, *The Ismā'īlīs*, 125–35, and Halm, *Reich*, 64–7, trans., 62–7.

18. Madelung, 'Ḥamdān Qarmaṭ and the Dā'ī Abū 'Alī,' 117.

19. For a full account see Halm, *Reich*, 67–86, trans., 66–88.

these unsettling events transpired in ʿIraq and Syria, the areas of Egypt, Yemen under Ibn Ḥawshab, and the Maghrib continued as before, still loyal to the central leadership. By 286/899 Abū ʿAbdallāh had been in the field among the Kutāma for six years. Moreover, he was far from the conflict. Still, he was presumably in constant communication with headquarters, quite possibly through his brother in Egypt. Ibn al-Haytham adds to our information about this contact a story – one told by Abū ʿAbdallāh himself – about a *dāʿī* named Abu'l-Ḥusayn who had come to him and stayed in the Kutāma region for several years before returning to the east. But Abū ʿAbdallāh had never personally met either the previous or the new Imam. By contrast Abu'l-ʿAbbās worked as a go-between and often visited Salamiya from his main post in Fusṭāṭ. Unlike Abū ʿAbdallāh, he knew the leadership personally and from direct experience.[20]

The revolt in Syria and the Imam's flight to Ramla occurred in 289/902; he was definitely in Ramla during a meteor shower on 28 October 902 (Dhu'l-Qaʿda 289).[21] At that moment Abū ʿAbdallāh, though by then approaching his tenth year with the Kutāma, had still not undertaken any major military campaigns. By contrast the foolhardiness of an early revolt in the east was now becoming obvious. First the Man with the She-camel and then his brother, the Man with the Mole, fell to ʿAbbasid forces. The consequence of both their actions, and those of the ʿAbbasids in response, sorely disrupted an already fractious *daʿwa* and put the Imam in serious jeopardy. He realized that he had little choice but to continue to move westward and away from his former base. In departing from Salamiya for Ramla he was accompanied by his son, by a major *dāʿī* who may have been his chief lieutenant – a person named Fīrūz – and by a number of servants or slaves, one of whom lived long enough both to become the chamberlain of the Fatimid court of his master and later to recount for posterity his experiences on

20. On this point see also below.
21. Halm, *Reich*, 76, trans., 75.

the Imam's flight to North Africa.[22]

When Ramla proved to be an insecure hiding place, the party moved to Fusṭāṭ in Egypt where the *da'wa* was in the capable hands of Abū 'Alī, who was then also the titular *bāb al-abwāb* ('gate of gates'), the highest rank in the organization except for that of Imam. The retinue of Abū 'Alī in Egypt also included Abu'l-'Abbās. They arrived there in Rabī' I 291/January–February 904.

By this time, Abū 'Abdallāh's forces had claimed their first victory in the conquest of Mīla (289/902) and, although still in a precarious position vis-à-vis the Aghlabids, an eventual triumph was now conceivable. Clearly, moreover, the Imam in Egypt recognized the likelihood of that outcome. Meanwhile, the 'Abbasids had sent a military expedition to Egypt which reached Fusṭāṭ on 1 Rabī' 292/11 January 905 for the purpose of replacing the semi-independent governor there. The new one took over on 2 April 905 (3 Jumādā II 292). Although as yet undetected by the authorities in Egypt, the Imam's position was again in jeopardy and he knew he would soon have to leave. His immediate circle thought they would surely go on to the Yemen but he decided in favour of the Maghrib, evidently impressed by what he had heard of Abū 'Abdallāh's growing strength and the possibility of complete victory there.

When the Imam announced his intention, Fīrūz absconded to Yemen on his own. Abū 'Alī implored the Imam to take him with the departing party but, aside from slaves and servants, only Abu'l-'Abbās, an obvious choice, went with him. The chamberlain Ja'far, who is the source for these details, was dispatched back to Salamiya to retrieve as much gold and other of the Imam's possessions as he could still find there. The Imam and

22. The *Sīrat Ja'far al-Ḥājib* (Arabic text ed. by W. Ivanow, *Bulletin of the Faculty of Arts*, University of Egypt, 4 (1936): 107–33, Eng. trans. Ivanow in *Ismaili Tradition Concerning the Rise of the Fatimids* (London, etc., 1942), 184–223, French trans. by M. Canard, 'L'autobiographie d'un chambellan du Mahdī 'Obeidallâh le Fâṭimide,' in *Hespéris*, 39 (1952): 279–330 (reprinted in his *Miscellanea Orientalia*, London, 1973, no. V). On this work see further below.

the rest joined a caravan in Alexandria heading west.[23] Half way to Libya they were attacked by brigands and, in the ensuing melée, Abu'l-'Abbās received a serious wound on the face for which he was thereafter called *al-Makhṭūm* (the Broken-nosed). Upon reaching Tripoli the Imam halted to await Ja'far.

But, to test the situation ahead of him, he ordered Abu'l-'Abbās to travel on to Qayrawan. Their collective disguise until then was a claim to be no more than a party of merchants, even though the unusual size and wealth of the group was apparently hard to ignore. The Aghlabid authorities must surely have harboured quite valid suspicions about these 'merchants.' Perhaps they also knew about their connection with Abū 'Abdallāh and the Berber rebellion to the west. In any case they promptly detained Abu'l-'Abbās and locked him up in the jail of Qayrawan. Apparently, though interrogated harshly, he simply continued to insist that he was nothing but a merchant from the east. That was mid-summer of 292/905. He was still in the Aghlabid prison when, in the spring of the following year, the revolt of Mudlij set him free.

Having been warned away from Aghlabid territory by the earlier arrest of Abu'l-'Abbās, the Imam was by this time long ensconced safely, more or less, in the distant town of Sijilmāsa. As soon as Ja'far had rejoined the Imam's party in Tripoli, he had moved on, well aware that attempting to travel directly through Aghlabid territory to Kutāma country would not succeed. Instead he went by a southern route arriving at Tūzur in the Qasṭīliya region of southern Tunisia on 1 Shawwāl 292/6 August 905. Fearing imminent capture, however, he did not linger there for very long but departed again along what was perhaps the only route open to him – that leading eventually to the Maghribi trading centre of Sijilmāsa some two months away. There, thanks to his wealth and noble status, he was accorded a fair measure of respect and for a long while was

23. The source for this portion of the Imam's journey is the *Istitār al-imām* by al-Naysābūrī (Arabic text ed. by W. Ivanow, *Bulletin of the Faculty of Arts*, University of Egypt, 4 (1936): 93–107; Eng. trans. Ivanow in *Ismaili Tradition Concerning the Rise of the Fatimids*, 157–83).

unrestricted by the local ruler who himself began to benefit from the attention and largesse of this new resident.

Soon after his arrival in Sijilmāsa, the Imam received a delegation from Abū ʿAbdallāh bringing both news of a major victory over Aghlabid forces and a sizeable share of the booty gained in it, including many newly minted dinars of a type that had not previously appeared in Sijilmāsa. Over the period of his stay in the far west there is no doubt also that messages and letters passed frequently between the *dāʿī* and the Imam, despite the distance between them and the danger of having to travel through often hostile territory in the middle.[24] But, in contrast to letters that could be hidden and kept secret, the Imam's open use of the new dinars might have exposed him. One person who noticed their presence was a noble merchant from Qayrawan, himself a Muṭṭalibī and, thus, a close relative and by tradition an ally of the Prophet's own Hāshimite family. This man, Abu'l-Ḥasan Aḥmad al-Muṭṭalibī, along with his son Abu'l-Qāsim, first encountered the Imam en route to Sijilmāsa where they became acquainted. The Imam befriended al-Muṭṭalibī and, discovering his pro-Shiʿi inclinations and sympathies, took him into the *daʿwa*, according to the direct testimony of the manservant Jaʿfar who was certainly present when it happened.[25] Non-Ismaʿili sources from North Africa confirm parts of this story. Apparently al-Muṭṭalibī often repeated the account of his meeting and friendship with the Imam in Sijilmāsa, his noticing the new dinars, and the Imam's approval and trust of him, and instructions to conceal their mutual accord and what he had learned about the mission of Abū ʿAbdallāh, the source of the dinars. Later, when al-Muṭṭalibī came to leave Sijilmāsa for Qayrawan, the Imam wrote letters addressed to Abū ʿAbdallāh as a reference for him in the eventuality of the final conquest.[26] Even prior to the

24. Al-Naysābūrī, *Istitār,* 106; Qāḍī al-Nuʿmān, *Iftitāḥ,* par. 126 and p. 124; Halm, *Reich,* 92, 102, trans., 95, 106.

25. *Sīrat Jaʿfar,* 119, Eng. trans. in *Rise,* 202, Canard trans., 302.

26. Ibn ʿIdhārī, *al-Bayān,* I, 139; *Sīrat Jaʿfar,* 121–5, 131, Eng. trans. in Ivanow, *Rise,* 205–12, 220, Canard trans., 305–9, 319.

arrival of the Imam in person, those same letters were to earn al-Muṭṭalibī great esteem and honour from the victors. Ibn al-Haytham recounts significant additional details to confirm the importance of this man and his role in these events and the role of the letters which carried the Imam's stamp and seal.

As Abū 'Abdallāh and his Berber army moved rather slowly towards their ultimate goal, the situation of the Imam in Sijilmāsa grew more precarious. The link between the two could not remain hidden for ever. Eventually, Ziyādatallāh informed al-Yasa' b. Midrār, the ruler of Sijilmāsa, exactly whom he was harbouring.[27] Al-Yasa' reacted by separating members of the Imam's party and placing them all under house arrest. The servants were tortured for information. Thus, Abū 'Abdallāh's rescue of the Imam became more and more imperative. By the time of his definitive victory, he well knew that the expedition to Sijilmāsa had become urgent. It is likely, nevertheless, that he also understood the danger inherent of leaving Qayrawan and Ifrīqiya unattended or merely governed by commanders untested in this kind of administration. He required a senior official who could represent the Isma'ili *da'wa* with great authority in the face of the local Arabs – a task evidently not within the capacities of his Kutāma followers. He therefore wrote to his brother Abu'l-'Abbās, who had retreated to Tripoli after his escape from Aghlabid detention three years earlier, requesting him to proceed to Raqqāda and sent with his letter 200 cavalry as an escort.[28]

Upon Abu'l-'Abbās's arrival, Abū 'Abdallāh had completed his preparations. He announced publicly that Abū Zākī, his long-time associate, would assume the regency. Abū Zākī's influence among and control over the Kutāma was essential, while Abu'l-'Abbās had no standing with them. But clearly it was understood that Abu'l-'Abbās, although reluctant in the beginning, would be the real power in crucial matters of

27. Qāḍī al-Nu'mān, *Iftitāḥ*, p. 165, 227; Halm, *Reich*, 121, trans., 129.

28. This information comes from the account of Ibn al-Haytham. See below pp. 107–9.

religious policy. Abū Mūsā, the other Berber chieftain closest to Abū 'Abdallāh, was ill at the time – a fact reported by Ibn al-Haytham – and had not been able to go with the army.

The army under Abū 'Abdallāh departed Raqqāda one Thursday in the middle of Ramaḍān 296/6 June 909 and arrived before Sijilmāsa on Saturday 6 Dhu'l-ḥijja/26 August 909.[29] Since Abū 'Abdallāh had never seen the Imam himself, he took with him the son of al-Muṭṭalibī who personally knew the Imam from the days he had spent in Sijilmāsa with his father. By then the city's ruler, al-Yasa', had become somewhat uncertain about the exact identity of the person sought by the advancing army and he at first sent out another merchant before whom Abū 'Abdallāh is reported to have dismounted in error. The problem was soon sorted out, however, and the Imam finally obtained his freedom. Ja'far the chamberlain, along with others of the Imam's retinue, were, however, still under arrest in the city. Ja'far's account provides precious details of the rescue in Sijilmāsa and of Abū 'Abdallāh's efforts to find and liberate the whole party, including most particularly the Imam's son, Abu'l-Qāsim. But, as Ja'far was himself not a witness to the actual liberation of the Imam since he was under detention, he repeats an account related to him by al-Muṭṭalibī's son, who had seen it all.[30]

Once freed, the Imam was soon publicly proclaimed caliph on 7 Dhu'l-ḥijja 296/27 August 909. Thereafter the army commenced a slow and careful march back to Raqqāda that was to take the better part of four months as they deliberately returned at leisure through Kutāma territory. As they moved they attended to various matters. When they finally reached the former

29. For these dates see Ibn 'Idhārī, *al-Bayān*, I, 152 and 153; Abū 'Abdallāh Muḥammad b. 'Alī Ibn Ḥammād, *Histoire des Rois 'Obaidides* (*Akhbār mulūk banī 'Ubayd wa sīratuhum*), ed. and trans. M. Vonderheyden (Algiers and Paris, 1927), 9; Halm, *Reich*, 125, trans., 135.

30. *Sīrat Ja'far*, 123–4, Eng. trans. in Ivanow, *Rise*, 209, and Halm, *Reich*, 125–6, trans., 134–5. In the letter given to al-Muṭṭalibī, the Imam had ordered Abū 'Abdallāh to bring with him the son for just such an eventuality, according to Ja'far.

enclave of Īkjān, the Imam insisted on receiving the funds that had been collected for him and were stored there. Some of the Kutāma chieftains who thought they had a right to a share in this fund resented his act. However, to those attuned to the practical requirements inherent to the imamate with respect to various dues and other financial obligations owed the Imam, his action would not have seemed inappropriate. As such monies belonged to the Imam and were to be disposed of as he, and he alone, determined.

Word eventually reached Abu'l-'Abbās that the party was on Kutāma lands and would soon be on its way toward the pass of Sabība some 90 kilometres southwest of Qayrawan. He and those around him decided to ride out to greet it there. Finally all met in a grand ceremony, after which the whole procession proceeded to Raqqāda reaching the city on 20 Rabī' II/4 January. The Imam settled into the palace formerly occupied by Abū 'Abdallāh and his son took over another. On the following day, a Friday, al-Mahdī's name and titles were proclaimed in the *khuṭba* for the first time in Qayrawan, Raqqāda, and the other areas of the old Aghlabid state. His triumph was complete.

The Religious Situation in Qayrawan Before the Fatimids

Nearly all the surviving evidence about the old conflict between Mālikīs and Ḥanafīs derives from authors who were ardently loyal to the Mālikī point of view. Moreover, the Maghrib itself became more and more exclusively Mālikī in the next century. Ibn al-Athīr notes that it was only with al-Mu'izz b. Bādīs, the fifth/eleventh century Zīrid ruler (407–454/1016–1062), that the Mālikī legal school was finally imposed on its people. He reports that earlier the Aghlabids had favoured the school of Abū Ḥanīfa.[31] Almost as if to confirm this trend, Mālikī *ṭabaqāt* works increasingly denied the validity or relevance of any other school in the Maghrib, and tended to erase any record of its

31. 'Izz al-Dīn Ibn al-Athīr, *al-Kāmil fi'l-ta'rīkh*, ed. C. J. Tornberg (Leiden, 1851–76, reprinted Beirut, 1965–67), 9: 257.

ever having been otherwise. Still, the earliest surviving sources, which are nonetheless preserved by Mālikī authors, reveal the clear presence of prominent and influential Ḥanafīs in Qayrawan. ʻArīb b. Saʻd's account in Ibn ʻIdhārī's *al-Bayān al-mughrib*[32] alone indicates a fairly vigorous scholarly tradition of Ḥanafī learning in that city. Fortunately, his data about this is corroborated, though quite uncharacteristically for a Mālikī author, by al-Khushanī's *Ṭabaqāt* which, in contrast to most works of its kind, includes biographical entries on some of the leading Ḥanafīs among the Mālikīs who are its main subject.[33]

Almost nowhere, however, is there any information among these accounts about other figures who might have been, for example, Shiʻi. To be sure, one highly important feature of al-Khushanī's work is a list he gives of those scholars of Qayrawan who converted or otherwise joined the Fatimids after they came to power. Obviously, in his mind such turncoats, many of whom were previously Ḥanafīs, were the worst sort of renegades and their motives for changing allegiances were most often suspect and highly immoral. In any case, because of the narrow, generally partisan focus of these sources, an accurate and complete description of the scholarly community in pre-Fatimid North Africa appears unobtainable.

Generally speaking, Ismaʻili sources could hardly be expected to add much more since they were primarily concerned with the revolution itself – the new dispensation – and not the prior intellectual climate of the state they conquered. Still, some interesting details of the situation just before the victory of Abū ʻAbdallāh are mentioned by Qāḍī al-Nuʻmān. However, he was primarily interested in presenting the victory in terms of the Ismaʻili *daʻwa*'s mobilization of the Berbers and the collapse of the Aghlabids, thus giving almost no credit to any other participants. Qāḍī al-Nuʻmān is much more apt to be silent about

32. The sections on the Aghlabids and earlier Fatimids in the *Bayān* are mostly by ʻArīb.

33. Al-Khushanī was born in or near Qayrawan, which he left only in 311/923 and thus he was an eyewitness to the Fatimid takeover. On him see Ch. Pellat, ʻal-Khushanīʼ in the *EI2*.

the local situation in Qayrawan and events there after the victory.[34] Therefore, his information contributed little to an accurate assessment of what had happened or was to happen in Qayrawan itself just before and after the takeover.

From Mālikī sources by themselves, the picture of Fatimid rule is one of severe persecution and harsh repression. Al-Khushanī reports that many suffered, including the ordinary people.[35] Al-Mālikī's *Ṭabaqāt*, the *Riyāḍ al-nufūs*, never fails to mention the punishments inflicted by Fatimid authorities on the local *fuqahā'* (Mālikīs). A double case of the martyrdom of two Mālikī scholars was given an ever more embellished prominence in subsequent accounts, leading, finally, to depictions of it that are pure hagiography and not history. Ibn al-Haytham also took note of the same incident which for him had the opposite meaning, that of heresy and of rebellion. It is true that the initial phase of Fatimid rule, even setting aside some exaggeration, was less kind and gentle on the Maghrib than it was much later on Egypt. But, despite the assertions of biased sources – or perhaps because of them – modern scholars have understood little about what actually happened in those first months and years and what was the local attitude, including what, if any, was the role in those events of the scholars of Qayrawan itself. It would have helped considerably to have available a source that spoke for the side of the local non-Mālikīs, possibly the Ḥanafīs but, of course, even better, for an indigenous Shi'i community. However, no such source was known to exist and the Ḥanafīs, having disappeared or gone over to the Fatimids after their triumph, ceased to be a presence and left no records of their own.

34. Based on the new information presented below, one might justifiably ask if Qāḍī al-Nu'mān did not purposely leave out what he knew about the role of those from Qayrawan who joined the *da'wa*.

35. Muḥammad b. al-Ḥārith b. Asad al-Khushanī, *Kitāb Ṭabaqāt 'ulamā' Ifrīqiya*, ed. Mohammed Ben Cheneb in *Classes des savants de l'Ifrīqiya* (Paris, 1915), 232. Some further details are provided by the contemporary Mālikī scholar Abu'l-'Arab al-Tamīmī in his *Kitāb al-miḥan*, ed. Yaḥyā Wahīb al-Jubūrī (2nd ed. Beirut, 1988).

In the circles of a city like Qayrawan in the third/ninth and fourth/tenth centuries, the *madhāhib* of the *fuqahā'* were designated by the eastern city of their founder. Thus, the two main factions were called the 'Iraqis (*al-'Irāqiyyūn, ahl al-'Irāq*), or occasionally the Kufans (*al-Kūfiyyūn*),[36] which always meant Ḥanafīs, or the partisans of Madina (*al-Madaniyyūn, ahl al-Madīna*), which indicated the Mālikīs. On the periphery of the larger Islamic world, religious affiliation was thus tied to a base at a distant centre back in the east. Yet, somewhat ironically, but certainly in keeping with this trend, upon the arrival of Abū 'Abdallāh and the Isma'ili *da'wa* beginning in 280/893, the local North African term for him was the 'Easterner' (*al-mashriqī*) since he had come to Ifrīqiya from the east. Those who joined his movement were labelled the 'Easterners' (*al-mashāriqa*), although nearly all were at that point native Berbers of the Kutāma tribe. If someone were to convert or otherwise come to adhere to the Isma'ili *da'wa*, the verb used was *tasharraqa* ('to become an Easterner'). Abū 'Abdallāh himself was known for a long time also as al-Ṣan'ānī ('the man from Ṣan'ā') even though he had spent less than one year of his life in that Yemeni city and actually hailed from Kufa.[37]

In part this distinctive label for the Isma'ilis may have begun among the Kutāma themselves as a positive way of noting the transference of an allegiance from a purely local tribal affiliation to that of a widespread movement which had its roots in the all-important eastern centre of Islam itself. Qāḍī al-Nu'mān, whose *Iftitāḥ al-da'wa* is the most important account of Abū 'Abdallāh's origin and early activities, reports this name for the Isma'ilis seemingly without embarrassment and perhaps with a touch of pride.[38] The use of the term in this way became common for all of the North African writers and it

36. 'Madhhab al-Kūfiyyīn,' al-Khushanī, 193.

37. Examples: Ibn 'Idhārī, *al-Bayān*, I, 124, 137.

38. Qāḍī al-Nu'mān, *Iftitāḥ*, paras 49 (p. 52) and 71 (p. 79). The fact that Idrīs 'Imad al-Dīn repeats this information in his history written in the fifteenth century (*'Uyūn al-akhbār*, ed. al-Ya'lāwī, 94 and also 273, 355) confirms this.

appears, for example, frequently in the Mālikī *ṭabaqāt* works. Al-Khushanī even devotes a chapter to 'A record of those scholars of Qayrawan who became Easterners (*man tasharraqa*).' For these Mālikīs who were entirely hostile witnesses, however, the terms must have been used to indicate a foreign innovation and heresy, one not acceptable to the local or traditional orthodoxy.[39] For the scholars of Qayrawan, to become an Easterner was not a good thing; the Isma'ilis were foreigners.

On the eve of Fatimid victory, the religious culture of the Aghlabid domain was, thus, controlled by scholars of either the Mālikī or the Ḥanafī legal schools. There were significant representatives of both traditions in the major cities. Although these were each respected Sunni schools, often the doctrines that separated them were the subject of fairly intense rivalry and enmity, particularly in those cases where the Ḥanafī authority also happened to espouse a Mu'tazilī theological position. The sources usually note this tendency by announcing that the person in question advocated the 'createdness of the Qur'an.' At the beginning of the third/ninth century the problem of opposing views of the law was solved by appointing two qadis for Ifrīqiya (i.e. Qayrawan), one Asad b. al-Furāt, who had studied with Mālik,[40] and the other Abū Muḥriz, who was considered an orthodox Ḥanafī. Later, with the appointment of the eminent Saḥnūn, the position of the Mālikīs hardened and the relationship between the schools grew far less fluid. Saḥnūn and his teachings, in fact, came to define the later Mālikī doctrine.

As mentioned, the Aghlabid court, unlike much of the common populace, tended to favour the Ḥanafīs and even the Mu'tazila. During the early reign of Ibrāhīm II (from 275/888) the grand qadi was Ibn 'Abdūn, a Ḥanafī, noted for his

39. Some examples: al-Qāḍī Abu'l-Faḍl 'Iyāḍ, *Tarājim Aghlabiyya mustakhraja min Madārik al-Qāḍī 'Iyāḍ*, ed. Muḥammad al-Ṭālibī, (Tunis, 1968), 283, 284, 369, 383, 390–1, 394.

40. He had also studied in 'Iraq with disciples of Abū Ḥanīfa and thus he was well qualified in both schools, although the distinction was in his time less strict than it became after the arrival of Saḥnūn.

severity against the Mālikīs.[41] In 280/893 he was replaced by the equally harsh Mālikī 'Īsā b. Miskīn, who persisted until near the end of this reign.[42] When Ibrāhīm II departed in 289/902 for the jihad in Sicily,[43] Muḥammad b. Aswad b. Shu'ayb al-Ṣadīnī was appointed as the new qadi. Al-Ṣadīnī was both Ḥanafī and Mu'tazilī and his policies were decidedly antagonistic to the traditionalist Mālikīs, some of whom suffered harshly as a result. This situation, however, did not last long, in part because of the animosity of the populace and in part because of the accession several months later of Ziyādatallāh III who, upon coming to power, chose to placate his Mālikī subjects with the appointment in 290/903 of Ḥimās b. Marwān b. Simāk al-Hamdānī, who had been a student of Saḥnūn.[44] But to satisfy the court itself a Ḥanafī, Muḥammad b. 'Abdallāh b. Jīmāl, was made qadi of Raqqāda in 293/905, to the eventual annoyance of Ḥimās who threatened to, and then finally did, quit his post in either 294/906 or 295/907.

These were serious conflicts which in many ways dominated the intellectual life of North African cities, especially Qayrawan and Raqqāda. The men just mentioned played an important part in the early life of Ibn al-Haytham who grew up in the midst of the controversy between the two sides and had met and knew personally many of these scholars and judges. Ibn 'Abdūn, al-Ṣadīnī, Ḥimās, and Ibn Jīmāl were still alive when the Fatimids took over, and they, together with many of the other local *fuqahā'*, were immediately confronted by the incoming government and subjected to its new religious policies.

41. Talbi, *Aghlabide*, 275, 697.

42. Ibid., 274–7.

43. Ibrāhīm II left for Sicily in Rajab 289/June 902 and died there in Dhu'l-Qa'da 289/23 Oct. 902. See Halm, *Reich*, 103–4, trans., 106–8.

44. On Ḥimās (222/837–303/915–16) in addition to the citations given below, see Talbi, *Aghlabide*, 549–51.

The Shi'is of Qayrawan

Less than six weeks after assuming power, Abū 'Abdallāh appointed a local figure, Muḥammad b. 'Umar al-Marwadhī, as qadi of Qayrawan.[45] Information previously available strongly hinted at this man's prior affiliation with Shi'ism but since, aside from this one case, almost no other evidence suggested that there were Shi'is in Qayrawan, it was quite possible, even reasonable, to doubt such a connection. Ibn al-Haytham, however, not only admits to the Zaydism of his own family but names several others among his circle who were clearly Shi'is of one kind or another. In fact the leading authority among them was this very al-Marwadhī. Ibn al-Haytham was a schoolmate of the same man's son. Other Shi'is included Muḥammad b. Khalaf, Ibrāhīm b. Ma'shar,[46] and Abu'l-Ḥasan al-Muṭṭalibī. Some time after his father's death, Ibn al-Haytham had, as one of his teachers, a certain Muḥammad al-Kūfī, then lately arrived from Sicily.[47] This man taught him Shi'ism, not of the vague and extremely moderate kind of his own Zaydi father,[48] but evidently of a much more radical form. He also maintained close contacts with other local Shi'is. Later he was appointed *khaṭīb* and imam of the congregational mosque by Abū 'Abdallāh.

From the new information alone, however, it would be difficult to estimate the number of Shi'is in Qayrawan or the extent of their influence. Certainly they were not many and they had always to conceal their true beliefs lest they lose the protection of the law. Ibn al-Haytham recounts how he was nearly deprived

45. Mid-Sha'bān 296/April 909.

46. This man, a resident of Qayrawan, was the owner of a work called *Kitāb yawm wa layla.* On one such book with this title, see W. Madelung, 'The Sources of Ismā'īlī Law,' *Journal of Near Eastern Studies,* 35 (1976): 29–40, on pp. 39–40.

47. The date is likely to fall somewhere between 285 and 290/898–903.

48. The father died in 285/898 and thus did not live to supervise his son's education beyond elementary reading of the Qur'an and other basic texts.

of his legitimate inheritance because the Mālikī qadi Ḥimās suspected his orthodoxy. Nonetheless, it is significant that there were some Shi'is, and that they were participants in elite scholarly circles. These Shi'is, for example, frequented the teaching sessions of the leading Ḥanafīs with whom they obviously shared a degree of mutual respect. When Ibn 'Abdūn, the most esteemed of the Ḥanafīs, died, al-Marwadhī, the Fatimid-appointed (and now an Isma'ili) judge said prayers over him. They were, in fact, old friends and colleagues. Ibn al-Haytham also confirms Fatimid regard for Ibn 'Abdūn even though he never converted (as did many other Ḥanafīs). Still, it is evident from Ibn al-Haytham's account that these Shi'is studied with the Ḥanafīs in large measure because they were not allowed either to teach or to study their own Shi'i law in public. Significantly, once he began to study Shi'i *fiqh* under al-Kūfī, Ibn al-Haytham ceased to attend and hear the sessions devoted to Ḥanafī law.

The presence of Shi'is in Qayrawan before the Fatimid takeover raises questions about other instances of Shi'ism in the Maghrib, particularly about the mission of the obscure al-Ḥulwānī mentioned in several places (among them Qāḍī al-Nu'mān's *Iftitāḥ al-da'wa*). Ibn al-Haytham also refers to this man who, in Isma'ili sources, is said to have been sent to the Maghrib by the Imam Ja'far al-Ṣādiq. However, these various accounts all name people who were converted by al-Ḥulwānī and yet who also met and supported Abū 'Abdallāh. The list is fairly substantial, including Ismā'īl b. Naṣr al-Ma'ādī, Ibn Ḥayyūn Abu'l-Mufattish, Abu'l-Qāsim al-Warfajūmī, Abū 'Abdallāh al-Andalusī,[49] the *dā'ī* and judge Aflaḥ al-Malūsī, and most significantly Ḥurayth al-Jīmalī and Mūsā b. Makārim, two members of the very party of Kutāmīs who first encountered Abū 'Abdallāh al-Shī'ī in Mecca and urged him to return with them to their homeland.[50] All these men were Shi'is *before* the

49. The latter three men are cited in par. 38 (p. 40) of the *Iftitāḥ* where Qāḍī al-Nu'mān states explicitly that *'kāna hā'ulā'i shī'a'*.

50. Qāḍī al-Nu'mān, *Iftitāḥ*, par. 168.

arrival of any form of the Fatimid Isma'ili *da'wa*, having been already converted by al-Ḥulwānī.[51] But, if so, al-Ḥulwānī cannot have been sent by Ja'far al-Ṣādiq, who died some 130 years earlier, but must have arrived much later.[52] It may be that the Fatimid authors, when they came to mention the influence of al-Ḥulwānī, preferred to credit Ja'far al-Ṣādiq, an Imam they recognized, with having sent him on this mission.

Religious Measures and Debates

The appointment of al-Marwadhī as qadi gave him the power to impose fairly strict adherence to Shi'i ritual and law, and the measures he took were known previously from various historical sources. It is now clear, however, that they were in line with his own previous Shi'i inclinations and not due solely to a policy brought and instigated by the Fatimids. Still, these changes of al-Marwadhī were supported by the two brothers and later confirmed by al-Mahdī at the beginning of 910 (297). Ibn al-Haytham provides an interesting description of the precise moment when the appointment of the new qadi was arranged in Sha'bān/April of the year before. He reports that the matter began with al-Muṭṭalibī's asking Abū 'Abdallāh on behalf of the people of Qayrawan that a qadi be appointed to supervise their affairs. Al-Muṭṭalibī had earlier met the future al-Mahdī and was close to him. The Imam's letters, which he carried with him and was to use when Abū 'Abdallāh's campaign finally succeeded, ensured him high status with the new government. Thus, al-Muṭṭalibī's request for a qadi was not to be ignored, despite the fact that the Isma'ili *da'wa* had never needed one before. According to Ibn al-Haytham, Abū 'Abdallāh first pointed to him as the most suitable candidate,

51. See, for example, Ibid., paras 38 (p. 40) and 168.

52. This Imam died in 148/765 and Abū 'Abdallāh, the vanguard of the Ismaili *da'wa*, reached Kutāma territory in 280/893. Even allowing that all those on this list except al-Malūsī were dead by the time of the Fatimid victory, al-Mahdī was still able to appoint al-Malūsī to a judgeship. Admittedly he was old by then, but not that old!

but Ibn al-Haytham proposed al-Marwadhī as the senior Shi'i scholar. Abū 'Abdallāh accepted this proposal without much thought but warned al-Marwadhī to forget any grudges lingering from former times. He rightly anticipated that, in his implementation of Shi'i law, al-Marwadhī would be subject to an urge for revenge against those responsible for the previous repression of the Shi'is in the city. Abū Mūsā, the Kutāma leader, protested this decision. He evidently resented the interference of an independent judge in his own authority over the town.

Over the following months, Shi'i rituals and institutions were increasingly imposed on everyone. The *adhān* was changed; the Shi'i phrase 'Come to the best of works' was inserted in place of 'Prayer is better than sleep.' The *tarāwīḥ* prayers led by an imam during Ramaḍān were forbidden. The Shi'a regard this practice as a reprehensible innovation of the second caliph 'Umar and thus not to be allowed. It is, however, considered sunna in Mālikī law.[53] In the new *khuṭba*, a prayer was added for 'Alī b. Abī Ṭālib immediately following that for the Prophet. Thereafter came benedictions for Fāṭima, al-Ḥasan, and al-Ḥusayn. In general the new qadi decreed that the practices of 'Umar and other Companions not confirmed by 'Alī and the family of the Prophet were unacceptable.[54] The implementation of these and other[55] changes and the suppression of Sunni practices by the newly appointed local Shi'i qadi with the eager support of the local Shi'is aroused much popular Sunni resentment against him personally. They were, however, fully in accord with the previous practice of Abū 'Abdallāh among the Kutāma Isma'ilis and with early Fatimid religious policy.

53. See Ibn 'Idhārī, *al-Bayān*, I, 137; Halm, *Reich*, 120, trans., 127–8; al-Mālikī, *Riyāḍ*, II, 55–6; A. J. Wensinck 'Tarāwīḥ' in the *EI2*.

54. On these changes see Halm, *Reich*, 219–20, trans., 243–4; al-Mālikī, *Riyāḍ*, II, 55–6 (and notes); Ibn 'Idhārī, *al-Bayān*, I, 151–2.

55. Such as the abolition of the *qunūt* prayers and the *qiyām al-layl*, as well as loud mourning. In general see Halm, *Reich*, 215–22 (particularly p. 219); trans., 239–47 (p. 243).

In addition to these changes, which would have been readily and immediately obvious to the general public, questions of law and the Shi'i religious interpretation of them were soon hotly debated among the scholars of Qayrawan. Abū 'Abdallāh saw to that almost from the moment of his arrival and his brother continued the practice. One record of the various 'debates' (also signified by the term *munāẓarāt*) between the brothers and the local (Mālikī) *fuqahā'* has long been available. That version comes from al-Khushanī and appears in his biography of Abū 'Uthmān Sa'īd b. al-Ḥaddād who is presented there as the courageous champion of orthodoxy against the heretics. It later became a part of Mālikī legend and proved how, in the face of an obvious mortal threat, Ibn al-Ḥaddād had upheld the truth.

In the new material supplied by Ibn al-Haytham, however, the picture changes considerably. Abū 'Abdallāh and his brother were fond of disputation and they indulged in it almost relentlessly. It was the principal means they used for teaching and propagating doctrine. Abū 'Abdallāh held such sessions with many individuals and groups: Ibn al-Haytham, the local Shi'is and Ḥanafīs, as well as the Mālikīs. The latter were not singled out, nor, it would seem, coerced into them. But what is striking about Ibn al-Haytham's report is his own role in these debates. With the permission and commission of the brothers, it was often he who confronted his fellow scholars of Qayrawan; he was thus acting for them and the Fatimids as well as for the Shi'i side in these public controversies.[56]

In the end, he says, Ibn al-Ḥaddād, who was obviously the main opponent in many of the debates, wrote what Ibn al-Haytham claims was an embellished account of them, and by lying about them made them seem what they were not.[57] Ibn

56. He specifically recounts his role in one debate mainly with Ḥanafīs on the inheritance of women and another with Ibn al-Ḥaddād about the meaning of the Prophet's declaration at Ghadīr Khumm.

57. A version of Ibn al-Ḥaddād's account is preserved in al-Khushanī, 148, 198–212; al-Mālikī, *Riyāḍ*, II, 57–115; 'Iyāḍ, *Madārik*, 351–63. See also Qāḍī al-Nu'mān, *Iftitāḥ*, 269–70.

al-Haytham also reports that he himself wrote a refutation of what Ibn al-Ḥaddād had put in his book.[58] He states clearly, moreover, that he was personally present at all of the debates this man had with either of the two brothers.

Despite the tone of scholarly respect and courtesy evident in some accounts of these debates, as the year wore on, the suppression of both Ḥanafī and Mālikī jurisprudence grew increasingly complete. Finally, it was forbidden to issue a ruling on the basis of the works of either Mālik or Abū Ḥanīfa. Ibn al-Haytham notes with pride that their books were soon all but worthless, and were sold for use in pharmacies to wrap prescriptions or exported to Andalus. The zeal of the local Shi'is was obviously not restrained but rather supported by Abu'l-'Abbās; they were thus willing instigators of a new mandate on behalf of their recently victorious Isma'ili rulers.

One incident, previously mentioned here, provides a useful way of illustrating the complex interactions of all these scholars and of the way older sentiments played a role in the new situation. It involves the two Mālikī *faqīhs*, cited earlier, who were arrested in Qayrawan, reportedly for slandering the Fatimids, and were subsequently put to death by the authorities. This case later became a highly celebrated example of martyrdom. What really happened is not, of course, quite so simple. The principal victim was a man known by the name Ibn al-Birdhawn. He had a reputation as a zealous agitator against the Ḥanafīs, having once been a student of Ibn al-Ḥaddād and, thus, a specialist in disputation. As early as 290/903, during that fairly brief period of Ḥanafī ascendancy when the qadi was one of their party, Ibn al-Birdhawn was detained and officially flogged. Apparently that punishment achieved little and when, soon after, the Mālikīs gained the upper hand again, he reverted to his old habits. But, when finally the Fatimids came to power and the Mālikīs were out, several leading Ḥanafīs –

58. That very account appears to be what Abū Ḥayyān al-Tawḥīdī alludes to in his *Kitāb al-imtā' wa'l-mu'ānasa*, ed. Aḥmad Amīn and Aḥmad al-Zayn (Beirut, n.d.), III, 195, referring there to Ibn al-Haytham and a *munāẓara* about the imamate.

the two named are Ibn Ẓafar and al-Kalāʿī – took their revenge by reporting to the authorities that Ibn al-Birdhawn used to praise Muʿāwiya and disparage ʿAlī. Ibn al-Hudhayl, the second of the two men, was accused of a similar crime. As a consequence, Ibn al-Birdhawn was sentenced to 500 lashes and then to die; the other man was sentenced to death alone. After their execution, carried out on the orders of the new governor of Qayrawan, Ibn Abī Khinzīr, they were publicly exposed and crucified. The execution took place in Ṣafar of 297/October–November 909 and provided the first martyrs for the Mālikīs who later made as much out of the event as possible.[59] Ibn al-Haytham also mentions the same incident and supplies the details concerning what these men were accused of, i.e. asserting publicly that ʿAlī had no right to claim the imamate and should not, therefore, have waged war against Muʿāwiya. This claim, which was distinctly at variance with orthodox Sunni doctrine predominant in the eastern Muslim world, reflected the strong pro-Umayyad sentiments among the Mālikīs in the Maghrib. Significantly, both the Ḥanafīs who had brought this affair to a head soon converted and joined the Fatimids.

It is now clear that the Fatimid revolution in the Maghrib and the local reaction to it was more complex than previously thought. Not only were some of the Kutāma already dedicated Shiʿis, even prior to the advent of the Ismaʿili *daʿwa* among them, but also some members of the elite in Qayrawan were either Zaydi or Imami. To be sure, these latter Shiʿis seem to have attached themselves to local Ḥanafī teachers since, in part, they were forced to hide their true religious attitudes. But those Ḥanafīs who later joined the Fatimids appear to have been naturally sympathetic to them for a variety of reasons, many

59. In the later *ṭabaqāt* works, both Ibn al-Birdhawn and Ibn al-Hudhayl receive generous amounts of attention. Ignoring historical impossibilities, the martyrdom was recast in dramatic form like a stage play. Brought before the Fatimid caliph al-Mahdī, who sits on his throne flanked by the brothers al-Shīʿī, the two Mālikīs must confess that al-Mahdī is himself the apostle of God, which they refuse to do and righteously accept death instead.

based on doctrinal affinities but others connected to their shared animosity toward the Mālikīs. What is not clear is to what extent the Ḥanafīs were aware of the Shi'ism of these associates of theirs. Nevertheless, the purely venal motives for their various conversions, attributed to them by al-Khushanī, are suspect; he was definitely not an unbiased observer. Forced conversion, certainly, was never at issue, despite a Fatimid policy from the beginning of insisting on Shi'i practices and norms in public life. But the assumption of power in its initial phase – that is, before the arrival of the Imam – brought with it an *ad hoc* policy in regard to the gradual imposition of Shi'i rules and regulations. The local Shi'is, once assured of a Fatimid victory and general support for their positions, seized the opportunity both for revenge against their previous oppressors and for a long sought ascendancy of their own. To a certain extent, the Ḥanafīs, particularly those with Mu'tazilī leanings, likewise used the Fatimid revolution to get back at the Mālikīs and gain their own advantage. For them, of course, conversion was ultimately the only avenue that remained open, although many were converted willingly. Not to participate fully with the new government would have left them in a difficult limbo since they evidently had no broad popular base in the Maghrib. Without government support and permission to practise law, they, like the Mālikīs who were themselves to suffer considerably over the ensuing decades, would have lost out completely. This is, in fact, what happened to them. But many, as with the local Shi'is, welcomed the Fatimids and were happy, at least initially, to support them and did so avidly and enthusiastically.

The Fall and Execution of the Brothers

Sadly, the *da'wa* that put the Fatimids in power suffered a major blow soon after its victory. Abū 'Abdallāh, his brother, and their two closest Kutāma allies, Abū Zākī and Abū Mūsā, were accused of conspiracy and disloyalty.[60] Less than fourteen

60. For a complete review of the information about this event see Halm, *Reich*, 148–56, trans., 159–68.

months from the euphoria of al-Mahdī's arrival and assumption of power, he ordered that the four be executed for treason, first Abū Mūsā, and then in rapid succession Abū Zākī, followed by the two brothers on Monday 15 Jumādā II 298/18 February 911.[61] The story of what actually happened, however, was, for different reasons, subject to exaggeration for polemical purposes, depending on the particular viewpoint of the source that related or preserved various accounts and explanations of the incident.

Moreover, the repercussions of this event, despite a degree of immediate serious unrest and some acts of open rebellion among the Kutāma Berbers, were relatively inconsequential given the previous importance and obvious centrality of those who were put to death. But the Imam must certainly have risked a great deal in moving so decisively against these men; they had been the architects of his triumph, and many of his Berber followers were beholden to them long before they had accepted him. To warrant such a drastic step, the threat to him and his rule must therefore have constituted a real and present danger.

One reason for the weak response from some members of the *da'wa* who might have felt the most disquiet over the execution of the brothers was al-Mahdī's deliberate policy of reassigning and thus dispersing his *dā'īs*. To cite an example, Abū 'Alī was finally allowed to leave Egypt to join the Imam at his new headquarters in Raqqāda, but was almost immediately sent off again on yet another mission to, of all places, Constantinople where he was taken prisoner by the Byzantines and detained for the next five years.[62] Ibn al-Haytham, the author of the memoir that reveals so much about the brothers and their stewardship of Fatimid government just after the initial

61. This is the date given by Qāḍī al-Nu'mān (*Iftitāḥ*, 316). 'Arīb (Ibn 'Idhārī, *al-Bayan*, I, 164) prefers Tuesday, 1 Dhu'l-ḥijja 298/31 July 911.

62. This information comes from an obituary for Abū 'Alī included by Idrīs in his *'Uyūn al-akhbār* (as edited by al-Ya'lāwī, 236–38, but for some reason omitted from the earlier edition of M. Ghālib). See Madelung, 'Ḥamdān Qarmaṭ and the Dā'ī Abū 'Alī.'

takeover, who was clearly quite devoted to them personally, was dispatched to Spain as an ambassador to the famous Andalusian renegade 'Umar b. Ḥafṣūn, who had just recognized al-Mahdī as the caliph in his domains.[63] Neither of these key figures, therefore, were present when the blow occurred.

The accounts given in the sources leave the precise cause of the tragedy obscure. Fatimid tradition suggests that it was Abu'l-'Abbās, portrayed as Abū 'Abdallāh's evil older brother, who instigated the troubles that resulted in the executions by convincing his brother that he had more of a right to lead than the Imam. According to this version, Abu'l-'Abbās resented his own and his brother's demotion, and he was able to instill a similar attitude in the mind of Abū 'Abdallāh and of his Berber companions. Thus, although Abū 'Abdallāh went along with the plot against the Imam and deserved his own death, he was not himself the principal culprit or the primary cause of his own misfortune.[64]

Another explanation appears in both Fatimid and anti-Fatimid sources. According to these, the Berber leaders, disgruntled by their loss of power and the relative neglect of their interests on the part of the new caliph who, to cite but one of their grievances, often passed over them and re-employed officials of the previous regime in his new government, began to question his right to the imamate. Abū Mūsā, the supreme chief of the Kutāma, in particular, is said to have voiced doubts about whether or not al-Mahdī was, in fact, the Mahdi and to have demanded that he produce a miracle to prove his title. In one anti-Fatimid version Abū 'Abdallāh advises his Berber followers to demand that the Imam show them the sign that should be written on his back between his shoulder blades

63. Ibn al-Haytham alludes to his own participation in this embassy. The event itself was recorded in Ibn al-Khaṭīb's *Kitāb a'māl al-a'lām*, ed. E. Lévi-Provençal (Beirut, 1956), 32. See also Halm, *Reich*, 250, trans., 280.

64. This is certainly the case as it is presented by Qāḍī al-Nu'mān, *Iftitāḥ*, paras 278–88 (pp. 306–19), which is the main official Isma'ili explanation for the background and cause of this event.

if he were really the Mahdi.[65] In one way or another this story appears, not only in the blatantly polemical context of the writings of the anti-Isma'ili Qāḍī 'Abd al-Jabbār,[66] but also in Qāḍī al-Nu'mān's *Iftitāḥ*, which probably serves in this instance as an officially sanctioned account of what happened and why.

The case against Abu'l-'Abbās seems implausible on the surface. As the depiction of him by Ibn al-Haytham clearly reveals, the older brother, though admittedly more scholarly and, thus, the beneficiary of a wider and broader education than Abū 'Abdallāh, was equally devoted to the Isma'ili *da'wa* and its cause. Moreover, and most importantly, Abu'l-'Abbās had substantial personal knowledge of al-Mahdī, whom he had known both in Syria and in Egypt, as well as on the journey across North Africa. Like his brother he had spent over twenty years in the service of the *da'wa* whose Imam and supreme leader was al-Mahdī. Where Abū 'Abdallāh and his Kutāma companions spoke about abstractions they had never seen, Abu'l-'Abbās must have been rather familiar with the actual qualities of the man for whom they all worked.

Quite different is the case of Abū Mūsā. There is evidence of widespread dissatisfaction with the conduct of al-Mahdī among the Kutāma from the very beginning. Qāḍī al-Nu'mān reports that when the Imam, on his way from Sijilmāsa to Raqqāda, passed through Īkjān, he ordered that the money gathered by the Kutāma *dā'īs* and shaykhs in support of the Isma'ili cause be surrendered and carried off with him. According to al-Nu'mān this aroused considerable resentment.[67] At the same time the Imam ordered the faithful Kutāma supporters of the *da'wa* to move with him to the capital. Many of them may have expected that the Imam would reside among them, his most loyal supporters, as Abū 'Abdallāh had done.

65. Ibn 'Idhārī, *al-Bayān*, I, 161–2.

66. 'Abd al-Jabbār b. Aḥmad al-Hamadhānī, *Tathbīt dalā'il al-nubuwwa*, ed. 'Abd al-Karīm 'Uthmān (Beirut, 1966), 380–91. A version also appears in Ibn 'Idhārī, *al-Bayān*, I, 161–2.

67. See Qāḍī al-Nu'mān, *Iftitāḥ*, 288–9; Halm, *Reich*, 135–6, trans., 144.

Al-Mahdī's common reliance on Arab officials and on slave servants, the Kutāma's own relegation to a lower rank and status, as well as his caliphal lifestyle, added to the discontent and soon led to charges that he did not fulfil the expectations connected with the advent of the promised Mahdi.

Abū Mūsā, as the chief of the Kutāma, could not have been indifferent to such dissatisfaction even though al-Mahdī kept him as the chief of his Berber army. He appears in Ibn al-Haytham's account as a proud man who jealously guarded his own power, a person who did not hesitate to censure Abū 'Abdallāh openly when the latter appointed an independent judge in Qayrawan who would interfere with his own government. It is therefore not unreasonable to think that Abū Mūsā would have dared to confront al-Mahdī, giving vent to the misgivings among his tribesmen, without realizing that the Imam was much less dependent on his support than Abū 'Abdallāh had been. Although the open confrontation seems to indicate that a concrete scheme of revolt did not exist at the time, the Imam acted to deprive any Kutāma rebellion of its potential leadership.

While Abū Mūsā may well have come to regret al-Mahdī's assumption of power and may have contemplated a revolt against him, Abu'l-'Abbās's role in the plot looks more as if it was based on a calculated smear. Perhaps because he had entered the local scene only in the final phase of the Fatimid takeover and, thus, had no immediate following there, it was easier to lay blame on him as an outsider than on his brother, who was revered by the Kutāma with whom he had lived as teacher and leader for over eighteen years. Significantly, in his reaction to the deaths of the two brothers, al-Mahdī is reported to have expressed regret over that of Abū 'Abdallāh, whom he continued to praise for his efforts on behalf of the *da'wa.* But in the case of Abu'l-'Abbās he merely offered condemnation and reproach. The story of his reaction may be largely accurate and the sentiments expressed by the Imam genuine, but it also served a purpose in publicly assigning blame for what happened while at the same time preserving the link to Abū

'Abdallāh's original mission and his personal success with it.[68] Although now, as then, it is impossible to read Ibn al-Haytham's memoirs without pondering the loss of the two men he describes with such reverent awe and personal respect, he himself does not allude directly or, possibly, even indirectly to the tragedy itself. And this judgment applies most strikingly in the case of Abu'l-'Abbās, the putative villain of subsequent events.

In yet another passage of Qāḍī al-Nu'mān's account of Abū 'Abdallāh's seditious activity, he quotes at length the latter's rather pointed advice to the Imam not to corrupt the Kutāma by offering them riches, by appointing them to lucrative positions, and not to order them, as he had done, to wear pompous official dress and ornament.[69] Abū 'Abdallāh, thus, warned the caliph about his very style of rule. But it is obvious that the plain ascetic demeanour and simple habits that Abū 'Abdallāh acquired from long years of work in the field among the tribesmen were not those of al-Mahdī, who as Fatimid caliph adopted the trappings of power and majesty and kept a distance between himself and them. Ibn al-Haytham remarks on these qualities of Abū 'Abdallāh who, it seemed, no amount of wealth and power could change. Abū 'Abdallāh, who knew the Berbers as well as any outsider, saw what troubles lay ahead,[70] but his advice could easily be taken as a ploy for his own return to command. According to Qāḍī al-Nu'mān, Abū 'Abdallāh had in fact suggested to the Imam that he leave the command of the Kutāma to him, in which case al-Mahdī would have been able to live at ease in his palace without being troubled by any of them.

It may be significant that Abū 'Alī, the old *dā'ī* who had

68. Al-Mahdī's words in this instance are quoted not only by Qāḍī al-Nu'mān, where they might be expected most, but by the anti-Fatimid 'Arīb (Ibn 'Idhārī, *al-Bayān*, I, 164–5) as well.

69. Qāḍī al-Nu'mān, *Iftitāḥ*, par. 279 (p. 308), quoted in full by Halm, *Reich*, 150, trans., 161.

70. The Berber disapproval of material wealth was also reflected in the revolt of the Kharijite Abū Yazīd, who took pride in his ascetic life style and castigated the Fatimid caliphs for amassing riches.

recruited the brothers and knew them well, was not nearby when the crisis occurred. As previously noted he had already been dispatched by al-Mahdī on a mission to Constantinople where the authorities detected his true purpose and put him in prison. However, when he was eventually released, he returned to North Africa and is reported to have commented that, had he been present, he could have prevented the tragedy. He used to say, 'Our Lord, the Commander of the Faithful, is like the sun whose light is bright and blinding such that, if it were not followed by the moon to moderate and cool its effects, no plant could develop properly on earth and the heat would overpower it.'[71] But whatever al-Mahdī actually believed or had been told about the matter, and whether or not it was entirely accurate, he regarded it as treason and acted accordingly.

The Role and Character of Abu'l-'Abbās

Given the effort to blacken his name and blame him for the corruption and downfall of his brother, the role of Abu'l-'Abbās deserves special attention here because it contrasts so completely with the picture that emerges from Ibn al-Haytham's account of him.[72] Clearly, despite his secondary position with

71. Quoted by Madelung in his article 'Ḥamdān Qarmaṭ and the Dā'ī Abū 'Alī' (p. 120) from the obituary of Abū 'Alī as preserved in the *'Uyūn al-akhbār* (ed. al-Ya'lāwī, p. 237).

72. For the known facts about Abu'l-'Abbās, see the following: al-Maqrīzī, *al-Muqaffā al-kabīr*, ed. M. al-Ya'lāwī (Beirut, 1991), vol. 5, 264–7; Ibn 'Idhārī, *al-Bayān*, I, 150–2; al-Naysābūrī, *Istitār al-imām*, in Ivanow, *Rise*, 182; *Sīrat Ja'far*, 116, 121–2, 123, Eng. trans. in *Rise*, 198, 206, 209, Canard trans., 295–305 (especially 298 n. 2); Qāḍī al-Nu'mān, *Iftitāḥ*, pp. 162, 260–3, 269–70, 275, 306–20; Qāḍī al-Nu'mān, *Kitāb al-Majālis wa'l-musāyarāt*, ed. al-Ḥabīb al-Faqī, Ibrāhīm Shabbūḥ and Muḥammad al-Ya'lāwī (Tunis, 1978), 183f; Idrīs, *'Uyūn*, ms. (as given by al-Yalāwī) pp. 112–13, 117, 132–3, 147–9, 161, 163–4, 167–8, 223; al-Khushanī, 199–210, trans., 288–304; Halm, *Reich*, 44, 61, 74, 89, 105, 117–20, 122, 133, 136, 151–6, 217, 332, trans., 39, 58, 73, 91, 109, 124–8, 130, 141, 145, 162, 165–8, 240, 375; and 'Abd al-Jabbār, *Tathbīt*, 380–91.

respect to the mission of Abū 'Abdallāh, Abu'l-'Abbās was an important figure and, from as far back as 278/891, was intimately linked to the central activities of the *da'wa.* There are, moreover, references to Abū 'Abdallāh's almost reverential regard for his older brother, whom he treated as his senior in more than chronological age. He is said, for example, to have stood up for Abu'l-'Abbās whenever they were together, and to have remained standing until his brother granted him permission to sit. Of the two, Abu'l-'Abbās was obviously the better educated.[73] Fatimid sources, such as the *Iftitāḥ*, agree on this, and the new account by Ibn al-Haytham bears ample witness to it. Qāḍī al-Nu'mān readily admits that Abu'l-'Abbās had a keener intellect and sharper wit and was more learned in the sciences than his brother.[74] Moreover, Abu'l-'Abbās seems to have read widely, not only in religious sciences, but also in a full range of classical Greek sciences and theories.

Ibn al-Haytham was quite convinced of his great merit. He says of him, 'I had not seen his like before, nor do I expect that I will meet another the equal of him, who combined in himself all the sciences, who had read through the doctrines of every school, who had investigated the doctrine of those who differ and fully comprehended the statements of both ally and opponent.' And in another place he remarks, 'This man has an even greater eminence than his brother. In terms of rank, he surpasses his brother in knowledge. He exceeds him in the excellence of his company, the nobility of his character and his civility ... .'

He was, moreover, deeply impressed with Abu'l-'Abbās's masterful stewardship of the new government during the more than seven months of his rule. Yet Ibn al-Haytham's portrait of Abu'l-'Abbās presents him as a reluctant leader, a person less at ease with public responsibilities than his brother. He, for example, at first insisted that he would not meet with or receive

73. See, for example, the comments of Qāḍī al-Nu'mān, *Iftitāḥ*, par. 243 (pp. 269–70); Halm, *Reich*, 118–19, trans., 126.

74. *Iftitāḥ*, 269–70. However, Qāḍī al-Nu'mān also notes that Abū 'Abdallāh was sounder in his judgement and the more pious of the two.

the visits of others until the Imam and his brother returned. Later he accepted only under pressure to host a general audience at the feast marking the end of Ramaḍān. Many, if not most, of his sessions with Ibn al-Haytham occurred in private with few other than servants in attendance.

It is interesting also that Abu'l-'Abbās, once freed from Aghlabid detention in 293/906, chose to retreat to Tripoli. For three years he remained there and did not attempt to reach either his brother or the Imam. Perhaps he had been ordered to do exactly that or knew well that it might be too difficult and even impossible to journey into the mountains where Abū 'Abdallāh and the Kutāma were. If he had been apprehended a second time en route to the west, it would have appeared a sure proof of his complicity. He might, however, have contemplated travelling on to Sijilmāsa but did not. Even when the final victory came, Abu'l-'Abbās did not set out immediately.

It is true that the fleeing Aghlabids blocked the path for a time although they soon enough reached Tripoli. There Ziyādatallāh confronted Abu'l-'Abbās for one last time. For most of those three years a party of Fatimids had waited in the city. Among them were the mother and sisters of the Imam under the care and protection of al-Khazarī, another *dā'ī* like Abu'l-'Abbās. The two *dā'īs*, in fact, often debated with each other in the mosque pretending to support the doctrines and opinions of opposite sides so as to deflect suspicion of any collusion between them. When Ziyādatallāh attempted in that last encounter to force a confession from Abu'l-'Abbās about his connection to Abū 'Abdallāh, the brother could argue that, if he had been related to the leader of the Berber rebellion, he would have gone over to them instead of travelling to Tripoli and, in any case, would have already proceeded to Raqqāda.[75]

But was he ordered to remain in Tripoli until granted explicit permission to join Abū 'Abdallāh, which he received only in time for him to arrive just before his brother's departure for

75. Qāḍī al-Nu'mān, *Iftitāḥ*, paras 235–7 (pp. 260–3); Halm, *Reich*, 117–18, trans., 125.

Sijilmāsa?[76] The chronology of the events as implied by the *Iftitāḥ*[77] does not accord with the observations of Ibn al-Haytham, who seems to indicate that Abu'l-'Abbās did not reach Raqqāda until just before his brother's departure. Even then his role evidently had not been clearly delineated by Abū 'Abdallāh, who may not have had much time to arrange matters of that sort, and his assumption of what authority he inherited began slowly and hesitantly.

Thus, the picture of Abu'l-'Abbās painted by the sources is of an urbane scholarly intellectual, more at ease in private social exchanges than with public responsibilities, and less inclined to take on an arduous missionary venture of the kind his brother pursued. In contrast to Abū 'Abdallāh, he took evident delight in the pleasures of a sumptuous meal. Obviously, fine living held an appeal for him. It may well have been indicative of his character that he remained in Egypt when his brother went first to the Yemen and then to the Maghrib. In this he was not unlike Ibn al-Haytham, whose scholarly interests were much the same, and who, despite great sympathy for the cause of Abū 'Abdallāh, had not left the urban security of his home in Qayrawan for the rugged existence of the rebels in the mountains – a point not lost on Abū 'Abdallāh who raised it against him early in their first meeting together. It seems, therefore, unlikely that Abu'l-'Abbās would have been moved by personal political ambition. At most he may have encouraged his brother in the aim of preserving his effective control over the Kutāma and, thus, have exposed himself to the suspicion

76. The distance between Raqqāda and Tripoli is somewhat over 600 kilometres or about fourteen stages. Therefore, although pigeons could swiftly deliver a note from one place to the other, a journey on land would have required about a month for a round trip. Abū 'Abdallāh cannot have sent for his brother until some time in Rajab 296/April 909 at the earliest and it could well have been later. That Abu'l-'Abbās did not reach Raqqāda before Ramaḍān (May–June), perhaps not until early June, is thus reasonable and likely. This explains why Ibn al-Haytham, who was frequently in attendance with Abū 'Abdallāh, did not meet Abu'l-'Abbās until after the former's departure in mid-Ramaḍān (6 June).

77. Pp. 269–70.

that he wanted to remove the Imam from political power.

2. IBN AL-HAYTHAM AND THE HISTORICAL SOURCES

The Sources Previously Known

An unusual array of surviving sources cover various aspects of the advent of the Fatimids in North Africa. Of those known previously, two provide a view of it from outside and two from inside. Yet all four, at least in origin, were contemporary or come from sources contemporary to the events in question or nearly so. Most importantly they represent separate accounts not dependent on each other. They are the history of Ibn ʿIdhārī entitled *al-Bayān al-mughrib fī akhbār mulūk al-Andalus wa'l-Maghrib,* the biographies collected by al-Khushanī in his *Kitāb Ṭabaqāt ʿulamāʾ Ifrīqiya,* Qāḍī al-Nuʿmān's official history of the founding of the Fatimid state, his *Iftitāḥ al-daʿwa wa ibtidāʾ al-dawla,* and finally the memoirs of al-Mahdī's chamberlain Jaʿfar. In addition there is a fair amount of information in other works that add to and complement what these four record. Moreover, quite significantly, and uncharacteristically for the Fatimids over the long run of their reign, the two inside accounts derived ultimately from the inner circles of the Ismaʿili organization. Later periods of Fatimid history were, to be sure, similarly chronicled or otherwise documented by witnesses, but these writings have all too frequently not survived. It is also true to a certain extent that, with the possible exception of al-Khushanī's text, the information in the other three primary sources comes to us second hand.

Abu'l-ʿAbbās Aḥmad b. Muḥammad b. ʿIdhārī al-Marrākushī lived long after the Fatimids.[78] He was active in the second half of the seventh/thirteenth and early eighth/fourteenth century. His *al-Bayān al-mughrib,* however, was based on and thus contains a good deal of valuable information from older

78. On him see J. Bosch-Vilá, 'Ibn ʿIdhārī' in the *EI2*.

chronicles, most notably, for the coming of the Fatimids, the chronicle of ʿArīb b. Saʿd. An Andalusian native, ʿArīb, who died about 370/980, wrote his own history of the Maghrib for the Umayyad court in Cordova and his basic outlook was thus pro-Umayyad. Nevertheless, like al-Khushanī, of whom he was a younger contemporary, he relied in all likelihood for a good part of his information concerning the Maghrib on Mālikī refugees who had fled from there to Spain. In any case, because of the insertion in it of whole passages from ʿArīb,[79] the work of Ibn ʿIdhārī is now the major source for the history of the later Aghlabids and the North African Fatimids. No other source provides as much information over the whole of the relevant time frame or as wide a geographical range.[80]

Quite separate from Ibn ʿIdhārī, the Mālikī *Ṭabaqāt* of Abū ʿAbdallāh Muḥammad b. al-Ḥārith al-Khushanī, who was born near Qayrawan where he was educated prior to departing in 311/923, offer a near contemporary eyewitness account of the lives and activities of many of the figures he thought fit to

79. From p. 134 of the edition the text is, in fact, based on the Gotha manuscript of a fragment of ʿArīb's chronicle in addition to the two manuscripts of Ibn ʿIdhārī. There are quite long and important texts marked by square brackets in the edition which are found only in the ʿArīb manuscript and which were evidently omitted by Ibn ʿIdhārī. Words or passages found only in the Ibn ʿIdhārī mss. are enclosed in parentheses in the edition, but they are, with a few exceptions, quite insignificant. Since the ʿArīb manuscript contains only a fragment of his chronicle, it is likely that most of the text up to p. 134 also goes back to ʿArīb. He should therefore be given full credit in quotations from the *Bayān* in the sections on Aghlabid and early Fatimid rule, especially those marked by square brackets.

80. Though not for the period in question here, one other important source for Ibn ʿIdhārī was the *History* (*Taʾrīkh Ifrīqiya waʾl-Maghrib*) of Abū Isḥāq Ibrāhīm al-Qayrawānī, usually called simply Ibn al-Raqīq, which is itself apparently lost. Ibn al-Raqīq, who died after 418/1027–8, worked for the Zīrids at a time when they were still ostensibly loyal and subservient to the Fatimids. He is thought to have visited Cairo during the reign of al-Ḥākim and to have been pro-Shiʿi. Ibn al-Raqīq likely had access to some Fatimid works, quite possibly those of Qāḍī al-Nuʿmān, but perhaps others. See M. Talbi, 'Ibn al-Raḳīḳ' in the *EI2*.

include in it. Although al-Khushanī eventually moved to Spain (where he died in 371/981) and to service there under the Umayyads, early in his life he had witnessed the Fatimid assumption of power and had seen the measures taken by them. Most importantly, in contrast to the *ṭabaqāt* works of the other Mālikī authorities, which naturally focus almost exclusively on the scholars and notables of this *madhhab*, al-Khushanī added to his own various sections on the Ḥanafīs, as well as accounts of those *fuqahā'* of Qayrawan who converted to the Isma'ili cause and also a special list of the scholars who were persecuted by the government.

Later Maghribi *ṭabaqāt* compilations, which were all Mālikī, never failed, of course, to point out the repression of their own by the Fatimids. The most important of these works, al-Mālikī's *Riyāḍ al-nufūs* and Qāḍī 'Iyāḍ's *Madārik*,[81] although rich in information about what happened to the members of this particular school under the Fatimids, both tend toward exaggeration and hagiography[82] and, regardless, depend on al-Khushanī for the details of the earliest encounters with the Isma'ilis as well as for the biographies of any of the scholars from Qayrawan under the last Aghlabids. Therefore, al-Khushanī's work has a historical value that is not always characteristic of items in the *ṭabaqāt* genre. He was certainly not unbiased but, nevertheless, he provides a viewpoint not given by 'Arīb or by the Isma'ili sources. Therefore he cannot be ignored. Still, because of his anti-Fatimid bias, most of the information he gives needs to be treated with caution. All along it would have helped immensely to have available some

81. Abū Bakr 'Abdallāh b. Muḥammad al-Mālikī, a native of Qayrawan, died about 460/1068 (according to Bakkūsh, the editor of his *Riyāḍ al-nufūs*) and the Qāḍī 'Iyāḍ b. Mūsā al-Sabtī (from Ceuta) died in 544/1149. On the latter see the article by M. Talbi in the *EI2*.

82. These later Mālikī writers, beginning with al-Mālikī's *Ṭabaqāt*, were evidently under moral pressure to justify the horrible massacres of Ismaili communities throughout the Maghrib instigated by the Mālikī *'ulamā'*. This may explain why they quote at length lurid and obviously fictitious tales about Fatimid atrocities and about Ismaili heresy and atheism.

balancing record giving the opposing view.

In contrast to the non-Isma'ili accounts of the rise of the Fatimids and the reaction to them that may be extracted from sources such as those just mentioned, Isma'ili and thus Fatimid records largely, if not entirely, disappeared from North Africa and later even from Egypt. They were preserved almost exclusively by that Yemeni branch of the post-Fatimid Isma'ili *da'wa* known as the Ṭayyibīs. Even now most copies derive from Indian Ṭayyibī libraries where the majority of such texts have been copied and preserved. But, while the history of Ibn 'Idhārī appeared in print as long ago as 1848–51[83] and the Arabic text of al-Khushanī in 1915, Isma'ili works have been slow to reach historians because of their relative inaccessibility. Thus, a balanced account of Fatimid achievements could not be contemplated until recently. Finally, in 1936, the Arabic text of Ja'far's *Sīra* was published (with an English translation in 1942; French 1952). Qāḍī al-Nu'mān's *Iftitāḥ al-da'wa*, however, though available to some scholars in manuscript earlier – it was put to good use, for example, by Mohamed Talbi in his *L'Emirat Aghlabide* (1966) – ultimately came out only in 1970, edited by Wadad Kadi (Dachraoui's edition in 1975).

However, even these two extremely valuable sources, rich as they are in detail, do not provide significant information needed for the whole picture. For example, for reasons not obvious in the text, Qāḍī al-Nu'mān, although quite thorough in his writing on the mission of Abū 'Abdallāh and its background, is less meticulous in his account from the point of his triumph onward. While he provides additional information, sometimes of great importance, such as the copies he includes of official decrees and other court proclamations from the earliest period of the new government, he is less attentive to events that took place in Raqqāda and Qayrawan for the period from Abū 'Abdallāh's assumption of power to the time when al-Mahdī

83. First edited by R. Dozy in his *Histoire de l'Afrique et de l'Éspagne* (Leiden, 1948–51), an edition that was superseded in 1948–51 by that of Colin and Lévi-Provençal.

took over. Perhaps, given that he provides such a wealth of information about other matters both before and after, his relative neglect of events in Qayrawan is not noteworthy. But did he also know about the memoirs of Ibn al-Haytham which certainly fill this gap amply? Or was he deliberately avoiding a discussion of the activities of Abu'l-'Abbās whom he overtly blames for corrupting Abū 'Abdallāh and causing the downfall of both as well as their Berber colleagues? Significantly, Qāḍī al-Nu'mān and his works were accorded an official status and were personally approved by the Imams al-Manṣūr and al-Mu'izz.

The *Sīra* of Ja'far represents a uniquely personal document, though not one written by the person who related the story but by a later author, Muḥammad b. Muḥammad al-Yamānī from the reign of the Fatimid caliph al-'Azīz who, nevertheless, offers it as a first-person memoir. However, if Ja'far, who was born within months of his master al-Mahdī in 260/874, had still been alive in the time of al-'Azīz (365–386/975–996), he would have then exceeded the age of one hundred. Even granted its authenticity in general, there are details in it that Ja'far could not recall precisely, as he admitted himself. Significantly, despite his later role as chamberlain, he was originally simply a servant and, thus, did not necessarily have accurate knowledge about sensitive matters as, for example, those connected to the workings of the *da'wa*. Still, he did personally witness major events or was present on important occasions.

Ibn al-Haytham and the Value of his Work

The *Kitāb al-Munāẓarāt* both provides an unexpected abundance of new information about a critically important period and at the same time fills in a chapter largely missing from the other sources. But recognition of its significance was delayed in part because the text did not survive on its own. Also, when it was first quoted in Isma'ili literature, it was not cited by a title but merely by author. Therefore, the true nature of the work in question remained unknown and became the subject of speculation. Accordingly, when S. M. Stern noticed the passages from it as they appear in Idrīs ʿImād al-Dīn's history of the Ismaʿili Imams, the *ʿUyūn al-akhbār*, he knew them only by the author without any way to recognize what work they might have come from.[84] It is now clear, however, that the three quotations given by Idrīs in the name of Ibn al-Aswad or Ibn al-Haytham all come from the *Kitāb al-Munāẓarāt*.

Idrīs, who lived from 794/1392 until 872/1468, was the nineteenth chief *dāʿī* of the Ṭayyibī Ismaʿilis in the Yemen.[85] His son al-Ḥasan became the twentieth *dāʿī* and was also the teacher of Ḥasan b. Nūḥ b. Yūsuf b. Muḥammad b. Ādam al-Hindī al-Bharūchī (d. 939/1533), the author of the extensive compilation of Ismaʿili texts called by him the *Azhār*. Born in India, he travelled to the Yemen to study with the leading Ṭayyibī authorities, most of whom continued to reside there.[86] He began the *Azhār* in 931/1524 and completed it after 935/1528. Fortunately, in the sixth part of the *Azhār*, al-Bharūchī, as he was wont to do with other works, simply copied Ibn al-Haytham's *Munāẓarāt* verbatim, even though only the beginning of it was germane to the subject he claimed to want to illustrate, namely the imamate of ʿAlī b. Abī Ṭālib. However, he stated clearly that the text contains an account of the discussions (the *munāẓarāt*) of Ibn al-Haytham with Abū ʿAbdallāh. This fact was thus known to anyone with access to the *Azhār* and it appears appropriately and correctly in Poonawala's

84. Stern, who was trying to identify material in the *ʿUyūn al-akhbār* that did not appear in any other known source, collected these quotations along with a number of others and they were eventually published together in his posthumous *Studies in Early Ismāʿīlism* (Jerusalem, 1983), 100–4. H. Halm subsequently offered the speculation that all of these items were from the same work, a lost *Sīrat al-Mahdī*, which he then ascribed to Ibn al-Haytham. See his 'Zwei fatimidische Quellen aus der Zeit des Kalifen al-Mahdī (909–934),' *Die Welt des Orients*, 19 (1988): 102–117.

85. On him see Ismail K. Poonawala's *Biobibliography of Ismāʿīlī Literature* (Malibu, Calif., 1977), 169–75, and 'Idrīs b. al-Ḥasan' also by Poonawala in the *EI2*, *Supplement*.

86. On him see Poonawala, *Biobibliography*, 178–83.

Biobibliography of Ismāʿīlī Literature.[87]

However, while the text and its author were known in this manner and copies of the *Azhār* existed, the work itself received little or no serious scrutiny, perhaps because its potential historical value was masked by its bland title which, in the absence of careful inspection, appeared to promise no more than yet another discussion of doctrine. In his record of these debates, interrogations and discussions, Ibn al-Haytham in fact reveals a great deal more than simple items of doctrine; but from the title alone this was hardly obvious and it has thus proved to be an unexpected benefit of the complete manuscript. Perhaps the most interesting of all the *Munāẓarāt*'s new material are the details it provides of the author's own background and his upbringing among the elite of Qayrawan, of his education and career, and of his impressions of the two brothers who played so pivotal a role in the Fatimid revolution. These are not the normal elements of a *munāẓara,* which is usually simply a work of disputation.

Moreover, while it ostensibly covers only the author's conversations with Abū ʿAbdallāh and Abu'l-ʿAbbās, much of Ibn al-Haytham's *Munāẓarāt* consists of stories that he told them about himself and about things that had happened to him. Thus, while these stories are in fact a part of various 'discussions' (the *munāẓarāt* of the title), they constitute at the same time elements of the author's own autobiography. In truth the narrative contains less of either of the two brothers than it does of Ibn al-Haytham. Many, if not the majority, of the passages in it record the words and statements the author made to someone else, not those of the men with whom he was conversing.

Thus, ultimately, the circumstances that prompted Ibn al-Haytham to write this work may reflect more than his desire to extol the virtues of the two brothers. From comments in it, moreover, it is clear that he cannot have written this work before the year 334/946, some thirty-seven years after the events he describes. By then he was about sixty years old and evidently

87. Ibid., pp. 34–5.

a well respected senior *dāʿī* of long standing and much service to the Ismaʿili *daʿwa* and the Imams. The year in question happens to coincide with the most dangerous and intense period of Abū Yazīd's revolt against the Fatimids. This Khariji rebel had taken Qayrawan that year and threatened the coastal capital city of al-Mahdiyya. In the same year, the Imam al-Qā'im died and his son succeeded, although, to avoid giving aid to the rebels, no public announcement of this fact was made for a while. The son quickly took to the field and began a long series of clashes with the enemy in which he was almost always victorious. He retook Qayrawan that same year (after Shawwāl 334/28 May 946).

Ibn al-Haytham mentions Abū Yazīd whom he, like all Fatimid writers, calls the Dajjāl ('the apocalyptic deceiver'). He also proudly notes that the 'son of the Imam' has taken the field against him. Surely, whether or not he personally knew that al-Qā'im had died, he could not put that fact in writing and therefore in these circumstances he used the officially allowed designation of his successor. Perhaps he did not know about it. Al-Manṣūr was not called by his eventual throne name until 336/947 after he had achieved total victory over Abū Yazīd.

One more item in Ibn al-Haytham's account has a bearing on the question of the date and circumstances of writing, namely his comment about the letter that Abu'l-ʿAbbās had written to the qadi al-Marwadhī, admonishing him to deal with members of the *daʿwa* with special care. Ibn al-Haytham says that he once owned the letter but had lost it among other possessions taken from him during the revolt of Abū Yazīd. Evidently he must refer to things that were in his own house in Qayrawan from which he had obviously had to flee. The house, which was known to belong to him, an Ismaʿili *dāʿī*, was without doubt ransacked by the invading forces (or possibly even the local population many of whom seized the occupation as an occasion for revenge). But Ibn al-Haytham could not have been sure of his specific losses before the re-entry of the Fatimid army at the end of May.

Why then did he decide at that moment to write the story of his first encounter with Abū 'Abdallāh and Abu'l-'Abbās? From the context it appears that he may have realized that the previous Imam was dead and that a new era under the son was about to begin. He obviously wanted to insure his place and position in the new *da'wa*, perhaps even to claim a higher rank. Thus, it was important in his view to rehearse for his reader, namely, the person to whom the work is addressed, who was probably above him in terms of influence among members of the innermost circle, including possibly the new Imam, his own credentials and his early membership and service in the *da'wa.* A subtext in his writing is the recurring theme of the high respect and regard due the *dā'īs* and their efforts which he hoped would be an inherent part of the next Imam's policies. Surely he hoped to benefit from it. If so, however, there is no sign that it worked in his favour. Al-Manṣūr and later al-Mu'izz gave preference to Qāḍī al-Nu'mān who may well have been a rival of Ibn al-Haytham.

The text of Ibn al-Haytham's memoir is, nonetheless, of inestimable significance, both for the history of the rise of the Fatimids in the Maghrib and for how the Isma'ili *da'wa* functioned in the first months following the victory of Abū 'Abdallāh. Incidental, but with almost equal claim to attention, is its depiction of the intellectual life of Qayrawan, the author's hometown, and that of his father and immediate ancestors.

One result of Ibn al-Haytham's extended discussion with Abū 'Abdallāh was his own conversion to the Isma'ili cause and his entry into the service of the *da'wa* as a *dā'ī.* Although the proselytizing role of the *da'wa* and its members is relatively clear from other accounts, none are as personal and direct. Here is perhaps the earliest account of what led one Isma'ili *dā'ī* to his own conversion, of what message he responded to, and how the senior *dā'ī* – in this case the masterful Abū 'Abdallāh, whose record of success as a missionary was, quite possibly, unsurpassed – convinced him to offer a pledge of total allegiance. The very act of making this covenant, although well known in the abstract, is here described in detail with its religious and doctrinal justification fully outlined by Abū 'Abdallāh himself.[88] To be sure, the interrogation by Abū 'Abdallāh of Ibn al-Haytham reveals more about the author's prior religious knowledge and opinions than the teachings of the *da'wa* to which he was being summoned. Still, the method of Abū 'Abdallāh and what questions he used in order to elicit from Ibn al-Haytham the answers he wanted is itself instructive and provides a unique window to the activities of these *dā'īs*.

The work also presents a carefully drawn portrait of Abu'l-'Abbās. Assuming that, in his discussions with Ibn al-Haytham, he, too, in part intended to further the Isma'ili cause rather than merely entertain his new protégé, Abu'l-'Abbās's methods in many ways constitute a striking contrast to those of his brother. The older brother was obviously erudite in matters that Abū 'Abdallāh had either never studied, or preferred to ignore. The education of the discussants in the second half of the text is a noteworthy feature of it: they had each read Aristotle, for example, and could, as they did, discuss fine points of his logic or his treatises on animals. They each knew Hippocrates, Dioscurides, and other ancient sages, as well as the Epistles of Paul and other books. It is, on the one hand, interesting to find such learning in the provincal city of Qayrawan already by the end of the third/ninth century, but it is possibly of even more significance, on the other hand, to discover this level of erudition in key figures of the *da'wa* of that time and place.

Another highly important fund of new information in this text is its account of the Shi'is of Qayrawan. However few and isolated they were, their existence was not previously known and could hardly have been suspected from other sources. Ibn al-Haytham was born into a Zaydi family and, although he himself admits that he left the Zaydis for the Shi'ism of the Imamis,

88. For what was known previously about the Ismaili practice of taking an oath from those who converted, see H. Halm's 'The Isma'ili Oath of Allegiance (*'ahd*) and the 'Sessions of Wisdom' (*majālis al-ḥikma*) in Fatimid Times' in F. Daftary ed., *Mediaeval Isma'ili History and Thought*, 91–115.

who were also represented in Qayrawan, he continued his links to a variety of Shi'i schools. When he finally met Abū 'Abdallāh, he had also departed from strict Imami doctrine by remaining undecided about the correct line of the Imams after Ja'far al-Ṣādiq. He was thus not a Twelver, as he carefully explained to Abū 'Abdallāh. Still, at a critical point in his life Ibn al-Haytham was almost deprived of his inheritance by a Mālikī judge. Had he not concealed his beliefs and books and sought the intervention of a powerful friend of his father, his troubles might have multiplied. The Shi'is living under Sunni rule, even those who came from a wealthy, noble background, as in the case of Ibn al-Haytham, possessed neither security from religiously motivated persecution nor open and free access to others of like mind. Nonetheless, he was close to al-Marwadhī, whom he personally recommended for the judgeship of Qayrawan, to the latter's son, to a few other Shi'is, and to yet others who were later to convert to Isma'ilism, among them prominent Ḥanafīs, a substantial number of whom soon became Isma'ilis. Ibn al-Haytham's personal encounters with, and depiction of individual scholars from Qayrawan, which he related to the two brothers, are unusually valuable and provide an inside view of the elite of that city on the eve of a dramatic change.

The Education and Career of Ibn al-Haytham

In answer to a series of questions put to him by Abū 'Abdallāh, Ibn al-Haytham recounts the details of his heritage. His family traced their lineage to Kufa and to noble northern Arab blood. He was descended from Qays b. 'Āṣim b. Sinān b. Khālid b. Minqar of the tribe of Tamīm. An ancestor, the grandfather of his grandfather's father, al-Haytham b. 'Abd al-Raḥmān, had first come to Qayrawan in the service of the 'Abbasid governor Yazīd b. Ḥātim. Yazīd's brother and successor in the governorship of the Maghrib, Rawḥ b. Ḥātim, released him from service and sent him home with 10,000 dinars. Soon, however, having raised an even larger sum and having obtained a commission from the ʿAbbasid caliph al-Hādī (or al-Rashīd), he returned and began to acquire estates and build houses. He constructed one of these on the Simāṭ al-Aʿẓam, the main street of Qayrawan. As late as the reign of al-Muʿizz this same house, obviously still identified with the author of these memoirs, is mentioned in passing in a Mālikī *ṭabaqāt* work as 'the house of the *dāʿī* Ibn Aswad.'[89]

Ibn al-Haytham's father died, he reports, in 285/898 when he was not yet at puberty, although he had by then read the Qur'an several times as well as other books on language, rare words, disputation, and legal reasoning. One would thus surmise that he was about eleven or twelve at this time, which places his birth in 273/886 or 274/887. After his father's death, he continued to study religious subjects, including Ḥanafī law, and began also to take an interest in the books of the ancients, copies of which he possessed in his library, among them the works of Plato and Aristotle. At one point, in order to master logic, he engaged a Jew named Yūsuf b. Yaḥyā al-Khurāsānī to teach him. Later, he received instruction from another teacher who was to stimulate his interest in the imamate and thus the scholarly investigation of Shiʿi literature and doctrine.

Thus, when he met Abū ʿAbdallāh, he was well versed in Shiʿism, as well as the sciences of the ancients that were to be of more concern to the latter's brother Abu'l-ʿAbbās. The brothers were obviously pleased to discover both the rich learning of Ibn al-Haytham and his eager devotion to the Shiʿi cause which they quickly determined to harness. He was drawn into service almost at once, one aspect of which involved his role in the frequent debates the two brothers set up with the local *fuqahā'*, both the Ḥanafīs and the Mālikīs. Ibn al-Haytham acted as the champion of the Shiʿi side in many of these encounters.

Later still, at the end of the period of his memoir, the author provides a strikingly vivid picture of the arrival of the Imam. Ibn al-Haytham's motive in doing so is, of course, partly to show how he was himself honoured on that occasion when he first

89. Al-Mālikī, *Riyāḍ*, II, 487–8.

met al-Mahdī. Finally, he adds a few notes about his association with prominent *dāʿīs* of the time such as Aflaḥ b. Hārūn al-Malūsī, a leading authority among the Kutāma who apparently impressed the author highly.

What Ibn al-Haytham does not state directly but only alludes to is his service not long after the coming of al-Mahdī as an ambassador – one of two *dāʿīs* – who were sent to Andalus to the famous rebel ʿUmar b. Ḥafṣūn. This ʿUmar held out in opposition to the Umayyad rulers for a long time and is reported to have converted back to the Christianity of his ancestors late in life. Nevertheless, when al-Mahdī declared his caliphate in the Maghrib, Ibn Ḥafṣūn recognized him as the caliph of the Muslims in his domain and had him cited in the *khuṭba* accordingly. Al-Mahdī sent a delegation to him consisting of two Ismaʿilis with robes of honour (*khilʿāt*) and they stayed with Ibn Ḥafṣūn for some time, even attending some of his battles against the Umayyads. Finally, the Andalusian sent them back with gifts for their master in return.[90] Evidently Ibn al-Haytham was one of the two delegates, as he himself suggests at the beginning of his memoir.

Another incident he mentions occurred subsequently when he was dispatched as a *dāʿī* to the western Maghrib. Bitterly, he casts blame on the Berber prince of Tāhart, Maṣāla, and his sister for what happened there. Maṣāla b. Ḥabūs ostensibly supported the Fatimids. However, ʿArīb[91] reports an incident in the year 309/921 when several *dāʿīs* were killed by the local people in Wansharīsh, an area under Maṣāla's control. Shortly thereafter, al-Mahdī cracked down hard on a large number of *dāʿīs*, many of whom were rounded up and imprisoned on the charge of having advocated antinomianism. This matter obviously caused great concern in the *daʿwa* at the time and, even many years later, Qāḍī al-Nuʿmān was forced to recall and discuss the incident when al-Manṣūr asked him about it, as he

90. These details are contained in the report of Ibn al-Khaṭīb, *Kitāb aʿmāl al-aʿlām*, ed. E. Lévi-Provençal, p. 32.

91. Ibn ʿIdhārī, *al-Bayān*, I, 185–6.

recorded in his *al-Majālis wa'l-musāyarāt.*[92] Although any suggestion that Ibn al-Haytham might have preached a disregard for the law of Islam appears totally unwarranted from the information about him in his own memoir,[93] he seems to have suffered himself in this purge and presumably held Maṣāla and his sister ultimately responsible for what had happened and believed that, despite their nominal recognition of the Fatimids, they were acting out of purely regional and personal motives to rid themselves of the *da'wa* and its influence in their territory. Thus, in his view, both the initial killings of the *dā'īs* in Wansharīsh and al-Mahdī's subsequent severe repression of additional *dā'īs* was caused by some plot or intimation set in motion by Maṣāla. It is significant that, when al-Manṣūr restored Fatimid rule in Tāhart in 336/947 following the rebellion of Abū Yazīd, the bodies of both Maṣāla, who had died long before in 312/924, and his brother Yaṣal, also long dead (d. 319/931), were exhumed and publicly burned.[94] The sister is apparently not mentioned in any other source.

Ibn al-Haytham in non-Isma'ili Sources

It would appear that there are only three known references to the author in non-Isma'ili sources, two under the name Ibn al-Aswad and one as Ibn al-Haytham. Evidently, he was known locally mainly by the former name and in other places by the latter, or by both as also in later Isma'ili literature, such as the *'Uyūn al-akhbār* of Idrīs. Abū Ḥayyān al-Tawḥīdī in his *al-Imtā' wa'l-mu'ānasa* comments about a debate on the subject of the imamate that allegedly had taken place between Ibn al-Haytham and Ibn al-Ḥaddād.[95] His information is second hand and not

92. See Qāḍī al-Nu'mān, *al-Majālis,* pp. 499–500.

93. Against this, it may be noted that Ibn al-Haytham, with obvious approval, reports the angry reaction of Abu'l-'Abbās to the punishment by the qadi al-Marwadhī of two *dā'īs* who were accused of antinominian conduct.

94. On the latter incident see Halm, *Reich,* 287–8, trans., 323.

95. *Al-Imtā',* III, 195. In the text of the *Imtā',* the name of Abū

quite precise, but is nonetheless undoubtedly based either on his having seen, or his informant's having seen, the account of these *munāẓarāt* that Ibn al-Haytham himself issued. The other two references were located by Muḥammad al-Ya'lāwī and were noted in the apparatus to his edition of the relevant portion of the *'Uyūn al-akhbār*.[96] One of these consists of a line in a poem composed by the Maghribi poet Abu'l-Qāsim al-Fazārī in ridicule of the Fatimids.[97] The other involves a story within the biography of a Mālikī shaykh and famous ascetic, whose student was forced by circumstances to travel home one night through the streets and quarters of Qayrawan after curfew. Miraculously, the prayers of the shaykh were so powerful that they protected the student; no dogs barked at him and the security patrols did not spot him even though he passed right in front of 'the house of the *dā'ī* Ibn Aswad.' This incident occurred in the reign of al-Mu'izz and is related in the *ṭabaqāt* of al-Mālikī.[98]

3. THE EDITION OF THE ARABIC TEXT

The present edition of the Arabic text of the *Kitāb al-Munāẓarāt* is based on three manuscript copies. These were taken from complete copies of volume six (*al-juz' al-sādis*) of al-Bharūchī's *Kitāb al-Azhār*. In each case we obtained and worked from a photocopy of the original and have not examined either the original manuscript itself or the rest of the volume. The text of the edition, however, retains the compiler's introduction and concluding comments.

The manuscripts are the following:

1. A manuscript of ninety-three pages, eighteen lines to a page,

'Uthmān Ibn al-Ḥaddād is deformed and appears as 'Uthmān b. Khālid.

96. P. 157, no. 16. Halm, *Reich*, trans., 243, 248–9 and his n. 381.

97. The full text of the poem appears in al-Mālikī's *Riyāḍ al-nufūs*, II, 494, and al-Ya'lāwī's *al-Adab bi-Ifrīqiya fi'l-'ahd al-Fāṭimī*, 219–20. On al-Fazārī himself see al-Ya'lāwī, 'al-Fazārī' in the *EI2*, *Supplement*.

98. Al-Mālikī, *Riyāḍ*, II, 487–8 (the biography of Abū Isḥāq Ibrāhīm b. Aḥmad al-Sibā'ī al-Muta'abbid who died in 356/967).

belonging to Professor Abbas Hamdani, copied in 1307/1889–90, by ʿĪsā b. Dāʾūd b. ʿAbd al-ʿAlī b. Ibrāhīm, and designated in the Arabic apparatus as *hāʾ*. This manuscript was assigned page numbers (not folio numbers) by the copyist and they have been retained in the edition, noted after an / in the text.

2. One of two manuscripts belonging to The Institute of Ismaili Studies in London. Containing forty-seven folios, sixteen lines to a page, it was copied in Shawwāl 1342/1924 and was formerly in the Chotu Lakhani Collection, Bombay. It is designated by a *lām* in the Arabic apparatus.
3. A manuscript of fifty-eight folios, between sixteen and nineteen lines per page, formerly belonging to the Ismaʿili Society of Bombay, now in The Institute of Ismaili Studies in London, from the eleventh/seventeenth century (according to A. Gacek, *Catalogue of Arabic Manuscripts in the Library of The Institute of Ismaili Studies*, vol. 1, p. 40). It is designated by an *alif* in the Arabic apparatus.

In all these manuscripts, which are quite recent in date, the salutary benedictions, such as *ṣallā Allāh ʿalayhi wa ālihi* and *ʿalayhi al-salām*, generally appear as abbreviations but they have been spelled out completely in this edition. The spelling of words that have retained an older, archaic form in these copies has also been modernized.

Three short passages from this text were quoted by Idrīs ʿImād al-Dīn in his *ʿUyūn al-akhbār*. These have been noted where appropriate and the texts as published in S. M. Stern's *Studies in Early Ismāʿīlism* and in al-Yaʿlāwī's edition of the relevant portion of the *ʿUyūn al-akhbār* have been compared.

4. THE TRANSLATION AND NOTES

The translation that follows is my work and thus I bear primary responsibility for it. Professor Wilferd Madelung, however, not only read and corrected my draft but provided any number of suggestions and annotations, many of which were subsequently incorporated in the notes and introduction. A full translation of Ibn al-Haytham's *Kitāb al-Munāẓarāt* not only allows it to be consulted by readers who have no access to the Arabic text but also serves as a vehicle for the numerous annotations and explanatory commentary it requires. Parts of the work cover quite obscure items that were, however, apparently well known to the original discussants and the person or persons for whom it was written some forty years afterward. By then, of course, a majority of the individuals mentioned in it were long dead; many of them, in fact, were leading figures – the most prominent of the local *fuqahā'*, for example – of the intellectual scene in Qayrawan at the end of the Aghlabid period. Moreover, the four men of greatest importance to the cause of the Fatimids were by then not only dead but were considered traitors whose end was hardly to be recalled with honour. Thus, the persons cited by Ibn al-Haytham might have presented a serious problem of identification. Fortunately, that did not prove to be the case. Most, but especially the Ḥanafīs and the Mālikīs, merited biographies in the *ṭabaqāt* works of al-Khushanī and other, later authorities.

Many other details in the text require explanations that are given here in the notes. A number of passages present special difficulties, particularly for the discussions between Abu'l-'Abbās and Ibn al-Haytham about the details of scientific, philosophical, or logical matters. For these, and especially for items of logic, we were able to draw on the expert assistance of several colleagues, most notably Dr. F. Zimmermann and Professor E. Rowson.

A point of special interest in the work is its title and consequently the meaning of the term *munāẓara*. I have translated it by the vague English term 'discussions' although that hardly indicates what is in it or what it is about. A *munāẓara* (plural *munāẓarāt*) is a debate or a disputation most often undertaken between two persons or parties in a formal setting. Its subject was often an issue or issues of scientific, juridical, or theological importance, and the outcome could be expected to result in the conversion of the losing side to that of the winner (if there was, in fact, a clear winner). These 'debates' also feature in a special genre of literature which either recorded an actual confrontation of this kind – frequently reconstructed for the benefit of the party that gained from it – or were simply created for that purpose in written form even though no real dispute had taken place. Eventually also the literary form became quite stylized.[99]

For Ibn al-Haytham his title points first of all to his several encounters with the brothers Abū 'Abdallāh and Abu'l-'Abbās. The very first of these begins, in fact, as a kind of 'debate' in which Abū 'Abdallāh assumes the role of questioner. Ibn al-Haytham is the respondent and he has the burden of taking responsibility for what he says, whereas his interrogator merely poses hypothetical queries designed to elicit from him information and eventually a commitment to a particular doctrine. In fact from that first debate we learn little about Abū 'Abdallāh's position. Subsequently, however, the form and content of the various debates between either brother and Ibn al-Haytham change and they become far less confrontational. Many are rather true discussions and exchanges of information without the pressure of urgency. Besides these, the author reports and comments on a variety of *munāẓarāt* of a slightly different character that occurred between the Fatimid authorities, including himself acting for them, and respresentatives of the local *fuqahā'*, both Ḥanafīs and Mālikīs. These encounters are also covered by the title of the work and by the term *munāẓarāt*, although many of them are not simple 'discussions' but instead formal 'debates.'

Note: In the translation we have preferred to follow the original text fairly closely, even literally, with one significant exception. At each mention of the Prophet, 'Alī b. Abī Ṭālib,

99. It also served a literary purpose as a device for the display of erudition and wit as in cases where two objects or two animals are made to vie with each other to establish which of them is the better. For a general discussion of the concept and use of *munāẓarāt* in Arabic literature, see E. Wagner, 'Munāẓara' in the *EI2*.

and other revered figures such as Jesus, Moses, and the former prophets and the imams and their most distinguished adherents, Ibn al-Haytham added a pious benediction which we have retained in the edition throughout but in the translation only for the first instance of it, or when the sense requires it, and thereafter omitted them in order not to impede the flow of the narrative unduly.

Paul E. Walker

Ibn al-Haytham

Kitāb al-Munāẓarāt

THE BOOK OF DISCUSSIONS

[from]

The Sixth Part of the *Book of Flowers and the Gathering Place of the Illuminations gleaned from the Gardens of Mysteries, the Congregations of Spiritual Fruits and Benefits,* composed by our master, Ḥasan b. Nūḥ,[1] may God sanctify his spirit and bestow on us his intercession and affection.

In the name of God, the Merciful, the Compassionate.
From Him we seek help.

Praise be to God who manifests His radiant proofs on the tongues of His pure saints, they who glorify God by revealing the truth and explaining it and by proving false the distortions of those who deny it. May the blessings of God be on his Apostle, the lord of those who came first and last, and on the noble born and most pure Imams. Having arrived at the completion of the Fifth Part of the *Book of Flowers*, we want to bring in here the discussions that took place between the *dāʿī* Abū ʿAbdallāh, the head of the *daʿwa* in the Maghrib, and Abū ʿAbdallāh Jaʿfar b. Aḥmad b. Muḥammad b. al-Aswad b. al-Haytham, may God pardon them both, because they are relevant to what we brought up in the previous part to demonstrate the imamate of the Commander of the Faithful, ʿAlī b. Abī Ṭālib, may the blessings of God be upon him, and to prove false what is asserted by those who put forth specious claims in order to usurp unjustly, nefariously, and viciously his noble position. Thus we relate as follows:

Abū ʿAbdallāh Jaʿfar b. Aḥmad b. Muḥammad, may God be pleased with him, said: May God embellish rectitude in your eyes and grant you success in your words and deeds. You have asked, may God guide your affairs, that I write for you an account of the discussions that took place between me and Abū ʿAbdallāh and his brother about the imamate and other matters, and the reasons for our leaving for al-Andalus and what happened between us and the one who rose there against the

1. Ḥasan b. Nūḥ b. Yūsuf b. Muḥammad b. Ādam al-Hindī al-Bharūchī (d. 939/1533), the author and compiler of the *Kitāb al-Azhār* (Mss. Hamdani Collection and The Institute of Ismaʿili Studies, London), was born in India. He travelled to the Yemen where he studied with the leading Ṭayyibī authorities, who continued to reside there. He began the *Azhār* in 931/1524 and completed it after 935/1528; on him see Poonawala, *Biobibliography*, pp. 178–83.

Umayyads,[2] and what we planted with those people and the inhabitants of Cordova about the superiority of 'Alī b. Abī Ṭālib, the Commander of the Faithful, may the blessing of God be upon him, and the excellence of the family of Muḥammad, peace be upon him, and the reason also for our going out to the Maghrib and what trial we were subjected to by Maṣāla and his accursed sister and their sympathizers against us among the party of the devil.[3] I will recall for you some of what I remember of all that. Although it was long ago and time has passed on well beyond the era in which that took place, and we have been beset by the occurrence of such tribulations and successions of crises as to make us forget even the recent history of a nearer time, deadening the mind, taking away reason, removing desires, and bringing on death, were it not that faith

2. The person in question here is the famous Andalusian renegade 'Umar b. Ḥafṣūn whose rebellion against the Umayyads lasted from 267/880 until his death in 306/918. See E. Lévi-Provençal, 'Omar b. Ḥafṣūn' in the *EI*. He declared for the Fatimids just after the ascension of al-Mahdī, who sent a delegation to him consisting of two of his *dā'īs* with robes of honour. Ibn Ḥafṣūn had begun to proclaim al-Mahdī as the caliph in the Friday *khuṭba* in the mosques under his control. On this incident, see Ibn al-Khaṭīb's *Kitāb a'māl al-a'lām*, ed. E. Lévi-Provençal (Beirut, 1956), 32, and Halm, *Reich*, 250, trans. 280.

3. This is Maṣāla b. Ḥabūs al-Miknāsī, a Berber tribal prince in Tāhart, who ostensibly supported the Fatimids. However, 'Arīb (Ibn 'Idhārī, *al-Bayān*, I, 185–6) reports an incident in the year 309/921 when several *dā'īs* were killed by the local people in Wansharīsh, an area under Maṣāla's control. Shortly thereafter, al-Mahdī cracked down on a large number of *dā'īs*, many of whom were rounded up and imprisoned. Apparently Ibn al-Haytham himself suffered in this purge and he believed that Maṣāla and his sister were ultimately responsible for what happened. On the charge of antinomianism levelled against these *dā'īs*, see Qāḍī al-Nu'mān's *Majālis*, 499; Ibn 'Idhārī, *al-Bayān*, I, 185–6; and Halm, *Reich*, 222–4, trans. 248–9. See also Qāḍī al-Nu'mān, *Iftitāḥ*, 328–9. It is significant and may confirm Ibn al-Haytham's suspicions that when al-Manṣūr restored Fatimid rule in Tāhart in 336/947, following the rebellion of Abū Yazīd, the bodies of both Maṣāla and his brother Yaṣal were exhumed and publicly burned. On the latter incident see Halm, *Reich*, 287–8, trans. 323. The sister is apparently not mentioned in any other source.

was born in the course of those very events, it might be forgotten. But the story of it remains in the memory and shall not be concealed.

In the company of Abū Mūsā Hārūn b. Yūnis al-Azāyī al-Masāltī,[4] we called upon Abū 'Abdallāh two days after his arrival in Raqqāda, and that was Monday, the third of Rajab in the year 296 [27 March 909]. My aim in going to him and my predilection in his favour was due to their unanimous agreement regarding his discernment, understanding, culture, intelligence, and knowledge. I had been staying with Abū Mūsā for those two days. He conveyed news of me to Abū 'Abdallāh and informed him about my seeking to visit him and what there was between him and me. On the third night Abū Mūsā set out with me on foot. We passed by the abode of Abū Zākī,[5] and Abū Mūsā sent in to him word that I was present. He came out and Abū Mūsā introduced me to him, and he greeted me. Thereupon, we entered into the courtyard of the palace in which Abū 'Abdallāh had settled. Then the door was opened for us and Abū Mūsā informed them of my name. The doorway to Abū 'Abdallāh was entrusted to fifty men of proper faith, understanding, and surety. They expressed their greetings and crowded about me, embracing me with the welcome of the people of faith who truly desire God's reward. Abū Mūsā then entered before me and informed Abū 'Abdallāh of my presence. He came out to me again and I now entered with him into his presence. Abū Mūsā said to me, 'Do not hold back but rather debate with him like your first debates with me. He will surely humour your entertaining a different opinion.'

Abū 'Abdallāh rested on a fine couch on which he was sitting, its covering a single *Yansānī* (*sic*) saddle. I extended him my greetings standing and thanked God for what He had

4. Abū Mūsā was one of the earliest supporters of Abū 'Abdallāh, having joined him in 280/893. On him see the introduction above and the references given there in note 4.

5. This is Abū Zākī Tammām b. Mu'ārik, another early supporter of Abū 'Abdallāh. See the introduction above and the references given there in note 4.

granted to us through his being close at hand and God's investing him and supporting him and giving him victory. There then sprang up in me such a flow of tears that I could not restrain them as I remembered our lord al-Ḥusayn b. ʿAlī, may the blessing of God be upon him, and what harm the criminals had done to him and what was inflicted on his followers. We were at that time still more tender of heart, damper of eye, and more copious in tears. Grief had given notice to our hearts, and our souls were wont to remember the humiliation of the family of Muḥammad, blessings be upon them, enfolding hearts with regret, sadness, and pain, and a rising anger against the enemies of God, those criminals. Each day prior to his arrival we had anticipated his days, and we had expected his advent with great longing. Hopes created in us the expectation of attaining that, and of the coming of victory and the vanquishing of the iniquitous. Among our Shiʿi companions, our watchword had been none other than the words of the poet:

When will I see the world without a determinist?
    And no Ḥarūrī[6] or opponent of ʿAlī?
When will I behold the sword that signifies
    the love of ʿAlī, the son of Abū Ṭālib?

Then he sat and made me come closer to him until my right knee was on his couch. At that I said to him, 'We have come to you as students hoping for the knowledge that you possess. It has been proven about the Apostle of God, may God's blessings be on him and his family, that he said, "Whosoever listens to the summoners of my family and does not respond positively to them, God will throw him down on his face in hellfire".'

He responded: 'Why then did you fail to join up with us and come to where we were?'

I answered: 'Fear, youth, and being too weak to undertake it, even though our hearts and prayers were with you.'

He said: 'That is weak support indeed! Whoever combines

6. A Kharijite.

with the heart his tongue and hand, he has truly fulfilled his obligation and done what is required of him. God, exalted is His mention, has declared, "Whosoever leaves his home as an emigrant to God and His Apostle and then death overtakes him, his recompense falls due with God" [Qur'an 4: 100], and He said also, "And for those who believe and do not emigrate, nothing obliges you to associate with them until they emigrate" [8: 72].'

So I replied: 'And He, glorified is His name, also said, "Do not deliver yourselves by your own hands into destruction" [2: 195], and God excused "those men who are weak and the women and children who do not have the means" [4: 98].'

He responded: 'If you are resigned to being in the position of women, children, and the weak among men, I hope that God will make a path for you hereafter.'

Then he said, 'You seek knowledge and guidance, and yet we regard the shedding of blood as lawful and we kill persons and take their wealth as booty.'

In response I said: 'You kill those whose blood God allows and the taking of whose possessions He permits. The Most High has said, "Most of them do not believe in God; they are polytheists" [12: 106], and He said, "If you obeyed most of those on the earth, they would lead you away from the path of God" [6: 116].'

He said: 'Those were the polytheists of Quraysh and the Arabs.'

I answered: 'But they were those about whom God, the Most High, said, "We have not found that most of them have a covenant" [7: 102], and He said, "It is not you they consider false but rather it is the signs of God that the wrongdoers repudiate" [6: 33]. Thus, He informed us that they approve of Muḥammad, may God's blessings be on him and his family, and yet they consider false the legatees that come after him, and thus they said, "We intended nothing but goodwill and prosperity. They are those who God knows what is in their hearts, so avoid them" [4: 62–3], and He said, "They are those whom God has cursed and for those whom God curses you will never find a supporter" [4: 52], and the Most High said, "Muḥammad is only an Apostle, before him there were other apostles; thus if he should die or be killed, would you turn on your heels? Whoever turns on his heels will not harm God in the least" [3: 144]. Thus, He warned that they would turn their backs except those whom God protected and He informed us that they had violated their contract. God also said, "Those who pledge allegiance to you pledge allegiance to God, and the hand of God is over their hands; thus whosoever breaks the covenant violates his own soul, and whosoever fulfils what he has promised to God will be granted a magnificent reward" [48: 10]. He thereby reported their violation of the covenant, their misgivings, and their disavowal, and it is confirmed about the Apostle of God that he once stood on the graves of the martyrs of Uḥud and said, "God have mercy on you, you are my true companions." At that 'Atīq[7] and 'Umar said to him, "Are we not your companions?" He replied, "Yes, but I do not know what you will bring about after me; truly, those among you who create mischief after I am gone or give shelter to the one who creates it, on him is the curse of God".'

He said: 'They were the hypocrites.'

I said: 'Rather they were the double-crossing, doubting deceivers who broke up the army of Usāma[8] and assumed control over the Apostle of God's commander, deposed him, and spread lies against him. Their most prominent man accepted the fraud when the apostates called him the successor of God's Apostle and accepted it from those who said this, even though the Apostle of God had cursed the one who attests to a lie and

7. Referring to Abū Bakr whose *ism* was said to have been 'Atīq.

8. Usāma b. Zayd b. al-Ḥāritha. Just before his death, the Prophet dispatched an army toward Syria and put it under the command of Usāma, the son of his adopted son Zayd. Shi'is accuse Abū Bakr and his supporters of withdrawing from the army after Muḥammad's death, thus weakening it, and then of deposing Usāma. See, for instance, Abān b. 'Uthmān al-Aḥmar, *al-Mab'ath wa'l-maghāzī*, ed. Rasūl Ja'fariyān (Qum, 1417/1996), 129.

those for whom it is attested. Sufficient as an offence is their assault against the Radiant [*al-Zahrā'*] Fāṭima, the daughter of the Apostle of God, and the blocking of her inheritance, the taking away of what was in her hands of the gifts of her father and his presents to her, and their repudiation of her testimony.'

He said: 'Truly God will not unite the community to agree on an error and, by their claim, they unanimously agreed on the leadership of Abū Bakr. The Apostle of God declared that, "My companions are like the stars; whichever of them you take as a model you will be guided rightly," and he said also, "There will occur among my companions trifling matters for which God will forgive them".'

I responded: 'A unanimous agreement is one in which there is no disagreement and that is in our favour against the [Sunni] sects, as in the unanimous agreement of all that 'Alī b. Abī Ṭālib was a distinguished, pious, and learned man who deserved the imamate, and we regard whoever preceded him as a wrong-doer. Thus, they are in agreement with us while we reject their claim. As for the consensus of those who agreed on Abū Bakr, it did not happen except after dissension, killing, and the thrust and parry of swords, and that certainly is not to be called a unanimous agreement. Their consensus with respect to Abū Bakr is no more valid than their consensus in favour of Yazīd b. Mu'āwiya or al-Ḥajjāj b. Yūsuf and 'Abd al-Malik b. Marwān.[9] The Shi'a have stated, "We are the community of Muḥammad," and the trifling matters of disagreement that exist among them lie in secondary details, and for those they are excused. All of them concur about Muḥammad, 'Alī, and the imams from the progeny of the Prophet. These other communities broke faith with the Prophet, repudiated his legatee, and murdered the offspring of the Apostle, the God-fearing. They are apostates

9. These three men were prominent in the Umayyad reign. Yazīd (d. 64/683) was the son and successor of Mu'āwiya, the founder of the Umayyad dynasty; al-Ḥajjāj (d. 95/714) was, among other positions, a major provincial governor known for his persecution of Shi'is (on him see A. Dietrich, 'al-Ḥadjdjādj b. Yūsuf,' *EI2*); and 'Abd al-Mālik b. Marwān (65–86/685–705) was the fifth of the Umayyad caliphs.

who have departed from the community of Muḥammad and they are the anthropomorphists, the Mu'tazila, the Murji'a, the Khawārij, and the rest of the sects. The trifling matters that are excused are the minor lapses which occur among the believers because of mutual competition and reproach. The Companions signified by the stars are the family of Muḥammad and whoever followed them in doing good such as Salmān, Miqdād, Abū Dharr, 'Ammār, Ḥamza, Ja'far, 'Ubayda b. al-Ḥārith, and others like them.[10] These are the veracious [*ṣiddīqūn*] and true witnesses before their Lord, and theirs is the reward and the light. Claiming the imamate and leadership ahead of God's friends and taking away the veil of Fāṭima, the mistress of all the women in creation, belongs among the major sins which cannot be expiated but constitute polytheism that nullifies any merit and which will not be forgiven.'

He said: 'How can you declare an unbeliever someone who, having been chosen by the people, claims the imamate?'

I said: 'On the basis of the Book of God, the Glorious and Mighty, who said, glorious is His mention, "Take not for yourselves a guardian apart from me" [17: 2], and the Most High said, "They say: Glory to You, it was not necessary for us to take protectors other than You" [25: 18], and "They say: Glory to You, You are our protector and not they" [34: 41]. Then God, the Most Sanctified, said, "Your Lord creates and chooses as He wills; they have no choice, glory to God, and He is far above the partners they ascribe to Him" [28: 68]. Thus, He put their choosing and agreeing in the class of polytheism which will not be forgiven. As for adopting them as guides, if that were confirmed from the Apostle of God, it would imply the permissibility of theft, treachery, and the murder of an inviolable person. For Mu'ādh and Abū Hurayra stole the funds of God, yet 'Umar reconciled with them and merely fined

10. The persons named here are, in order, Salmān al-Fārisī, al-Miqdād b. 'Amr, Abū Dharr al-Ghiffārī, 'Ammār b. Yāsir, Ḥamza b. 'Abd al-Muṭṭalib, Ja'far b. Abī Ṭālib, and 'Ubayda b. al-Ḥārith b. al-Muṭṭalib. They were all Companions and were either members of the Prophet's family or loyal supporters and upholders of its rights.

them.[11] Abū Bakr killed members of the community of Muḥammad and called them the people of apostasy [*ahl al-ridda*]. He allowed the false testimony against Fāṭima, peace be upon her. In regard to [the inheritance of] the grandfather, he issued seventy-two rules, each different from the others, and repented of them all when he died.[12] He burned al-Fujā'a by fire and he regretted that as well.[13] Hence, by which of his statements are we to be guided? 'Uthmān tore down the house of Ja'far b. Abī Ṭālib, peace be upon him, and included it in the mosque [of Madina] but did not consult its owners or give them its value, considering that lawful and acting high-handedly.'

He said: 'Surely 'Alī b. Abī Ṭālib had killed Muslims and done other things like that.'

I responded: 'Alī b. Abī Ṭālib had authorization for the fighting and he never fought without a sound argument and a command that had issued from the Apostle of God. The Apostle of God, for example, said to 'Ā'isha, "You will fight with 'Alī, at which time you will be so wrong towards him that even the dogs of al-Ḥaw'ab will bark at you"; and he said to 'Ammār, may God be pleased with him, "The seditious faction will kill

11. Abū Hurayra, a prominent Companion, who had been appointed governor of Baḥrayn by 'Umar, was deposed, and a large sum of money was found in his personal possession, which was confiscated. Nonetheless, 'Umar tried to reappoint him a second time. See 'Abū Hurayra' by J. Robson in the *EI2*. Mu'ādh is probably Mu'ādh b. Jabal who was governor of Ḥimṣ under 'Umar.

12. It is usually 'Umar who is accused by Shi'i authors of having issued numerous contradictory rulings in the matter of the grandfather's inheritance. See 'Abd al-Ḥusayn Aḥmad al-Amīnī, *al-Ghadīr* (Beirut, 1967), VI, 115–18. Here, however, clearly Abū Bakr is meant.

13. Al-Fujā'a was Bujayra b. Ilyās of the Banū Sulaym. He was granted a commission to fight the apostates by Abū Bakr but, when he also killed and plundered Muslims, Abū Bakr had him seized and burned. See Muḥammad b. Jarīr al-Ṭabarī, *Ta'rīkh al-rusul wa'l-mulūk*, ed. M. J. de Goeje et al. (Leiden, 1879–1901), I, 1903–4, trans. Donner, 79–81; Caskel, II, 228–9; Aḥmad b. Yaḥyā al-Balādhurī, *Futūḥ al-buldān*, ed. M. J. de Goeje (Leiden, 1866), 98.

you"; and he said to 'Alī, "You will fight the violators, the unjust, and the schismatics"; and he informed his Companions that, "Among you is someone who will fight over the interpretation of the Qur'an just as I fought over its revelation," and each one of them thought of himself. So he said, "Nay, the mender of the sandal," and he pointed to 'Alī and said to 'Alī, "When the most wretched of them is sent, this [beard] will be dyed by that [blood]," meaning thereby his killer Ibn Muljam, may God curse him. 'Alī was protected from sin in accord with the appeal of the Apostle of God on the day of Ghadīr Khumm when he said, "Whosoever I am the master of, then 'Alī is his master. Oh God, take as a friend whoever befriends him and consider an enemy whoever is his enemy; assist those who assist him, forsake those who forsake him; make the truth circulate with him wherever he turns." Thus, the actions of 'Alī are all right because they result from the command of the Apostle of God on the authority of God, the Most High. He stated to 'Alī, "You are my brother," and fraternized among his Companions twice and thus he said to him "You are my brother" twice. He also said to him after that, "You are to me as was Hārūn (Aaron) to Mūsā (Moses)." He meant by this that his community would break its covenant with him just as the community of Moses broke with Hārūn. Everyone who opposed 'Alī or made war against him – thus breaking his oath to him – was opposing God and His Apostle and making war upon them both.'

He said: 'But is it not the case that the Shi'a say that he intended by his statement, "You are to me as Hārūn was to Moses," a confirmation of the succession, since Moses had said to his brother, "Take my place among my people" [7: 142]?'

I said: 'Certainly that is so. We only mention the violation in order for us to assert the righteousness of 'Alī in every action of his and the import of the hadith is both this and that.'

He said: 'On what basis have you chosen to uphold the imamate of 'Alī and not the others whom the people selected, when they were the senior leaders of Islam and the Muslims, and were the Companions of the Apostle and his kinsfolk who emigrated to Madina and to Ethiopia, and among them one entered the cave with the Apostle of God and himself comforted him. The Apostle of God used to say, "The funds of no one benefited me like those of Abū Bakr"; this in addition to his [Muḥammad's] preference for him and his giving his daughter to him in marriage, the most beloved of his wives. Among those to whom I have alluded there is no one but that his early merits are obvious, and his positions in the faith are famous, and his glorious acts well known and acknowledged.'

I said to him: 'We know about them only the defeats of Ḥunayn, Khaybar, and Dhāt al-Salāsil, and the sorrow of Abū Bakr in the cave is sufficient, and his alarm and fear to the point that God censured him and characterized him with sorrow and lack of tranquillity. The early merits of 'Alī b. Abī Ṭālib in comparison to his are, by contrast, merits and excellences that one recalls and are noble deeds of the kind about which one can boast. As for his giving his daughter to him in marriage, Māriya the Copt was better than she, because the Apostle of God caused Māriya to bear a child while none of the 'consorts of Joseph' [*ṣuwayḥibāt Yūsuf*][14] bore him any offspring that is mentioned. As for Khadīja, may God be pleased with her, she cannot be compared to these women. Khadīja compares only to Maryam, the daughter of 'Imrān, peace be upon her. A son-in-law's marriage tie with God's Apostle is better than being related through a wife of his because God, glorious is His mention, said: "He is the One who created man from water and made for him kinship and marriage tie" [25: 54]. Those who are tied to the Apostle of God by marriage with his daughter are his descendants, his offspring, and his two grandsons al-Ḥasan and al-Ḥusayn, peace be upon them both. The Apostle of God allied with those others by marrying their daughters in order to curb their vehemence. Not one of these women

14. This refers to an angry reproach of Muḥammad on his death bed addressed to 'Ā'isha in which he called her and women in general *ṣawāḥib Yūsuf*. See Ṭabarī, I, 1811.

bore him children because the bearing of children to the prophets cannot occur except by the pious and pure woman. These, however, were like the wife of Noah and the wife of Lot. Since they were not pure, God debarred them from bearing children to the Apostle of God.'

He said: 'But how can you remove them from the state of purity since God said, "Oh women of the Prophet, you are not like any of the other women; if you fear God, do not be too submissive in your speech lest those in whose heart is a disease lust after you. Say only what is appropriate. Stay in your homes and do not display your finery ostentatiously as did women in the former days of ignorance. Observe your prayers and give alms. Obey God and His Apostle. God only desires to remove from you impurity, you who are members of the family, and to render you most pure" [33: 32–3].'

So I said: 'The women of the Prophet here are his family because they are from one stock, whereas his wives are from several different houses, and a relationship of marriage is discontinuous but relationship for members of his own house persists. A report confirms that this verse was revealed while the Apostle of God was in the abode of Umm Salama, may God be pleased with her, and then he gathered together his family in his cloak, and they were himself, 'Alī, Fāṭima, and their two sons, may the blessings of God be upon them all. About them God, the Mighty and Glorious, revealed in His Book the verse of mutual imprecation [*al-mubāhala*], "Say, come let us gather together our sons, your sons, and our women and your women, and ourselves and yourselves and then pray humbly [*nabtahilu*]" (to the end of the verse) [3: 61].[15] Those mentioned are the members of Prophet's house and his women and himself, and the members of his house are his children, his pure offspring, and the imams from his own progeny, peace be upon them. The Apostle of God said on that day, "These are the members of my house".'

15. The remainder of the verse reads, 'so that we call forth the curse of God upon those who lie.'

He said: 'This may be construed more broadly to include those you mention and others from the whole of the community, and thus the community is the family and they are the sons, daughters, wives and offspring.'

I said: 'The real meaning is not the same as the metaphorical, and the consensus is closer to us than is disagreement, since the one who advocates the general meaning thereby attests to the merit of the particular and that the specific deserves these terms, whereas we will not acknowledge his claim until he brings a proof from someone other than those who share his claim – from those who are above suspicion and not suspect in their testimony.'

He said: 'The Book of God testifies on their behalf to this fact. God, the Mighty and Glorious, said, "Banish the family of Lot from your town" [27: 56] and He said, "Enter the family of Pharaoh into the harshest of punishments" [40: 46].'

I said: 'This is a recital of a statement by someone who does not really understand what he is saying, but God, the Most High, was specific about the family. He made them the chosen, not the common people but instead the progeny. Thus He, Glorious is the Speaker, said, "God chose Adam, Noah, the family of Abraham, and the family of 'Imrān over all the world, offspring one of another, and God is All-hearing and All-knowing" [3: 33–4]; and He said, "Peace be upon the house of Yāsīn" [37: 130]; and He said, "The mercy and grace of God be upon you members of the house" [11: 73]. The Apostle of God has elaborated this as His having imposed on his community the duty of loving the members of his family and praying for its Prophet. They asked, "What form should the prayer for you take, O, Apostle of God?" He replied, "Say, O, God, bless Muḥammad and the family of Muḥammad; have mercy on Muḥammad and the family of Muḥammad; sanctify Muḥammad and the family of Muḥammad with the best of that with which You blessed, granted mercy, and sanctified Abraham and the family of Abraham." And God has confirmed this when He, glorious is His praise, said, "Or do the people envy what out of His bounty God has brought to them? We have provided the family of Abraham the book and the wisdom, and We have given them a great kingdom“ [4: 54]. This is specific and not general. He, the Most High, also stated, “Say, I ask for it no payment except the love of the close relatives” [42: 23], and the Most High said, “Give those of close relationship their due and also the poor and the traveller in need” [30: 38]. Thus He provided for them a portion of the booty, and those who have shares in the booty are the family and they are the close relatives for whom God, the Mighty and Glorious, has imposed a duty to love and pray for them. He said, “And fear God by whom you question one another and the wombs” [4:1]. Thus, God confirmed this and explained and clarified it and made it close at hand.'

He said: 'What proof do you have of the excellence of 'Alī, peace be upon him, and his worthiness for the imamate you have mentioned?'

I said: 'Every word of ours previously stated is in fact a proof, but our real proof is the Book, the Sunna, the consensus, reason, reflection, the revelation, and historical report. All of these certify it to the person who considers carefully, thinks it over, and listens attentively as a true witness and avoids personal bias.'

He said: 'With respect to historical reports and the revelation, they may be construed in the general sense, and the opponent can also invoke them in an argument with you.'

I answered: 'It is necessary for someone who discusses the imamate to be of sound faith and a piety that restrains him from putting forward claims for something that does not belong to him, and that he be thoroughly familiar with the reported accounts and neither repudiate them nor steal them from their owners. When the disputant is like this, that is, he does not repudiate or steal, and does not claim something that does not belong to him, we prove it by citing what no other can claim. Thus, it is firmly reported that 'Alī was the brother of the Apostle of God, who established brotherhood between the two of themselves when he fraternized as brothers among his Companions on two occasions. He said to him, "You, 'Alī, are my brother and you are to me in the position of Hārūn in respect to Moses," and he stated in reference to him, "Whosoever I am the master of, 'Alī is his master." He prayed for him and for his party and he cursed those who would forsake him and make war against him. He removed all of his Companions from his neighbourhood and left behind only 'Alī, when he evicted the polytheists of the Quraysh from the vicinity of the sacred sanctuary. Thus, he removed all of them from himself and kept behind 'Alī alone in his presence. In the sura, "Does there not pass over man ...,"[16] there is sufficient mention of him and of God's promising him paradise. And God promised him paradise, and there is the statement of the Most High, "Your protectors are God, His Apostle, and those who believe, who observe prayer and give alms, while they kneel down in worship" [5: 55], and the verse of confidential discourse in which is His statement, "O you who believe, if you have a private conference with the Apostle, pay something as alms for your conference" [58: 12]. No one did this except 'Alī alone. There is also the Exalted's statement, "Do you consider providing water [*siqāya*] for the pilgrims and repair of the sacred mosque to be like believing in God and the Last Day and fighting on behalf of God? They are not equal with God. God does not guide those who do wrong" [9: 19]. The whole of this verse to its end was revealed about 'Alī and al-'Abbās and Shayba.[17] God, the Mighty and Glorious, judged 'Alī superior to both of them. Also there is the verse of mutual imprecation. All that and similar passages in the Qur'an are about 'Alī and all those who oppose nevertheless confirm that

16. *Sūrat al-insān* (no. 76), which begins with these words.

17. Al-'Abbās, the Prophet's uncle, held the hereditary right of *siqāya*, the privilege of providing water for the pilgrims. This right was restored to him upon the conquest of Makka by the Muslims. Shayba b. 'Uthmān b. Abī Ṭalḥa was a member of the Banū 'Abd al-Dār who were collectively the guardians or keepers (*sadana*) of the Ka'ba, and this Shayba is reported to have been one of those confirmed in this role (along with his cousin 'Uthmān) by the Prophet at the conquest of Makka. See M. Gaudefroy-Demombynes, 'Shayba, Banū,' in the *EI2*.

this is about him and do not deny it, praise be to God, Lord of the two worlds.

As for implied and obscure indications or examples and allusions, they are incalculably numerous, such as the statement of God's Apostle about him, "'Alī is among you like the ark of Noah; whoever sails upon it is saved and whoever stays away from it, sinks and is destroyed," and his saying, "I am leaving with you two weighty items such that if you cleave to them, you will not fall into error, the Book of God and my descendants, the members of my family." And there is the statement of the Most High, "And he made this a word to remain among his descendants" [43: 28]. All of this is quite clear and well known and is in addition to the early merits, knowledge, jihad, and nearness to the Apostle of God in which 'Alī stands alone. Thus, he combined in himself every excellence by which one merits the imamate because of his closeness to God, the Mighty and Glorious, and that he was owed the obedience linked to the Apostle in the statement of the Most High, 'Obey God and obey the Apostle and those with authority among you' [4: 59]. There was thus combined in 'Alī the excellence of every one who had any excellence, whereas God, the Mighty and Glorious, singled him out to have what none of them have. He had purity of birth, superiority of knowledge and kinship, and about 'Alī, God revealed, "Is then the man who believes no better than the wicked; no they are not equal" [32: 18]. None are the like of 'Alī and he resembles no one else of those who are believers after him and were termed abominable prior to finding faith. And about him and his companions, God, the Exalted, revealed, "... men who have been true to their covenant with God. Of them some have already redeemed their pledge; others still wait but have not changed in the least" [33: 23]. They have all agreed that this verse was revealed about 'Alī, Ḥamza, 'Ubayda b. al-Ḥārith b. al-Muṭṭalib, and Ja'far b. Abī Ṭālib, peace be upon them all.'

He said to me: 'The Islam of 'Alī, according to your opponents, was like the Islam of a child who does not truly believe.'

I replied: "Alī's submission [*islām*] was in response to the summons of God's Apostle by the command of God, the Mighty and Glorious, and he was not a child devoid of belief but rather he was thirteen years old. Boys of eleven years have produced children just as women have attained puberty at ten. The Apostle of God commanded that youths be taught prayers from the age of six and five, and to discipline them for prayers from seven. 'Alī had then passed these limits. The Apostle of God was not one who would deceive himself about the religion of God and disclose it to someone who will not believe anything. It has been universally agreed that the Apostle of God entered the ravine with him, and with them was Khadīja. They remained in it three years and seven months, eating poor bread and date pits, and cracking bones and splitting them apart. If 'Alī had not been a believer, he would have abandoned this hardship in favour of ease and joined his uncles and kin. Moreover, no one relates that the Apostle of God summoned any of the young boys of the Banū Hāshim or others. In this is a proof that 'Alī was the remnant of God on His earth after Muḥammad and that from him came the progeny of the Apostle of God. He was the summons of Abraham, peace be upon him, and however the ignorant belittle his case, that merely increases his excellence.'

He said: 'How could this be, given that the one who benefits from Islam is the adult who prefers what he enters to what he leaves, because of a proof whose evidence is plain to him or a sign that is firm in his perception and whose explanation is for him sound?'

I said: 'But the adult may enter it out of fright and fear and humiliation and of being overpowered, and his Islam might be for worldly gain or leadership over the people of this world, or in order to attain status with the one who rules over them. A child gains nothing of this kind by entering Islam, and especially not 'Alī b. Abī Ṭālib in particular since his father was the supporter of the Apostle of God and the one who stood up for him and defended him. Thus, 'Alī was loved by the Apostle of God and was his chosen, his intimate, and the one brought up by him. For that reason he selected him to be his associate and his legatee, and singled him out by adopting him as his brother, turning over to him the government of his community after him, designating him as successor and approving of him, and choosing him as deputy and friend. Furthermore, the virtue of the Islam of the young boy is confirmed in the Book of God. An example of that is Abraham who was properly guided by inferences when he was only thirteen; "and he said, I will not hold dear those that fade away" [6: 76]. The setting of the stars was for him a proof of their having come into being and that the exalted Creator, glory be to Him, does not set or cease or move about or belong to a place. Similarly, Abraham desired the Islam of his sons and to acquaint them with faith prior to their reaching maturity and before they would know and worship the idols. That was confirmed in the mind of Abraham by the word of God and His making it clear in the statement of Him who has no partner, "And Abraham was tried by his Lord with certain edicts which he carried out;" He then said, "I will make you the leader [*imām*] of the people;" He asked, "And also from my offspring?" He said, "My assurance does not apply to the evildoers" [2: 124]. At that Abraham desired more and he said, "Preserve me and my children from worshipping idols" [14: 35], and he said, "My Lord give me a righteous son" [37: 100]. God, the Mighty and Glorious, thus informed Abraham that the imamate will not be inherited by someone who embraces polytheism nor one who reaches maturity as a polytheist, even if he then accepts faith and Islam. None will inherit the imamate who is not pure from the beginning. Likewise was Moses, peace be upon him, of such purity in his birth that the milk of harlots was forbidden him in order that he be as pure in his nursing as he was in his birth. Likewise was Jesus, peace be upon him, in the purity of his beginnings, and similarly Muḥammad, may God bless him and his family, and 'Alī, peace be upon him, after him. One aspect of the complete purity of 'Alī is that his grandmother and the grandmother of Muḥammad was the same woman, the mother of 'Abdallāh, father of Muḥammad. The mother of Abū Ṭālib was the same woman and they were thus full brothers.'

He said: 'The Qur'an denies what you have just mentioned. In reference to Muḥammad, God has said, "And did He not find you in error and guide you?" [93: 7]; and He said, "There was Abraham who said to his father and his people: I dissociate myself from what you worship" [43: 26]; and He said in reference to the mother of Moses, "Had We not strengthened her heart so that she remained a believer?" [28: 10]; and "Abraham said to his father Āzar: Do you take idols to be gods?" [6: 74].'

I said: 'Being in error can be divided into various types, one of which is forgetting, as when God, the Mighty and Glorious, said, "If either of the two makes a mistake, the other will remember" [2: 282]. There is going astray in some matter or losing one's way as when Moses said, "Would that my Lord guide me on the smooth path" [28: 22]. Error might be associated with love and passion as when the son of Jacob said, "Truly you are still under your former delusion," [12: 95] meaning his love and passion for Joseph. Similarly, paternity could be a paternal concern for upbringing, or the paternity of leadership, or of instruction. The mother of Moses, when she saw her son, thus almost gave him away until God, the Most High, supported her in order to increase her in faith with regard to Moses and beyond her faith in the law of Abraham. If she had shown her sorrow, she would have pointed him out to the people of Pharaoh, but God supported her. When something can be construed in two ways, it is necessary to attribute to the friends of God the better of them and exempt them from the more abominable of the two.

With regard to the proofs of intellect and reasoning, there is the need of the people for someone to govern them, take charge of their affairs, establish their pilgrimage, feasts, Friday prayers, collect alms, restrain the wrongdoer, and render justice to the wronged. God has confirmed this in His saying, "Of their goods take alms in order to cleanse and purify them through it" [9: 103], and He said, "If they, when they injured themselves, had come to you and they had sought God's forgiveness and the Apostle had sought forgiveness for them, they would have found God most forgiving and merciful" [4: 64].

Since the imposition of obligatory duties remains after the departure of the Apostle of God, the continuation of those who preserve them and are entrusted with the commands of the prophets on behalf of God, the Most High, continues to be necessary. Through them prayers are established and through them are maintained the obligatory duties and the pilgrimage. God, the Mighty and Glorious, said about Abraham, "O our Lord, I have settled some of my offspring in a valley without vegetation in the vicinity of Your sacred house so that they, O our Lord, may establish regular prayers; dispose the heart of the people kindly toward them" [14: 37]. Through them the pilgrimage will be completed; whoever recognizes them, his pilgrimage will have been completed. Another proof is that God, the Mighty and Glorious, began creation with a viceregent [*khalīfa*] before creating the species of which they are a part because of His knowing about their need for someone to govern them, in the same way as He began by creating milk for nursing before the coming out of the foetus because of His knowing of its need for nourishment prior to its creation. God, the Exalted, said, "As He began you so will you return, some guided and some He rightly left in error for they took satans as protectors instead of God" [7: 29–30]. God began creation with His viceregent and made it necessary that He bring again another like him among them until he inherits the earth and those on it. The Most High said, "Just as We brought about the first of creation, so shall We restore it, a promise of Ours that We shall truly carry out, and We wrote in the Psalms after the message [of Moses] that the earth will be inherited by My righteous servants" [21: 104–5]. Thus, God made the earth an inheritance of His friends, to repeat in it after each imam another imam. Thus, whoever is guided to God's friends has won "and whoever takes satan as protector" [4: 119] "an evil consort has he" [4: 38].'[18]

18. This latter phrase is preceded in this verse by 'He that takes satan as his consort [*qarīn*].'

He said: 'All of what you have mentioned proves the need for the imam, but what is your proof with regard to his name, his attribute, lineage, and status? And if it were like that, all doubts about him would be precluded and all would be in agreement about him.'

I said: 'Indeed God, the Most High, wanted humans to acquire cognition and make deductions in order to earn a reward. "If God had wanted it, all those on the earth would have believed to a person" [10: 99], but He preferred to put them to the test and to try them by a thorough examination, so as to distinguish the malicious from the good. Thus, by being subjected to testing and acquiring merit by being examined, the true nature of the human appears in the same way that fire extracts the dross in the gold and silver. The trial is the elixir for the human, just as fire is that by means of which minerals are tested. The person of intelligence infers derivative matters from root principles. Since we all were in agreement about the Prophet, it is necessary for us to seek the imam after the Prophet in the origins of that particular prophet and we seek information about the imam from the Prophet's place, and in his offspring, among his descendants, the closest of the people to him, and those of greatest benefit. If the people had wanted to make such a deduction, God, the Most High, would have guided them. Yet the Prophet set forth, indicated, and coined examples and then even declared outright, explained explicitly, and spoke plainly. However, the community gave the lie to the legatee, discredited the Prophet, and aspired to assume leadership over the people of the source of divine inspiration. Thus, after his death they fled away from nearness to God's Apostle. They provoked the common people and the masses to revolt, entered the Hall of the Banū Sā'ida,[19] and abandoned the abode of inspiration, the place where the angels had descended and the assembling point of the Qur'an. If only they had gathered around the corpse of God's Apostle and at his grave site, and if

19. The hall (*saqīfa*) of the Banū Sā'ida was the place in Madina where Abū Bakr was elected caliph in the absence of 'Alī.

they had met with the uncle of the Prophet, and the son of his uncle and his son-in-law, his offspring, his wives, daughters, and with the worshippers of the community, the ascetics of the religion such as Salmān, al-Miqdād, Abū Dharr, ʿAmmār, and had beseeched God, the Exalted, to grant them success in choosing the one whom they would put in charge, if indeed, as they claimed, the Apostle of God had not appointed a legatee. But, if the Apostle of God made a will or made an allusion or accepted a man among them as his brother, it was obligatory to invest him and to submit to him. Nevertheless, they seized upon the preoccupation of the Banū Hāshim and the grief of ʿAlī and on their concern for the Apostle of God. They gathered together for criticism of the Apostle of God and in disrespect for his family. Of the greatest wonder was the role in this of those most distant from the Prophet and not the closest. If the Prophet were to have ordered them to do that rather than his family, it would have been obligatory at least to perform the funeral for God's Apostle and display grief for him a single day and only then gather with the members of his family in order to choose. Instead they went astray "and caused many to go astray; they have strayed themselves from the even path" [5: 77]. If we wanted to assert the nomination of the imam after Muḥammad that would be possible.

He said: 'How is that?'

I said: 'God, the Mighty and Glorious, said, "And what of someone who stands before a clear sign from his Lord and a witness from Him recites it" [11: 17], meaning a witness from his family. There is no freeborn male from those in his family except ʿAlī alone, because the Apostle of God said, "The slave cannot act as imam to the freeborn," and he said, "The caliphate is forbidden to the freedmen [*ṭulaqā'*] and to the sons of the freedmen."[20] God, the Mighty and Glorious, said, "God has revealed to you as a remembrance an Apostle to recite for you the clear and obvious signs of God" [65: 10–11]. Thus, He

20. The *ṭulaqā'* were the Makkans who were still not Muslim at the time of the conquest of Makka and were thus considered freed war slaves.

called His Apostle Muḥammad a "remembrance." Then the Exalted said, "Consult the people of remembrance if you do not know" [16: 43]. There was none in the family of Muḥammad that someone might consult other than 'Alī alone, and the Most High said, "Are those who know the equal of those who do not know?" [39: 9]. He also commanded that the people of knowledge be consulted, and 'Alī, following Muḥammad, is the one referred to here. The Most High said, "Then We bequeathed the Book to those of Our servants We have chosen" [35: 32]. 'Alī is the one with knowledge, and the heir of the bequest. Most of the religion consists of allusion and parables, and this is explanation and clarification. Hence, we are able to declare that 'Alī b. Abī Ṭālib is the person designated for the imamate following the Apostle of God on the basis of God, the Most High, having said, "In the mother of the Book which is with Us, he is 'Alī, full of wisdom" [43: 4]; and God's statement, "We appointed for them 'Alī as a voice of truth" [19: 50]; and His statement, "This is the straight path of 'Alī" [15: 41].[21] For the person of intelligence, the indication given in these phrases is enough and does not need to be clarified or explained.'

He said: 'The specialists in language would preclude your saying this and would oppose you in what you intend by it. Grammatical rules do not allow what you claim on behalf of 'Alī or that he is meant by *'aliyyan* or that he is *'aliyyun*, full of wisdom; and moreover, there were in the family other scholars of perfect knowledge such as 'Abdallāh b. 'Abbās.'[22]

21. The author's understanding of these verses depends on an irregular interpretation or reading of them, as pointed out in the objection of Abū 'Abdallāh. They would otherwise be rendered: 'It is in the mother of the Book with Us, sublime indeed [*'aliyyun*] and full of wisdom,' 'We appointed them a voice of sublime [*'aliyyan*] truth,' and 'This is a path straight to Me [*'alayya*].'

22. 'Abdallāh b. al-'Abbās (d. 68/687–8) was, like 'Alī, a first cousin of the Prophet as the son of his paternal uncle al-'Abbās. He is generally considered one the of greatest scholars among the first generation of Muslims. On him, see L. Veccia Vaglieri, ''Abd Allāh b. al-'Abbās,' in the *EI2*.

I said: 'As for the freedmen and their sons, they have no share in the imamate nor any portion of it and no priority in Islam or in jihad on behalf of God. All of this, however, is combined in 'Alī. The rules of grammar are whatever conveys the truth. The nominative and genitive consist in whatever puts it in the proper places with sound meanings in accordance with the intention of God, the Mighty and Glorious, and thus the nominative is for His friends and the genitive is for His enemies. These people claim to be reading the letters of the language correctly grammatically, and yet they are ignorant of what God, the Mighty and Glorious, intended in regard to meanings, applications, and examples. The allusions, symbols, and implications are God's, the Mighty and Glorious, and only those possessing knowledge will comprehend them.'

He then smiled and motioned to Abū Mūsā and Abū Zākī. Badr the eunuch asked permission to have enter some of our colleagues whom he had summoned to join the faith before me.[23] They were al-Marwadhī,[24] his son Aḥmad,[25] Isḥaq b. Abi'l-Minhāl,[26] and Abū Ḥabīb b. Rashīd.[27] However, he did not allow

23. That is, they had been summoned to join the Isma'ili community before the author.

24. Muḥammad b. 'Umar b. Yaḥyā b. 'Abd al-A'lā al-Marwadhī, who will be mentioned again, was to become the first Fatimid qadi of Qayrawan. He died, however, in 303/915–16, apparently under torture. On him, in addition to the information given later, see Ibn 'Idhārī, *al-Bayān*, I, 151–2, 159, 169, 173 (notice of his death), 189; Qāḍī al-Nu'mān, *Iftitāḥ*, 247; 'Iyāḍ, *Madārik*, index; al-Khushanī, 239, trans. 333–4; Idrīs, *'Uyūn*, 117, 134, 171; *Sīrat Ja'far*, 131, Eng. trans. in Ivanow, *Rise*, 220, Canard, French trans., 319; al-Mālikī, *Riyāḍ*, II, 41, 48, 54, 55–6, 60, 155.

25. Aḥmad, the son of al-Marwadhī, was, as will become apparent, a school friend and companion of the author. On him, see Idrīs, *'Uyūn*, 311 (n. 151), Ibn 'Idhārī, *al-Bayān*, I, 215; *Sīrat Jawdhar*, French trans. *Vie de l'ustadh Jaudhar* by M. Canard, (Algiers, 1958), 77 (n. 105), Halm, *Reich*, 439 ('al-Marwarrūḍī'), trans. 426.

26. Isḥāq b. Abi'l-Minhāl was a local Ḥanafī jurist. Following the events reported here, he became an Isma'ili and, according to Ibn al-Athīr, al-Mahdī appointed him qadi of Sicily. Later he served as the qadi

them to come in and said for them to be patient. Then he said, 'So who was after 'Alī b. Abī Ṭālib?'

I said: 'His son al-Ḥasan b. 'Alī.'

He said: 'Then who?'

I said: 'Al-Ḥusayn b. 'Alī.'

He said: 'Then who?'

I said: ''Alī b. al-Ḥusayn, Zayn al-'Ābidīn.'

He said: 'Why have you taken it away from the brothers and passed it on to the son of a brother?'

I said: 'Since close relationship to the Apostle of God is one of the pillars of the imamate, and Muḥammad b. al-Ḥanafiyya was distant from the Apostle of God, whereas 'Alī b. al-Ḥusayn was a descendant of Fāṭima, the daughter of the Apostle of God. There is a confirmed report from the Apostle of God that he pointed to al-Ḥusayn, peace be upon him, and said to him, "From your lineage will come the Qā'im, the Mahdī," and he informed Jābir b. 'Abdallāh al-Anṣārī[28] that he [Jābir] would see the fourth Imam [to come] from his descendants, and he ordered Jābir to extend to him greetings from himself and say to him, "You are the splitter [*al-Bāqir*] who splits open the knowledge most thoroughly".'

He said: 'It is confirmed of 'Alī that he said, "Muḥammad is my son in truth," and he gave him the standard at the Battles of Ṣiffīn and the Camel; and other intimate matters than these are reported; and that he jested with him alone and he signalled to him as he did not with others.'

I said: ''Alī b. al-Ḥusayn, peace be upon him, combined in himself all knowledge and ascetic piety, and he was of the very flesh of the Apostle of God. God proscribed for His Apostle

of Qayrawan under al-Mahdī from 307/919 until 311/923, and then again from 312/924 until his death in the reign of al-Qā'im. See Ibn 'Idhārī, *al-Bayān*, I, 182, 188, 189, 205; 'Iyāḍ, *Madārik*, 369, 386; al-Khushanī, 225, 240, trans. 319, 334–5; Ibn al-Athīr, *al-Kāmil*, VIII, 49–50; Halm, *Reich*, 221, trans. 246.

27. No other information about this man is available.

28. A prominent Madinan Companion of the Prophet. On him, see M. J. Kister, 'Djābir b. 'Abd Allāh' in the *EI2*, *Supplement*.

whatever women 'Alī b. al-Ḥusayn touched. The Apostle of God was his grandfather, and God states – and He is the Most Truthful of Speakers and the Most Judicious of Judges – "Those related by blood have prior rights among you" [8: 75 and 31: 34], and He said, "Give to relatives what is due them" [30: 34]. Muḥammad b. al-Ḥanafiyya submitted to 'Alī b. al-Ḥusayn and made his own withdrawal clear to him and followed his orders. Muḥammad b. al-Ḥanafiyya had only been a cover for 'Alī b. al-Ḥusayn and, when 'Alī attained maturity, he submitted to him.'

He said: 'Then who?'

I said: 'Muḥammad b. 'Alī, Bāqir al-'Ilm.'

He said: 'And what about Zayd? He was the older[29] and he waged war on behalf of God and expended himself. A person who wages war and strives openly is not the like of someone who hides himself and lets down a protective curtain.'

I said: 'Zayd disavowed any right of his own and did not claim anything. He acknowledged his brother Muḥammad b. 'Alī, peace be upon him, and it is confirmed that Ja'far b. Muḥammad [al-Ṣādiq], may the blessings of God be upon him, said, 'May God have mercy on my uncle Zayd; if he had prevailed, he would have surrendered the command to us.' Muḥammad b. 'Alī informed his brother that he would be the one killed in Kufa and crucified on the refuse dump, and said to him on the day of his farewell, "O brother, I am sure that I sense on you the odour of the martyr's blood." He answered, "God has completed what will be." Zayd only saw a recurring dream in which someone was saying to him, "O Zayd, rise against Hishām the squint-eyed. It is better for you than worshipping." When that had happened to him repeatedly, he rose up.'[30]

He said: 'I see that his rising by the order of God is confirmed in your eyes. Therefore, is he the imam?'

I said: 'The imamate is not a matter of dreams and aspirations

29. This is mistaken. Zayd was in fact at least eighteen years younger than Muḥammad al-Bāqir.

30. Zayd's revolt occurred in 122/740 during the reign of the Umayyad caliph Hishām.

and not everything belongs to someone because he is ordered to do something in his sleep. Zayd did not claim the imamate but was instead a supporter and venerator of his brother.'

He said: 'So if he had claimed it, would he have been the imam?'

I said: 'If he had made the claim, his claim would have been false if Muḥammad b. 'Alī denied it, because the sign was with Muḥammad b. 'Alī and with him also was the immanence and the knowledge.'

He said: 'And what is the sign of the imamate?'

I said: 'For each imam there is a sign through which he makes clear his veracity and the falseness of any one else who claims it. God, the Mighty and Glorious, does not bestow His signs on those who lie. Moreover, it is indispensable for each imam to have a miracle, and knowledge is the best of all miracles, in the same way that the Qur'an is the most wondrous of miracles and the most miraculous of signs. Zayd used to say, "He who wants to wage holy war should join me and he who wants knowledge should go to the son of my brother," meaning Ja'far b. Muḥammad al-Ṣādiq. The Prophet fed a whole group of people from food that would not have satisfied even one person. He called a tree to himself and it advanced to him. Water flowed suddenly from between his fingers; the moon split for him; and other examples of miracles which could not have come from anyone but God.'

He said: 'On this matter one could go on at length, but who came after Muḥammad?'

I said: 'Ja'far b. Muḥammad.'

He said: 'Then who?'

I said: 'At this point I stop. My certainty and knowledge end. It is my hope that with you there is a recognition of who came after Ja'far.'

He said: 'Those associates of yours whom we summoned yesterday designated the imams after Ja'far, tracing them to Mūsā his son and then after him among his descendants up to Muḥammad b. al-Ḥasan.'

I said: 'We are aware of this. I held as they do but then have parted from them some four years ago and they know this fact.'

He said: 'Why did you choose the doctrine of the Wāqifa?'[31]

I said: 'I saw that the Shī'a were united on Ja'far after disagreeing and that they broke apart after Ja'far regarding his son. Each sect backed one of them [his sons] because of the excellence he displayed. I decided that I would stop at what they had agreed upon and begin to seek the truth of the matter.'

He said: 'Speak about their disagreements.' Abū Mūsā then stood up and asked him to excuse me. He requested that he take care of my need. But Abū 'Abdallāh said, 'Leave me to talk. His need will be fulfilled. I have had close to eighteen years with you in which I have debated no one. This one has what we want. Let me debate with him. Surely if this one stands firmly with you, God will rescue through him a great mass of people.' Then he said to me, 'Mention their disagreement.'

I said: 'Without any restriction?'

He said: 'There is no restriction on you. Speak.'

I said:[32] 'After Ja'far, the Shi'a broke up into four sects. Of them one upheld the imamate of 'Abdallāh b. Ja'far, noting that he was the eldest of his sons and that it was on account of him that Ja'far was called Abū [the father of] 'Abdallāh. It was he who washed his father when he died. These people are the

31. The Wāqifa are those who 'stop' the imamate with some particular imam and do not recognize any imams after him.

32. Ibn al-Haytham's answer to this question contains some remarkable pieces of new information, particularly in regard to the groups that supported the imamate of Ismā'īl and Muḥammad b. Ismā'īl. Thus, the name al-Mubārak as the *mawlā* of Ismā'īl who became the chief of a sect called the Mubārakiyya, which is attested in works of al-Nawbakhtī (*Firaq al-Shī'a*, ed. H. Ritter. Istanbul, 1931, 67–8) and al-Qummī (*Kitāb al-maqālāt wa'l-firaq*, ed. Muḥammad Jawād Mashkūr. Tehran, 1963, 79–80), is not given elsewhere in full, nor is the information on these groups as detailed in the other accounts. Still it is noteworthy that, although Ibn al-Haytham wrote this passage long after he had become an Isma'ili *dā'ī*, he does not offer it as the official Isma'ili or Fatimid version but rather as a recollection of only what he actually knew about the matter when he first spoke to Abū 'Abdallāh, not what he learned about it later after his conversion.

Faṭḥiyya; 'Abdallāh was broad-headed [*afṭaḥ al-ra's*]. His brothers regarded him highly, and with veneration and respect. When, however, 'Abdallāh died, they restored the imamate to Mūsā and thus passed it from one brother to another. Another group had supported the imamate of Ismā'īl. And according to them, he is alive to this day. Some of them did, in fact, affirm his death during the lifetime of Ja'far, while others denied his death and said that Ja'far caused it to appear as though he had died in order to hide him, but that Ja'far had actually interred a teak log [*sāja*] and announced to the people that this was Ismā'īl. He even performed prayers for him and buried him. Among these also were some who said that Mūsā is a speaking [*nāṭiq*] imam and Ismā'īl is a silent [*ṣāmit*] imam and that obedience to both is obligatory. Yet others insisted that the imamate reverted to Muḥammad b. Ismā'īl during the lifetime of Ja'far and that Ja'far had pointed to the son of Ismā'īl, peace be upon him. Others of them claimed that for each imam there is an intermediary [*wāsiṭa*] and, if one is ignorant of the imam, obedience to the intermediary becomes obligatory. One sect thus upheld the imamate of al-Mubārak b. 'Alī al-'Abdī, who was the 'gate' [*bāb*][33] for Ismā'īl, and said that Ja'far ordered al-Mubārak to adopt an abode of emigration [*dār al-hijra*] in Khurāsān between Kābul and Qandahār. When al-Mubārak died, he bequeathed his position to his son Muḥammad b. al-Mubārak. Most of the Shi'a turned away from the son of al-Mubārak and accepted the imamate of Ismā'īl solely and said that he was still alive. Another group admitted that he had died but held that God would restore him to life and return him to the world, whereupon he will fill it with justice. They also said that the believer is not harmed by the loss of the imam if he acknowledges the true teachings of the imams and abstains concerning knowledge of the imam. Others of them

33. The term *bāb* literally means gate and here indicates the chief representative or chief deputy of the Imam. All access to the Imam depends on his *bāb* who is therefore the highest in rank of his followers. He would be the 'intermediary' (*wāsiṭa*).

maintained that Muḥammad b. Ismāʿīl was alive and that ʿAbdallāh b. Maymūn b. Muslim b. ʿAqīl [b. Abī Ṭālib] was his *bāb.* Yet others held that Muḥammad had died and that the imamate had passed to ʿAbdallāh b. Maymūn from ʿAbdallāh b. Jaʿfar because ʿAbdallāh did not leave offspring and thus surrendered the control of affairs to his *bāb*, ʿAbdallāh b. Maymūn.

The mass of the Shiʿa affirmed the imamate in Mūsā, then in his son, ʿAlī b. Mūsā al-Riḍā. It was he whom [the caliph] al-Ma'mūn killed after first making him his son-in-law by marrying him to his daughter. Thereafter, it went to his son, Muḥammad b. ʿAlī, then to al-Ḥasan b. Muḥammad, then to Muḥammad b. al-Ḥasan, and they are the Continuators [Wāṣila], the Ithnāʿashariyya. They claim that the imamate consists of twelve imams, and that it was transferred solely from father to son and did not revert to a brother because the imamate does not remain among brothers following the case of al-Ḥasan and al-Ḥusayn. Among them there are some who trace the imamate to Muḥammad b. Jaʿfar, although Muḥammad did not leave a male heir. Yet others claim that Mūsā is alive; they are the Cutters [Qaṭʿiyya].'[34]

He said: 'Is it not true that the Mūsā'iyya insist that al-Ḥasan died and left a pregnant slave girl and that after him this Muḥammad b. al-Ḥasan, whose existence they assert, was born to him?'

I said: 'That is what they say.'

He said: 'But how could the imam depart and the world be left to itself without an imam?'

I said: 'They maintain that it was delegated to the *bāb*s until the imam would be born and would attain maturity in the same way that Muḥammad b. al-Ḥanafiyya was the *bāb* for ʿAlī b. al-Ḥusayn [Zayn al-ʿĀbidīn] until he reached his maturity.

34. Normally this group is called Wāqifa, i.e., those who 'stop' the imamate with Mūsā (because he is still alive and thus remains the Imam) and not those who 'cut' (*qaṭaʿa*) his imamate upon his death. Here the name is to be understood in contrast to Wāṣila, which means those who continue the imamate among the descendants of Mūsā.

Similarly Yūsha' b. Nūn (Joshua) was a veil for [Eleazar] the son of Hārūn (Aaron).'[35]

He said: 'A foetus cannot compare to a child not yet mature because the foetus might abort or disappear or be stillborn or come out female, and 'Alī b. al-Ḥusayn existed and likewise with the son of Hārūn. The foetus is essentially non-existent and the non-existent is not like the existent. A male youth may reach maturity at eleven years as similarly a female may come to puberty at ten years. 'Alī b. al-Ḥusayn was at that time thirteen.'

I said: 'They have affirmed his having been born and abstain concerning the time and place of his birth. They claim evidence that the number of imams is twelve, although no one else says that this is the case or produces the same evidence that they do.'

He said: 'What is their evidence?'

I said: 'They maintain that only God, the Most High, creates souls and horizons and that He created in the heavens twelve divisions of the zodiac and a year consisting of twelve months. In every day there are twelve hours and likewise in the night. The members of the body subservient to the heart are twelve, and the regions of the terrestrial world are twelve.'

When I mentioned the like of this, he wanted to get down from the couch and said, 'People can claim that about others than the descendants of Mūsā.'

Abū Mūsā and those present rose for him, and I stood out of respect for him if he should get down. But he kept his place with his feet on the floor. He said: 'Why do they not speak of thirteen and make the argument on the basis of God, the Most High, saying, 'I saw eleven stars and the sun and moon; I saw

35. Ibn al-Haytham refers here to Eleazar (Arabic: al-'Ayzār) who inherited the status of his father Aaron (Hārūn), although it was Joshua who assumed immediate command. Thereafter, the priestly lineage continued among Eleazar's (and, accordingly, Aaron's) descendants, not Joshua's. Presumably, the doctrine of those Ibn al-Haytham is describing recognizes that Aaron, as the brother of Moses, is the founder of a line of imams through his son Eleazar.

them bowing down to me' [12: 4]. That is thirteen and there is fourteen. Why do they not argue on the basis of God, the Most High's, statement, "By the dawn and the ten nights and the even and the odd and by the night when it passes on; is there in that an oath for the man of discrimination" [89: 11–15]? That is fourteen and fifteen. And why do they not propose nineteen and support it on the basis of God, the Most High, saying, "And over it are nineteen" [74: 30]? Or why do they not use twenty and make the argument from God, the Most High's statement, "If there are twenty patient men among you" [8: 65]. And why do they not cite thirty and support it by God's words, "thirty nights" [7: 142]? Why don't they uphold forty and cite as proof the statement of God, the Mighty and Glorious, "forty nights" [2: 51], or why not fifty and claim it on the basis of the words of the Apostle of God about the collective oath concerning murder [*qasāma*][36] "fifty men," and in the statement of God, the Exalted, "fifty thousand years" [70: 4]? Why do they not argue the case for sixty by God's, the Mighty and Glorious, statement, "sixty indigent persons" [58: 4]? Why do they not say seventy and support it by God, the Mighty and Glorious's words, "And Moses chose of his people seventy men" [7: 155]? Or why not uphold eighty and argue by God's words, "eighty lashes" [24: 4]? Why not ninety-nine based on God's statement, "ninety-nine ewes" [38: 23]? Why don't they say a hundred and make the argument from God's words, "The woman and man guilty of adultery should be flogged each one hundred lashes" [24: 2]? He went on extensively in this sense, expounding considerably, and said much more. He explained it all with a wondrous clarity that I had not known nor heard of prior to that moment. By God I could not compare him with anything but a flowing river, or a man reading a sheet held in his hand, written in his own handwriting, which he comprehends and whose meanings he recognizes to be sound. He pointed out their arguments and evidence, refuted their claims,

36. On this oath and its use, see the section on *kasāma* in the article by J. Pedersen and Y. Linant de Bellefonds on 'Ḳasam' in the *EI2*.

and demolished their contentions on behalf of that claim.'

I said: 'One must accept what you have cited, but there is enough even in a part of what you said to destroy their claim.'

Following that he summoned me to the faith and he gave permission for our colleagues whom he had summoned before me to enter into his presence. Thus, they joined in the *da'wa*. When it was time for the oath, he said, 'Know, may God have mercy on you, that this oath is a sunna from God in respect to His people and His servants. God took it from His prophets, and each prophet took it from his own community. The proof for this is from the Book of God, since He says, "When We took a covenant from the prophets, from you, from Noah and Abraham and Moses and Jesus, the son of Mary, and We took from them a solemn pledge" [33: 7]; and His saying, "When We took the pledge of the tribe of Israel not to worship any except God" [2: 83]; and His statement, "God took a pledge from the tribe of Israel and We sent among them twelve leaders" [5: 12]; and His saying, "From those who said that they were Christians, We took their pledge" [5: 14]; and His saying, "When We took your pledge not to shed each other's blood" [2: 84]; and His statement to the Apostle of God, "Those who swear allegiance to you, swear allegiance to God Himself, His hand above theirs; whoever violates it violates himself and whoever remains true to what he promised to God shall be due a great reward" [48: 10].' Thereafter he reviewed everything in the Qur'an mentioning the covenant and fidelity to it. He said, 'There is no religion except on the basis of covenant. Of whomever God has not taken a covenant, has no one to guard him nor any religion to restrain him. Prior to this "you were a dissolute people" [48:12].' He said, 'Truly God has said, "God has purchased from the believers their souls and their wealth in exchange for paradise when they will fight on behalf of God, killing and being killed, a promise He made truly in the Torah, the Gospels and the Qur'an. And who is truer to his covenant than God? Rejoice therefore in your pledge of allegiance which you have pledged to Him. That is a wondrous triumph" [9: 111].' And He said, '"God was pleased with the believers when they swore allegiance to you under the tree" (to the end of the verse) [48: 18].'[37] Then he said, 'Today you have pledged allegiance to God and you are truly His servants and you have acknowledged Muḥammad and pledged allegiance to him.' He continued, 'God has explained that He was not satisfied with the worship of those who came first except upon their pledging allegiance to Muḥammad, His Prophet. How could He then approve your worship without a pledge?'

I said: 'By God, O by God, I had never heard this and yet I have read all that reached us concerning the teachings of the sects and the many doctrines of both heretics and believers, but I had never heard of this. Surely, it is quite obviously true, and its proof and veracity are certainly evident. We used to think and maintain that God extracted the descendants of Adam from his back and took from them the covenant.'

He said: 'This is wrong and no proof will support it, nor would an intelligent person consider it to be valid, since God, the Most High, says, "Be mindful of the favour God showed you and of His pledge with which He bound you when you said: we hear and we obey" [5: 7]. How could it be that He reminded them of something they could not remember, and then they gave Him this understandable reply. No, it is as we see it; it was those from before you.'

I said: 'There is no religion in the absence of a covenant.'

He said: 'That is correct. Have you not heard God's words, "None shall have the power of intercession except those who have taken a covenant with the Most Merciful" [19: 87], and, "They said, the fire will touch us only for a limited number of days; say, have you taken a covenant with God – God will never go back on His covenant – or do you assert of God what you have no knowledge of?" [2: 80]. Thus, the covenant is a precondition for worship and an intercession for him with God.

37. The verse continues, 'He knew what was in their hearts; He sent down upon them tranquillity and He rewarded them with a speedy victory.'

Whoever violates it has a painful punishment. The covenant is the means. God, the Most High, said, 'O you who believe, fear God and seek the means to approach Him' [5: 35].'

I said: 'Praise be to God, we have faith and believe. We would not have been led rightly if it were not that God guided us by the arrival of the apostles of our Lord with the truth.'

Once he had discussed everything that pertains to the covenant, he said, 'May God have mercy on you, you should know that the imams are seven.' He then cited everything that provides evidence of sevens out of all that God has created, fashioned, and produced in the way of the spheres, the shining stars, Ursa major and minor, the climes, the days, the heavens, and the earths, the limbs and sensory organs. Next he divided the Qur'an into sevenths from *al-Baqara* to "Say, He is God the One" [112: 1]. Then he mentioned *al-Ḥamd*[38] and that it is the seven oft-repeated verses [*mathānī*] and he proved all this with reference to individual letters and the alphabetic order. He arranged them section by section, thereby making known in each section the true intent of God and His purpose and the ultimate aim of His command. When he had covered this completely, explaining it all and putting it in proper order, he said, 'Understand that for each imam there are twelve visible diurnal *ḥujja*s and twelve concealed and hidden nocturnal *ḥujja*s.' He established this fact on the basis of all that we had mentioned about the hours, the territories of the world, the months, and the signs of the zodiac, the limbs of the body, the intestines, and the heart, and that they [the *ḥujja*s] are the veil of the imam and are his mouthpieces and gateways, his deputies, and the messengers from him to the *dā'ī*s, who in turn convey the message to the believers. He proved this by reference to matters which had previously been incomprehensible and which, before these demonstrations and explanations for it, had appeared unreasonable.

I said: 'There is no god but God; this, by God, is a clear

38. *Sūrat al-fātiḥa.*

explanation and is a comfort for what is in the breast; and it is guidance and a mercy for the believers.'

He then took up the order of 'There is no god but God, Muḥammad is the Apostle of God.' He divided it on the basis of the twelve limits [*ḥudūd*],[39] then on seven and nineteen, then four limits, indicating that they are a single word in which is the oneness and all other limits. He commented on the hadith of the Apostle of God in regard to whoever says 'There is no god but God' that he has spared his property and blood and is relieved of the burden of paying the poll tax [*jizya*]. Whoever utters it with perfect sincerity enters paradise. He mentioned that being sincere in this regard implies understanding its limits. I knew at that moment that I had not previously uttered it with complete sincerity. Prior to this I had noticed in some treatise of doctrine that the one on whose behalf the Silent One [*ṣāmit*] testifies is the Lord of the Truth [*ṣāḥib al-ḥaqq*]. I mentioned this fact to him.

He said: 'We testify by the Silent One, the Speaker, the mountain, the tree, the heavens, the earth, the letters, the word, and the long and short suras.'

I said: 'What is your opinion if the Twelvers maintain that the twelve are the imams and the seven are *ḥujjas*?'

He said: 'That doctrine does them wrong because seven is masculine and twelve is feminine. The seven is spirits and the twelve is houses and abodes. God, the Mighty and Glorious, said, "Like a grain of wheat which brings forth seven spikes and on each spike is a hundred grains" [2: 261].' Then he brought up 'In the name of God, the Merciful, the Compassionate,' and next began to explain the whole of the Qur'an beginning with *al-Ḥamd* and going on to the end of it. I heard then the like of what I had never heard before. He explained a variety of matters in *al-Ḥamd* and the meaning of extolling, praising highly, expressing gratitude, and what the prayer for Muḥammad consists of and how it is perfectly done, how to obey the commandment of God in praying for Muḥammad,

39. *Ḥudūd*, limits, here signifies the ranks of the *da'wa*.

God bless him, and that the person who says, 'O God, pray over Muḥammad and the family of Muḥammad,' has commanded his Creator to do what his Creator ordered him to do. Then he adduced a proof of this and demonstrated it and made it clear. He said, 'Do you believe that, if a man commands you to give someone something and you answer him, "You give it to him," are you carrying out the command of the commander or not?'

I said: 'No.'

He said: 'It is the same with these people in the prayer for Muḥammad. No one acknowledges Muḥammad but the person who understands the prayer for him, and no one recognizes Muḥammad who does not understand in what way Muḥammad conveyed his message to all humankind, even though he never went beyond the borders of the Hijaz.'

Then he began to explain *al-Baqara* and he mentioned *alif, lām, mīm,* and the suras which open with letters of obscure meaning,[40] the *rā'āt,*[41] the *ḥawāmīm,*[42] the *lawāmīm,*[43] *ṭā' hā',*[44] *ṭā' sīn,*[45] *ṭā' sīn mīm,*[46] *yā' sīn,*[47] *kāf hā' yā' 'ayn ṣād,*[48] and *ṣād.*[49]

I said: 'Praise be to God and there is no god but God.'

He said: 'The listener is more bored than the reciter. The morning approaches and you do not know how to stay awake all night. I know that it will be difficult for you for three nights, then you will not be bothered. But we have need of you.'

I said: 'God forbid that hearing this would bore anyone. This is tender and fresh knowledge, the like of which we have never

40. On the so-called mysterious letters that open twenty-nine suras in the Qur'an and the various theories about their significance, see A. T. Welch, 'al-Ḳur'ān,' *EI2* (section 4d).

41. Verses whose opening letters are the letter *rā',* i.e., suras 10–15.

42. Verses with the letters *ḥā', waw* and *mīm,* i.e., suras 40–46.

43. Suras 2, 3, 7, 29, 30–32.

44. Sura 20.

45. Sura 27.

46. Suras 26 and 28.

47. Sura 36.

48. Sura 19.

49. Sura 38.

heard before.'

Then he brought up prayer and its limits, and the call to prayer and its number, and ablution and purification, and making ablutions with sand [*tayammum*]. He arranged the meaning, explained it, pointed out similarities, and detailed aspects. He mentioned fasting, pilgrimage, the Ka'ba, the Black Stone [*al-ḥajar*], Zamzam, al-Ṣafā, al-Marwa, the Sanctuary, the pebbles [*jimār*], the cattle for sacrifice [*hady*], the rituals of the pilgrimage [*manāsik*], the Holy Places [*mashā'ir*], the circumambulations, Minā, 'Arafāt, the Maqām, the covering for the Ka'ba [*kiswat al-bayt*], and what each of these indicates. He said, 'A person who fasts and does not understand, and who prays and does not understand, or performs the pilgrimage and does not understand, is someone who acts but does not know. God, the Most High, said, "To fast is better for you if you only knew it" [2: 184]; and He said, "Woe to those who pray but are heedless of their prayers" [107: 4–5]; and He said, "Has the story of the overwhelming not reached you? Faces on the day will be humiliated, labouring and weary, roasted in a scorching fire, watered from a boiling spring" [88: 1–5], that is, from water that pours out into a vessel; it is the knowledge of transmission and reports, which is action without knowledge. The flowing spring is that whose sources and wellsprings flow from God to His friends and His *ḥujjas*.'

He let it be known that action without knowledge is not sound and outward performance is not valid without inner understanding. A body that has no spirit in it is useless; the body without spirit is dead. He brought up the interior of the body of the human and its face, spirit, soul, back, belly, five external senses and the internal senses and their excellence and that these external senses are the servants of the internal senses.[50] On this matter he spoke in rhyme, with mastery, and went on at length. He mentioned the hadith of the Prophet, 'There is no verse of the Book of God that does not have an outward and an

50. For early references to the internal senses, see Bālīnūs, *Sirr al-khalīqa*, index, and *Pseudo-Ammonius*, 230, index under *ḥāssa/ḥawāss*.

inner meaning; for every letter there is a rank; for every rank there is an origin.' He made the outward aspect of it represent its revealed form and its inner aspect its cryptic meaning and its allegorical interpretation. He said unprecedented things, and explained and clarified all with demonstrations.

Then he said: 'What do you hold in regard to the imam? Is it possible that he commit major sins, offend, and kill a soul whom God made unlawful, and other such things?'

I said: 'The imam who is guided and supported by the holy spirit cannot possibly be ascribed this kind of thing, and the commission of major sins cannot be attributed to him nor any abominable or sinful act.'

He said: 'What is the holy spirit?'

I said: 'A power with which God supports his prophets and friends.'

He said: 'So also the imams?'

I said: 'The distinction between the imam and the prophet is the intermediaries through which they receive what they receive from God. The intermediaries for the prophet are spiritual beings, and the intermediaries for the imams are human prophets.'

He said: 'Does the prophet show partiality to the imam and single him out for things he denies to others?'

I said: 'It is allowed to the prophet to single out, just as God, the Most High, singled him out, and to choose, just as God chose him. A part of the knowledge of the prophets is generally shared by everyone, and the noble and the less noble are equal in it. Another part of his knowledge is given by him specifically to the one whom God, the Most High, identifies to him. What pertains to the laws and the acts prescribed by them and to confirming the oneness of God is available to all the people equally. Of what pertains to knowledge in which the people excel one another, the imam may inform the community, and one of them might preserve whereas the rest forget it. It is related that when God, the Mighty and Glorious, revealed "so that ears retain it as a remembrance" [69: 12], the

Apostle of God said, "O God, make it the ear of 'Alī b. Abī Ṭālib".'

He said: 'How could the Prophet, God bless him and his family, comprehend the speech of the angels?'

I said: 'By means of a spirit from the holy spirit additional in him which has the form of the angels. The angel may assume forms, as it is confirmed in the report that Gabriel, peace be upon him, used to appear in the form of Diḥya al-Kalbī.[51] Thus, it is by an increase in power that they make contact with the angels.'

He said: 'How is it possible that offences be ascribed to them or mistakes be attributed to them, and forgetting, carelessness, and inadvertence?'

I said: 'What offences are these?'

He said: 'God, the Most High, said, "And Adam disobeyed his Lord and allowed himself to be seduced" [20: 121]; and He said about Joseph, "Surely she desired him and he desired her" [12: 24]; and there is Moses and his asking for that in which his people would be destroyed, and the statement of God, the Mighty and Glorious, about Muḥammad, His own Prophet, "So that God may forgive your past and future sins" [48: 2].'

I said: 'All that you mention may be construed in various ways and interpreted, and it is necessary that we attribute to the prophets of God the very best of these ways, and that we consider them above the worst of them, and that we distinguish between the offences [*dhunūb*] of the prophets and those of others.'

He said: 'What can you say once you have labelled them as offences?'

I said: 'We have agreed that offences is a term that includes minor forgivable sins, and major sins about which forgiveness depends on the will of God, and polytheism which will never be forgiven. Some sins involve intention and premeditation;

51. Diḥya b. Khalīfa al-Kalbī, a Companion of the Prophet, was said to be so handsome that the angel adopted his form when he appeared among humans. See H. Lammens and Ch. Pellat, 'Diḥya' and 'Djabrā'īl' by J. Pedersen in the *EI2*.

others, inadvertence, negligence, error, or forgetting; yet others are mere thoughts without deliberation or lust. Some are by choice and desire for pleasure. The offences of the common worshippers involve lust, premeditation, intention, choice, and the contravention of the command of God, intentionally opposing Him, whereas the offences of the prophets, peace be upon them all, involve only inadvertence, negligence, forgetting, and thoughts without deliberate intent or for pleasure. In so doing they are not opposing God, the Most High, given that these acts are also subject to interpretation. For example, Adam, peace be upon him, did not act deliberately but merely forgot. He trusted the one speaking to him and presumed the best of him at that moment. When he realized the lapse and mistake, he shed tears of remorse and begged for forgiveness. God's saying, "he went astray" [*fa-ghawā*] does not imply seduction, but that he was separated from the command of God, the Most High, just as it is said "the calf went astray" [*ghawā al-faṣīl*] when the milk was withheld from it. Thus, Adam felt shame in front of his Lord, and that shame separated him from God. Then God forgave him and thereafter guided him. Every offence that God, the Most High, forgives is not called an offence once it is forgiven, but instead it becomes a mercy as in God's, the Most High, saying, "God will change the evil acts of those into good" [25: 70]. In regard to Joseph, he never desired an act of disobedience, but instead we hold that she[52] desired a disobedient act and he wished to correct and reprimand her. There are people who hold that there is advance and deferment [in the Qur'anic passage and they interpret it as meaning] "were it not that he saw the sign of his Lord, he would have desired her."[53] Since the sign came first, he was prevented from offending. The sign was the immunity from sin [*'iṣma*]. Since this immunity came first, the desire was barred. As for Moses, he did not ask in the sense that his people asked and he was

52. Referring to the wife of Joseph's Egyptian master who attempted to seduce him.

53. The discussion is about Qur'an 12: 24 and its context.

not unaware that God, the Most High, cannot be perceived by the senses, and that God does not have limits, or that what has no limit does not possess a shape, and what has no shape has no form, and what has no form cannot not be perceived by the senses. He asked only in apology for his people. Moses, however, was the foremost of those who believe that eyesight cannot perceive God, the Exalted. Similarly, the offences of Muḥammad have the character of inadvertence as, for example, it was possible for him to be inattentive about praying or forgetful in regard to the Qur'an but without intent and deliberation.'

He said: 'How could Adam have been inattentive or forgetful given that God had explained things to him? The Most High said, "This one is an enemy to you and your wife" [20: 118], and he [Satan] is the one who said to Adam, "Your Lord has forbidden you this tree" (to the end)[54] [7: 20]. He was addressed by the enemy who had been forbidden to him, so how can you ascribe forgetfulness to him?' But then he said, 'Return to the question.'

He said: 'What if the imam does what you have exempted him of doing and intentionally perpetrates a major sin and murders someone whose murder is forbidden?'

I said: 'The question is impossible; an imam does not do anything of the kind.'

He said: 'But if he did?'

I said: 'After his sign and confirming proof have been established that he is the imam to whom obedience is a duty?'

He said: 'Yes.'

I said: 'Obeying him is obligatory, and we should not doubt him or think badly of him, and we must not carry out his actions without his permission.'

He said as if reproaching me: 'Would you really obey someone who commits grave sins and enormities and murders a person whom God, the Most High, made inviolate?'

Our colleagues whom he had summoned before me

54. The verse continues, 'lest you should become angels or become one of those who live forever.'

answered him, trying to excuse me. They said to him, 'Your exaltation induced him to answer in this way since you pressed him, but no one would say such things.'

He reprimanded them for what they were saying and said, 'Hold back. What prompts you to speak? Permission was requested for you to enter last night, but I was loath to let you enter to me.' Then, however, he turned to me with leniency and relaxation. He said, 'What did you say to this?'

I said: 'The master should repeat the question.'

He said: 'The imam who commits grave sins and kills a person whom God, the Most High, made inviolate?'

I pronounced the question impossible and only intensified in my denial. However, he insisted that the act could actually happen. I said again, 'Following upon the continuation of his sign and proof?'

He said: 'Yes.'

I said: 'Obeying him is necessary and also approving of his actions. We do not repudiate his acts, but we act as he does only with his permission.'

He said: 'Can you establish this on the basis of anything?'

I said: 'Yes, I have read in some scripture that when someone who knows does something, do not do the like of it but do whatever he commands of you. And in the Book of God, there is the story of Moses and the knowing and righteous worshipper who killed an innocent person and scuttled the boat. Moses repudiated his act but God approved of it.[55] Since Moses repudiated an act which was pleasing to God, it is even more appropriate for us that we not repudiate the act of the imam, nor fault him, and not be hasty in regard to him, or consider him ignorant or incapable.' By God, I had not before this been guided to this answer. I was not aware of it and had not heard it before, but God aided me to it when the need arose.

He said to me: 'Well done and nicely spoken, may God bless you,' and he said to those present – among whom was Ibrāhīm al-Yamānī, who was called the lesser master[56] – 'Seeing how

55. These events come from Qur'an 18: 71–76.

56. Ibrāhīm b. Muḥammad al-Yamānī or (according to Qāḍī al-

well he articulates and expresses what he means in regard to every matter, I would not compare him with anyone but Abu'l-Ḥusayn.' Then he said to me, 'This Abu'l-Ḥusayn with whom I compare you was a man who came to us from the east and whom the lords [*awliyā'*] had sent. He stayed with me some years in the territory of the Kutāma. You look like him, are the same age, and have the same manner of speaking.'[57]

I kissed his hand and expressed thanks for his words of praise and approval. His mealtime arrived, and the washing water was brought to him. He ordered me to wash, which I did, and then Abū Mūsā and Abū Zākī washed. A bare table of *khalanj* wood was brought in which was then set up in front of him, and another was set up near it. Four trays of Chinese porcelain were put before him which turned out to be [...][58] surrounded by the meat of young chickens. He ordered me to sit at the table, and our colleagues sat separately at that other table. They produced a great quantity of food, featuring various kinds of meat in different dishes. Then he washed, and I wanted to get up to go wash. He said to me, 'Stay where you are and don't leave.' Later I withdrew to the abode of Abū Mūsā.

Nu'mān) Ibrāhīm b. Isḥāq al-Zabīdī was sent from Ṣan'ā' to accompany Abū 'Abdallāh throughout his mission in North Africa in place of 'Abdallāh b. Abi'l-Malāḥif, who had to return to the Yemen for family reasons. Since the Kutāma referred to Abū 'Abdallāh as the lord or master (*al-sayyid*), they simply called Ibrāhīm the lesser lord (*al-sayyid al-ṣaghīr*). See Qāḍī al-Nu'mān, *Iftitāḥ*, 31–2, Dachraoui's introduction, 47, n. 3; Ibn 'Idhārī, *al-Bayān*, I, 153; Idrīs, *'Uyūn*, 84; Halm, *Reich*, 124, trans. 132.

57. There is no other information about who this Abu'l-Ḥusayn might have been. It is noteworthy, however, that at least one *dā'ī* had come to Abū 'Abdallāh from the east during this period and had also returned east. The mission in North Africa evidently was never out of touch with headquarters. One prominent *dā'ī* of this same period was the Abu'l-Ḥusayn b. al-Aswad who became involved, against his will, with the Ṣāḥib al-Shāma in Syria. Perhaps they are the same. See Halm, *Reich*, 79–81, trans. 79–81; al-Naysābūrī, *Istitār al-imām*, in Ivanow, *Rise*, 163–72; Arabic, 99–101, 104.

58. A word or words are missing in the text.

When it was afternoon I again entered to him. He inquired about me and said, 'How are you feeling about what you heard? Do you disapprove of anything?'

I said: 'God forbid it!'

He said: 'If you disapprove of anything, ask about it and do not leave it be lest it constitute a rejection. Know that there are four attitudes: recognition, affirmation, rejection, and disapproval. The first evidence of affirmation is recognition and the first evidence of rejection is disapproval. When recognition increases in strength, it becomes affirmation.'

I said: 'O master, what is the name of the Imam and who is he and whose son is he?'

He said: 'There will be another time for that.'

I said: 'Bestow or withhold without an accounting.'

After some silence he said: 'The Imam is Muḥammad b. Ismā'īl b. Ja'far.'

I said: 'The period is long; today is a hundred and forty years from the death of Ja'far, and Ismā'īl is said to have died in the lifetime of his father.'

He said: 'Would you deny that he might live a thousand years when Noah lived among his people for a thousand years?'

I said: 'We don't deny it because of following your lead and believing in your declaration. We affirm that this is a cover for another.'

He said: 'God does whatever He wishes.'

I said to him: 'Certainly there is among the reports from the Prophet that he said, "The Mahdī will have my name and the name of his father will be that of my father".'

He said: 'He meant by "his father" Ismā'īl the son of Abraham, his ancestor, whom he takes here as a father.'

He wrote a letter to his brother Abu'l-'Abbās in Tripoli giving him permission to come.[59] He sent also two hundred horsemen

59. Abu'l-'Abbās had escaped from Aghlabid detention in Qayrawan during the revolt there of Mudlij b. Zakariyyā', a disaffected former Aghlabid commander, in Jumādā II 293/March 906. See Qāḍī al-Nu'mān, *Sharḥ al-akhbār*, III, 430, and *Iftitāḥ*, 260; Ivanow, *Rise* (Arabic text, p.

under Tamīm al-Wasqānī.[60] At that time Bahrām the gardener entered to him with three trays of red roses arranged uniformly. On each tray, there was a censer of wondrous manufacture on which the roses revolved about a lion. He gave one to me and another to Shabīb al-Qammūdī, the governor of Ṭubna.[61] He had summoned him that first night before me. Shabīb kissed it and returned it to the tray and departed. When I wanted to leave, I kissed it and put it back. He said to me, 'Depart with it to your place.' Thus, I went out with it in my hand and passed into the gallery of his palace where there were men belonging to the Banu'l-Aghlab and other men as well. They gathered around me and offered congratulations to me. They expressed an esteem for me that I had never known before that moment. I realized that he had meant to ennoble me by means of those roses and thus to honour me. That was exactly what he wanted when I departed with it. So I hid it and in the morning I went to him, taking with me a donation. I had calculated my fifth and assessed my estates, and I presented it to him as what I wanted to donate. That pleased him, and I let him know what I hoped to pay to him as the fifth[62] and that I had made an assessment of my estates, but that a portion of it was subject to the land tax. He said, 'Do not pay land tax to me; on your kind

34); and Halm, *Reich*, 105, trans. 109, and 118, trans. 118. Mudlij's revolt is reported in Ibn 'Idhārī, *al-Bayān*, I, 139. See also Talbi, *Aghlabide*, 657ff. Abu'l-'Abbās thereafter returned eastward to Tripoli where he stayed for the next three years, waiting for his brother's eventual victory and permission to join him.

60. Tamīm al-Wasqānī or al-Wasfānī (so in Idrīs, *'Uyūn*, p. 261) appears also as the commander of a Kutāma horse troop much later under al-Qā'im in 332/943–4.

61. This Shabīb must be Shabīb b. Abī Shaddād al-Qammūdī, who had been either governor or commandant of the Aghlabid garrison in Ṭubna. Evidently he went over to the Fatimid side. See Idrīs, *'Uyūn*, 117–18; Ibn 'Idhārī, *al-Bayān*, I, 140; Qāḍī al-Nu'mān, *Iftitāḥ*, 170, 172, 174, 175–6 and Dachraoui's introduction, 90 no. 5.

62. Isma'ilis commonly gave a fifth (*khums*) of their gains as a donation to the Imam. For details see Qāḍī al-Nu'mān, *Kitāb al-himma fī ādāb atbā' al-a'imma*, ed. M. Kāmil Ḥusayn (Cairo [1948]), 68–73.

there is no land tax.' He exempted me of it and ordered that the land tax I had been subjected to for Nīna and Qanshiyya[63] in regard to two houses henceforth not apply to me. He said, 'I have not cancelled the land tax for anyone else but for you and Ibn 'Imrān al-Ṭubnī,[64] in regard to Ṭubna.'[65]

Then he asked me about my *kunya*. He said, 'I know your name, are you not called Ja'far?'

I said: 'Yes.'

He said: 'What about your *kunya*?'

I said: 'Abū Bakr.'

He said: 'This is amazing! Here is a Shi'i, the son of a Shi'i, who accepts the *kunya* Abū Bakr.'

I said: 'It is up to you.'

He said: 'Your name is Ja'far, and from today you shall have the *kunya* Abū 'Abdallāh so that, for you, a fine name will be associated with a fine *kunya*.' It was as if, by God, I had never had the *kunya* Abū Bakr, and yet those who knew me and those who did not know me from far and wide had known that fact. Then he said, 'Were those who came before you of your religious doctrine?'

I said: 'They were Zaydis who disassociated from 'Uthmān and Mu'āwiya but who did not renounce Abū Bakr and 'Umar. They said, 'We hold back from whomever 'Alī b. Abī Ṭālib held back and we dissociate from those he dissociated from.' They were wont to uphold the superiority of 'Alī b. Abī Ṭālib but they allowed putting the person of lesser excellence ahead of him.'

Then he asked me about our ancestors. I said, 'My ancestors were from Kufa. My grandfather al-Haytham b. 'Abd al-Raḥmān came here with Yazīd b. Ḥātim.[66] My clan were a

63. No information is available about such places. Perhaps these names are not correct.

64. Nothing is known about this man.

65. On the remission of the land tax in Ṭubna, see Ibn 'Idhārī, *al-Bayān*, I, 141–2; Halm, *Reich*, 106–7, trans. 111.

66. Yazīd b. Ḥātim was governor of the Maghrib from 154 or 155/771 to 170/786–7 on behalf of the 'Abbasids.

part of Muḍar. The grandfather of my grandfather was Qays b. 'Āṣim b. [Sinān b.] Khālid b. Minqar.'[67]

He said: 'Was then al-Haytham, the one who first came, your grandfather?'

I said: 'He was the grandfather of the father of my grandfather, the fifth back from my father. We have heard that al-Haytham was exempted from serving Rawḥ b. Ḥātim.[68] He was a friend of his whom he preferred to his peers. He presented to him ten thousand dinars and excused him from service and gave him leave to return to Kufa. So he went back to Kufa but returned with a large sum of money along with a decree from either al-Hādī or Hārūn[69] to Rawḥ to honour, protect, and aid him in whatever he might want to build. He had made plans for three locations, one in Qayrawan on the Simāṭ al-A'ẓam,[70] one at Bāb Salam,[71] and one at Mawqif al-Tibn.[72] Thus, he settled, built, and set up estates in many areas and on the coast. These are those that you have exempted me from paying the land tax for. And others were in the eastern province and in Qarna, Bāja, and he set up a large garden which is known as the Palace of Abū Hārūn, near by the Two Towers.[73]

67. Qays was a tribal chief of Tamīm and is said to have died in 47/667. On him see 'Ḳays b. 'Āṣim' by M. J. Kister in the *EI2*. On the genealogy see Caskel, I, table 76; al-Balādhurī, *Ansāb*, VII/i, pp. 37–47.

68. Rawḥ was governor of the Maghrib after his brother from 170/786–7 to 174/790–1.

69. These two were 'Abbasid caliphs. Al-Hādī ruled from 169/785 to 170/786; Hārūn al-Rashīd from 170/786 to 193/809.

70. The Simāṭ al-A'ẓam was the main thoroughfare of Qayrawan and ran from the Bāb Tūnis in the north to the Bāb Abi'l-Rabī' in the south. The author's house on that street acquired his name and, during the reign of al-Mu'izz, there is mention of an itinerary followed by a young man that passed by 'the Dār of Ibn Aswad the *dā'ī*.' See al-Mālikī, *Riyāḍ*, II, 487–8; H. R. Idris, *La Berbérie orientale sous les Zīrīdes, xe-xiie siècles* (Paris, 1962), 419.

71. The Bāb Salam or Bāb Aslam was one of two gates to Qayrawan on the western side.

72. Mawqif al-Tibn (station of straw) is not mentioned elsewhere.

73. Bāja is a well-known town about 170 km northwest of Qayrawan and Qarna (or Qurna) is the town of Coreva/Coreba, a small fortified

All that is still in our hands to this day with the exception of Bāja, which is said to have been taken over by the army.'

He said: 'You have left the religious doctrine of your forefathers and improved upon them according to what I have heard from you. You are piercing gems.'

I said: 'My father died in the year 285 [898] when I had not yet reached majority. I had gone through the Qur'an several times. He possessed many books and was competent in various areas of language, uncommon words, disputation, and jurisprudence. Through him I became especially fond of jurisprudence and disputation and I set aside these books and commenced careful study and investigation of them. Each day and night I devoted myself to memorizing ten topics in the legal reasoning of Abū Ḥanīfa and five in disputation, the doctrine of the unity of God, of the creation of the Qur'ān, the denial of anthropomorphism, that capacity accompanies the act, the doctrine of the creation of acts, theological discussions of knowledge, faith, and the promise and the threat. He also endeared to me the study of the books of the ancients, and I occupied myself with Aristotle's *Book of Logic.* I possess many of his books and the books of Plato and others. In order to hear jurisprudence, I would regularly visit Ibn 'Abdūn[74] and Ibn

enclave between Tunis and al-Urbus. On the latter see Talbi, *Aghlabide,* 198 and 201. It has not been possible to identify the other places mentioned here or confirm the reading of these names. However, there was an Abū Hārūn who was governor of Qayrawan under the first of the Aghlabids and, according to a reference in Qāḍī al-Nu'mān's *Iftitāḥ,* (p. 58), there was an area called the Hārūniyya located between Qayrawan and the Qaṣr al-Qadīm.

74. Ibn 'Abdūn is Abu'l-'Abbās Muḥammad b. 'Abdallāh al-Ru'aynī. He was the leading Ḥanafī jurist in Qayrawan and had been chief qadi for some thirty months, starting in 275/888–9 during the reign of the Aghlabid Ibrāhīm b. Aḥmad (ruled 261/875–289/902) and was known for his severity toward the Mālikīs. He died in 297/910, and al-Marwadhī, the new Fatimid qadi and an old friend, led prayers for him. See al-Khushanī, 187–90, trans. 274–7; 'Iyāḍ, *Madārik,* index; Ibn 'Idhārī, *al-Bayān,* I, 121 161; Qāḍī al-Nu'mān, *Iftitāḥ,* 70, Dachraoui, intro., 59 n. 2; R. Roy and L. Poinssot, *Inscriptions arabes de Kairouan,* épitaphe no. 89 (vol. 2, pt. 1, pp. 171–3).

Ma'mar.[75] I heard hadith from Abū Ja'far b. Abān and from Ziyād al-Lu'lu'ī.[76] But most often I would frequent those associated with the science of theology. At that a Jew known as Yūsuf b. Yaḥyā al-Khurāsānī got in touch with me. He was so well versed in logic that I had no need to frequent anyone else.[77] He visited me regularly until there came to us, after having departed from Sicily, as an expatriate, a man known as Muḥammad al-Kūfī.[78] Word of me had reached him and so he got in touch with me. In him I found a man who understood theology [*kalām*] and disputation. So I supported him and made gifts to

75. Abū Sa'īd Khalaf b. Ma'mar b. Manṣūr was counted among the Ḥanafīs of Qayrawan. His father was best known for his connection to Asad b. al-Furāt, a scholar with Ḥanafī tendencies, but he was also on good terms with Saḥnūn, the most prominent of the Mālikīs in his time. Ma'mar, however, had also been noted for disparaging Mu'āwiya and proclaiming the virtues of 'Alī and as denying, in accordance with Shi'i doctrine and against the Sunni position, the validity of the *ṭalāq al-bid'a*. Ibn al-Haytham describes the son later as teaching his father's book on *fiqh* to himself and others. He joined the Fatimids soon after the advent of Abū 'Abdallāh in Qayrawan and died in 303/915–16. See Ibn 'Idhārī, *al-Bayān*, I, 173 (an obituary notice for both father and son); 'Iyāḍ, *Madārik*, index; al-Khushanī, 112–13, 193, trans. 192–4, 281; al-Mālikī, *Riyāḍ*, I, 264, 266.

76. Nothing is known about Ibn Abān. Whether Ziyād al-Lu'lu'ī may be identical with Muḥammad b. Abi'l-Haytham al-Lu'lu'ī, a *faqīh* whose death in the year 294/907 is noted in Ibn 'Idhārī's *al-Bayān* (I, 144), must be considered doubtful.

77. There is no other information about this Jewish teacher of logic.

78. This man, whose role in the author's education as a Shi'i is of great significance, is evidently the same as the person called al-Kūfī whom Abū 'Abdallāh appointed *khaṭīb* of the mosque of Qayrawan in a story related later in the text. He is most likely also identical with the Zaydi authority mentioned by Qāḍī al-Nu'mān as Abū 'Abdallāh Muḥammad b. Sallām b. Sayyār al-Kūfī, who was known to 'Arīb (Ibn 'Idhārī, *al-Bayān*, I, 188) as Muḥammad b. Sallām b. Sayyār al-Barqī al-Hamadānī (perhaps originally from Barqarūd, a centre of Shi'ism in the region of Hamadān). Noting his death in the year 310/922–3, 'Arīb says explicitly *kāna mutafaqqihan 'alā madhhab al-shī'a*. See Madelung, 'The Sources of Ismā'īlī Law,' 31 and 35; 'Notes on Non-Ismā'īlī Shiism in the Maghrib,' *Studia Islamica* 44 (1976): 87–97, p. 97.

him. He used to frequent me but, after my companionship with him had lasted some time, I realized that I was myself more knowledgeable than he, and my kindness toward him diminished and he sensed that in me.'

So he [al-Kūfī] said to me one day, 'Have you investigated the matter of the imamate?'

I said: 'My father taught me to uphold the superiority of 'Alī over the others, and that the imamate resides among his offspring, but I seldom took up the subject with him and held that the imamate was a well-known matter.'

He laughed and shook his head and said to me, 'The investigation of the imamate is an enormous subject that opens up important issues of which you had no inkling. All of that about which you busied yourself including disputation, speculation, and legal reasoning is ultimately referred to the subject of the imamate. If your mind were opened to the intricacies of the imamate, you would abandon all the sciences and concentrate on it. The true sciences concern four topics only and they are the doctrine of the unity of God, prophecy, the imamate, and the negation of anthropomorphism.'

I said: 'Discuss it.' So he discoursed thirty days about the root principles and derivative matters until all that was firmly established and also that the imamate is one of the pillars of the religion connected to prophecy.

Next he spoke about dissociation [*barā'a*], but I did not respond to him and said, 'In regard to those who have died, there is no need for us to mention of them their evil acts nor even their good ones.'

He said: 'Not so, until you know the superiority of those you accept as leaders and the wickedness of those whom you regard as enemies.' Then he discussed with me disassociation for thirty days. At the end he said to me, 'Do you see that you must consider someone who steals these clothes of yours or robs you of this ledger as unjust and as a wrongdoer, must impugn him and not accept his testimony?'

I said: 'Yes, certainly.'

He said: 'You treat the person who stole clothes from you

with a value of two dinars as a wrongdoer and yet you desist in regard to someone who violated the religion of God, repudiated the Sunna of the Apostle of God, assumed power over the friend of God, tore aside the veil of Fāṭima, daughter of God's Apostle, cancelled her inheritance, took away what was in her hands as a gift from her father, the Apostle of God, murdered her, killed the infant of hers in her womb, and did many things of this kind and incited other to do so.'

I said: 'The truth, by God, is what you have stated.' I then accepted him as my patron and embraced him and he me. He wept and I wept. Thereafter he took great pains with me and stuck with me. I left aside the investigation of everything else that I had been studying and which had been diverting me. I took to reading the treatises on the imamate by Hishām b. al-Ḥakam[79] and on the virtues of 'Alī, may the blessings of God be upon him, and the vices of Abū Bakr, 'Umar, and 'Uthmān

Then one day he came to me while I was praying the afternoon prayer at the time of assembly. When I had greeted him, he said to me, 'Which prayer is this?'

I said: 'The afternoon prayer.'

He said to me: 'This is not the time for the afternoon prayer according to the tradition of the Shi'a.'

I said: 'Do they have times other than these times?'

He said: 'Yes, we have sciences and a religious law and duties and norms and a call to prayer and prayer. All that you have which accords with the doctrine of Abū Ḥanīfa and Mālik is wrong and misguided.'

I said to him: 'Complete for me your favour to me and let me know who here belongs to the Shi'a.' He brought me a

79. Hishām b. al-Ḥakam was a major Shi'i theologian and author from the period of Ja'far al-Ṣādiq and thereafter. He died in 179/795–6. Among his works mentioned here, one was presumably his *Kitāb ikhtilāf al-nās fi'l-imāma* which was an important source on the earlier Shi'a for many of the later writers. On him see 'Hishām b. al-Ḥakam' by W. Madelung in the *EI2*.

copy of the *Book of a Day and Night* on which was the name of Ibrāhīm b. Ma'shar.[80] He was my neighbour and an associate of mine who sat with us. I memorized the text of it entirely. I was then occupied with it and used to carry out all that was in it about prayer and legal knowledge. He brought me a book that was a collection about bequests, punishments, religious duties written in the hand of Muḥammad b. 'Umar al-Marwadhī. He often sat with us and his son was my companion in our sessions with Ibn 'Abdūn and others.

I said to him: 'Alas, these are our revered elders and they were associates of my father before me.'

He said to me: 'It is they who urged me to work with you.'

I revealed this to them and asked them for the books, so they allowed me their books. I made contact with Muḥammad b. Khalaf, who was one of the most trustworthy, pious, and ascetic of the Shi'a.[81] I gained from him knowledge of many books and I occupied myself with the legal doctrine of the family of Muḥammad and abandoned the study of the books of Abū Ḥanīfa. By God, I did not resume listening to anything involving those sciences. I and my companion Aḥmad ceased reading the treatises of Abū Ḥanīfa with Ibn 'Abdūn. But we used to frequent him and read with him the commentary of Abū 'Ubayd and the transmissions of Ibn Qutayba[?][82] and other

80. *Kitāb yawm wa layla.* The title *Kitāb yawm wa layla* is common. It refers to the ritual obligations for a single day and night. It is uncertain which particular book is meant here. For one example that might fit the context, see Madelung, 'Sources of Ismā'īlī Law,' 39–40.

81. The identity of this man is uncertain. He may, however, be the son of Khalaf b. Ma'mar b. Manṣūr, who, as noted, had Shi'i sympathies and formally converted to Fatimid Isma'ilism after the arrival of Abū 'Abdallāh. 'Arīb mentions a son of Khalaf without giving his name (Ibn 'Idhārī, *al-Bayān*, I, 173). The assertion of al-Khushanī that Khalaf was compelled to convert because his son was accused of having immersed his hands in the loot of Aghlabid property must be taken with caution and may be a Mālikī smear.

82. Abu 'Ubayd al-Qāsim b. Sallām, ca. 154/770–224/838, was a renowned traditionist and scholar of the Qur'an. Abū Muḥammad 'Abdallāh b. Muslim Ibn Qutayba, 213/828–276/889, was a theologian

transmissions, and books of legal scholars about judgments, and books of explanation. He used to show preference for us and place us ahead of others. Whenever we came, he would silence whoever was then reading, and we would read what we wanted and would sit if we wanted to or would leave. We were that way until your auspicious and blessed advent intervened.

Abū 'Abdallāh said: 'Is this man [al-Kūfī] still living today?'

I said: 'He is present, and tomorrow we will bring him to you, God, the Most High, so willing.' In the morning I presented him to Abū 'Abdallāh, and the latter informed him of my gratitude for his instruction.

He said to him: 'He requited you when he mentioned you and thanked you, and he is your means to what is even better. Thus, he requited you with what is more worthy.' And then he summoned him to the faith in my presence.

Abu'l-Ḥasan al-Muṭṭalibī[83] made a request of him and mentioned that the people of Qayrawan had asked him to seek on their behalf his appointment of a judge over them. He then pointed to me, but I said, 'Al-Marwadhī, our senior master, is the more worthy.' Our view then concurred on this man. So he appointed him and said to him, 'Guard against grudges and, in the case of any blood between you and anyone in the era of ignorance [*al-jāhiliyya*],[84] regard it as non-existent.' He then invested him with the office. Word of this reached Abū Mūsā Hārūn b. Yūnus and he came in to find me in the hall of the palace with al-Marwadhī. We greeted him, but he expressed disapproval of what he had heard about my excusing myself and our concurrence in support of al-Marwadhī.

He said to me: 'By God, this act of yours will certainly come to plague you. The city is mine and its governor is a part of my

and widely known writer of works of *adab*. On him see G. Lecomte, 'Ibn Ḳutayba' in the *EI2*.

83. On al-Muṭṭalibī see the account of his encounter with Abu'l-'Abbās below.

84. Normally the term *jāhiliyya* refers to the pre-Islamic era, but here the period of Sunni rule prior to the arrival of Abū 'Abdallāh is meant.

da'wa. It should be you, if it is to be.' That pleased me. Then he went in, but he was strongly averse to the appointment of al-Marwadhī. Abū 'Abdallāh spoke first and said to him, 'Al-Muṭṭalibī mentioned to me the need of the people for someone to supervise their markets and scales, and so we appointed the one known as al-Marwadhī.' He replied, 'What need have we for this? Did the Apostle of God have a judge? We want only to return them to our belief and our sunna as we did in Ṭubna and elsewhere.'[85] He replied, 'What harm is there to us if we appoint a sweeper for every garbage heap?'

Then he asked me to bring him books on shares of inheritance and religious law. I produced them for him. He was at the time debating with Ibn 'Abdūn, Sa'īd b. al-Ḥaddād,[86] Mūsā al-Qaṭṭān,[87] al-Ṣadīnī,[88] and Ḥimās[89] about the shares of

85. On the measures taken by Abū 'Abdallāh in Ṭubna with respect to the collection of canonical taxes and no others, see Ibn 'Idhārī, *al-Bayān*, I, 141–2; Halm, *Reich*, 106–7, trans., 111.

86. Abū 'Uthmān Sa'īd b. al-Ḥaddād (219–302/834–915) will be mentioned again. He was a Mālikī jurist and follower of Saḥnūn from whom he related directly, but he specialized also in disputations and refutation. See Ibn 'Idhārī, *al-Bayān*, I, 172; 'Iyāḍ, *Madārik*, (biography no. 127), 351–63 and index; al-Khushanī, 148–52, 198–212 and index; al-Mālikī, *Riyāḍ*, II, 57–115.

87. Abu'l-Aswad Mūsā b. 'Abd al-Raḥmān al-Qaṭṭān was a Mālikī jurist and an associate of Muḥammad b. Saḥnūn. He had once been qadi of Tripoli and died in 306/918–19 at the age of 71. Ibn 'Idhārī, *al-Bayān*, I, 181; al-Khushanī, 159, 229; al-Mālikī, *Riyāḍ*, II, 63, 78, 79; 'Iyāḍ, *Madārik*, 189, 203, 281, 311, 344, 357, 363–5, 374, 389.

88. Muḥammad b. Aswad b. Shu'ayb al-Ṣadīnī of the Berber tribe of Ṣadīna was a Ḥanafī jurist with Mu'tazilī tendencies. In 289/902 he replaced the Mālikī 'Īsā b. Miskīn as chief qadi of Qayrawan, only to be deposed and replaced in 290/903. He died in 304/916–17. 'Iyāḍ, *Madārik*, 285, 344, 390, 411, 474; Ibn 'Idhārī, *al-Bayān*, I, 162, 175; al-Mālikī, *Riyāḍ*, I, 472, II, 36, 37, 38, 129; al-Khushanī, 194, 238, trans. 282–3, 333; Qāḍī al-Nu'mān, *Iftitāḥ*, 154–5, and Dachraoui, intro., 81 no. 7.

89. Ḥimās b. Marwān b. Simāk al-Hamdānī was a Mālikī jurist and student of Saḥnūn who became qadi after al-Ṣadīnī in 290/903. His tenure lasted until 294 or 295/907–8 when he quit in disagreement or

inheritance and the acquisition by the daughter of the whole of the estate, and about the imamate and other matters. He said to me, 'If a believer is called to the faith, he becomes like the *muḥrim*[90] to whom the hunting of land animals is not permitted or the killing of game, or approaching women and perfume, until he departs from his state of consecration. But you are here with me, a believer worthy of our permitting you to dispute with them and argue against them and make legal rulings according to the words of the family of Muḥammad and to prevent them from reading the books of Abū Ḥanīfa and Mālik.'

I said: 'O our master, the month of Ramaḍān is about to begin. 'Alī had wanted to end the innovation of 'Umar in regard to praying the night prayer with an imam.[91] I hope that God will, through you, satisfy this desire. Therefore instruct Abū 'Alī to stop that practice.'

So he said: 'Yes, by God, we will do it.' He ordered Abū 'Alī b. Abī Khinzīr[92] and al-Marwadhī to end that practice, and he gave permission for the sweeping of the mosques and providing

annoyance with the appointment of the Ḥanafī Ibn Jīmāl as qadi of Raqqāda. See Ibn 'Idhārī, *al-Bayān*, I, 136, 140, 143, 173; 'Iyāḍ, *Madārik*, 340–50 and index; Qāḍī al-Nu'mān, *Iftitāḥ*, 155, 201–3, Dachraoui intro., 82 and n. 4, 98–9; al-Khushanī, 153, 238, trans. 241–2, 333; Talbi, *Aghlabide*, 549–51.

90. A pilgrim to Makka who has entered the state of consecration (*iḥrām*).

91. These are the *tarāwīḥ* prayers popular in Sunni ritual although, by common admission, when performed with an imam, they were an innovation ascribed to the caliph 'Umar. They are, however, considered sunna in Mālikī law. See 'Tarāwīḥ' by A. J. Wensinck in the *EI2*.

92. Abū 'Alī al-Ḥasan b. Aḥmad b. Abī Khinzīr, of an Arab family from Mīla, had just been appointed the new governor of Qayrawan on behalf of Abū 'Abdallāh. Later he was appointed governor of Sicily by the Fatimid caliph al-Mahdī. On him and his brothers, one of whom, Khalaf b. Aḥmad, was the governor of Qaṣr al-Qadīm and the other, 'Alī b. Aḥmad, accompanied him to Sicily, see Qāḍī al-Nu'mān's *Iftitāḥ*, paras 134, 135, 219, and 221; Ibn 'Idhārī, *al-Bayān*, I, 151, 168, 171; Abu'l-'Arab, 174–5; 'Iyāḍ, *Madārik*, bio. no. 144; and Talbi, *Aghlabide*, 627–8, n. 5.

a plentiful supply of oil, and for the people to assemble for the obligatory prayer only and not to pray supererogatory prayers with an imam. When the month of Ramaḍān had begun, he had that carried out according to his wish; and his decision was executed and we attended the obligatory prayer with al-Marwadhī. The imam recited, 'By the heavens of the sign of the zodiac and the promised day,' to the words of the Most High, 'slain were the men of the pit' [85: 1–4]. But he choked on the rest of his recitation and made an allusion to what prayers and night rituals they were precluded from performing.[93] I pointed this out to al-Marwadhī. He said, 'You are right, by God, he intended nothing else.' He wanted to make him descend from the pulpit for it then and there and to have him arrested.

I said: 'Don't do this tonight; dismiss him tomorrow.'

The master learned what he had done, and he appointed al-Kūfī, our companion, to give the Friday sermon and lead the prayers. In a dream prior to the entry of the master, al-Kūfī had dreamed that al-Shi'i entered Qayrawan and that he spurred his mount to the point of entering the Friday mosque and dismounted at the pulpit. He then gave him a Sulūqī dog, and al-Kūfī had grasped him fast by his halter at the foot of the pulpit. I had given him an interpretation of this dream, telling him, 'Al-Shi'i will enter and put you in charge of the Friday sermon.' He laughed and said, 'How could that be?' I said, 'The Sulūqī dog is praiseworthy, and a dog barks and bites and warns and points out strangers. The preacher, too, makes matters clear and points out and warns.' I mentioned the dream of al-Kūfī to al-Marwadhī and also informed the master of that. He then appointed him to give the Friday sermon and lead prayers and provided for him a salary of five dinars per month

93. On the 'men of the pit' (*aṣḥāb al-ukhdūd*) mentioned in the Qur'an 85:4, see the article by R. Paret in the *EI2*. The implied allusion is to the faithful mentioned thereafter in verse 6, about whom verse 7 states: 'They held a grudge against them merely because they believed in God, the Mighty, the Praiseworthy.'

.I met together with Ibn ʿAbdūn, al-Ṣadīnī, Ibn Jīmāl[94] and al-Kalāʿī[95] along with al-Ḥusaynī al-Jazarī.[96] With them I conducted an inquiry into the question of the acquisition by the daughter of the whole of the estate.[97] Ibn ʿAbdūn said, 'She receives half according to the word of God, but, if the matter is to be based on anything else, say whatever you like.' I said, 'She receives half when there are two parents and the two parents receive a third, each one of them having then a sixth. The remaining sixth reverts to her because she would be subject to a shortfall below the half in the event that there were,

94. Abu'l-ʿAbbās Muḥammad b. ʿAbdallāh b. Jīmāl was a Ḥanafī. There are conflicting reports about exactly when he was appointed qadi and of which city. Ibn ʿIdhārī's *al-Bayān* (I, 140) claims that he was appointed over Raqqāda in 293/905–6, a post he continued to hold until the fall of the Aghlabids, and in the next year, 294/906–7, he replaced Ḥimās as chief qadi of Qayrawan. Yet one year thereafter in 295/907–8, Ibn al-Khashshāb, a Mālikī took over the qadiship of Qayrawan. Pro-Mālikī sources consider Ibn Jīmāl to have been unqualified but Qāḍī al-Nuʿmān, whose account is the clearest, indicates that his appointment pleased the members of the ruler's family and court. Ibn ʿIdhārī, *al-Bayān*, I, 140, 143; al-Khushanī, 196, 239, trans. 284–5, 333; ʿIyāḍ, *Madārik*, 262, 263, 346, 348; Qāḍī al-Nuʿmān, *Iftitāḥ*, 200–1; Talbi, *Aghlabide*, 550ff.

95. Muḥammad al-Kalāʿī was a Ḥanafī expert in disputation and theology who upheld the creation of the Qur'an and wrote a refutation of a book by Ibn al-Ḥaddād that upheld the uncreated nature of the Qur'an. According to al-Khushanī he converted after the coming of the Fatimids, and this fact is confirmed by Ibn al-Haytham. Note also his role in the affair of Ibn al-Birdhawn to be discussed later. Al-Khushanī, 215, 221–2, trans. 316; Ibn ʿIdhārī, *al-Bayān*, I, 155.

96. It has not been possible to identify this man, although he seems to have had a fairly high standing in local society. The *nisba* might also be read al-Khazarī, but this seems less likely since it implies that a Ḥusaynī had once resided with the Khazars. Later in the text there are references to Abū Jaʿfar al-Khazarī (which also might be read al-Jazarī), who is a known figure in the Ismaʿili *daʿwa* and was personally charged with escorting the Imam's womenfolk from Salamiya to North Africa. He cannot be the same person.

97. In Shiʿi law, the daughter may inherit the full estate in the absence of a spouse or parents of the deceased, while in Sunni law her portion cannot exceed the half accorded her by the Qur'an (4:11).

along with her, a husband or wife. Whoever is subject to a shortfall has the best right to the surplus share; but God, the Most High, in fact makes her inherit the whole in His Book.'

He said: 'Where is there a reference to that in the Book of God?'

I said: 'In the statement of the Most High, "If a man dies without a child but he has a sister, she receives half of what he leaves and he is her heir if she has no children" [4: 176]. God, the Most High, allows no inheritance to the brother or the sister in the case of children, and thus we allow nothing to the agnates since God gives no inheritance to either brother or sister.'

Ibn Jīmāl said: 'It is as if, by God, I had never heard that passage in the Book of God.'

Ibn 'Abdūn said to him: 'Hold on, the child here means a male child!'

I said: 'God rejects what you mention; He, the Most High, said, "You receive half of what your wives leave, if they have no children" [4: 12]. Thus, the daughter keeps the husband from the half and the wife from the fourth. Therefore, if she keeps him from it, she is the child with whom no brother or sister or none of the agnates inherits. That was upheld by both Ibn 'Abbās and Ibn Mas'ūd.'

The Shaykh al-Ḥusaynī said to him: 'He has, by God, proven it against you and, by God, has beaten you decisively.' Ibn 'Abdūn became angry and did not speak until we entered upon Abū 'Abdallāh and they greeted him. When they had departed, I informed him about what had happened between me and them. He said, 'Why didn't you mention this in his presence?' I replied, 'I was honouring him, since he had become angry and was scowling over the manner in which the Shaykh al-Ḥusaynī made clear to him that the proof was decisively against him.' My saying that pleased him.

I was constantly in attendance upon Abū 'Abdallāh and frequently visiting him. He was a man firm of character, single-minded in pursuit of justice, veracity and abstinence from worldly pleasures; his food was always the same as were his clothes; he was neither haughty nor despotic nor given to gluttony, but instead had a great desire for summoning those who might respond to the faith and to make every conceivable effort for the salvation of their souls.

One day his blood became so inflamed he feared for himself because of its excessiveness. Ziyād[98] said to him, 'Discharge it and thereby get rid of it.' Then he bled him in my presence, yet Abū 'Abdallāh did not increase any food nor did he ask for any more than he was accustomed to, except for some eggs we cooked for him in front of him and he sipped their yokes.

I was present at his debates with Sa'īd b. al-Ḥaddād and others and I requested of him one day to debate Ibn al-Ḥaddād. He sought to interpret the hadith of the Apostle of God who said to 'Alī, 'Whoever I am the master of, 'Alī is his master.' So Abū 'Abdallāh said to him, 'Is 'Alī your master [*mawlā*]?'

Ibn al-Ḥaddād said: 'Yes, he is my friend [*mawlā*] in the same sense that I am his friend [*mawlā*].'

Thereupon I took him up on the matter and said to him, 'So you are the friend of the Prophet in the same sense that the Prophet is your *mawlā*. Hence, you hold more authority [*awlā*] over the Prophet than he holds over himself, just as the Prophet holds more authority over you than you hold over yourself. The Apostle of God put the authority God had delegated to him over His community in the hands of 'Alī and, according to the Most High's statement, "The Prophet holds more authority [*awlā*] over the believers than they have over themselves" [33: 6]. At that time, 'Umar said to 'Alī, "You have become my patron [*mawlā*] and the patron of every believing man and woman".'

He begged to be excused from the debate and said, 'O

98. Ziyād b. Khalfūn al-Mutaṭabbib was the leading physician of Qayrawan. He was murdered by a rival in 308/920–1. On him see Ibn 'Idhārī's *al-Bayān*, I, 183; Abū 'Ubayd al-Bakrī, *al-Masālik wa'l-mamālik*, ed. W. MacGuckin de Slane (Algiers, 1857), 24; and L. Leclerc, *Histoire de la médecine arabe* (Paris, 1876), I, 410.

master, you have entered a number of cities other than ours and you left the inhabitants of them with the beliefs they held.'

Abū 'Abdallāh said: '"There is no compulsion in religion" [2: 256].' Then he told me, 'Let them be. You will debate with them and dazzle them. I will merely say what Shu'ayb said, "And a party of you are those who believe in the message I have been sent with and a party which does not believe. Therefore be patient until God judges between us; He is the best of judges" [7: 87].'

This Sa'īd b. al-Ḥaddād wrote a small book in which he mentioned his debates with Abū 'Abdallāh and Abu'l-'Abbās and distributed it everywhere, but he added to them and thus lied, in fact, in his composition. However, I was present at all of his sessions with both of them at that time and I have seen his book.[99] I have also written a refutation of it and followed it up with a comprehensive statement to prove the falseness of his doctrines and what he sought to establish in regard to the principles of legal analogy, the imamate of the person inferior in excellence, and other notions of his, and it was dispersed among a group of his associates.

I related to Abū 'Abdallāh the story of a conversation we had had with Ibn al-Ḥaddād. We had gone in to see him one day. With me was Aḥmad b. al-Marwadhī and Ibn Ḥayyūn.[100] Yūsuf

99. Ibn al-Ḥaddād's pamphlet is quoted by al-Khushanī in his entry on Ibn al-Ḥaddād (pp. 198–212) and later by al-Mālikī in his *Riyāḍ* (II, 57–115) and by other authors. The version of al-Mālikī is now the most useful of them, in part because of the editor's copious annotation to it. However, while this one version survived and was thus widely known among the later Mālikīs, neither Ibn al-Ḥaddād's nor Ibn al-Haytham's original versions are available.

100. The identity of this man and even the reading of the name in the mss. is in doubt. Assuming that the reading is as given here, he may be identical with Qāḍī al-Nu'mān. The latter would have to be born around 280/893, much earlier than is commonly assumed. He would then have been 83 at the time of his death in 363/974, not an unreasonable age. His father, a remote possibility, is known to have been an old man at that time and also by his own claim a Mālikī. Thus it seems unlikely that he

b. Danqas was also with us.[101] We found him in his portico sitting alone. That was after the demotion of Ibn Miskīn[102] and the appointment to the judgeship of al-Ṣadīnī. We used to feel freer in the time of the 'Iraqis.[103] We said, 'A question?' He said, 'Ask.' We said, 'Please tell us about the words of God, the Mighty and Glorious, "Creator of every thing." Is it general or particular?' He was silent a while and then said, 'This is one of the questions of the innovators.[104] If you belong to them, you are proscribed everything but leaving us.' We said to him, 'You are a foolish, ignorant old man. Someone setting himself up in your position gives a proper answer and does not revile. The innovation is in you, and the inconceivable is what you uphold; anthropomorphism is your creed; multiplicity of numbers in God and in the entitative qualities in His attributes is your doctrine. Your belief is that God has a likeness; yet it is God who says, "Like unto Him is nothing" [42: 11].' I will never forget his dread of us and his humiliation fearing that we might turn violent against him, and thus we left him. Later he sought out Ibn Danqas al-Isrā'īlī and asked him, 'Who were those people who were with you?' So he informed him who we were. He

would have joined with the young Ibn al-Haytham and the son of al-Marwadhī to embarrass Ibn al-Ḥaddād.

101. Later this man's name appears again with the added *nisba* al-Isrā'īlī, indicating that he was a Jew. Otherwise no information is available about him, and the vocalization of the name D-n-q-s is uncertain.

102. 'Īsā b. Miskīn was a Mālikī. He died in 295/907–8 (Ibn 'Idhārī, *al-Bayān*, I, 145). On him see al-Khushanī, 142, 193, trans. 227, 332; Ibn 'Idhārī, *al-Bayān*, I, 204; al-Mālikī, *Riyāḍ*, index; 'Iyāḍ, *Madārik*, index and his biography (no. 53, pp. 233–53); and Talbi, *Aghlabide*, 540–1.

103. Referring to the Ḥanafīs. This period of Ḥanafī ascendancy occurred in 289–90/902–3. 'Īsā b. Miskīn, the Mālikī chief judge was deposed in 289/902 and al-Ṣadīnī assumed it then, but he was deposed himself in 290/903. According to Abu'l-'Arab (*al-Miḥan*, 464), Ibn al-Ḥaddād was imprisoned and shackled by the Ḥanafī Ibn 'Abdūn when the latter was qadi.

104. The question posed by Ibn al-Haytham and his friend was evidently designed to refute the Sunni traditionalist dogma that the Qur'an is uncreated. Ibn al-Ḥaddād recognized the purpose behind it and refused to give a proper answer.

said, 'Yes, it must be so.'

I recounted for him [Abū 'Abdallāh] also the story of my affair with Ḥimās the judge. I was once involved in litigation before him concerning the inheritance from my father. He imposed on me an absolution. None of our elders withheld it from me, but he kept putting me off, and my opponent who was known as Ibn al-Tustarī[105] thus did harm to me. He told the judge, 'He dissociates from the pious ancestors,' and he incited him against me, seeking the help of some others in that. One day I exerted pressure on him to make the ruling for me. He told me, 'Be patient until we write to Egypt for an answer in this matter.'[106] I said to him, 'How can it be that the legal scholars of Ifrīqiya are incapable of deciding, so that you need to consult the jurisprudents of Egypt? The case is perfectly clear. A man made a bequest to a man and set a condition in his bequest that, when his son so and so attains maturity, he becomes the sole executor in respect to his other children, and the other executors are discharged when this son of his reaches maturity. You ask of me absolution, and yet men have borne witness before you, most of whom you hold to be too noble to sit in front of you and whom you raise to your own sitting place.' He became upset, lost his temper and said, 'You have pernicious doctrines,' repeating it to me. 'It has reached me that you dissociate from the pious ancestors [*salaf*], uphold the createdness of the Qur'an, repudiate Abū Bakr and 'Umar, and the Jews keep your company.' I said to him, 'You are the judge of Ifrīqiya and the jurisprudent [*faqīh*] of the Madinans [Mālikīs] and yet some of them accuse you of pernicious doctrines and assign you to the Shukūkiyya.'[107] He grew more enraged and furious,

105. The identity of this Ibn al-Tustarī is uncertain. A possibility is the Abu'l-'Abbās al-Tustarī mentioned by al-Khushanī (p. 232, trans. 327). See further below, n. 116.

106. Perhaps it is significant in this context that, following the death of his teacher Saḥnūn, Ḥimās visited Egypt where he studied in the circle of Ibn 'Abd al-Ḥakam.

107. Shukūkiyya refers to those traditionalists who, according to their

began to foam at the mouth, and ordered my arrest. When I arrived at the jail, his doorkeeper said to me, 'Be patient and don't go up, he will not proceed against you.' However, I insisted on ascending, so he pulled me and tore the clothes I was wearing. Ibn Za'lān the one-eyed came over to me and seated me in his place, and therefore I was sitting in it when the doorkeeper asked me what was the matter with me. I was still sitting there when al-Ṣabī,[108] his doorkeeper, yelled at me and the commissioner [*wakīl*] himself asked me to get down. I got down and al-Ṣabī, his doorkeeper, said to me, 'Do you vilify the judge in his seat of judgment? If he did not know you or were unfamiliar with you and your ancestors, would you not have come to grief and would we not be grieving for you?' I said, 'What have I said? I said this to him in reverence since he is the judge and yet he is the one being slandered. It is more likely that something should be said about us that is not true of us and that they attribute to us what is not our doctrine.' Thus, God warded off his evil.

It happened one day that I was walking toward the Bāb al-Rabī' when I chanced upon a piece of paper in the alley and picked it up. I was used to picking up any piece of paper I saw in order to ascertain what was on it. Lo and behold, it was from my brother and his brother-in-law, my opponent, written to the judge, urging him to investigate my books. They were telling him that, if the judge would prolong his imprisonment, they would bring to him various books by the Rāfiḍa[109] and the upholders of the eternity of the world [*dahriyya*]. I retraced my steps at once and gave up whatever I wanted at the Bāb al-Rabī'. I gathered my books and delivered them to some women who were at the time my paternal aunts and the paternal aunts

Murji'ī opponents, have doubts about their status of belief and hold it obligatory to add the phrase *in shā' Allāh* (if God so wills) to the affirmation 'I am a believer' (thus saying: *Ana mu'min in shā' Allāh*).

108. The name of the doorkeeper appears in the mss. as al-Ṣabī, the boy. He is otherwise unknown. Perhaps the name should be read al-Ḍabbī.

109. Rāfiḍa, rejectionists, was a common Sunni nickname for Shi'is.

of my father. Two days later, as I departed late in the evening from the house of Abū Sa'īd, the son of al-Ma'mar b. al-Manṣūr, where we had been listening to him read the book of his father on religious law – he was upholding the nullity of the irregular divorce [*ṭalāq al-bid'a*][110] – I came upon al-Ṣabī, my opponent, and my brother inspecting my books. They, however, found only the books of my father on religious law, the campaigns of the Prophet [*maghāzī*], rare words [*gharīb*], poetry, the works of al-Jāḥiẓ,[111] the works of Abū 'Ubayd and Ibn Qutayba, and the books of al-Mawṣilī[112] and others. I thundered and flashed and went to put myself under the protection of the superintendent of the postal service, who had been a student of my father. I informed him of my story in a note. He ordered that I be admitted. He recognized me and wept when I mentioned my father. On my behalf, he wrote a decree which he dispatched with a courier in the name of Ziyādatallāh b. al-Aghlab[113] to the effect that, 'Ja'far b. Aḥmad b. Muḥammad b. al-Aswad b. al-Haytham has reported that you have accepted the statement of his opponents against him and that you ordered the inspection of his books. I disapprove of this most strongly and I forbid you from scrutinizing publicly the religious doctrines of the people. It is your duty to uphold harmony, accord, and the like.' The letter reached Ḥimās; and he read it, became agitated, and excused himself from jurisdiction between us. He said to his colleagues, 'They have pursued this lawsuit as of today for two years.[114] I am returning it to them so that they settle their

110. The *ṭalāq al-bid'a* is an irrevocable divorce based on uttering the required three declarations repudiating the wife on one single occasion. The Shi'a prohibit this.

111. Abū 'Uthmān 'Amr b. Baḥr al-Jāḥiẓ, ca. 160/776–255/868–9, was a famous Mu'tazilī theologian and prose writer. See Ch. Pellat, 'al-Djāḥiẓ' in the *EI2*.

112. Perhaps this is Isḥāq b. Ibrāhīm al-Mawṣilī (d. 235/850), a well-known scholar and musician. On him see the article by J. W. Fück in the *EI2*.

113. He was the last of the Aghlabid governors. His reign commenced in 290/903.

114. For clarification it is useful to note that the father died in 285/

differences. I will not judge between them in any matter.' There was much rancour in my heart against him until God caused him to be humbled and humiliated and strengthened me against him. Thereby did we ward him off; and he now behaved humbly toward us, sought help against us, and submitted to us. He wrote us a letter pleading for mercy on him and he sent his two sons Ḥamūd and Sālim to me.[115] I fell down in prostration to God and I thanked God for what He had given us, and that He supported, led and guided us. I made a commitment to them and to their father that nothing but good should ever come to him from me. Thus, we foresook the rancour and the malice, and we relied solely on God, the Most High, the best patron and the most excellent of supporters.

Abū 'Abdallāh was delighted with all this that I had just related to him and he commanded his governor to take care of Ibn Za'lān and confirm him in the post of commissioner of the prison. He said, 'And whosoever relies on God, He will suffice him.'

I had suffered from Ibn al-Tustarī's constant hostility against me and his alienating my aunts from me to the point that they were induced to treat me unfairly.[116] He caused them to incline

898, prior to the maturity of the author, and that Ḥimās became the qadi in 290/903.

115. The two sons of Ḥimās both merited notices in the Mālikī *ṭabaqāt* works, although neither was especially distinguished. Sālim died in 307/919–20 and Ḥamūd in 309/921–2. On Ḥamūd, see al-Khushanī, 178, trans. 266; 'Iyāḍ, *Madārik*, 345, 348, 400–1. For Sālim, see al-Khushanī, 160, 178, trans. 245, 266; al-Mālikī, *Riyāḍ*, I, 517, II, 118; 'Iyāḍ, *Madārik*, 343, 345, 399–400.

116. The only al-Tustarī mentioned by al-Khushanī was included by him as one of the scholars who were subjected to persecution by the government. This Abu'l-'Abbās al-Tustarī was beaten, tortured, and his possessions were confiscated. These facts appear to match Ibn al-Haytham's claim about his eventual revenge and the recovering of what was previously his. Ibn al-Haytham's account shows that al-Tustarī was not such an innocent victim of government persecution as he is presented by al-Khushanī.

toward my brother and my opponent and he incited them against me. However, Abū 'Abdallāh said to me, 'Do not grieve about that; God will cause you to inherit those and other things.' Thus, by God, I saw that happen. The days increased my power and status and humiliated and diminished them. Everything that was once in their possession either from forced sale or inheritance was restored to me. Our Lord is to be thanked both for His aid and His affliction, for hardship as well as prosperity. But then, after all that, we underwent a trial which consolation could not make good and steadfastness of patience was incapable of enduring. I witnessed a time like the poet said:

> How much have I tasted over time of hardship and ease;
> In the children of time, there are heads and there are tails.
> Events wondrous in decrease and increase;
> In its action time is but the father of wonders.

Another one said:

> Sufficient for a man in this world, even though he be resolute,
> is the alteration of conditions and the lowering of ranks.
> Power at one moment changes to disgrace and poverty and
> that is truly of the most marvellous and wondrous things.
> Therefore be steadfast in the face of events and submit to a
> Master of the Age whose advent is the hope against these calamities.

Many were the times I asked Abū 'Abdallāh about the creation of the Qur'an, capacity, creation of the act, the promise and the threat, and about the doctrine of the Murji'a concerning works and faith.[117] He always said, 'A person will come to you who will satisfy you in regard to this and other matters.' But then he said to me, 'What do the Murji'a say about faith?'

I said: 'They say that affirmation and belief are faith and

117. On this early Islamic movement and its doctrines in general, see W. Madelung, 'Murdji'a' in the *EI2*.

that the non-performance of any work does not damage nor do offences nullify it, as also the performance of good actions in no way benefits the unbeliever. God will inevitably show mercy to the offenders, just as He will inevitably punish the polytheists. The Mu'tazila and the Ibāḍiyya uphold the implementation of the threat and say that it is like the promise in terms of obligation and necessity, and that the threat and the promise are a communication and communication is never abrogated nor is it subject to interpretation. Some of them label the offender an unbeliever because of ingratitude toward God. Others call the sinner an iniquitous polytheist and all polytheists are iniquitous. Yet others do not term him a polytheist. They have various interpretations for all of this. The proponents of authorization [*tafwīḍ*][118] maintain that those believers who offend are subject to the will of God, there being no inevitability that God will inflict punishment on them as it is likewise not obligatory on Him to grant them mercy, but instead they are in a state of suspension between grace and justice. If He punishes them, He will be just; if He forgives them, He will be bestowing a grace. It is not said about the desisting from carrying out a threat that He went back on His word, but it is said in regard to not fulfilling a promise that He broke His word, because the promise is one of the rights of the servants, granted to them by God as a reward, whereas the threat is a right of God's. If He refrains, it is in favour of being gracious by virtue of not carrying it out. They compare this to a man who promises another man a gift and threatens someone with punishment. If he should forgo punishing him, he will be praised for it and not blamed, but if he breaks his promise, he will be called a miser and false in his promises. Does one not see that God described Himself as being good, compassionate, forbearing, merciful, beneficent, and forgiving? God is only merciful to the offenders and forgives only those who go astray, but against those who do good, there is no option.'

118. *Tafwīḍ* here is not the delegation of power, but rather seems to mean leaving the authority to God either to punish or to forgive.

He said: 'And what do the Shi'a say about faith?'

I said: 'They say as Ja'far b. Muḥammad al-Ṣādiq said that faith is work in its entirety and that affirmation is part of that work because it involves a statement made by the tongue and acting in accord with belief. Forming an intent [*niyya*], prayer, almsgiving, fasting, and pilgrimage are actions required of the limbs.'

He approved of that and said: 'Faith consists of knowledge and action. A person who knows and does not act will have no benefit from his knowledge, nor does he understand its reality. A person who acts but does not know does not understand the reality of his action, and it will be of no benefit to him. This should be projected into outward and inner meanings. A person who does not know the inner meaning inside its outward form is lacking in knowledge. Someone who does not observe the external meaning, exposes his own secret and his intellect is incomplete. A person who exposes his inner meaning will never become complete. He cannot become a summoner [*dāʿī*], nor can one be assured that he will ever procure what continues to be incumbent on him.'

Next he said: 'As for the threat, when you allow not carrying it out and forgiving, it is a falsehood in your mind in regard to the person who murdered an imam or a prophet or about the person who killed 'Alī b. Abī Ṭālib and killed al-Ḥusayn b. 'Alī. It is the same in regard to the person who usurped the position of 'Alī and wronged him and who tore away the veil of Fāṭima. The Apostle of God had said, '"Fāṭima is a piece of my flesh; whoever angers her angers me. On him are the curse of God, the angels, and the people altogether."'

I said: 'They maintain that these are polytheists not believers, unbelievers and not Muslims, and persons who consider lawful or who purposely declare licit things God has forbidden. Whoever advocates what God has forbidden is not a believer in God. Likewise, if we presumed the offence of a believer who affirmed the Imam, who acknowledged his Lord and His Apostle, such as Abū Dharr and others, if he were to slip, thereby falling into a grave offence, it is necessary not to affirm absolutely an exemplary and enduring punishment for him as if he were in the company of Pharaoh and Hāmān and other wrongdoers like these two.'

He said: 'You only allow the will of God in regard to those who agree with you about your Imam and your doctrines?'

I said: 'That is what we hold.'

He said: 'That is confusion on your part and departs from the general consensus. The communication from God, the Mighty and Glorious, conveys a universal application and it is not licit for you to particularize it through interpretation.'

I said: 'We do not particularize except on the basis of a communication from God, the Mighty and Glorious, in His words, "God will not forgive those who associate gods with Him, but He will forgive any lesser matter of whomever He may wish' [4: 48]. Whoever declares lawful the things God, the Most High, has forbidden is a deliberately acting polytheist who will not be forgiven, but every offence short of polytheism may be subject to God's will."' He said: 'Then it is inevitable that God's will applies generally to all the people in the community and, in regard to the murders of 'Alī and al-Ḥusayn, you are forced to admit that God's will applies to them as well.'

I could not find a way out of his statement except by also reversing the judgment for the offences of the saints, such as Abū Dharr and others or the brothers of Joseph and their like. However, I said then, 'God, the Most High, said, "And the reward for evil is an evil like it" [42: 40], not by the torment of hellfire and eternal punishment, and He said, "Whenever their skins are totally burned We will give them other skins in exchange" [4: 56], "for them there will maces of iron" [22: 21], and their drink "will melt whatever is in their bellies" [22: 20]. The perpetrator of a grave sin does not deserve all of this, nor is it the same as the act of the person who consumes the property of the orphan or commits adultery or steals.'

He said: 'Likewise also, if you relate these forms of punishment to polytheism, it is not the same.'

I said: 'Contravening the God who created and then put in order, who measured out and then guided, and who brought forth existence from non-existence, is of greater magnitude than the commission of a grave sin. Therefore, the punishment is greater of a heretic in regard to God, who associates gods with Him, and who worships what the hands of humans have made such as stone statues, crosses, and stone altars.'

He said: 'Similarly the perpetrator of a grave offence contravenes the God who feeds, brings water, causes death, gives life, who sustains, and provides wealth.'

I said: 'How do you deal with the words of God, the Most High, "they will not be treated unjustly for the slightest thing" [4: 49],[119] and "and whoever has done an atom's weight of good shall see it; and whoever has done an atom's weight of evil shall see it" [99: 7–8]? Thus, if this person is to be punished for a grave sin, the promise is annulled, the good deeds go in vain, and the evil deeds cancel out the good deeds. But the Qur'an denies the loss of good deeds by evil ones. The Most High thus said, "God will change the evil deeds of such persons into good ones" [25: 70].'

He said: 'He, the Most High, also said, "those who will lose most for their deeds" [18: 103].'

I said: 'They forfeited them because of unbelief and hypocrisy, but affirming God's unity, prophecy, and the imamate cancels all offence, and forgiving it is within God's power for anyone who affirms Him, His apostles, and the imams. God confirmed this in His revelation. The Most High said, "Whoever associates other gods with God has been forbidden paradise" [5: 72]. He did not say the like in regard to the perpetrators of an offence but rather made them inevitably subject to His will.'

He said: 'Similarly, the will must apply in the case of the Jews and the Christians, since He says, "The Jews and Christians say: we are the children of God and beloved of Him; say: why then does He punish you for your sins; no, instead, you are mortal humans and a part of those He created. He will forgive whomever He wishes and He will punish whomever He

119. Also Qur'an 4: 77 and 17: 71.

wishes" [5: 18].'

I said: 'This verse affirms their punishment, not their being subject to will in regard to the forgiveness of their offences and their polytheism.'

He said: 'How is that?'

I said: 'In His statement denying that they are the beloved of God, when He says, "Say, why then does He punish you for your sins?" After that, being subject to will is possible in respect to the health of their bodies, their being ill, poor, or rich. The will perhaps applied to those who died in the lifetime of Moses from among those in his community; and prior to the appearance of Jesus, God's will was perhaps applicable to them because they had not yet earned the designation of unbelief until after they rejected belief in Jesus.'

He said: 'Likewise you make God's will obligatory in the punishment of the hypocrites and, according to you, their being treated mercifully is a possibility on the basis of His words, "He will punish the hypocrites if He wishes or He may forgive them" [33: 24].'

I said: 'Punishment here is an equivocal name for the punishment of this world as in God's saying, "Fight them, God will punish them at your hands" [9: 14].'

He said: 'These are the words of God, "Hopeless will be those who are burdened with iniquity" [20: 111], and His statement, "Do not contend for those who betray their own souls, for God does not love those who are treacherous and wicked" [4: 107].' He gave many such examples and went on at length.

I said: 'In these examples He is not speaking in dispute against the offenders, but out of God's considering it grave that His servants would try to prevent Him going back on His word and thus interpret Him and pass judgment on Him, as if God has no will to choose and no exception in regard to punishing whomever He wishes or to being merciful on whomever He wishes.'

He said: 'These are swords made of reeds that will cut nothing. The proof for all this lies in its inner meaning and I hope you will attain it, should God, the Most High, be willing. Then you will know the promise and the threat and the reality of that.'

We were wont to drink with him from the source of life and to graze freely in the meadows of paradise, 'gardens and springs,' 'a noble station,'[120] and 'a great variety of fruit uncut and not forbidden' [56:32–33], until he left in quest of the noble Imam, the great lord, the adornment of the country, the sun of worshippers, the dome of time. Thereupon, and for that reason, I said farewell to him.

He told me: 'I have commended you.' I supposed that he meant to Abū Zākī. I remained at home a few days and then went out and I found all of our colleagues along with al-Marwadhī at the abode of Abū Zākī. He made room for me next to himself. Then our colleagues went away, and he kept me with him. He produced for me some bound volumes on one of which was inscribed, *Book of Recognition, Affirmation, Denial, and Disapproval* [*Kitāb al-ma'rifa wa'l-iqrār wa'l-jaḥd wa'l-inkār*]. There was another bound volume containing a poem called *The Container of Jewels* [*Dhāt al-jawāhir*] in which there were sciences, the doctrine of the unity of God, esoteric symbols, and the wisdom of a sage. I read to him from them what had been obscure to him and I expounded for him those of its meanings that had been difficult for him to understand. He was delighted with all this and said, 'I shall bring you together with a guest who is noble unto God.' I thanked him for his words and for this utterance with which he addressed me.

I said to him: 'My affairs were begun with Abū Mūsā and I hope to complete them with you and at your hands.' He rose and left me in his place. He entered a wing of the palace which had been closed off by a wooden partition and concealed by a covering. Then he came out and called to me. I then entered into an apartment in the palace.

120. Here the author alludes to Qur'an 44:52 and 51:15, and other verses that describe paradise (as in 25:57–58 and 44:25–26).

Here ends the First Part of the Discussions, praise be to God, Lord of the worlds, and may God bless His Apostle Muḥammad, and his family, the righteous and veracious members of his offspring, and peace.

There follows:

THE SECOND PART OF THE BOOK OF DISCUSSIONS

In the name of God, the Merciful, the Compassionate, and may God bless Muḥammad and the family of Muḥammad.

Abū ʿAbdallāh Jaʿfar b. Aḥmad b. al-Aswad said: Together with Abū Zākī Tammām b. Muʿārik, I entered upon Abu'l-ʿAbbās in the month of Ramaḍān, three days after Abū ʿAbdallāh had departed.[121] He stood up for me, walked toward me, and embraced me. I kissed his hand and then he kissed mine.[122] He said to me, 'You are Ibn al-Aswad. Your master has commended you to me and I had asked Abū Zākī about you.' Then he sat down again in his place and drew me near to him. He had me sit up on a cushion on his right and made me comfortable for the disputation. He then produced a letter from his brother to himself in which he related on behalf of Ziyād the physician[123] a prescription that he had made for the disease of Abū Mūsā Hārūn b. Yūnus – Abū ʿAbdallāh had left him behind in a state of illness – and said that, if one of six things happened to him: nose-bleeding, sweating, diarrhoea, or vomiting,[124] this would be a sign of recovery, but the crisis for him would be the

121. Abū ʿAbdallāh departed for Sijilmāsa on a Thursday, 15 Ramaḍān 296/6 June 909, and arrived there on 6 of Dhu'l-ḥijja/26 August. See Ibn ʿIdhārī, *al-Bayān*, I, 152 and 153; Ibn Ḥammād, 9; Halm, *Reich*, 125, trans. 135.

122. On this protocol and its importance, alluded to here earlier, see Qāḍī al-Nuʿmān, *Iftitāḥ*, par. 227; Halm, *Reich*, 116, trans. 122–3.

123. Ziyād, the physician mentioned before, had gone with Abū ʿAbdallāh and the army. See Ibn ʿIdhārī, *al-Bayān*, I, 153.

124. Note that there are only four things mentioned in the text and not six as specified. The text is probably incomplete here.

occurrence of nose-bleeding and diarrhoea following that. 'So put what Ziyād recommended to the test and write to me about what happens to him and his condition and if he finds relief, as he must not stay behind but join us, for our hearts are attached to him.' Then Abu'l-'Abbās said to me, 'These physicians, does this knowledge come to them from their own minds, or from experiments, or revelation, or inspiration, or from the legacy of prophets? This would necessitate the presence of prophets among them even though we have no memory of them.'[125]

I said: 'In regard to the role of experimentation in respect to the fundamental principles, this is absurd since that would involve the perdition of some people and the benefit of others, and experimenting would prove false for one group while sound in another. When it is sound in one case and false in another, Hippocrates has said, 'Life is short, experiment risky, the time acute, judgment difficult, and the art long.'[126] Experiment can play a part in some derivative matters in such a way that one may infer something from another like it and judge it on the basis of what applies to another of its same type. They experimented with dissection in order to learn the true nature of the arteries and other such things. As for their own minds, they did not lead them to the science of medicine and the different kinds of beneficial and lethal drugs and the

125. This general question was frequently debated and itself had a history. See for example the discussion of it in Isḥāq b. Ḥunayn's *Ta'rīkh al-aṭibbā'*, ed. F. Rosenthal, *Oriens*, 7 (1954): 55–80, pp. 62–4.

126. This is the first of Hippocrates' *Aphorisms*, the meaning of which is not entirely clear or agreed upon. On it see the study by F. Rosenthal of its history in Arabic ('Life is Short, the Art is Long,' in the *Bulletin of the History of Medicine* 40 [1966]: 226–45), and also F. Rosenthal's, *The Classical Heritage in Islam* (Berkeley, 1975), 186–7. The Arabic text here contains an unusual rendering of the Greek original: 'the time is acute' (*al-zamān ḥadīd*), rather than the more common: 'the time is narrow' (*al-waqt ḍayyiq*). However, it is closer in meaning to the original *kairos oxys*. It is the same reading as that given by al-Ya'qūbī's *Ta'rīkh*, ed. M. T. Houtsma, I, 107, but not that of the published Arabic translation, *al-Fuṣūl*, ed. J. Tytler, p. 1.

variety of them in various countries. Some kinds exist in India; others are in rivers and seas, as in, for example, the lake of Tiberias; and there are substances like sealing clay [*ṭīn makhtūm*], *ṭabāshīr*,[127] yellow amber [*kahrubā*],[128] and pearls. Recognition of these things is not available to the mind without a learned sage who makes their benefits known and these are the prophets, peace be upon them. God instructed Adam as to the benefits and the harm of each thing and its source and its name; and Adam's knowledge was inherited in the earth through the hands of those like him among the friends of God, that is, his descendants and the prophets who came after him.'

He said: 'Were these people themselves prophets?'

I said: 'They were the followers of the prophets. It is said that Idrīs, peace be upon him, was the one who revealed the knowledge of astronomy and arithmetic and that he was called Hermes in the language of the Greeks.[129] It is quite possible that these figures have names among the non-Arabs that are not the names for them among the Arabs. I have seen where Plato calls Asclepius [Saqliyūfus] the Master of Sanctification [*ṣāḥib al-taqdīs*]. Aristotle he refers to as the One whose Prayer was Accepted [*al-mustajāb*] and Socrates as thc Founder of Life's Proper Ways [*wāḍi' al-siyar*]. These people used to venerate Marwās the sage, and it is related of Plato that he "left behind Kardāūs [Critias?]" in the temple as if the meaning were, "he backed him".'

He said: 'But their books bespeak a disregard for the masters of religious laws and of making the mind the sole arbitrator.'

I said: 'I have read words by Empedocles[?] affirming the existence of an imitated teacher and of the need on the part of the people for him so that he would set up for them the rule of

127. 'A substance of a silicious nature produced in the bamboo, used in medicine,' as defined in F. Steingass, *A Comprehensive Persian-English Dictionary*. For more detail consult A. Dietrich, 'Ṭabāshīr' in the *EI2*.

128. On yellow amber in this context, see M. Plessner, 'Kahrubā' in the *EI2*.

129. On Hermes and Idrīs see M. Plessner, 'Hirmis' and G. Vajda, 'Idrīs' in the *EI2*.

law. He also remarked that there is a language for the people in each age and for each language there is a code of conduct by which they are led. All of them are in agreement about pious behaviour and the censure of disorder. They urge abstinence, acknowledge justice, forbid adultery and lying, uphold a prohibition against murder, and prohibit all abominations. They say, moreover, that everything you detest having done to yourself must not be done to anyone else.'

He said: 'Have you noticed any evidence among them of prayer?'

I said: 'Yes, I observed that the Ḥarnāniyya have a law and a prayer that is attributed to Mālik b. Sinān the Ḥarnānī.'[130]

He said: 'Are you familiar with it? He belongs to the people of this language and not to the ancients.'

I said: 'And I have seen a passage of Galen in which it is stated, "We have been subjected to eating unleavened bread seven days each year." This indicates that he was within the law of Moses. Socrates said, "Whosoever concerns himself with the pursuit of knowledge and education, his preoccupation with that will preserve him from offences and his bad actions will be few." Socrates denounced the idols so often he was killed for that reason and forced to drink the poison. When he was told, "Flee to Rome," he replied, "I will not leave the truth here, and in Rome there are some who hate me." May it be enough for you what Socrates said about the Creator and his repudiation of anthropomorphism. When he was asked about the Creator, he said, "What has no limit has no form, and what has no shape and no form is not perceived by the senses." It was said to him, "Describe for us the Creator." He replied, "A discourse about what cannot be perceived is ignorance, and a discussion about what cannot be attained by mind is wrong."'[131]

130. The reading of Ḥarnāniyya/Ḥarnānī is unclear in the mss. but can be confirmed on the basis of Ibn al-Nadīm's *Fihrist* (Cairo, n.d.), (*maqāla* 9.1: Arabic, 456ff, Dodge trans., 745ff) where Ḥarnāniyya is a variant for Ḥarrāniyya, i. e., the Ṣābians of Ḥarrān.

131. On these details about Socrates, see Alon, *Socrates Arabus*, specifically i (his life), pp. 96–8, 106–12, 117, 124, 126; ii (his teachings), nos

He said: 'But they uphold a doctrine of the eternity of prime matter and nature?'

I said: 'Eternity, according to them, is divided into five types.[132] The Creator is eternal by His essence, not because of a cause that is other than He. Prime matter is of two kinds in their view. The first prime matter is eternal through a relation to the eternity of its Creator. It is above the realm of intellect, the realm of rational soul, and the realm of animal soul and vegetative soul. From second prime matter come the four elements. Following upon the effects of first prime matter, there is intellect. Eternal duration is subsequent to the actions of intellect, and time is subsequent to the actions of second prime matter. That to which eternity is subsequent does not fall under the senses, but that to which time is subsequent is perceptible to the senses.'

He said to me: 'Have you read the Epistles [*Mayāmīr*] of Paul?'

I said: 'Yes, and I have a copy.'

He then launched forth into the substance of them, and it was as if he had a copy in front of him and he went over it chapter by chapter. He mentioned that a Christian had recited it to him. Next he referred to the book of Balīnūs.[133] He expressed his high regard for it and asked me about it.

1.2, 10, 561f, p. 104 n.1.

132. The doctrine expressed in this statement about eternity does not appear to match exactly any other known Arabic text. On this general question see 'Ḳidam' by R. Arnaldez in the *EI2*. The problem of a matter prior to intellect out of which intellect is, comes, or is formed may go back to Plotinus's attribution to Aristotle of an intelligible matter, which raises an issue in Aristotle that is still discussed and which also may have influenced Isaac Israeli and Ibn Gabirol. On this see D. De Smet, *La Quiétude de l'Intellect: Néoplatonisme et gnose ismaélienne dans l'oeuvre de Ḥamîd ad-Dîn al-Kirmânî (Xe/XIes.)* (Leuven, 1995), 255–9.

133. Presumably Ibn al-Haytham is referring to the *Sirr al-khalīqa*, the main work ascribed to Balīnūs (pseudo-Apollonius of Tyana) which was well known at this time. See the nearly contemporary discussion about it and its author by Abū Bakr b. Zakariyyā' al-Rāzī and the Isma'ili *dāʿī* Abū Ḥātim al-Rāzī recorded in the latter's *A'lām al-nubūwwa*, pp. 107–8 and 275–6. The Arabic of the *Sirr* was edited by U. Weisser (Aleppo, 1979) and summarized with a discussion in her *Das Buch über das Geheimis der*

I said: 'I have a copy.'

He asked me to show him this book.

I said: 'He opposes in it the proponents of astrology and claims that Saturn alone exercised control over this and that, and then later Jupiter joined him.'[134]

He said: 'There are various meanings he has that you will learn, God willing.' Then he mentioned the books of logic. He did not set much store by them and disapproved their teaching about what is possible. He said, 'How could there be between two contraries a quality that is other than they? Were that necessary, it would follow that there is between ice and fire a quality that is neither fire nor ice, and likewise between truth and falsehood, right and wrong.'

I said to him: 'He meant by his statement only that the root principles are three: that whose existence is necessary, that whose existence is impossible, and that whose existence is possible. An example is writing in regard to a single human being who may write or not write, or like a tree which can be burned by fire, cut by an iron implement, or uprooted by the wind. Fire may be extinguished with water or with sand, or it is possible that the fire is stayed from its nature by a miracle of God. But that does not happen in every age or at the hands of all people.'

He said: 'Is the inversion of nature possible?'

I said: 'Yes, but not all that can be done has to happen. We have observed events happening that transform the natures from their defined forms, such as the transformation of blood into yellow bile, its burning into black bile, and you can transmute phlegm from its normal nature also, and transform water into air, and air may turn into fire. We therefore must affirm that God has the power to alter the natural properties and to invert what is necessary into something not so and what is im-

Schöpfung (Berlin, 1980). See also M. Plessner, 'Balīnūs' in the *EI2*.

134. This statement about the initial primacy of Saturn matches a doctrine cited in the *Sirr al-khalīqa* (ed. Weisser, II, 6.1f).

possible into its opposite, just as it is possible for the elements to undergo transmutation.'

He said: 'Is it not the case that, when the existence of the contingent is possible, it becomes necessary, so that the contingent is the necessary or else it is the impossible?'

I said: 'That is the case when it is particular to a specific thing and not general for all things. Not every contingent thing is either necessary or impossible, since purely in their essence the necessary does not become impossible, or the impossible necessary, and the contingent either necessary or impossible. This can only happen as a result of a quality from God, the Mighty and Glorious.'

He said: 'Is it then possible for a human to become a donkey?'

I said: 'It is possible; God has changed some people into monkeys and pigs.'[135]

He said: 'Is it possible for a donkey to become a human and a monkey and a pig to become human?'

I said: 'If He wishes, He does it. But, whenever God changes a man into a pig, that is, on God's part, a punishment and an expression of anger with him, and His restoring him is an act of mercy and grace and being pleased with him. It is impossible that God would become pleased with someone with whom he is angry, but it is possible that He return him to a form more vile than a pig, as for example, into vermin of the earth, insects of salt marshes, and vermin of the sea.'

He smiled and said to me: 'Have you read the book on metempsychosis produced by the Shi'a?'[136]

I said: 'Indeed, I read the one they have and those of others who uphold metempsychosis and transmigration. Metempsychosis [*naskh*] is not the same as transmigration [*maskh*].

135. This is a reference to Qur'an 5:60: 'Those whom God has cursed, and with whom He is angry, and some of whom He has turned into monkeys and pigs ....'

136. *Kitāb al-tanāsukh.* It is not known what particular book is meant here. The Imami Shi'i author al-Ḥasan b. Mūsā al-Nawbakhtī wrote a refutation of metempsychosis, *al-Radd 'alā aṣḥāb al-tanāsukh* (See H. Ritter's introduction to al-Nawbakhtī's *Firaq al-shī'a*, p. *bā' ẓā'*.)

Metempsychosis follows humanity, and transmigration follows after metempsychosis.'

He said: 'How is that?'

I said: 'Metempsychosis involves the return of the human in another human form, and transmigration implies his leaving human form for that of the beasts.'

He said: 'Is there a cause for this?'

I said: 'There is a cause for this according to them. They say that, if there was in the person goodness which predominated over evil, by the power of God, the Most High, he returns as a human but, if there was no good in him, God transforms him into one of the beasts and he is subject to repeated return under God's curse and chastisement.'

Next he took up the books of logic and spoke at length about them. He cursed Ibn Qutayba and mentioned his disparagement of the books on logic.

I said: 'Ibn Qutayba was one of the Sunni masses and the rabble who cursed the Shi'a. He once said, "If they were birds, they would be vultures and, if they were beasts, they would be donkeys." He reported from al-Sha'bī[137] that he had said, "If I wanted to fill my house with gold and silver from them, I would relate to them reports about 'Alī b. Abī Ṭālib".'

He said: 'May the curse of God be upon Ibn Qutayba. He did not attach any shame to them by this but rather praised them. It is sufficient merit for the servant when he is guided to the people of excellence and acknowledges the reality of their virtues and spends his wealth on them. Can there be any shame on those who acknowledge the superiority of God and His friends?'

Then I said: 'One might not be grateful to the master of logic[138] for anything other than what he said about the three principles and their propositions, and what they go back to as

137. On this famous Kufan traditionist who died between 103/721 and 110/728, see G. H. A. Juynboll, 'al-Sha'bī' in the *EI2*.

138. The *ṣāḥib al-manṭiq* or 'author of the logic', i.e. Aristotle.

the indefinite, the delimited, the specific, the true, the false, the affirmative, and the negative, and how the mutually contradictory differ and the way in which nullification is set opposite affirmation in a statement compounded of noun and particle. The indefinite is what expresses neither the whole nor the part. The delimited is what distinguishes the whole and the part. The specific is what specifies one case only. We say, for example, "so and so is a writer." The indefinite form is "men are writers"; the delimited is "each one of the people is a writer," and what follows this of negation and affirmation, and what follows that of the three dimensions of time: past, present, and future. The quantifiers [*al-aswār*][139] of discourse are four: all, not all, some, and not any,[140] and what is engendered from these in the way of simple propositions, metathetic[141] propositions, delimited and unquantified propositions, binary, ternary, and quaternary propositions and the contraries of them, their opposites, their truth and falsity. There is also his dictum that each thing inquired about can be investigated according to four things: whether it exists or does not exist, then what is that existent either defined or not defined, then in what manner is it, and finally for what reason is it. "Is it?" follows from "how is it?" in the same way that "what is it?" follows from "why is it?" So, "is it?" and "what is it?" are simple and active, and the howness and whyness are composite and passive. Thus, the combination of 'how' is with 'is it?', and the compounds of the secondary simple proposition consisting of those in combination are with "why is it?" Thus, "is it?" and "how is it?" are qualifiers, and "what is it?" and "why is it?" are qualifications which one investigates by means of definition and species, and are answered by the respondent with respect to definition and species as he prefers, while the former are delimited by yes

139. See Ibn al-Muqaffa', *Manṭiq*, ed. M. T. Dānishpazhūh, (Tehran, 1978) 46 and 75. *Aswār* is plural of *sūr*, an old term for quantifier. See F. Zimmermann's *Al-Farabi's Commentary and Short Treatise on Aristotle's* De Interpretatione (London, 1981), index, under 'quantifier.'

140. Or: every, not every, some(one), and no(ne).

141. Greek *metatheseos*, i.e., metathetic propositions.

and no. Also a virtue of logic and a reason for needing it is its division of discourse into four modes: command, question, inquiry, and statement. Three of these do not involve truth or falseness; the statement alone contains what is true or false.'[142]

He said to me: 'The translator was mistaken. They are command, question, answer, and statement.'

I expressed my approval of this remark of his. Then I said, 'Fine also is his statement that the four comprises the existence of the ten that God made the categories of all things. This is represented by our saying one, then two, then three, then four. When you arrange the numbers successively, it becomes ten. The ten is thus comprised in the number four.[143] Each thing exists in ten, and each substance and accident exists in it. Thus, substance, quantity, quality, relationship, where, when, position, possession, action, and affection are the ten categories that form species and definitions.[144] When the speaker has understood them, he will not mix up his discourse, as do speakers engaged in disputation who in their discourse jumble together definition and delimitation, and the specific and the general.'

He said: 'What is the fault of the disputants when they do that as long as their arguments are valid, since the arguments shift as freely as language itself?'

I said: 'If a speaker cites letters of raising [*ḥurūf al-raf'*], should he introduce particles of lowering [*ḥurūf al-khafḍ*] along with them or argue on the basis of them to the exclusion of the letters of raising?'

He said: 'This is not necessary. Often the letters revert once what causes them to turn back meets them, such as the *hā'* that refers back [*hā' al-rāji'a*] and the four (prefixed) additional

142. A similar distinction is cited by Ibn al-Qutayba in his *Adab al-kātib*, ed. M. Grünert, p. 4, '*wa l-kalāmu arba'atun amrun wa-khabarun wa-'stikhbārun wa-raghbatun wa-thalāthatun lā yadkhuluhu l-ṣidqu wa- l-kidhbu wa-wāḥidun yadkhuluhu l-ṣidqu wa- l-kidhbu wa-huwa l-khabaru.*'

143. That is, one plus two plus three plus four equals ten.

144. On the categories and the various terms used in Arabic for them, see J. N. Mattock, 'Maḳūlāt' in the *EI2* .

letters [*zawā'id*].'[145]

I said: 'In a similar way, the meanings of quantity are in quality, since quantity is what possesses number and it is divided into two, the conjunctive and the disjunctive. The conjunctive comprises five divisions which are line, plane, body, time, and place. The disjunctive comprises the two categories of number and speech, and they both evolve one by one, just as they exist one thing following the other, and not as though their individual parts persist until the whole of them is comprised together. Instead hearing comprises it and the heart comprehends it, while the tongue separates it. Quality is what exists in its entirety such as whiteness, blackness, power, and weakness. Relationship is what relates it to others such as father and son or master and slave. One of the two beings put in a relationship may be the other. However, one cannot be called a son unless the father exists, nor can he be called a father without there being a son. It is the same with master and slave. Relationship is also where one attaches to the other as in saying master of the slave and slave of the master. In the opposite, one does not attach to the other. One cannot say the hot of the cold or the cold of the hot. With regard to existence and non-existence, non-existence attaches to existence, but existence does not attach to non-existence, as one may say the blind of sight but not the sight of the blind. One says the death of life but not the life of death. Non-existence is what takes the place of existence, just as blindness takes the place of sight.'

He said: 'Are darkness and light opposites or are they like non-existence and existence?'

I said: 'Darkness is the non-existence of light because darkness and light cannot be found together in the way that the opposites black and white and heat and cold cannot be found together. Likewise, blindness and sight are not found together.'

145. This discussion is about the discontinuation of grammatical governance in Arabic sentences. The governance may be broken by the occurrence of a pronominal suffix referring back to a noun (*hā' al-rāji'a*) or of a pronominal prefix in the present tense of the verb (*al-zawā'id al-arba'a: alif, tā', yā', nūn*).

He said: 'But you may see both darkness and light in one place.'

I said: 'The darkness in that case results from the failure of light to reach there. You have surely observed that we take the light of a fire and with it remove the darkness, but we cannot find anyone who takes the darkness and repels the light with it.'

He said: 'Body consists of darkness, and sight of light; yet they are joined in the same place.'

I said: 'Do you think that, if we were in the dark of night, the sight would see anything? This indicates that body is altogether darkness and that sight is a locus for the reception of the sunlight and other forms of light.'

He said: 'Then you have confirmed that darkness exists and light exists, and they are opposites, and not non-existent and existent. Similarly, darkness is a name for something, and light is a name for something and, as long as their two names exist together, they are contraries.'

I said: 'Light is a term for itself only; it is nothing for anything else.'

He said: 'What about "where" and "when" and the remaining qualifiers? Go back to them.'

I said: 'These six are the rest of the qualifiers: "where" is a composite of substance with place, "when" is the compounding of substance with time, "possession" a compounding of substance with substance, "position" the combination of substance with substance, "action" is substance with quality, "affection" is substance with quality also.'

He said: 'What is the meaning of his saying substance and accident, mass and body, and why is the accident called accident, and the body body, and substance substance, and why is the thing called a thing?'

I said to him: 'Body is called body because of its being composite and unified and because it has length, breadth, and depth. Body is the composite compounded from substance and accident and everything perceived by the senses, since body is composed of these two things. Substance is what subsists by itself and is the substrate for other things. Accident is what accedes to the substance and accedes to the body of discontinuous accidents such as greenness, yellowness, or blueness. And God, the Mighty and Glorious, is He who brings into existence the accident in the substance because He willed the temporality of the perceptible body.'

He said: 'Since you have defined substance as that which subsists by itself and God subsists by Himself, the two are alike.'

I said: 'The difference between them is that one cannot say about God that He is a substrate or subject to affection, whereas one says of substance that it is a substrate susceptible of being affected and susceptible to contraries.'

He said: 'What then may God be called?'

I said: 'It is permissible that we call Him "thing" just as He called Himself, but we do not call Him a body because body is susceptible of being affected. The agent does not resemble his act and, thus, the Maker of substance is not called substance or accident or body.'

He said: 'Is not "thing" also His act and creation? He has said, "Creator of every thing."[146] Therefore, based on your analogy, it is necessary that we not call Him thing in the same way we do not call Him substancc.'

I said: '"Thing" is an affirmation of its own self and a term for its specific identity. Body, however, is a term for something else in composition. He called Himself "thing" in the same way as He called Himself "living" and "knowing." When we say "nothing," we deny the reality itself. It is the same when we say "not living" and "not knowing." Have you not noticed that, when someone says, "I do not worship anything," he denies worship altogether, but someone who says, "I do not worship a body" and "I do not worship an idol," is not denying the true object of worship who is the Creator of everything. In the same way if he says, "I know nothing" and "I have no power over anything," he denies having power and knowledge. However, someone

146. God says this referring to Himself in the Qur'an at 6: 102, 13: 16, 39: 62, and 40: 62.

who says, "I do not know somebody" and "I am not able to free a slave," does not deny everything. "Thing" is a term that applies generally to everything known and everything mentioned. Body is specific to bodies only.'

Then he resumed the discussion of logic. He reviewed the univocal nouns, synonyms, ambiguous nouns, derived and divergent nouns, and the definitions of each of them, and he spoke at length about them. He discussed also the stipulations of the *Book of Analytics*[147] and the divisions of its chapters and propositions, and was brilliant and masterful. He also asked me about contradiction and opposition and metathetic propositions.

I said: 'With regard to the metathetic propositions, they are those that undergo a change from their first definition, so that whereas they are defined, they become undefined by the addition of the particles of negation. An example is for us to say, "The human can write," which is an indefinite proposition that is possible, not necessary, in respect to all people. The indefinite is that which none of the four quantifiers restricts, namely all, not all, some, and not one. Thus, whatever is not contained by one of these four is indefinite and unlimited. These metathetic propositions have two terms: a subject which is your saying "human" and a predicate which is your saying "can write" because it is predicated of human. When we add to the predicated term which is "can write," the particle "not" [*lā*], and we say "humans cannot write," the proposition is changed from its original form. For this reason it is called metathetic because of its change from its original form. Among these metathetic propositions, some are affirmative and some are negative. Our saying "humans cannot write" is affirmative, and our saying "humans cannot not write" is negative.'

He said: 'There may be among them those that are negative and particular, and affirmative and particular. The metathetic is divided into two, either affirmative or negative, and the particular is divided likewise.' He was astonishing and went to

147. Presumably Ibn al-Haytham means here the *Analytica priora*, which was later known in Arabic as the *Kitāb al-qiyās*.

great lengths in discussing the simple and metathetic propositions. Then he said, 'Which is more dissimilar, the contradictory or the opposite?'

I said: 'Whatever is at variance with the proposition in terms of both quantity and quality is greater in dissimilarity than what differs from it in terms of quality alone. The contradictory, thus, is more dissimilar because it differs from the proposition in two aspects, in quantity, that is, in respect to the whole and part, and in quality, that is, in respect to affirmation and negation.

Then he performed the afternoon prayer and he commanded me to stay with him, and we performed the prayer. Then he went out, but soon summoned me. He did not nap or take a rest but launched into an explanation of the inner meaning of what we had been discussing about the three, the four, and the ten, the necessary, the possible and the impossible, the elements, and the creation of humans, their composition, the number of their limbs, their arteries, and joints, to such a degree that you would have said that he knew even the number of hairs on their head. Next he spoke about what resemblances there are in the human being among its various parts and also the divergences of its parts. He mentioned rivers and what is like them in the human being – these being the arteries – and mountains and salt marshes [*al-sibākh*]. Thus, he connected each thing in the human to what resembles, and is like it. And he mentioned that the human is the microcosm. He went on describing that until such a point that I saw the whole of the heaven and the earth in the human being. Next he brought up the liver, heart, stomach, intestines, lungs, brain, the natural and instrumental powers and all of the bodily tools. By God, if he had been Hippocrates, the founder of medicine, he could not have added to it. Then he made associations between medicine and the stars and calculation and philosophical knowledge of metaphysics and mathematics,[148] until he had made out of

148. An alternate reading, suggested by F. Zimmermann, would be *al-siyāsiyyāt* (governance or politics) in place of *al-riyāḍiyyāt* (mathematics).

this an all-inclusive circle in which no part is independent of the rest. Then he mentioned the medicinal plants and their habitats, their trees, their names and their qualities. It was as if the book of Dioscurides was there in front of him.

Next he expounded the religious law and the excellence of what the Prophet Muḥammad had imparted, and that whatever the precursors had said and what the ancients related and what they had explained at length and overlooked concerning points, planes and mass, God, the Mighty and Glorious, had unified for His Apostle in the letter *alif.* He further spoke about the letters of the alphabet and mentioned the *bā'*, *yā'* and *kāf*, and why the script of the Arabs is linear and why the first script consisted of letters in isolation and in reverse. Next he began a discussion of the religious laws and he started with the words 'There is no god but God; Muḥammad is the Apostle of God.' He commented how it commences with a particle of negation and then makes an affirmation after the negation, and what God, the Mighty and Glorious, brought together for Muḥammad in these words about the definition of truth, the explanation of wisdom, and the order of the stations of religious exhortation. I beheld a man of perfect faculties who combined many disparate, solid, and grand sciences, but with flexibility, natural ease, and high-minded companionship, while he lacked avarice and jealousy and did not conceal his meanings nor veil the gems of his phrases. His mere indication was explanation, and his explanation always brought comprehension. Then he recited, 'We have created mankind from a seed of clay' (to the end of the verse) [23: 12] and commented on it, explained its meanings, ordered them, established them firmly, and connected them to evidence in the Book of God like them. Thus he recited, 'We poured out the water abundantly, then We split the earth in fissures and made plants grow in them from grains, grapes, reeds, olives, and palms, and dense gardens, and fruit and fodder' [80: 25–31], and it was in its arrangement like its mate. Then he confirmed and verified it on the basis of others like it also, as for example, the saying of the Most High, 'We have created above you seven pathways;

We are never inattentive to our creation' [23: 17], and 'seven, one above the other,'[149] and 'seven firmaments.'[150] He expanded, he illuminated, he explained, and he made the difficult easy and the distant near at hand. He brought out the sum of what God intended in a definitive statement. Next he mentioned the praiseworthy satan and the blameworthy satan and the rebellious man, and the satans, the humans, and the jinn.

I heard then what I had never heard and I remarked, 'This is knowledge that opens up sciences, a doorway that opens many doors.' So I said, 'Praise be to God.' He said, 'What is the praise that belongs to God in your standing up and sitting down, in times of your happiness and in times of your distress?' Then he said, 'We will not demand nor charge you with answering until after you understand.' Then he explained it. I realized that, prior to that moment, I had not understood it in its proper meaning. I said, 'Praise be to God truly,' as I said, 'There is no god but God' sincerely. Then I moved to stand up.

He said: 'Don't leave. You will stay with us tonight, and keep us company.'

I said: 'I have with me a riding mount and a servant boy.'

He instructed Abū Zākī: 'Order someone to take charge of the mount and servant,' and said to me, 'Stay put! I hope that you will be the praiseworthy man; you will be a proof of God.' I kissed his hand and he kissed mine, and he continued to speak about the Qur'an and its various meanings with sincere purpose and a pure heart, nothing distracting him until the stars appeared in clusters. Then he said, 'The time for prayer has arrived.'

I remarked to myself: 'A Shi'i who has learned the doctrines of the Shi'a.' And I said, 'The Shi'a do not break the fast until they see the stars.' He then mentioned the *Book of a Day and Night* and offered a summary of it and its contents, and the prayer of Ja'far al-Ṭayyār,[151] peace be upon him, and what

149. See Qur'an 71: 15 or 67: 3.

150. See Qur'an 78: 12.9-

151. This is Ja'far b. Abī Ṭālib, 'Alī's brother, who is reported to have

prayers he performed during the nights of Ramaḍān as supererogatory prayers and that the extent of them comprised a thousand *rak'as*. He rose in eminence in my heart and became great in my eyes. I had not seen his like before, nor do I expect that I will ever meet another the equal of him, who combined in himself all the sciences, who had read through the doctrines of every school, who had investigated the doctrines of those who differ, and fully comprehended the statements of both ally and opponent.

He retired to a chamber in the palace and performed the prayer. Then he summoned Sulaymān the eunuch[152] and ordered him to bring me in, along with Abū Zākī. As I entered, he commanded Sulaymān to remove my boots, and I went out again to remove them. He said, 'Take your place,' drawing me near to him and showing me hospitality and kindness. Sulaymān took off the boots, folded the *ṭaylasān*[153] and turban, and brought out the wash water in a silver vessel. He then brought out a new gilded dining table, and another table carried by two servants was brought in on which was a bamboo cover that concealed all of it. A servant removed the covering revealing an array of food in gilded Chinese bowls. There followed a continuous succession of hot food of marvellous concoction. After a quenching drink of water, the food continued to come to me, and plenty of succulent sweets were provided such as an

been called *al-Ṭayyār fi'l-janna* or *Dhu'l-janāḥayn* by the Prophet after he was killed at the Battle of Mu'ta in the year 8/629. On him see L. Veccia Vaglieri, 'Dja'far b. Abī Ṭālib' in the *EI2*.

152. There is a remote possibility that this Sulaymān (*al-khādim*, the eunuch) passed into the possession of the caliph al-Mahdī and is mentioned in the *Sīrat Jawdhar* (see pp. 35–6, trans., 46) as a Slav (Ṣaqlabī) who was a leader of al-Mahdī's Slavic slaves. During the invasion of Egypt in 307/919–20, the Fatimid fleet was commanded by Sulaymān al-Khādim al-Ṣaqlabī. At the Battle of Abukir that same year, he was captured by 'Abbasid forces and later put to death in Baghdad on the orders of the caliph al-Muqtadir. Ibn al-Athīr, *al-Kāmil*, VIII, 114; Ibn 'Idhārī, *al-Bayān* I, 181–2; Idrīs, *'Uyūn* 193 n. 76, 234 and n. 160.

153. The *ṭaylasān* was a shawl-like garment worn over the head and shoulders.

almond dish [*lūzanj*] and a *fālūdhaj* sugar confection.[154] He was serving me with his own hand and he said, 'This is not the food of someone fasting.' Then he spoke about the types of food and fragrances, the kinds of birds, the varieties of land and sea animals, those apparent and those concealed, and which of them are commendable and which blameworthy.

Next the table was taken away and wash water was brought to us, and he washed. I wanted to wash somewhere off to the side, but he told me, 'Stay where you are.' So I washed in my place. Then he had a new table brought in different from the former. It was arrayed with various platters, some on top of others, with a variety of succulent fruits such as apples, pears, grapes, shelled fresh almonds, and sugar-candy. He mentioned the fruits and their varieties and their differing as to tastes even though they are watered by the same water. He noted that, in the case of some of them, one eats its exterior and discards the interior, whereas, for others, one consumes the interior and throws away the exterior. For yet others, one eats both its exterior and its interior. He cited the cause for all this and other cases like it and its inner meaning. He spoke of the animal and how its feet are the inverse of our hands and our feet its hands. He observed that man is like an inverted tree, his head being its root and his arteries its top. His legs are its branches and he is watered from his head. The palm tree is similar to him in that, when its head is cut off, it perishes. Next he spoke about the bees and the difference in their honey and its varieties, and their knowledge of winds that are harmful to them, and about ants knowing of the approach of rainstorms and of their coming to an end. He noted many of the benefits of animals, and I realized that he had read Aristotle's *Book of the Animal*.[155] Next he took up the minerals and the characteristics of glass,

154. *Fālūdhaj* is a dish made of starch, honey, and water.

155. This is a reference to a series of books by Aristotle: *Historia animalium*, *De partibus animalium*, and *De generatione animalium*, which were commonly grouped together in the Arabic tradition. They were translated possibly by Ibn al-Biṭrīq (perhaps revised by Ḥunayn b. Isḥāq). See F. E. Peters, *Aristoteles arabus* (Leiden, 1968), 47–8. See also the

its source, its kinds of white, red, and yellow, and the cutting and grinding of it. It was as if he worked with the glass makers and had grown up in their trade.

Then the table was lifted away; he washed his hands and we washed ours. We then began again, and he started to comment on the sura of Joseph, peace be upon him. I heard what I had not heard nor had ever entered the mind of man. I thanked God, the Most High, for the grace of His bounty that He had bestowed on us and for His goodness and the blessings He had granted us. He followed with a discussion of the *rā'āt, lawāmīm* and *hawāmīm* suras and the glorifications of God [in uttering the phrase *subḥān Allāh*], all put in a wondrous sequence, a marvellous discourse, an extraordinary manner, and a diction that exceeded perfection and comprehensiveness. Then he said, as had his brother, 'We fear to have bored you since the listener is more apt to be bored than the one reciting.' I said, 'This is lush and fresh; it will not cause boredom, as God, the Most High, said, "You shall have in it what the souls desire and delights the eyes" [43: 71]. These are "hidden pearls" [52:24].'[156] He was happy with what he heard me say and he observed in it my delight and vigour. He continued with his discussion until the ninth hour of the night.

Then he said: 'You are not familiar with thc night vigil – just as his brother had said – but we have need of you.' He ordered Abū Zākī to let me sleep in his place during the day. He furnished me with a new cloak and a new garment of camel hair. Abū Zākī slept in front of me, and it was not as long as an hour when I heard him call for Sulaymān. Abū Zākī and Sulaymān then went to him. He said to Sulaymān, 'Get someone to fetch me a calm gentle riding mount for us to ride. We will visit Abū Mūsā while it is still dawn.' The mount was brought and presented to him. I went to him and bid him good morning with a wish for his health and continued happiness. He said, 'We have

introduction by R. Kruk to the edition of *The Arabic Version of Aristotle's* Parts of Animals (Amsterdam, 1979).

156. Also Qur'an 56:23. Note the context of this phrase in both these Qur'anic passages.

kept you awake.'

I said: 'It was the best night I have spent awake, the one of greatest benefit and of the best outcome.' When he attempted to ride, the mount would not go and he fell off. Abū Zākī and the servants noticed and took hold of him. He said, 'Woe to you, we do not ride enough; it has been some time since we have ridden. Do any of these people have an Egyptian donkey?' They said, 'Certainly.' He was supplied a quick donkey which they saddled, and he rode it while Abū Zākī and two servants proceeded alongside. Sulaymān was left behind with me. I slept a little, and then he returned while it was still dawning. He performed his prayer and slept until the advent of full daylight. Then he went out and sat in his daytime place of yesterday and resumed the discussion of the Qur'an, and science, wisdom, and good exhortation. I spent that day with him also and he detained me there. So I stayed with him for the night, and we broke the fast with him the second night in the same condition as before, with a great variety of fruits and food and with the continuation of his affection, kindness, and generosity.

I remarked: 'This man has an even greater eminence than his brother. In terms of rank, he surpasses his brother in knowledge. He exceeds him in the excellence of his company and the nobility of his character and his civility.' And he was even more hospitable than the day before. But he sensed in me a flagging at the end of the second day and he ordered for me a drink of rose petal extract and I broke the fast without him.

He said to me: 'This and the broth we have prepared will fortify the stomach, whet the appetite for the food, and dissolve the sharpness of the bile.' So I made use of it and tasted that night more of it than I had tasted before.

When the third day dawned and he sat, Abū Zākī came in and told him, 'Al-Marwadhī, the judge, and Abu'l-Ḥasan al-Muṭṭalibī and Abu'l-Ḥasan al-Ja'farī[157] are here.' He said, 'No, no one is

157. Abu'l-Ḥasan al-Ja'farī, who is mentioned here and later in connection with the affair of Ibn al-Birdhawn and Ibn al-Hudhayl, seems

to come to me or make an appearance, until the lord and the shaykh arrive.[158] Send them away.' So I went out to them with Abū Zākī.

Al-Marwadhī said: 'We inquired about you and looked for you. We were informed that you were here and we realized that you have found a benefit that distinguishes you alone.'

I said: 'You will – God, the Most High, willing – attain it and share with us in it.' I conversed with them for a while and they departed. I said to al-Muṭṭalibī, 'Come back again. We will employ a ruse to have you enter. I will expect you in the portico.' Al-Muṭṭalibī pretended that he would enter a room Abū 'Abdallāh had assigned us and in which we used to stay for the siesta. When al-Muṭṭalibī returned to me in the portico, I went in to Abu'l-'Abbās and recounted the story of al-Muṭṭalibī[159]

to have been close to Abu'l-'Abbās in Tripoli in the period just before the Fatimid victory. However, in contrast to Abu'l-'Abbās and Abū Ja'far al-Khazarī, two of the others in Tripoli at that time, he must have come to Raqqāda before either of them, since he had already had an audience with Abū 'Abdallāh. Perhaps Qayrawan was his home town. He was evidently a descendant of Ja'far b. Abī Ṭālib.

158. Abu'l-'Abbās refers here to the Imam as the lord (*sayyid*) and to his brother as the shaykh.

159. En route to Sijilmāsa al-Mahdī encountered this man and his son who were apparently merchants travelling in the same direction. After a number of conversations, al-Mahdī decided that the man was pro-Shi'i and therefore trustworthy. When al-Muṭṭalibī noticed that al-Mahdī possessed some unusual dinars that had been sent to him by Abū 'Abdallāh, the Imam took him into his confidence and had him join the movement. Thereafter, when he left again for the east, al-Mahdī gave him letters that requested his followers to accept al-Muṭṭalibī as a supporter of their cause. These are the letters mentioned here. Al-Muṭṭalibī's son Abu'l-Qāsim, having known al-Mahdī in Sijilmāsa and thus being able to recognize him in person, unlike Abū 'Abdallāh who had never before met him, was to be taken along by Abū 'Abdallāh when he went to rescue the Imam. See further the introduction above. These details are confirmed by the *Sīrat Ja'far* (p. 119, Eng. trans. in Ivanow, *Rise*, 202, Canard trans., 302) and Ibn 'Idhārī, *al-Bayān*, I, 139 (with full genealogy which, however, needs to be corrected to read, in part, 'Alī b. Yazīd b. Rukāna b. 'Abd Yazīd b. Hāshim b. al-Muṭṭalib). Halm, *Reich*, 125–6, trans. 134–5. Also *Sīrat Ja'far*, 121–5, 131, Eng. trans. in Ivanow, *Rise*,

and the respect of the master for him and how, whenever he came to him, he stood up from his place and made him sit with himself. But, when al-Ja'farī entered to him, he sat apart and he threw him a pillow.

He said: 'Why did he do that given that al-Ja'farī is closer to us?'

I said: 'There was a close acquaintance between him and the Imam in Sijilmāsa, and the Imam's protection covers him.'

He denied this.

I said: 'I am not telling you anything but what I have observed, and I read his letter to him concerning taking care of his needs.'

He rejected that as a lie.

I told him: 'He is in the portico alone.'

He said: 'We have dismissed them. Between us and al-Ja'farī, there is a close association from Tripoli.' Then he said to me, 'It is as if you would like him to enter.'

I said: 'It is up to you.'

He said: 'Have him enter.'

I went out to him and let him know what had just been mentioned concerning him.

He said: 'The letters are present with me.'

He entered to him and Abu'l-'Abbās rose to meet him. He had him sit apart and threw him a pillow, and I left him. There then occurred a lengthy conversation between them until he said to him, 'An old man like you who speaks lies!' And he displayed irritation with him. But al-Muṭṭalibī told him, 'These letters of his are with me,' and he produced the two letters for him. When he saw the seals, Abu'l-'Abbās stood up for him immediately and embraced him. He wept profusely and sat him with him on his own rug. They conversed together until late afternoon. Then I went in to him and he said to me, 'He spoke the truth and you also. You have done us a great favour,' and he gave permission for him to come with me at any time he

205–12, 220, Canard trans., 305–9, 319; al-Mālikī, *Riyāḍ*, II, 49; Ibn 'Idhārī, *al-Bayān*, I, 199 (recording his death in the year 318/930).

wanted. Al-Muṭṭalibī departed and I departed with him toward Qayrawan. Abu'l-'Abbās called me back and handed me a flask in which there was the drink of rose extract and two engraved cups that were masterfully made.

He said: 'This is rose oil of scammony and that violet oil of scammony. It has taken on the power of scammony, but nothing of the substance of scammony is in it that would be used.'

I thanked him for it, and he ordered the servant to carry it, together with the cloak in which I spent the night and the camel hair garment, until he had conveyed it to the boy. We departed then for Qayrawan, but I used to visit him frequently thereafter.

When[160] it was the evening prior to the feast, Abū Zākī, Sahl b. Birkās,[161] and Ibn al-Qadīm[162] jointly urged him to sit for the people on the day of the feast and to allow them to come in to him. But he disliked the idea and refused to do it. They told him, 'Your sitting is one of those acts by means of which you will restore the reign and repudiate the slanders. The army has been slandered with revolting stories that we loath to relate to you. Your holding such a session will offset that.' He

160. The passage that commences here appears also in Idrīs's *'Uyūn*, 133 (pp. 157–8) and from that source it was first published by S. M. Stern in his *Studies in Early Ismā'īlism*, 100–1. Also Halm, *Reich*, 133–4, trans., 141–2.

161. Sahl b. Birkās was one of Abū 'Abdallāh's followers. See Qāḍī al-Nu'mān, *Iftitāḥ*, 99, 100, 101, 102, 103, 104–7; al-Ya'lāwī's note to Idrīs's *'Uyūn*, p. 157 n. 17; also Talbi, *Aghlabide*, 614.

162. This is Abu'l-Qāsim 'Abdallāh b. Muḥammad known as Ibn al-Qadīm. He was an official in the Aghlabid government and fled to Egypt but returned fairly quickly and joined the Fatimids. Al-Mahdī was favourably disposed toward him and appointed him to act as a general supervisor of all the central offices (*dawāwīn*) and governorates. That lasted until he became somehow embroiled in the conspiracy surrounding Abū 'Abdallāh and Abu'l-'Abbās and was executed in 299/summer 911. See Ibn 'Idhārī, *al-Bayān*, I, 159, 167; Qāḍī al-Nu'mān, *Iftitāḥ*, 264–7, 315–16 (his being put to death in connection with the affair ofAbū 'Abdallāh and Abu'l-'Abbās); al-Ya'lāwī's note 18 to Idrīs, *'Uyūn*, p. 157; *Sīrat Ja'far*, 132, Eng. trans. in Ivanow, *Rise*, 221, Canard trans., 320 and n. 3; and Halm, *Reich*, 141, 157–8, trans. 151, 170.

then responded affirmatively and ordered the preparation of foods and the purchase of sheep. When the people had performed prayers, they departed, and they entered to him to offer their greetings. Next he ordered food for them and they ate. He preached to them and lectured and promised them every benefit in the immediate world and the reward of the next. The people departed uttering praises and thanking God for the sermons, benefactions, and blessings he had given and reiterated for them. Next he sat for the purpose of summoning to the faith [the *da'wa*] and the prominent people hastened to him. He strengthened the power of al-Marwadhī and ordered him to proclaim the doctrine of the family of Muḥammad and that no one should profess anything on the basis of the books of Mālik and Abū Ḥanīfa. He gave instructions to issue legal opinions in accord with those his brother had ordered me to issue. He said, 'Join together in your affairs and in union. Settle the differences between you and you will be happy and successful. Your cause will then surpass the others.' The people hastened to him and responded to his summons. Among them were Abū Sa'īd b. al-Ma'mar b. Manṣūr, the jurisprudent, the Banū Abu'l-Minhāl and al-Kalā'ī, the descendants of Abū Muḥriz, the judge,[163] 'Imrān b. Abī Khālid, a collection of my kin and brothers, the Banū Khallād,[164] the Banū al-

163. Abū Muḥriz al-Kilābī, a Ḥanafī, was qadi of Qayrawan jointly with Asad b. al-Furāt early in the 3rd/9th century. Abū Muḥriz was appointed qadi about 203/818–19 and died in 214/829. See Talbi, *Aghlabide*, 182–3, 411; Ibn 'Idhārī, *al-Bayān*, I, 97, 104; Abu'l-'Arab, *Ṭabaqāt*, 84–5; al-Mālikī, *Riyāḍ*, I, 189–96. Already in the year 220/835 his son Aḥmad was briefly the qadi of Ifrīqiya (Ibn 'Idhārī, *al-Bayān*, I, 105 and 106). Much later, after the Fatimid takeover, in the year 303/915–16, al-Mahdī put in charge of the *kharāj* a certain Abū Ma'mar 'Imrān b. Aḥmad b. 'Abdallāh b. Abī Muḥriz, the qadi (Ibn 'Idhārī, *al-Bayān*, I, 173), and for the year 307/919–20, 'Arīb records the death of Muḥammad b. 'Abdallāh b. al-Qāḍī Aḥmad b. Muḥriz (Ibn 'Idhārī, *al-Bayān*, I, 182). The first of these men must have converted as reported in this passage and perhaps also the second, as well as others from this family.

164. Al-Khushanī (p. 224, trans. 319) mentions two individuals, Qāsim b. Khallād al-Wāsiṭī and Abū Rubda b. Khallād, Qāsim's nephew, both

Shawādhikī,[165] and the Banū al-'Irāqī. No theologian or specialist in disputation or jurisprudence, no merchant, no one desirous was left who did not respond to his summons and seek to draw close to him and make contact with him. The prominent men of the country, the legal scholars of the Kufans and Madinans and the people of hadith went to see him. He was wont to honour Ibn 'Abdūn and favour him over the others because of his comprehension of the law and his understanding and knowledge of hadith and uncommon reports, the writing of epistles, of language, and documents. Several sessions of debate took place between him and Sa'īd b. al-Ḥaddād and Mūsā al-Qaṭṭān on the imamate, the elevation of the less excellent, the identity of the sunna, fasting, and maintaining chastity. He often spoke about me among them and said both in my absence and presence, 'I have not seen among you anyone but this young man, nor is there among you anyone like him.' Ibn 'Abdūn and Ibn Ẓafar,[166] and our colleagues and masters from among the Ḥanafīs were delighted with this and would tell him, 'He is one of our boys. We used to observe this blessing and saw him with eyes expecting growth and advancement.' On his part, this was a means of drawing me closer, of attracting attention to me, and of stabilizing and managing others. He used to detain me each day to eat with him, and many were the times I would spend the night with him. Thus, we benefited from his knowledge and literary accomplishments – a benefit the value of which has not disappeared nor has its merit diminished.

originally Ḥanafī, who now became Isma'ilis.

165. 'Iyāḍ's *Madārik* (ed. Talbi, no. 116, p. 335) contains a biographical notice for a certain Sa'īd b. Ḥamdūn al-Tamīmī, who was known as Ibn al-Shawādhikī and who died in 295/907–8. 'Iyāḍ regarded him as devoutly religious and a proper Mālikī who related from Saḥnūn. Nevertheless, Ibn al-Haytham probably refers here to members of this same family.

166. Abu'l-Faḍl Ibn Ẓafar was a Ḥanafī expert in disputation with Mu'tazilī leanings. See al-Khushanī, 221, trans. 316, also p. 215 for his role in the affair of Ibn al-Birdhawn.

Then the Shaykh Abū Ja'far Aḥmad b. Muḥammad al-Khazarī came to him.[167] Al-Khazarī esteemed Abu'l-'Abbās, exalted him highly, and showed deep respect for him. He would say whenever the people had gathered together in his presence, 'Among you this man is the staff of Moses "that swallows up the falsehoods they utter".'[168]

I had sought his help in the matter of some kinsmen of ours that 'Uqba, the mounted guardsman,[169] had seized in the district of Qammūda.[170] Al-Khazarī said to me, 'Cut off your evil kinsman in the same way you cut off gangrene because, if you leave gangrene without cutting it off, it develops and increases until you have to cut off a more vital member in its place.' Abu'l-'Abbās told him, 'Glory be to God, how would the people then understand his excellence in my eyes and his place with us? Rather, let them be released for his sake.' He ordered them set

167. Abū Ja'far al-Khazarī (possibly al-Jazarī) was a high-ranking *dā'ī* who had been specifically delegated, along with a family servant, by the Imam to escort the women of his family (his mother, sisters, daughters, and others) from Salamiya to the Maghrib. This party had reached Tripoli fairly early, and they waited there for the final outcome of Abū 'Abdallāh's revolt. During the period when both this Abū Ja'far and Abu'l-'Abbās were together in Tripoli, they would confront each other in public debate, each taking an opposite side and pretending to curse the other so as to deflect any suspicion of collusion. After the victory of the Fatimids, Abū Ja'far and the Imam's family made their way to Raqqāda. In the sources, however, there is some confusion about whether this happened before or after the arrival there of al-Mahdī. Ibn al-Haytham here indicates that at least Abū Ja'far reached Raqqāda prior to the Imam. The *Sīrat Ja'far* includes a double reference to the arrival of the Imam's family (pp. 123 and 132–3) and an expression of some doubt about when it happened. Slightly later, but still in 297/910, Abū Ja'far was appointed director of the treasury by the caliph. He died in 301/913–14, and al-Qā'im said prayers for him. On him see Qāḍī al-Nu'mān, *Iftitāḥ*, 261–2, 261 n. 3, 299 n. 3; Idrīs, *'Uyūn*, 135–6, 192 (short obituary notice); Ibn 'Idhārī, *al-Bayān*, I, 159; *Sīrat Ja'far*, 110–11, 123, 132–3, Eng. trans. in Ivanow, *Rise*, 190, 209, 222, Canard trans., 287, 308–9, 321; also Halm, *Reich*, 118, 139, 141, trans. 125, 148, 151.

168. Qur'an 7: 117 and 26: 45.

169. Nothing further is known about this man.

170. On the district of Qammūda, see H. R. Idris, *La Berbérie*, 429–30.

free. I thanked him for his kind words and act, and every one present there thanked him also. He would treat the people of his *da'wa* with generosity, look out for them, and give orders for their protection and their being favoured, and would recommend them to governors and judges. He also ordered me to protect them and bring them close to me. They were in the habit of assembling at my house and frequenting me, and I related to them the books of law and of the virtues of the family of Muḥammad. A group copied those books from me. He asked me to copy them for Abū Dujāna, the judge of Tripoli, and also requested me to copy them for Mufarrij al-Aṭrābulusī, a guest from Tripoli then staying with him, toward whom he showed hospitality and had set up in a room of the palace with him.

I was with him one day when two men of his *da'wa* came to him to raise a complaint against al-Marwadhī for having beaten and paraded them around the markets. He was troubled and angry and he became agitated by the distress and concern for them that arose in him. Then he said to me, 'Will you not take care of this matter for me?' He took a sheet of paper and, after the invocation of God, the Mighty and Glorious, wrote, 'May God return you to His obedience, in this matter we have succumbed to amazement at you. You have allowed the exposure of believers and violated their dignity and have claimed that the two of them are wicked and harmful. You have thus stated, as the ancients said to Noah, peace be upon him, "And we do not see any following you except those who are the most contemptible of us, those rashly inconsiderate" [11: 27] and, "Are we to believe in you when your followers are contemptible" [26: 111]. God, the Mighty and Glorious, reported about the statement of His enemies and their preoccupation with His friends while they are in His chastisement, and hellfire burns their faces, "And they will say, what happened to us, we do not see the men we once took to be wicked" [38: 62]. It is the same with us in regard to someone who yesterday cut short a prayer and a fast, then committed adultery, and then repents in the morning.

So do not be deceived by the world. Many are those who have acknowledged the virtues of this house, but then turn away from them and return to what is undutiful. "God is not unaware of what you do."[171] It was once said to Jesus, "Why do you appeal to tax-collectors and sinners and not to the scholars and learned men?" He said, "If the scholars do not respond to us, and we do not summon the tax-collectors and sinners who do respond to us, then whom shall we summon?"[172] We are only tutors and teachers. Those who properly accept our instruction, we raise in station and give a new life. Those who do not respond to our teaching, we reject. We employ with those we summon the utmost politeness that we possess. We command you from today forward not to investigate any person who has become one of us until after you consult with us about him. But we will abstain from looking further into the action of yours concerning these men that upset us. Peace.'

I delivered the letter to him and then took it home with me. It was preserved among my books until it was lost with those things of ours that disappeared in the days of the Dajjāl,[173] on whom may the anger of God fall.

Unity prevailed then, dissent was healed, virtue widespread, knowledge sought, the desirous were many, the word of truth lofty, the word of the believers accepted, sincere advice to the believer readily given. How much of the funds from the pillaging of Raqqāda and other places were received due to them![174]

171. Qur'an 2: 74, 75, 140, 149 and 3: 99.

172. The statement attributed to Jesus here depends on the incident of the tax collectors and sinners related in Matthew 9.9–13.

173. Referring to Abū Yazīd Makhlad b. Kaydād, the Kharijite rebel who became famous as the *ṣāḥib al-ḥimār* (master of the donkey). He is usually cited in Fatimid works simply as the Dajjāl. His revolt commenced in 332/943 and he first entered Qayrawan in 333/944–5. Al-Qā'im died in 334/946 and his son, who was to take the throne name al-Manṣūr (The Victor) only after having defeated Abū Yazīd, was able to retake Qayrawan shortly thereafter. The final victory over Abū Yazīd did not occur until Muḥarram 336/August 947.

174. When the last of the Aghlabid rulers absconded to Egypt, he and

Many were the hypocrites who were exposed, and they in turn revealed those of the Aghlabid family who had hidden. How many were slain and captured! During that time we heard nothing about any celebrity of women, nor any praise and boasting of the tyrants and leaders, nor any longing for Mālik and his partisans, nor of concern for anyone else. The truth ascended and was manifest; the false was hidden and scorned. Among them some were beaten, disgraced, made to fear, shunned, and despised.

When news of the lord who had been dismissed began to penetrate and these people started agitating and breathing heavily, it was established of two men[175] that they had revealed some of the rancour and envy they were concealing by speaking of the superiority of Mu'āwiya over the lord of mankind, and that 'Alī had gone out to make war against Mu'āwiya and to seek the imamate, but that the one who seeks the rulership

his party carried away everything they could manage. One large shipment of funds, however, was eventually intercepted and returned. Also in the two-day interval between the departure of the Aghlabid and the arrival of Abū 'Abdallāh's troops, the populace plundered Raqqāda freely. It is unclear exactly which of these incidents the author is referring to (perhaps it is both). See Halm, *Reich*, 115, trans. 122; Ibn 'Idhārī, *al-Bayān*, I, 151; and Qāḍī al-Nu'mān, *Iftitāḥ*, par. 223 (p. 304) which states 'He [Abū Abdallāh] ordered the search for the plunder of Raqqāda. Thus, he retrieved much of it from the hands of the people and those it was sought from, and a great sum of goods was thereby amassed.'

175. These two men were Ibrāhīm b. Muḥammad al-Ḍabbī, known as Ibn al-Birdhawn, and Abū Bakr b. al-Hudhayl, both executed in Ṣafar of 297/Oct.–Nov. 909. The latter of the two seems insignificant in the sources although, because this incident later became a major case of martyrdom in the view of the Mālikīs, both merited biographies in the later *ṭabaqāt* works. See 'Iyāḍ, *Madārik*, 390–4 (biography of Ibn al-Birdhawn), 394–5 (biography of Ibn al-Hudhayl); al-Mālikī, *Riyāḍ*, II, 47–9 and 49–51. Ibn al-Birdhawn was apparently an agitator against the Ḥanafīs, who hated him for it. He was also a student of Ibn al-Ḥaddād. In the earlier period of Ḥanafī dominance under al-Ṣadīnī, he was arrested and officially beaten. After the Fatimid takeover, the Ḥanafīs, namely Ibn Ẓafar and al-Kalā'ī, denounced him again, this time for his pro-Umayyad propaganda, and this led to his death. Ibn 'Idhārī, *al-Bayān*, I, 154–5; al-Khushanī, 215–16, trans. 310–11.

has no right to what he seeks.[176] Abu'l-'Abbās gave the order to kill them and then tie them to the tails of two mules to drag them through Qayrawan. They were killed, and that was done to them, and their disgrace was publicly proclaimed. Al-Ja'farī had objected on behalf of one of the two who was known as Ibn al-Hudhayl and he made a request for him prior to his execution. Al-Khazarī, however, rebuked him and let him hear words that would be ugly to repeat. As a result, all those who had had aspirations restrained them and all those who had come out openly concealed themselves and reverted to humility in disgrace. The books of Mālik and Abū Ḥanīfa were sold to physicians, pharmacists, and druggists who, out of disregard and contempt for them and despair of anything in them being of benefit, used them as wrapping paper. Some were sent to al-Andalus and to the east.

We continued to enjoy bounty and an honoured position in that same manner until a letter[177] came from his brother announcing the arrival of our master, peace be upon him, to Īkjān in the country of the Kutāma, the homeland of the religion and fount of the faith.[178] Then he made preparations to go out to meet him. The dawn broke and morning appeared, the day came upon us and the night went away, souls were delighted and hearts radiant at the arrival of his news. Such joy it held it cannot be forgotten, a glowing splendour inextinguishable, a

176. It is noteworthy that the argument put forward by the Mālikī Ibn al-Birdhawn was in conflict with the traditionalist Sunni creed which, ever since the time of Ibn Ḥanbal, recognized 'Alī as the fourth of the Rightly-Guided caliphs and as just in his war with Mu'āwiya. Ibn al-Birdhawn's position reflects the pro-Umayyad attitude still prevalent among the Mālikīs in the Maghrib.

177. The following passage, like the one noted earlier, was quoted by Idrīs (*'Uyūn*, 148–9 [pp. 169–70]) and published in Stern's *Studies in Early Ismā'īlism* (pp. 101–2). Halm has translated it in *Reich*, 136–7, trans., 145–6.

178. The text of this letter is quoted by Qāḍī al-Nu'mān, *Iftitāḥ* (pp. 289–90), followed by a description of the great meeting that took place shortly thereafter (pp. 291–2).

light that cannot be concealed. It was he whose excellence could not be hidden and 'the truth has now arrived and falsehood has perished' [17: 81]. The stars declined and the Alive and Self-subsistent appeared. Abu'l-'Abbās went out and we went out with him and met the lord on the mountain pass of Sabība.[179] I cannot forget his auspicious appearance, the splendour of his light, the brightness of his face, the elevation of his rank, the perfection of his build, and the resplendent beauty in his dawn. If I were to say that the lights that shine were created from the surplus of his light, I would have voiced the truth and the manifest reality. Abu'l-'Abbās dismounted before him, may the blessings of God be upon him, and kissed the earth. He lay on the ground in front of him, and his brother Abū 'Abdallāh dismounted for him, as did all of the friends from the Kutāma and the others of their followers. No one was left riding except the Commander of the Faithful, may the blessings of God be upon him, the sun most radiant, and [his son] the shining moon and glittering light, Abu'l-Qāsim. These two, may the blessings of God be on them both, were the light of the world. Our master Abu'l-Qāsim was just behind al-Mahdī. Then Abū 'Abdallāh greeted his brother. Abū 'Abdallāh brought me close to our master and said to him, 'O master of ours, this is the person whose story I related to you in Sijilmāsa.' Abu'l-'Abbās spoke and expressed thanks and praise. I will never forget the words of our master, 'May God be gracious toward you and bless us through you and thank you for your effort. You all are truly of our Shi'a, and of the people of our loyalty, and of those who have loved us in the past.' Next the people mounted, and the Commander of the Faithful proceeded to march. He drew Abu'l-'Abbās near to himself and he ordered me to accompany him. The earth began to shine with his light and the world was illuminated by his advent, and the Maghrib excelled because of his presence in it and his having taken possession of it. We were then in successive bliss whose beginnings were praiseworthy and whose later parts were joyous in

179. Sabība lies about 90 km west-southwest of Qayrawan.

glorious might and in firm stability with an erudite sage and a king who is gentle and compassionate with the believers, merciful 'in a shade extended, water poured, fruits that abound uncut and not forbidden' [56:30–33].

We were together with the shaykhs of the Kutāma, their *dāʿīs*, learned men, and the devotees of religion among their men, 'on raised mats' [56:34], 'with set drinking glasses, arrayed cushions, unfolded carpets' [88:14], 'under a thornless lote tree, stacked acacias, shade extended, water poured out' [56:28–31] that we drank among them 'in a cup from a running spring, white, a pleasure for those who drink' [37: 45–46], there being no headiness in it nor accusation of offence, 'reclining between strands of gold and brocade' [18:31]. We plucked from the fruits of their thoughts and inhaled from the fragrances of their flowers matters whose benefit was great with me and whose outcome was lofty. The mercy of God be upon all the believers who have gained certitude, are true to their covenant, and patient, and God is compassionate and merciful to us and to them all.

There was no duly authorized *dāʿī* among them but that I learned from him with the permission of the shaykh Abū Mūsā. I harvested from their fruits both the exterior and the interior, and there was not one of them who did not stay with me and visit my home. And whatever I may forget, I shall[180] never forget the *dāʿī* of Malūsa, the shaykh of the community and their legal authority, Aflaḥ b. Hārūn al-ʿIbānī.[181] He combined his

180. The passage that follows here was also quoted by Idrīs (*ʿUyūn*, pp. 211–13) and published in Stern's *Studies in Early Ismāʿīlism*, 102–4.

181. The praising of Aflaḥ by the author is particularly noteworthy because he was a Kutāmī. As a *dāʿī* of the prominence accorded him by the author, he is evidence of a learned elite among the Kutāma. Al-Mahdī first appointed him qadi of Raqqāda in 297/910. He died apparently in 310/922 at the time holding the post of qadi of Raqqāda and possibly al-Mahdiyya. Previously he may have been qadi of Tripoli, perhaps from the time of the conquest in 297/910 until shortly before his death. Idrīs, *ʿUyūn*, 192, 211, 213; Ibn ʿIdhārī, *al-Bayān*, I, 159, 173; al-Khushanī, 240, trans., 335; Dachraoui, *Califat*, 405–6; Halm, *Reich*, 332, trans., 375.

activity as a *dāʿī* with the sciences of the religious law, and he reached back to the time of Abū Maʿshar and al-Ḥulwānī, and transmitted on their authority from al-Ḥalabī.[182] I frequently met with him and visited him. He stayed with me many times and copied many books on law, traditions, and the virtues and speeches of our master and our lord, the Commander of the Faithful, ʿAlī b. Abī Ṭālib, may the blessings of God be upon him and on the imams among his offspring. I heard from him the summons for the women and what types of proofs he would address to them that their minds will accept and retain. He would say, 'God has the convincing proof' [6: 149]. He said, 'This means the proof with which the scholar addresses the one he teaches or the ignorant person, using only what that person comprehends.' He would address women and employ

182. In his investigation for 'The Sources of Ismāʿīlī Law' (*Journal of Near Eastern Studies*, 35 [1976]: 29–40), Madelung found that Qāḍī al-Nuʿmān cited two works by al-Ḥalabī, a *Kitāb al-Masāʾil* and a *Jāmiʿ*. He gives a possible identification there for this al-Ḥalabī as 'Ubaydallāh al-Ḥalabī, who transmitted directly from Jaʿfar al-Ṣādiq and who died in the latter's lifetime. See pp. 30, 34–5. Al-Ḥulwānī is reported to have been sent by the Imam Jaʿfar to the Maghrib, along with a certain Abū Sufyān, in 145/762 to spread Shiʿism there. See Qāḍī al-Nuʿmān, *Iftitāḥ*, pp. 26–9, 34, 41–2, 131–2, 182. Al-Ḥulwānī, who is specifically reported to have converted many of the Kutāma, is said also to have lived such a long time that persons who related directly from him were still alive when Abū ʿAbdallāh arrived in the Maghrib. But it is virtually impossible that Aflaḥ and the others extended back to the time of al-Ḥulwānī if he in fact came at the time of the Imam Jaʿfar since the time elapsed was a century and a half or more. The list of those who are reported to have known al-Ḥulwānī or were converted to Shiʿism by him include the following: Abū Ḥayyūn known as Abu'l-Mufattish (Qāḍī al-Nuʿmān, *Iftitāḥ*, 29, 38, 39, 40, 42), Abū Sufyān (a colleague of al-Ḥulwānī, *Iftitāḥ* 28, 29), Umm Mūsā bint al-Ḥulwānī (his daughter, *Iftitāḥ*, 29, 133), Yaḥyā b. Yūsuf known as Ibn al-Aṣamm al-Ijjānī, (*Iftitāḥ*, 132), Ismāʿīl b. Naṣr al-Maʿādī, Abu'l-Qāsim al-Warfajūmī, Abū ʿAbdallāh al-Andalusī, the *dāʿī* and judge Aflaḥ al-Malūsī, and Ḥurayth al-Jīmalī and Mūsā b. Makārim, two members of the party of Kutāmīs who first encountered Abū ʿAbdallāh al-Shīʿī in Makka and urged him to return with them to their homeland. The name Abū Maʿshar here has no parallel elsewhere and he is otherwise unknown.

as evidence in their case items of their jewellery, rings, earrings, headgear, necklaces, anklets, bracelets, dresses, head binding.[183] Next he would cite examples pertaining to spinning, weaving, costume, and hair, and other items that suit the natural disposition of women. He would speak to the craftsman using the terms of his craft and thus, for example, address the tailor by reference to his needle, his thread, his patch, and his scissors. He addressed the shepherd using references to his staff, his cloak, his horn, and his two-pouched travelling bag.[184] Today I know of no one who can do that or of anyone to take my place in it or who has preserved the memory of it as I have. All that was due to the success given by my Lord and Creator and my Benefactor and Sustainer. May God's mercy be upon him. Whenever he spoke, in his speech he was humble toward God, seeking what is with Him, and was tender of heart, amply tearful, and moist of tongue, and he mentioned God submissively, humbly, and affectionately. Of his maxims and his recommendations to me, I remember that he once said, 'Be wary of placing your trust in anyone until he is firmly established. When he is firmly established, what he was concealing, as well as what he was making public, will both become manifest in him.'

It has reached me that the Commander of the Faithful al-Mahdī bi-llāh was apprised of Aflaḥ's fine voice, excellence in recitation, and sincerity of intention. He had entrusted him with supervising the judicature in al-Mahdiyya, Raqqāda, and other areas in the whole of his domain. He was indeed pious,

183. *'Ijār*, alternately *mi'jar*, 'a thing which a woman binds on the head,' Lane, *Arabic-English Lexicon*. See also al-Ya'lāwī (Idrīs, *'Uyūn*, p. 212).

184. Or possibly 'his sash', depending on the reading of this word and the exact meaning of *kurziyyatihi*. The other items are things the shepherd carries on himself. Dozy (*Supplément aux dictionnaries Arabes*) cites the form *kurziyya* meaning something like a strip of cloth used as a turban or a belt. According to Dozy it is a Maghribi term. Thus the reading of the two mss. with *kurziyyatihi* appears to be correct. Another possible reading would be *kurzayhi*, but the word *kurz*, singular, already designates a double pouch like a *khurj*, itself a (saddle) bag with two pouches (although *khurjān*, dual, is also known for the same double pouched bag; see Lane, *Arabic-English Lexicon*).

chaste, righteous, devout, and virtuous. Once, longing to see him, al-Mahdī gave an order to search for him and he commanded the doorkeepers to admit him mounted. The Commander of the Faithful was at the moment indisposed with one of his illnesses. Accordingly, Aflaḥ went in until he dismounted at the gate to the inner sanctuary of the great palace. He was then asked to go in to him. Al-Mahdī drew him close, welcomed him, and urged him to speak, but he was awed and overpowered by the emotion of it. But al-Mahdī gave him permission to speak, and he then spoke. Thereupon, the Commander of the Faithful said to him, 'Silence.' He was silent, and the Commander of the Faithful spoke, while Aflaḥ burst into tears until the weeping overwhelmed him. What he heard from al-Mahdī impressed him profoundly and was of great significance in his ears. Then in front of him he rubbed his cheeks and suggested to al-Mahdī that he pray for his death.

He said: 'Woe to you, why so?'

Aflaḥ answered, 'O my master, you have placed me in a lofty position in relation to you. This is a noble station and a speech so privy that 'none may touch it except those who are purified' [56:79] and I fear for myself that I may stumble. My dying in this state of purity would be a most unsullied circumstance and a most glorious situation. Therefore, I ask of you, O my master, by the Majesty that you pray for me.'

Al-Mahdī said: 'O Aflaḥ, do not afflict me with the loss of you.'

He said: 'O my master, the meeting place is with God.'

Then al-Mahdī wept and said to him, 'May God choose for you the best.'

Aflaḥ departed that day and retired. We congratulated him for what we had heard of this meeting and he related some of it to us. He died that same month, may the mercy of God be upon him and His pleasure.[185]

While we were in those pleasing conditions and that pure

185. Aflaḥ died in 310/922.

situation, suddenly there croaked among us the croaker of discord and the disquieter of fates. Disasters followed successively night and day. The word became disunited, passions multiplied, opinions differed, matters were contested, and dreaded fear ensued. Resolution dwindled and deviation was mixed with guidance, and doubt with certainty – except for those of the devout whom God safeguarded – and rebellion gained ascendancy. The remnants of the men of the Aghlabids achieved what they were after by scattering, dissension, and help in fleeing, and in their goal of causing confusion and sedition.[186] Those drinking places were closed and the fires of war lit. These loathsome events continued widely and in succession. The she-camels ten months with young were left untended[187] and 'convents, churches, oratories, and mosques in which the name of God was often mentioned were razed' [22:40]. The river shrank, the stars grew dim,[188] the rains stopped, the sun of day was altered, the clouds multiplied, and storm clouds piled up, earthquakes and darkness descended, and thunderbolts, lightning and thundering succeeded each other without relent. God prolonged my days until in the passing of time I saw wonders, and the one did well who said:[189]

I had hoped that I would die and not witness
atop the minbars a preacher for Umayya.
But God prolonged my days and they lasted long
until I saw through time wondrous things.

And I say just as the first one said:

My ambition refuses anything but to rise to the summit even
though the vicissitudes of events may lower my head.

186. A revolt instigated by the Aghlabids followed the killing of Abū 'Abdallāh. See Qāḍī al-Nu'mān, *Iftitāḥ*, 320–2.

187. See Qur'an 81: 4.

188. See Qur'an 81: 2.

189. These two lines of poetry are ascribed to the poetess Bakkāra al-Hilāliyya in *al-'Iqd al-farīd* by Ibn 'Abd Rabbihi (Cairo, 1940, vol. 2, p. 105; Beirut, 1983, vol. 1, p. 347).

We endured the terrors and tasted, after our master, al-Mahdī, may the blessings of God be upon him, the sweetness of the age and its bitterness, and we fluctuated between its two halves. We were as Ibn Durayd said:[190]

If dreams intimated to me what I shall meet awake,
ruin would deal me a fatal blow.
Though my toughness fends off weeping from my eyes,
the heart is stuck in the throes of lament.
Should I die, my days are finite and every thing that reaches
its limit comes to an end.
I did not know, but time is passionately fond of severing
what is joint and of shattering powers.
I accept by force, and on the basis of force he becomes
content who was outraged at the changes of destiny.
I have milked the two sides of the age, at times it was bitter
for me and at others sweet.
If hard stone were touched by some of what my heart has
encountered, it would pierce the solid mass of the rock.

As for today, we say as did the ancients:

Time passes and life does harm,
the age repeats unpleasant lessons;
Enduring anxiety and grievous worry,
and a world that announces to you that no one is free.
And the best the faithful can employ in disasters is
the forbearance of the patient.

I say: 'O I would wish,' but is there any hope for something begun by 'would that!' Will those days be auspicious for me when I put my trust in God, the Mighty and Glorious, and am I assured that the highest of ranks will be restored? Bounties increase by seeking the protection of the rightly guiding imams,

190. This quotation is taken from the lengthy *Maqṣūra* poem of Ibn Durayd (223/837–321/933). See *Dīwān Ibn Durayd wa sharḥ maqṣūratihi lil-Khaṭīb al-Tabrīzī*, where the lines given here are nos 13, 12, 249, 27, 25, 183, and 9 respectively with slight variations for nos 249 and 9.

may the blessings of God and His peace be upon them, and by submitting to them and accepting their command in prosperity and adversity, in times of hardship and of ease. In bearing witness and testimony through them, salvation before the Judge on the promised day becomes a reality.

We were in that condition until the son of the Imam,[191] the ornament of the people, and the adornment of the days, departed to rectify what was corrupt, reveal what was concealed, illuminate what had become obscure, and rebuild what had been destroyed. He cut what temptation had produced and mowed over what had been caused to sprout until the truth began to bloom, and the dawn shone again, and that darkness was lifted. God, the Mighty and Glorious, never stops afflicting His servants by prosperity and adversity as a trial and a test, and because of what He intends and knows. God, thus, caused him to assume control over the faith so that he raised its beacon again and strengthened its buttresses, firmed its anchorages, and secured its pillars. He weakened the power of those who opposed him, destroyed their pillars, put out their fires, and with those who are rightly guided fought against those who went astray until God made the religion mighty. He gained success with the friends of God, and they returned after retreat, and came forward after having turned back, and professed his doctrine, and submitted after abstaining. Through them God supported the religion and destroyed the building of the hypocrites; through them for His friend He rectified the corruption; and through them He reinvigorated the servants. The pathways of truth appeared for the believers, and he made the guidance shine for those who would be guided and those seeking direction. Praise be to God, the Lord of the worlds, and the

191. The 'son of the Imam' is the future caliph al-Manṣūr who was then already the unproclaimed Imam since his father al-Qā'im had recently died, although the death was kept secret for the time being. Ibn al-Haytham therefore must have written this work during the period between the death of al-Qā'im on Sunday, 13 Shawwāl 334/17 May 946 and the public announcement of the succession on 29 Muḥarram 336/19 August 947.

curse of God be upon all wrongdoers, the first and the last. May God bless Muḥammad, the Prophet, and the imams from his family, the pure, the good and the elect, a blessing everlasting and continuous to the Day of Judgment.

The Book of Discussions is thus concluded. Praise be to God,[192] the Lord of the worlds and may God bless Muḥammad, seal of the prophets and master of the apostles, and his brother and legatee ʿAlī b. Abī Ṭālib, the noblest of legatees, and the imams from the descendants of them both, the good and pure, and our master, lord, and owner and ruler of our affairs and the extended rope to which the Imam commanded us to cling, the descendant of the Imam al-Ṭayyib Abu'l-Qāsim,[193] Commander of the Faithful, may the blessings of God be upon him, and on his pure forefathers, and his most noble sons who are expected until the day of judgment. May He grant them all peace. God is sufficient for us, how excellent a guardian is He.

192. This concluding passage is by Ḥasan b. Nūḥ al-Bharuchī, the compiler of the *Kitāb al-Azhār*. He is the transmitter of Ibn al-Haytham's text as mentioned at the beginning of the translation above, n. 1.

193. Al-Ṭayyib, son of the Fatimid caliph al-Āmir (d. 524/1130), disappeared as an infant. He is the last known Imam of the Ṭayyibī Ismaʿilis.

Bibliography

Abān b. ʿUthmān al-Aḥmar, *al-Mabʿath wa'l-maghāzī*, ed. Rasūl Jaʿfariyān. Qum, 1417/[1996].

ʿAbd al-Jabbār b. Aḥmad al-Hamadhānī, al-Qāḍī, *Tathbīt dalā'il al-nubuwwa*, ed. ʿAbd al-Karīm ʿUthmān. Beirut, 1966.

Abu'l-ʿArab, Muḥammad b. Aḥmad b. Tamīm al-Tamīmī, *Kitāb al-miḥan*, ed. Yaḥyā Wahīb al-Jubūrī, 2nd ed. Beirut, 1988.

——*Kitāb ṭabaqāt ʿulamā' Ifrqiya*, ed. Mohammed Ben Cheneb in *Classes des savants de l'Ifrīqīya*. Paris, 1915. French trans. *Classes des savants de l'Ifrīqīya*, Ben Cheneb. Algiers, 1920.

Alon, Ilai, *Socrates Arabus: Life and Teachings*. Jerusalem, 1995.

al-Amīnī, ʿAbd al-Ḥusayn Aḥmad, *al-Ghadīr*. Beirut, 1967

Ammonius (pseudo), *Kitāb Ammūniyūs fī ārā' al-falāsifa bi-'khtilāf al-aqāwīl fi'l-mabādi'*, ed. and trans. Ulrich Rudolph. Stuttgart, 1989.

al-Bakrī, Abū ʿUbayd, *al-Masālik wa'l-mamālik*, ed. W. MacGuckin de Slane. Algiers, 1857.

al-Balādhurī, Aḥmad b. Yaḥyā, Futūḥ al-buldān, ed. M. J. de Goeje. Leiden, 1866.

Balīnūs (pseudo-Apollonius), *Sirr al-khalīqa*, ed. Ursula Weisser, *Buch über das Geheimis der Schöpfung*. Aleppo, 1979.

al-Bharūjī (Bharūchī), Ḥasan b. Nūḥ al-Hindī, *Kitāb al-Azhār*. Mss. Hamdani Collection and The Institute of Ismaʿili Studies, London.

Caskel, Werner, *Ğamharat an-Nasab: Das genealogische Werk des Hišām ibn Muḥammad al-Kalbī*. Leiden, 1966. 2 vols.

Dachraoui, Farhat, *Le Califat Fatimide au Maghreb, 296–362/909–973: histoire, politique et institutions*. Tunis, 1981.

Daftary, Farhad, *The Ismā'īlīs: Their History and Doctrines.* Cambridge, 1990.

De Smet, Daniel, *La Quiétude de l'Intellect: Néoplatonisme et gnose ismaélienne dans l'oeuvre de Ḥamîd ad-Dîn al-Kirmânî (Xe/XIe s.).* Leuven, 1995.

Dozy, R., *Supplément aux dictionnaries Arabes.* Leiden and Paris, 1927.

EI. Encyclopaedia of Islam. Leiden/Leipzig, 1913–38.

EI2. Encyclopaedia of Islam, New Edition. Leiden, 1960- .

Gacek, Adam, *Catalogue of Arabic Manuscripts in the Library of the Institute of Isma'ili Studies,* vol. 1. London, 1984.

Halm, Heinz, 'The Isma'ili Oath of Allegiance (*'ahd*) and the 'Sessions of Wisdom' (*majālis al-ḥikma*) in Fatimid Times,' in F. Daftary ed., *Mediaeval Isma'ili History and Thought.* Cambridge, 1996, pp. 91–115.

——*Das Reich des Mahdi: Der Aufstieg der Fatimiden (875–973),* Munich, 1991; Eng. trans. *The Empire of the Mahdi: The Rise of the Fatimids,* by M. Bonner. Leiden, 1996.

——'Zwei fatimidische Quellen aus der Zeit des Kalifen al-Mahdī (909–934),' *Die Welt des Orients,* 19 (1988): 102–117.

Hamdani, Sumaiya, 'The Batin in the Zahir: Fatimid-Sunni Polemics in Tenth-Century North Africa.' Unpublished MESA paper.

Hippocrates, *Al-Fusūl: The Aphorisms of Hippocrates,* trans. into Arabic by Honain Ben Ishak, ed. John Tytler. Calcutta, 1832.

Ibn 'Abd Rabbihi, Aḥmad b. Muḥammd, *al-'Iqd al-farīd.* Cairo, 1940; Beirut, 1983.

Ibn al-Athīr, 'Izz al-Dīn, *al-Kāmil fi'l-ta'rīkh,* ed. C.J. Tornberg. Beirut, 1965–67.

Ibn Durayd, Muḥammad b. Ḥasan, *Dīwān Ibn Durayd wa sharḥ maqṣūratihi lil-Khaṭīb al-Tabrīzī.* Beirut, 1995.

Ibn Ḥammād, Abū 'Abdallāh Muḥammad b. 'Alī, *Histoire des Rois 'Obaidides (Akhbār mulūk banī 'Ubayd wa sīratuhum),* ed. and trans. M. Vonderheyden. Algiers and Paris, 1927.

Ibn Ḥawqal, Abu'l-Qāsim b. 'Alī, *Kitāb Ṣūrat al-arḍ,* ed. J. H. Kramers. Leiden, 1938. French trans. *Configuration de la terre* by G. Wiet. Beirut and Paris, 1964, 2 vols.

Ibn al-Haytham, Ja'far b. al-Aswad, *Kitāb al-Munāẓarāt.* Mss., see al-Bharūjī.

Ibn Ḥunayn, Isḥāq, *Ta'rīkh al-aṭibbā',* ed. F. Rosenthal, *Oriens,* 7 (1954): 55–80.

Ibn 'Idhārī, Abu'l-'Abbās Aḥmad b. Muḥammad al-Marrākushī, *al-*

Bayān al-mughrib fī akhbār al-Andalus wa'l-Maghrib. Vol. 1, ed. G. S. Colin and É. Lévi-Provençal. Leiden, 1948.

Ibn al-Khaṭīb, Lisān al-Dīn, *Ta'rīkh Isbāniya al-Islāmiyya, aw Kitāb a'māl al-a'lām,* ed. E. Lévi-Provençal. Beirut, 1956.

Ibn al-Muqaffa', *Manṭiq,* ed. M. T. Dānishpazhūh. Tehran, 1978.

Ibn al-Nadīm, *Fihrist,* Cairo, n.d.; Eng. trans. Bayrad Dodge, *The Fihrist of al-Nadīm.* New York, 1970. 2 vols.

Ibn al-Qutayba, *Adab al-kātib,* ed. M. Grünert. Leiden, 1900.

Idris, Hadi Roger, *La Berbérie orientale sous les Zīrīdes, xe-xiie siècles.* Paris, 1962. 2 vols.

——'Contribution à l'histoire de l'Ifriḳiya. Tableau de la vie intellectuelle et administrative à Kairouan sous le Aġlabites et les Fatimides ... d'après le Riyāḍ En Nufūs de Abū Bakr El Mālikī,' *Revue des Etudes Islamiques,* 9 (1935): 105–178 and 273–305 and 10 (1936): 45–104.

Idrīs 'Imād al-Dīn, *'Uyūn al-akhbār,* ed. M. al-Ya'lāwī as *Tā'rīkh al-khulafā' al-Fāṭimiyyīn bi'l-Maghrib: al-qism al-khāṣṣ min kitāb 'Uyūn al-akhbār.* Beirut, 1985.

Ivanow, Wladimir, *Isma'ili Tradition Concerning the Rise of the Fatimids.* London, etc., 1942.

'Iyāḍ, al-Qāḍī Abu'l-Faḍl, *Tarājim Aghlabiyya mustakhraja min Madārik al-Qāḍī 'Iyāḍ,* ed. Muḥammad al-Ṭālbī. Tunis, 1968.

Ja'far al-Ḥājib, see al-Yamānī.

al-Jawdharī, Abū 'Alī Manṣūr al-'Azīzī, *Sīrat al-ustādh Jawdhar,* ed. M. Kāmil Ḥusayn and M. 'Abd al-Hādī Sha'īra. Cairo, 1954. French trans. *Vie de l'ustadh Jaudhar* by M. Canard. Algiers, 1958.

al-Khushanī, Muḥammad b. al-Ḥārith b. Asad, *Kitāb Ṭabaqāt 'ulamā' Ifrīqiya,* ed. Mohammed Ben Cheneb in *Classes des savants de l'Ifrīqiya.* Paris, 1915. French trans. Ben Cheneb, *Classes des savants de l'Ifrīqīya.* Algiers, 1920.

Kruk, Remke, *The Arabic Version of Aristotle's* Parts of Animals. Amsterdam, 1979.

Lane, Edward William, *Arabic-English Lexicon.* New York, 1956.

Leclerc, Lucien, *Histoire de la médecine arabe.* Paris, 1876.

Madelung, Wilferd, 'Fatimiden und Baḥrainqarmaṭen,' *Der Islam* 34 (1959): 34–88; slightly revised Eng. trans., 'The Fatimids and the Qarmaṭīs of Baḥrayn' in F. Daftary, ed., *Mediaeval Isma'ili History and Thought.* Cambridge, 1996, pp. 21–73.

——'Ḥamdān Qarmaṭ and the Dā'ī Abū 'Alī,' *Proceedings of the 17th Congress of the UEAI* [Union Européenne des Arabisants et

Islamisants]. St. Petersburg, 1997, pp. 115–24.
——'Das Imamat in der frühen Isma'ilitischen Lehre,' *Der Islam,* 37 (1961): 43–135.
——'Notes on Non-Ismā'īlī Shiism in the Maghrib,' *Studia Islamica,* 44 (1976): 87–97; reprinted in his *Religious Schools and Sects,* article XIV.
——'The Religious Policy of the Fatimids toward their Sunnī Subjects in the Maghrib,' in M. Barrucand, ed., *L'Egypte Fatimide, son art et son histoire.* Paris, 1999, pp. 97–104.
——*Religious Schools and Sects in Medieval Islam.* London, 1985.
——'The Sources of Ismā'īlī Law,' *Journal of Near Eastern Studies,* 35 (1976): 29–40; reprinted in his *Religious Schools and Sects,* article XVIII.
al-Maqrīzī, Tāqī al-Dīn Abu'l-'Abbās, *Kitāb al-Muqaffā al-kabīr,* ed. M. al-Ya'lāwī. Beirut, 1991. 8 vols.
al-Mālikī, Abū Bakr, *Kitāb Riyāḍ al-nufūs fī ṭabaqāt 'ulamā' al-Qayrawān wa-Ifrīqiya,* ed. Bashīr al-Bakkūsh. Beirut, 1981–83.
al-Nawbakhtī, al-Ḥasan b. Mūsā, *Firaq al-Shī'a,* ed. H. Ritter. Istanbul, 1931.
al-Naysābūrī, Aḥmad b. Ibrāhīm, *Istitār al-imām,* Arabic text ed. by W. Ivanow, *Bulletin of the Faculty of Arts,* University of Egypt, 4 (1936): 93–107; Eng. trans. W. Ivanow in *Isma'ili Traditions Concerning the Rise of the Fatimids,* pp. 157–83.
Peters, F. E., *Aristoteles arabus.* Leiden, 1968.
Poonawala, Ismail K., *Biobibliography of Ismā'īlī Literature.* Malibu, Calif., 1977.
——'al-Qāḍī al-Nu'mān's Works and the Sources,' *Bulletin of the School of Oriental and African Studies,* 36 (1973): 109–15.
——'A Reconsideration of al-Qāḍī al-Nu'mān's *Madhhab,*' *Bulletin of the School of Oriental and African Studies,* 37 (1974): 572–9.
Qāḍī al-Nu'mān, Abū Ḥanīfa Muḥammad, *Iftitāḥ al-da'wa wa ibtidā' al-dawla,* ed. Wadad Kadi. Beirut, 1970; and Farhat Dachraoui. Tunis, 1975.
——*Kitāb al-Himma fī ādāb atbā' al-a'imma,* ed. M. Kāmil Ḥusayn. Cairo [1948].
——*Kitāb al-Majālis wa'l-musāyarāt,* ed. al-Ḥabīb al-Faqī, Ibrāhīm Shabbūḥ and Muḥammad al-Ya'lāwī. Tunis, 1978.
——*Sharḥ al-akhbār fī faḍā'il al-a'imma al-aṭhār,* ed. Muḥammad al-Ḥusaynī al-Jalālī. Beirut, 1994. 3 vols.
al-Qummī, Sa'd b. 'Abdallāh, *Kitāb al-Maqālāt wa'l-firaq,* ed.

Muḥammad Jawād Mashkūr. Tehran, 1963.
al-Rāzī, Abū Ḥātim, *A'lām al-nubuwwa*, ed. Salah al-Sawy and Gholam-Reza Aavani. Tehran, 1977.
Rosenthal, Franz, *The Classical Heritage in Islam*. Berkeley, 1975.
——'Life is Short, the Art is Long,' *Bulletin of the History of Medicine*, 40 (1966): 226–45.
Roy, Bernard, and Paule Poinssot, *Inscriptions arabes de Kairouan*. Paris, 1950–58.
Sīrat Ja'far, see al-Yamānī.
Sīrat Jawdhar, see al-Jawdharī.
Steingass, F., *A Comprehensive Persian-English Dictionary*. Beirut, 1970.
Stern, Samuel M., *Studies in Early Ismā'īlism*. Jerusalem, 1983.
al-Ṭabarī, Muḥammad b. Jarīr, *Ta'rīkh al-rusul wa'l-mulūk*, ed. M. J. de Goeje et al. Leiden, 1879–1901. Eng. trans. of vol. X: *The Conquest of Arabia*, by Fred M. Donner. Albany, N.Y., 1993.
Talbi, Mohamed, *L'Emirat Aghlabide (184–296/800–909)*. Paris, 1966.
al-Tawḥīdī, Abū Ḥayyān, *Kitāb al-Imtā' wa'l-mu'ānasa*, ed. Aḥmad Amīn and Aḥmad al-Zayn. Beirut, n.d. 3 vols.
Wolfson, Harry Austryn, *Crescas' Critique of Aristotle*. Cambridge, 1971.
al-Ya'lāwī, Muḥammad, *al-Adab bi-Ifrīqiya fi'l-'ahd al-Fāṭimī*. Beirut, 1986.
al-Yamānī, Muḥammad b. Muḥammad, *Sīrat Ja'far al-Ḥājib*, Arabic text ed. by W. Ivanow, *Bulletin of the Faculty of Arts*, University of Egypt, 4 (1936): 107–33; Eng. trans. Ivanow in *Isma'ili Tradition Concerning the Rise of the Fatimids*, pp. 184–223; French trans. M. Canard, 'L'autobiographie d'un chambellan du Mahdî 'Obeidallâh le Fāṭimide,' in *Hespéris*, 39 (1952): 279–330, reprinted in his *Miscellanea Orientalia*, London, 1973, article V.
al-Ya'qūbī, Aḥmad b. Abī Ya'qūb, *Ta'rīkh*, ed. M. T. Houtsma. Leiden, 1883.
Zimmermann, Fritz W., *Al-Farabi's Commentary and Short Treatise on Aristotle's* De Interpretatione. London, 1981.

Index

كتاب المناظرات

كتاب المناظرات

لأبي عبد الله جعفر بن أحمد بن محمد
بن الأسود بن الهيثم

الجزء السادس

من

كتاب الأزهار

ومجمع الأنوار الملقوطة من بساتين الأسرار مجامع الفواكه الروحانية والثمار

تأليف

سيدنا[1] حسن بن نوح

قدس الله روحه ورزقنا شفاعته وأنسه

بسم الله الرحمن الرحيم

وبه نستعين

الحمد لله مُظهر حججه الباهرات على ألسن أوليائه الصافين المسبحين، في إظهار الحق والتبيين، وإبطال تمويهات المُبطلين، وصلى الله على رسوله سيد الأولين والآخرين، وعلى الأئمة الطيبين الطاهرين.

---

[1] سيدنا: سيدي، ل.

وإنا لما فرغنا من إتمام الجزء الخامس من كتاب الأزهار أردنا أن نورد المناظرات التي جرت بين الداعي[1] أبي عبد الله صاحب دعوة المغرب وبين أبي عبد الله جعفر بن أحمد بن محمد بن الأسود بن الهيثم[2] عفا الله عنهما لكونها مناسبة لما أوردنا قبل هذا الجزء[3] في إثبات إمامة أمير المؤمنين علي بن أبي طالب صلوات الله عليه وإبطال ما ادعاه المبطلون[4] المدعون ظلمًا وافتراءً وتوثباً على مقامه الشريف واعتداءً.

فنقول: قال أبو عبد الله جعفر بن أحمد بن محمد رضي الله عنه: زيّن الله / [2] الإنصاف في عينك ووفقك في قولك وفعلك، سألتَ أرشد الله أمرك أن أكتب لك ما جرى بيني وبين أبي عبد الله وأخيه من المناظرات في الإمامة وغير ذلك، وسبب خروجنا إلى الأندلس وما جرى بيننا وبين القائم على بني أمية وما زرعناه عندهم وعند أهل قرطبة من فضل علي بن أبي طالب امير المؤمنين[5] صلوات الله عليه وفضل آل محمد عليه السلام، وعن سبب خروجنا إلى المغرب وما امتحنا به من مصالة[6] وأخته اللعينة ومماليهما[7] علينا من حزب

---

[1] الداعي: الداعيين، ه.

[2] الهيثم: + الاندلسي، ل.

[3] الجزء: الباب، ل.

[4] المبطلون: -، ل إ.

[5] امير المؤمنين: -، ه.

[6] مصالة: مضالة، ل ه إ.

[7] ومماليهما: وممايلتهم، ه إ ل.

الضلال. وسأذكر لك بعض الذي حفظناه من ذلك، فقد طال عهده وقدم الزمان به وبعد الوقت الذي كان ذلك فيه وطرقنا[١] من حوادث[٢] المحن وتوالي الفتن ما ينسينا القريب العهد من الأخبار المحدثة ويميت الخاطر ويذهب الفطنة ويبعد الأمنية ويقرب المنية، غير أنّ ولادة الدين من ذلك لا تنسى وأخبارها فتذكر ولا تخفى.

دخلنا إلى أبي عبد الله بعد نزوله برقّادة بيومين،[٣] وذلك في يوم الاثنين لثلاث خلون من رجب سنة ست وتسعين[٤] ومائتين، مع أبي موسى هارون بن يونس[٥] الأزايي[٦] المَسَالْتِي إذ كان قصدي إليه واختياري له للذي أجمعوا على فهمه وفقهه وأدبه ولبه وعلمه. فكنتُ عند أبي موسى ذينك[٧] اليومين، فنقل خبري إليه وعرفه بقصدي له وما جرى بيني / ٣ وبينه. فلما كان الليلة الثالثة مضى معي أبو موسى راجلاً، فجاز بدار أبي زاكي فوجّه إليه معرفاً له بحضوري، فخرج فعرّفه بي فسلم عليّ. ثم دخلنا إلى صحن القصر الذي نزل به

---

[١] وطرقنا: وطرقتنا، ل ه إ.

[٢] حوادث: الحوادث، ل.

[٣] بيومين: ليومين، ه ل إ.

[٤] سنة ست وتسعين: ستة وتسعين، ل.

[٥] يونس: يوسف، ه.

[٦] الازايي: الزائر (؟)، ل ه.

[٧] ذينك: ذلك، ه ل إ.

أبو عبد الله، ففتح لنا[١] الباب وعرفهم باسمي، وكان يتولى باب أبي[٢] عبد الله خمسون رجلاً من أهل الدين والبصائر[٣] واليقين، فسلموا وتزاحموا عليّ وحيّوني تحية أهل الدين الراغبين في ثواب الله المؤمنين. ثم دخل قبلي فعرّفه بي. ثم رجع إليّ فدخلتُ معه إليه.

وقال لي[٤]: لا ترجع عنه وناظره بأول[٥] مناظراتك معي، فإنّه يتقلد لك الخلاف. فقام عن سرير لطيف كان جالسًا عليه فرشه[٦] بَرذَعة واحدة ينساني (كذا). فسلمتُ عليه قائمًا وحمدتُ الله على ما وهب لنا من قربه وعلى تمكين الله له وتأييده ونصره، وهاج لي من البكاء ما لم أطق حبسه وذكرتُ مولانا الحسين بن علي صلوات الله عليه وما نال منه المجرمون وحل على أوليائه. وكنا حينئذ أرق قلوبًا واندى[٧] عيونًا وأغزر دموعًا، قد أشعرت الكآبة قلوبنا وتعاهدت نفوسنا تذكار ذل آل محمد صلوات عليهم، فاشتمل على القلوب الأسف والحزن والألم[٨] والقيام على أعداء الله المجرمين، وكنا

---

[١] لنا (او له): لهم، ه إ ل.

[٢] باب ابي: بابي، ه.

[٣] البصائر: :البصيرة، ل.

[٤] لي: -، ل.

[٥] باول: بادل، ه ل إ.

[٦] فرشه: فرشة، ل.

[٧] اندى: انداء، ل إ.

[٨] الالم: الامل، ه إ.

كل يوم قبل وصوله نتمنى أيامه ونتقرب بالاماني زمانه[١]، وتحدثنا الآمال بدرك ذلك وحضور الفتح والظفر بالظالمين، / ٤ وما كان شعارنا مع أصحابنا المتشيعين إلاّ قول الشاعر:

مَتَى أرَى الدنيَا بِلا مُجْبِر وَلا حَرُوريّ وَلا نَاصِب
مَتَى أرَى[٢] السَيفَ دَلِيلاً عَلَى حُبِّ عَلِيّ ابْنِ أبي طَالِبِ

ثم جلس وأدناني حتى صارت ركبتي اليمنى[٣] على سريره.

فقلت: أتيناك طالبين وفيما عندك من العلم راغبين، وقد ثبت عن رسول الله صلى الله عليه وآله أنّه قال: من سمع دعاة[٤] أهل بيتي ولم يجبهم أكبَّه[٥] الله على وجهه في النار.

قال: فلِمَ تخلفتم عن اللحوق بنا والمصير إلينا؟.

قلت: الخوف والحداثة والضعف عن الحيلة في ذلك وقلوبنا معك ودعاؤنا لك.

فقال: ذلك نصر ضعيف، ومن اجتمع له مع القلب اللسان واليد فقد كمل فرضه وأدى ما وجب عليه، والله قد قال جل ذكره: «وَمَن يَخْرُجْ مِن بَيْتِهِ مُهَاجِراً إِلَى اللهِ وَرَسُولِهِ ثُمَّ يُدْرِكْهُ المَوْتُ فَقَدْ وَقَعَ

---

[١] زمانه: -، إ.

[٢] اري: ار، ل.

[٣] اليمنى: اليمين، ل إ.

[٤] دعاة: دعوة و دعاة، ل.

[٥] اكبه: كبد، إ؛ اكبر (؟)، ه ل.

أجْـرُهُ عَلَى اللهِ»[١]، وقـال: «وَالَّذِينَ آمَنُوا وَلَمْ يُهَـاجِـرُوا مَـا لَكُم مِن وَلاَيَتِهِم مِن شَيْءٍ حَتَّى يُهَاجِرُوا»[٢].

فـقلت: وقـد قـال جل اسـمـه: «وَلاَ تُلْقُـوا بِأَيدِيكُم إِلَى التَـهْلُكَةِ»[٣] وعـذر الله «المُسْتَـضْـعَـفِينَ مِنَ الرِجَالِ وَالنِسَـاءِ وَالوِلْدَانِ الذِينَ لا يَسْتَطِيعُونَ حِيلَةً»[٤].

قـال: أمـا إذا رضيـتم بمحل النسـاء والولدان والضـعـفـاء من الرجال فأرجو من الله أن يجعل لكم بعد هذا سـبيلاً. ثم قـال: أنت تطلب علمًا وهدى ونحن نسـتحل الدمـاء ونقـتل النفس[٥] ونسـتبيح الأموال.

فـقلت: تقـتل من أباح / ٥ الله دمـه وأحل مـاله، قـال تعـالى: «وَمَا يُؤْمِنُ أَكْـثَرُهُم بِاللهِ إلاَّ وَهُم مُـشْرِكُونَ»[٦] وقـال: «وَإِن تُطِعِ أَكْـثَرَ مَن فِي الأَرْضِ يُضِلُّوكَ عَن سَبِيلِ اللهِ»[٧].

فقال: أولئك مشركو قريش والعرب.

فقلت: بل هؤلاء الذين قال الله تعالى: «وَمَا وَجَدْنَا لِأَكْثَرِهِم

---

[١] القرآن ٤:١٠٠.

[٢] القرآن ٨:٧٢.

[٣] القرآن ٢:١٩٥.

[٤] القرآن ٤:٩٨.

[٥] النفس: الانفس، ه.

[٦] القرآن ١٢:١٠٦.

[٧] القرآن ٦:١١٦.

من عَـهْـدٍ »[١] وقـال: « فَـإنَّـهُم لاَ يُكَذِّبُونَكَ وَلَكِنَّ الظالمينَ بِآيَاتِ الله يَجْـحَـدُونَ »[٢]، فـأعـلمنا أنّهم يقـرّون بمحـمـد صلى الله عليـه وآله ويكذبون بالأوصياء من بعده ويقولون: « إنْ أرَدْنَا إلاّ إحْسَانًا وَتَوفيقًا، أولَئِكَ الذِينَ يَعْلَمُ اللهُ مَـا فِي قُلُوبِهِم فَـأعْـرِضْ عَنهُم »[٣]. وقـال: « أولَئِكَ الّذِينَ لَعَنَهُمُ اللهُ وَمَن يَلْعَنِ اللهُ فَلَن تَجِدَ لَهُ نَصِيراً »[٤]، وقال تعالى: « وَمَا مُحَمَّدٌ إلاَّ رَسُولٌ قَدْ خَلَتْ مِن قَبْلِه الرُسُلُ أفَإنْ مَاتَ أو قُتِلَ انقَلَبْتُم عَلَى أعْقَابِكُم وَمَن يَنقَلِبْ عَلَى عَقِبَيْـه فَلَن يَضُرَّ اللهَ شَيئًا »[٥]، فأخبر أنهم ينقلبون إلا من عصم الله وأخبرنا أنّهم ينكثون وقال: « إنَّ الّذين يُبَايِعُونَكَ إنَّمَا يُبَايِعُونَ اللهَ يَدُ الله فَوقَ أيْدِيهِم، فَمَن نَكَثَ فَإنَّمَا يَنْكُثُ عَلَى نَفْسِه وَمَن أوْفَى بِمَا عَاهَدَ عَلَيه اللهَ فَسَيُؤْتِيه أجْراً عَظِيمًا »[٦]، فأخبر بنكثهم وارتيابهم وجحودهم وثبت عن رسول الله صلى الله عليه وآله أنه وقف على قبور شهداء أُحُد، فقال: رحمكم الله أنتم أصحابي حقًا، قال له صلى الله عليه وآله عتيق وعمر: أوما[٧] نحن أصحابك؟، قال: بلى ولكن لا أدري ما تحدثون

[١] القرآن ٧:١٠٢.

[٢] القرآن ٦:٣٣.

[٣] القرآن ٤:٦٢-٦٣.

[٤] القرآن ٤:٥٢.

[٥] القرآن ٣:١٤٤.

[٦] القرآن ٤٨:١٠.

[٧] أوما: وما، ه.

بعدي، / ٦ ألا ومن أحدث منكم بعدي حدثًا أو آوى محدثًا فعليه لعنة الله.

قال: هم[١] المنافقون.

قلت: بل المخادعون المراءون المرتابون الذين كسروا جيش أسامة وتأمروا على أمير[٢] رسول الله صلى الله عليه وآله وعزلوه وتقوّلوا عليه وقبل كبيرهم الزور إذ سماه المرتدون خليفة رسول الله فقبل ذلك من قائله وقد لعن رسول الله صلى الله عليه وآله شاهد الزور والمشهود له، وكفى حدثًا هجومهم على الزهراء فاطمة بنت رسول الله صلى الله عليه وآله وقطع ميراثها وانتزاع ما في يديها من نحلة أبيها وهبته لها وإبطالهم شهودها.

فقال: إنّ الله لا يجمع الأمة على ضلالٍ وقد أجمعوا بزعمهم على ولاية أبي بكر، ورسول الله صلى الله عليه وآله يقول: أصحابي كالنجوم بأيهم اقتديتم اهتديتم، وقال صلى الله عليه وآله: يكون بين أصحابي هنيهات يغفرها الله لهم.

فقلت: الإجماع ما لم يكن فيه الاختلاف وذلك لنا دون الفرق كإجماع الجميع أن علي بن أبي طالب صلوات الله عليه فاضل زاهد عالم يستحق الإمامة ونحن نظلم من تقدم عليه، فإجماعهم معنا ونحن منكرون لهم. وأما إجماع من أجمع على أبي بكر فلم يكن إلا بعد الاختلاف والقتل والضرب وسلّ السيوف، وهذا لا يسمى إجماعًا. وما إجماعهم على أبي بكر إلا كإجماعهم على يزيد بن معاوية وعلى

---

[١] هم: -، ه.

[٢] أمير: أمين، ه.

الحجاج بن يوسف وعبد الملك بن مروان. وقد قالت / ٧ الشيعة: نحن أمة محمد صلى الله عليه وآله، والهنيهات ما بينهم من الاختلاف في الفروع وذلك مغفور لهم. فكلهم مقرّون بمحمد وعلي والأئمة من عقب النبي صلى الله عليه وآله، وهذه الأمم كفرت بالنبي وجحدت الوصي وقتلت ولد الرسول التقي. فهم مرتدون خارجون عن أمة محمد صلى الله عليه وآله وهم المشبّهة والمعتزلة والمرجئة[١] والخوارج وسائر الفرق، والهنيهات المغفورة صغائر الذنوب التي تكون بين المؤمنين من التنافس والعتاب، والأصحاب الممثلون بالنجوم هم آل محمد صلى الله عليه وآله ومن تبعهم بإحسان مثل سلمان ومقداد وأبي ذر وعمار وحمزة وجعفر وعبيدة بن الحارث وأمثالهم، فهؤلاء هم[٢] الصدّيقون والشهداء عند ربهم لهم أجرهم ونورهم. والدعوى في الإمامة والترؤس[٣] على أولياء الله وكشف ستر فاطمة سيدة نساء الخلق أجمعين فمن الكبائر التي لا تكفّر بل من الشرك المحبط[٤] الذي لا يغفر.

قال: وكيف كفّرتَ من ادعى الإمامة وقد اختارته الجماعة؟

قلت: بكتاب الله جل وعز، قال الله جل ذكره: «أَلاَّ تَتَّخِذُوا مِن دُونِي وَكِيلاً»[٥]، وقال تعالى: «قَالُوا سُبْحَانَكَ مَا كَانَ يَنْبَغِي لَنَا

---

[١] المرجئة: المرجئية، ه.

[٢] هم: -، ل.

[٣] والترؤس: والتوثب + (في الهامش) الترؤس، ل.

[٤] المحبط: المحيط، ل إ.

[٥] القرآن ١٧:٢.

أنْ نَتَّخذَ مِن دُونِكَ مِن أوْلِيَاءَ»[١]، و«قَالُوا سُبْحَانَكَ أنْتَ وَلِيُّنَا مِن دُونِهِم»[٢]، ثم قال الله سبحانه: «وَرَبُّكَ يَخْلُقُ مَا يَشَاءُ وَيَخْتَارُ مَا كَانَ لَهُمُ الخِيَرَةُ سُبْحَانَ اللهِ وَتَعَالَى عَمَّا يُشْرِكُونَ»[٣]. فجعل اختيارهم وإجماعهم من / ٨ الشرك الذي لا يغفر، وأما الاقتداء بهم فلو صح هذا عن رسول الله صلى الله عليه وآله لكان فيه إباحة السرقة والخيانة وقتل النفس المحرمة وقد سرق معاذ[٤] وأبو هريرة مال[٥] الله وصالحهما عمر وأغرمهما[٦] وقتل أبو بكر أمة محمد ولقبهم بأهل الردة واستحلّ[٧] شهادة الزور على فاطمة عليها السلام وحَكَمَ في الجَدّ باثنين وسبعين حكمًا مخالفًا[٨] بعضها بعضًا وندم عليها كلها[٩] عند موته وأحرق الفجاءة بالنار وندم على ذلك. فبأي قوله نقتدي؟ وهدم عثمان دار جعفر بن أبي طالب عليه السلام وأدخلها في المسجد ولم يشاور أصحابها وأعطاهم ثمنها استحلالاً

---

[١] القرآن ١٨:٢٥.

[٢] القرآن ٣٤:٤١.

[٣] القرآن ٢٨:٦٨.

[٤] معاذ: ابو معاذ، ه.

[٥] مال: قال، إ.

[٦] وصالحهما ... واغرمهما: وصالحهم ... واغرمهم، ه ل إ.

[٧] استحل: استحلوا، ل إ.

[٨] مخالفا: مخالفة، ه ل إ.

[٩] ندم عليها كلها: قدم على ذلك كلها، ل.

واستكباراً[١].

قال: وإن علي بن أبي طالب صلوات الله عليه قد قتل المسلمين و‹فعل› غير ذلك.

فقلت: علي بن أبي طالب مأذون له في القتال ولم يقاتل إلا بحجة وأمر قد تقدم من رسول الله صلى الله عليه وآله وقد قال رسول الله صلى الله عليه وآله لعائشة: ستقاتلين عليًا وأنت ظالمة له حتى تنبحك كلاب الحَوْأب[٢]، وقال لعمار رضي الله عنه: ستقتلك[٣] الفئة الباغية، وقال لعلي صلوات الله عليه: تقاتل الناكثين والقاسطين والمارقين، وقال لأصحابه: إن فيكم من يقاتل على تأويل القرآن كما قاتلت أنا[٤] على تنزيله، فكلٌ ذكر نفسَه، فقال: بل خاصف النعل، وأشار إلى علي عليه السلام وقال لعلي[٥] عليهما السلام: متى يبعث أشقاها فيخضب هذه من هذا، يريد قاتله ابن ملجم لعنه الله وعلي عليه السلام معصوم /[٩] من الخطاء بدعوة رسول الله يوم غدير خُم إذ قال: من كنت مولاه فعلي مولاه اللهم والِ من والاه وعادِ من عاداه وانصر من نصره واخذل من خذله وأدر الحق معه حيث دار. ففعْل علي عليه السلام كله حق لأنّه بأمر[٦] رسول الله صلى الله عليه وآله عن

---

[١] استكباراً: استظهاراً، إ ل ه.

[٢] الحوأب: الحوب، ل إ.

[٣] ستقتلك: تقتلك، ل إ.

[٤] انا: –، ل

[٥] لعلي: على، ل.

[٦] بامر: امر به، ه.

الله تعالى وقوله لعلي عليه السلام: أنت أخي، وآخى بين أصحابه مرتين فقال له: أنت أخي، مرتين وقال له بعد ذلك: وأنت مني كهارون[١] من موسى. يريد بذلك أن أمته تنكث عليه كما نكثت[٢] أمة موسى على هارون، وكل من خالف عليًا عليه السلام أو حاربه ناكثًا عليه فقد خالف الله ورسوله وحاربهما.

فقال: أولم تقل الشيعة: إنه أراد بقوله: أنت مني كهارون من موسى، توكيد[٣] الخلافة لقول موسى لأخيه: «اخْلُفني فِي قَومِي»[٤]؟

فقلت: بلى، وكذلك هو، إنما ذكرنا النكث لنوجب[٥] صدق علي صلوات الله عليه في كل[٦] أفعاله، واحتمال[٧] الحديث هذا وذلك.

فقال: ولم اخترت القول بإمامة علي دون غيره ممن اختارته الجماعة وهم مشيخة[٨] الإسلام والمسلمين وأصحاب الرسول

---

[١] كهارون: بمنزلة هارون، ل.

[٢] نكثت: نكث، ل.

[٣] توكيد: يؤكد، ل ه إ.

[٤] القرآن ٧:١٤٢.

[٥] لنوجب: لتوجب، ل.

[٦] كل: -، ل.

[٧] واحتمال: واحتماله، ه.

[٨] وهم مشيخة: ومشيخة، ل.

والعشيرة[1] هاجروا إلى المدينة وإلى الحبشة ومنهم من دخل مع رسول الله صلى الله عليه وآله الغار وواساه بنفسه، وكان رسول الله صلى الله عليه يقول: ما نفعني مال أحد كمال أبي بكر، مع أثَرته وتزويجه ابنته أعزّ نسائه عليه، وما من أوميت إليه إلا وسوابقه في الخير ظاهرة ومقاماته في الدين مشهورة وآثاره معلومة مفهومة. /١٠

فقلت له: ما نعرف منهم إلا الهزائم من حُنين وخيبر وذات السلاسل، وكفى حزن أبي بكر في الغار وقلقه[2] وخوفه حتى ذمه الله وخصه بالحزن وحرمه السكينة، وسوابق علي بن أبي طالب عليه السلام قبله هي السوابق والفضائل التي تذكر والمكارم التي بمثلها يفتخر، وأما تزويجه ابنته فمارية القبطية أفضل منها لأن رسول الله صلى الله عليه وآله أولد مارية ولم يولد له من صويحبات يوسف شيء مذكور، وأما خديجة رضي الله عنها فليست تقاس بهن وإنما شبّه خديجة مريم بنت عمران عليها السلام، وصهر رسول الله أفضل من الختن لأن الله يقول جل ذكره: «وَهُوَ الَّذِي خَلَقَ مِنَ المَاءِ بَشَراً فَجَعَلَهُ نَسَباً وَصِهْراً»[3]، فمن صهر رسول الله ذريته وولده وسبطاه الحسن والحسين عليهما السلام[4]، وإنما خاتنهم رسول الله صلى الله عليه وآله ليكف بأسهم ولم يولد له من إحداهن لأن ولادة الأنبياء لا تكون إلا من

---

[1] العشيرة: العشرة، ه إ.

[2] قلقه: علقه، إ.

[3] القرآن ٢٥:٥٤.

[4] عليهما السلام: + وعلى الائمة من ولد الحسين، ل إ.

الطاهرات الصالحات وهُنّ[١] مثل امرأة نوح وامرأة لوط، ولما لم تكن[٢] طاهرات حرّمهن الله الولادة من رسول الله صلى الله عليه وآله.

قال: وكيف تخرجهن من الطهارة والله يقول: «يَا نِسَاءَ النَّبِيِّ لَسْتُنَّ كَأَحَدٍ مِنَ النِسَاءِ إِنِ اتَّقَيْتُنَّ فَلا تَخْضَعْنَ بِالقَوْلِ فَيَطْمَعَ الَّذِي فِي قَلْبِهِ مَرَضٌ وَقُلْنَ قَولاً مَعْرُوفًا وَقَرْنَ فِي بُيُوتِكُنَّ وَلاَ تَبَرَّجْنَ تَبَرُّجَ / ١١ الجَاهِلِيَّةِ الأُولَى وَأَقِمْنَ الصَّلاةَ وَآتِينَ الزَّكَاةَ وَأَطِعْنَ اللهَ وَرَسُولَهَ إِنَّمَا يُرِيدُ اللهُ لِيُذْهِبَ عَنْكُم الرِجْسَ أَهْلَ البَيتِ وَيُطَهِّرَكُم تَطْهِيراً»[٣].

فقلت له: نساء النبي هاهنا أهل بيته لأنهن من بيت واحد وأزواجه من بيوتات مختلفة وسبب النكاح ينقطع وسبب أهل بيته لا ينقطع، وقد ثبت الخبر[٤] أن هذه الآية نزلت ورسول الله في بيت أم سلمة رضي الله عنها فجمع أهله في كسائه وهم هو وعلي وفاطمة وولداهما صلوات الله عليهم أجمعين وفيهم أنزل الله عز وجل في كتابه[٥] آية المباهلة «فَقُلْ تَعَالَوا نَدْعُ أَبْنَائَنَا وَأَبْنَائَكُم وَنِسَاءَنَا وَنِسَاءَكُم وَأَنْفُسَنَا وَأَنْفُسَكُم ثُمَّ نَبْتَهِلْ» الآية[٦]، فهؤلاء أهل بيت

---

[١] وهنّ: وهما، ه ل إ.

[٢] تكن: يكن، ه إ.

[٣] القرآن ٣٣: ٣٢-٣٣.

[٤] وقد ثبت الخبر: وقد ثبت، ه؛ وقد ثبت في الخبر، ل.

[٥] في كتابه: -، ل إ.

[٦] القرآن ٣: ٦١.

النبي ونساؤه ونفسه وأهل بيته ولده وخالصته والأئمة من ذريته[١] عليهم السلام، وقال رسول الله صلى الله عليه وآله ذلك اليوم: هؤلاء أهل بيتي.

فقال: هذا يحتمل العموم فيمن ذكرت وغيرهم من جميع الأمة، فالأمة هم الآل وهم البنون والبنات والنساء والأولاد.[٢]

فقلت: الحقيقة غير المجاز والإجماع أولى بنا من الاختلاف، فمن ادعى معنى العموم فهو مقرّ بفضل الخصوص واستحقاق الخاص لهذه الأسماء، ونحن منكرون له حتى يأتي بالبيان من غير أهل دعواه ممن لا يتّهم ولا هو ظنين في شهادة.

فقال: كتاب الله يشهد لهم بهذا، قال الله عز وجل: «أَخْرِجُوا آلَ لُوطٍ مِن قَرْيَتِكُم»[٣] وقال: «أدخلُوا آلَ فِرْعَونَ أَشَدَّ العَذَابِ»[٤].

فقلت: هذه حكاية من قول / ١٢ من جهل ما يقول، ولكن الله تعالى قد خصّ الآل فجعلهم الصفوة لا العامة بل هم[٥] الذرية، فقال جل من قائل: «إِنَّ اللهَ اصْطَفَى آدَمَ وَنُوحًا وَآلَ إِبْرَاهِيمَ وَآلَ عِمْرَانَ عَلَى العَالَمِينَ ذُرِّيَّةً بَعْضُهَا مِن بَعْضٍ وَاللهُ سَمِيعٌ عَلِيمٌ»[٦] وقال: «سَلامٌ

---

[١] ذريته: ذريتهم، ه إ ل.

[٢] وهم البنون والبنات والنساء والاولاد: وهم البنون والنساء والاولاد، ه؛ وهم البنون والبنات والاولاد، إ.

[٣] القرآن ٢٧:٥٦.

[٤] القرآن ٤٠:٤٦.

[٥] بل هم: باسم، إ.

[٦] القرآن ٣:٣٣-٣٤.

عَلَى إِل يَاسِينَ»[١] وقال: «رَحْمَةُ اللهِ وَبَرَكَاتُهُ عَلَيكُم أَهْلَ البَيتِ»[٢]، وقد فسّر رسول الله صلى الله عليه وآله ذلك إذ فرض له على أمته مودّة أهل بيته والصلاة على نبيه، فقالوا: كيف الصلاة عليك يا رسول الله؟ قال: قولوا: اللهم صل على محمد وعلى آل محمد وارحم محمداً وآل محمد وبارك على محمد وعلى آل محمد أفضل ما صليت ورحمت وباركت على إبراهيم وعلى آل إبراهيم. وقد أكد الله ذلك فقال جل ثناؤه: «أَمْ يَحْسُدُونَ النَاسَ عَلَى مَا آتَاهُم اللهُ مِن فَضْلِه فَقَدْ آتَينَا آلَ إِبْرَاهِيمَ الكِتَابَ وَالحِكْمَةَ وَآتَينَاهُم مُلْكًا عَظِيمًا»[٣]، فهذا خاص لا عام فقوله[٤] تعالى: «قُلْ لاَ أَسْئَلُكُم عَلَيهِ أَجْرًا إِلاَّ المَوَدَّةَ فِي القُرْبَى»[٥] وقال تعالى: «فَآتِ ذَا القُرْبَى حَقَّهُ وَالمِسْكِينَ وَابْنَ السَبِيلِ»[٦]، فجعل لهم حظاً في المغانم، فأهل السهم في المغانم هم الآل وهم القربى الذين افترض الله عز وجل مودّتهم والصلاة عليهم، وقال: «وَاتَّقُوا اللهَ الَّذِي تَسَاءَلُونَ بِهِ وَالأَرْحَامَ»[٧] فأكد الله هذا وبينه وأوضحه وقرّبه.

فقال: ما دليلك على فضل علي عليه السلام واستحقاقه لما

[١] القرآن ٣٧: ١٣٠.

[٢] القرآن ١١:٧٣.

[٣] القرآن ٤:٥٤.

[٤] فقول: وقول، ه.

[٥] القرآن ٤٢:٢٣.

[٦] القرآن ٣٠:٣٨.

[٧] القرآن ٤:١.

ذكرت من الإمامة؟

قلت: كل ما تقدم لنا فهو دليل، ولكن دليلنا الكتاب والسنة /١٣ والإجماع والعقل والنظر[١] والتنزيل والخبر، كل ذلك يشهد لمن تدبر وفكر وألقى السمع وهو شهيد[٢] وترك الهوى.

قال: أما الخبر والتنزيل فيحتمل[٣] العموم ويدعيه الخصم معك.

قلت: ينبغي لمن تكلم في الإمامة أن يكون له دين وورع يحجزه[٤] عن الدعوى فيما ليس له وأن يعلم الروايات فلا يجحدها ولا يسرقها لأصحابها. فإذا كان المناظر هكذا[٥] لم يجحد ولم يسرق ولم يدّع ما ليس له فنحن[٦] ندل عليه بما لا يدعيه غيرنا، فقد ثبت الخبر أن علياً صلوات الله عليه أخو رسول الله آخى بينه وبينه إذ[٧] آخى بين أصحابه مرتين وقال له: أنت يا علي أخي وأنت مني بمنزلة هارون من موسى، وقوله فيه: من كنت مولاه فعلي مولاه، ودعا له

---

[١] والنظر: -، ل.

[٢] وهو شهيد: -، إ.

[٣] فيحتمل: فيحتمله، ه.

[٤] يحجزه : يحجره، إ.

[٥] هكذا: هذا، ل إ.

[٦] فنحن: ونحن، ه إ ل.

[٧] اذ: اذا، ه ل إ.

ولحزبه ولعن[1] من خذله وحاربه وأخرج جميع أصحابه من جواره وترك علياً عليه السلام وحده لما[2] أخرج مشركي قريش من جوار الحرم. كذلك أخرج الجميع من جواره وترك عليًا عليه السلام وحده معه[3]، وكفى ما في سورة: هل أتى على الإنسان من ذكره ووعد الله له بالجنة وقوله تعالى: «إِنَّمَا وَلِيُّكُمُ اللهُ وَرَسُولُهُ وَالَّذِينَ آمَنُوا الَّذِينَ يُقِيمُونَ الصَّلاَةَ وَيُؤْتُونَ الزَّكَاةَ وَهُم رَاكِعُونَ»[4]، وآية النجوى قوله تعالى: «يَا أَيُّهَا الَّذِينَ آمَنُوا إِذَا نَاجَيْتُمُ الرَّسُولَ فَقَدِّمُوا بَيْنَ يَدَي نَجْوَاكُم صَدَقَةً»[5]. فلم يفعل هذا غير علي[6] عليه السلام وحده، وقوله سبحانه: «أَجَعَلْتُم سِقَايَةَ الحَاجِّ وَعِمَارَةَ المَسْجِدِ الحَرَامِ كَمَنْ آمَنَ بِالله وَاليَوْمِ الآخِرِ وَ / ١٤ جَاهَدَ فِي سَبِيلِ الله لاَ يَسْتَوُونَ عِندَ الله وَاللهُ لا يَهْدِي القَوْمَ الظَّالِمِينَ»[7] الآية[8] كلها إلى آخرها نزلت في علي عليه السلام والعباس وشيبة، فحكم الله عز وجل لعلي صلوات الله عليه بالفضل عليهما، وآية المباهلة، كل هذا في القرآن وأمثاله ففي علي

---

[1] لعن: دعى، ه.

[2] لما: كما، ه إ ل.

[3] وحده معه: معه وحده، ل إ.

[4] القرآن ٥:٥٥.

[5] القرآن ٥٨:١٢.

[6] علي: + بن أبي طالب، ل.

[7] القرآن ٩:١٩.

[8] الاية: الايات، ه إ ل.

صلوات الله عليه أنزلت[١] وجميع المخالفين مقرّون له بهذا غير منكرين والحمد لله رب العالمين. وأما المضمرات الغامضات والأمثال والكنايات فكثير لا يحصى مثل قول رسول الله صلى الله عليه وآله فيه: علي فيكم كسفينة نوح من ركبها نجا ومن تخلف عنها غرق وهلك، وقوله صلى الله عليه وآله: إنّي تارك فيكم الثقلَين ما إن تمسكتم بهما لن تضلّوا كتاب الله وعترتي أهل بيتي، وقوله تعالى: «وَجَعَلَهَا كَلِمَةً بَاقِيَةً فِي عَقِبِهِ»[٢]. فكل هذا واضح مشهور مع ما قد انفرد به علي صلوات الله عليه من السوابق والعلم والجهاد والقربى من رسول الله صلى الله عليه وآله، فاجتمع فيه عليه السلام كل الفضائل التي بها يستحق الإمامة لقربه من الله عز وجل وأنه المفترض الطاعة المقْرون برسول الله صلى الله عليه وآله ‹في› قوله تعالى: «أَطِيعُوا اللهَ وَأَطِيعُوا الرَّسُولَ وَأُولِي الأَمْرِ مِنكُم»[٣]، فاجتمع في علي عليه السلام فضل كل ذي فضل واختصه الله عز وجل بما ليس فيهم، فله طهارة النشأة[٤] وفضل العلم والقربى، وفي علي عليه السلام أنزل الله: «أَفَمَن كَانَ مُؤْمِنًا كَمَن كَانَ فَاسِقًا لاَ يَسْتَوُونَ»،[٥] فلا يماثل علي عليه السلام ولا يشبه /[١٥] بغيره ممن آمن بعده وسُمّي قبل إيمانه فاسقًا، وفيه وفي أصحابه أنزل الله سبحانه: «رِجَالٌ صَدَقُوا مَا عَاهَدُوا

---

[١] انزلت: انزل، ل إ.

[٢] القرآن ٤٣:٢٨.

[٣] القرآن ٤:٥٩.

[٤] النشأة: المنشأة، ه.

[٥] القرآن ٣٢:١٨.

اللهَ عَلَيهِ فَمِنهُم مَن قَضَى نَحْبَهُ وَمِنهُم مَن يَنْتَظِرُ وَمَا بَدَّلُوا تَبْدِيلاً »[١]، وقد أجمعوا أن هذه الآية أنزلت في علي عليه السلام وحمزة وعبيدة ابن الحارث بن المطلب[٢] وجعفر بن أبي طالب عليهم السلام.

فقال لي: إسلام علي عليه السلام عند خصمائك كإسلام الطفل الذي لا يعتقد.

فقلت: إسلام علي عليه السلام بدعوة من رسول الله صلى الله عليه وآله بأمر الله عز وجل ولم يكن طفلاً غير معتقد، بل كان ابن ثلاث عشرة[٣] سنة وقد يولد للغلام ابن أحد عشرة سنة[٤] كما قد تبلغ المرأة ابنة عشر سنين، وقد أمر رسول الله صلى الله عليه وآله بتعليم الصبيان الصلاة[٥] أبناء ست سنين وخمس ويؤدبون عليها أبناء سبع، فعلي عليه السلام قد جاز هذه الحدود، ولم يكن رسول الله صلى الله عليه وآله ممن يغرر بنفسه[٦] ويغرر بدين الله ويطلع عليه من لا يعتقد شيئًا، وقد أجمعوا أن رسول الله صلى الله عليه وآله، دخل معه الشعب ومعهما[٧] خديجة فأقاموا فيه ثلاث سنين وسبعة أشهر يأكلون

---

[١] القرآن ٣٣:٢٣.

[٢] المطلب: عبد المطلب، ه إ ل.

[٣] ثلاث عشرة: ثلاثة عشر، إ ل.

[٤] ابن احد عشرة سنة: ابن احدى عشر سنة، ه؛ ابن احد عشرة، ل إ.

[٥] الصلاة: -، ه.

[٦] ممن يغرر بنفسه: غرر بنفسه، إ.

[٧] معهما: معه، ل ه.

الفثّ والنوى ويسحقون العظام ويشقّونها[1]، فلو كان علي عليه السلام غير معتقد لخرج من الضيق إلى السعة ولحق بأعمامه وقرابته، وأيضًا فلم يرو أحد أن رسول الله صلى الله عليه وآله دعا أحداً من صبيان بني هاشم ولا غيرهم، وفي هذا دليل أن عليًا عليه السلام بقية الله في أرضه بعد محمد صلى الله عليه وآله وأن[2] منه ذرية رسول /١٦ الله صلى الله عليه وآله وأنه دعوة إبراهيم عليه السلام، وكل ما قلل الجهلة[3] سببه كان ذلك أزيد في فضله.

فقال: وكيف يكون ذلك، وإنما ينتفع بإسلام الكامل الذي يؤثر ما دخل فيه على ما خرج منه بحجة بَانَ له برهانها أو آية ثبتت[4] في إدراكه وصح بيانها له؟

فقلت: بل الكامل يمكن دخوله فرقًا وخوفًا من الذل والغلبة ويكون إسلامه للدنيا والترؤس على أهلها والتمكن مع القائم عليهم فيها، والصغير لا يحتمل دخوله في الإسلام من هذه الوجوه شيئًا ولا سيما علي بن أبي طالب خاصة ‹و›أبوه ناصر رسول الله والقائم له[5] والذابّ عنه، فهو حبيب رسول الله وصفوته وخاصته وتربيته ولذلك اتّخذه وزيراً ووصيًا وخصّه بأخوته وأسلم إليه ولاء أمته من بعده واستخلفه ورضيه واتّخذه وكيلاً ووليًا، ومع هذا فإنّ فضل إسلام

---

[1] يشقونها: يسقونها، ل؛ يستقونها، ه؛ إ، غير واضح.

[2] وان: وانه، ل.

[3] قلل الجهلة: قلد الله لجهالة، ل.

[4] ثبتت: تثبت، ل؛ ثبت، إ.

[5] له: -، ل إ.

الصغير مؤكد في كتاب الله، فمن ذلك إبراهيم اهتدى بالاستدلال وهو ابن ثلاث عشرة[١] سنة و«قَالَ لاَ أُحِبُّ الآفِلِينَ»[٢] وكان الافول عنده دليلاً على الحدث وأن الخالق سبحانه غير آفل ولا زائل ولا منتقل ولا ذو مكان، وكذلك رغب إبراهيم[٣] عليه السلام في إسلام ولده وتعريفهم الإيمان[٤] قبل البلوغ وقبل أن يعرفوا الأصنام ويعبدوا الأوثان، وتأكد ذلك عند إبراهيم عليه السلام بقول الله وتبيينه في قوله لا شريك له: «وَإِذِ ابْتَلَى إِبْرَاهِيمَ رَبُّهُ بِكَلِمَاتٍ فَأَتَمَّهُنَّ / ١٧ قَالَ إِنِّي جَاعِلُكَ لِلنَّاسِ إِمَامًا قَالَ وَمِن ذُرِّيَّتِي قَالَ لا يَنَالُ عَهْدِي الظَّالِمِينَ»[٥]، فعند ذلك رغب إبراهيم عليه السلام وقال: «وَاجْنُبْنِي وَبَنِيَّ أَنْ نَعْبُدَ الأَصْنَامَ»[٦] وقال: «رَبِّ هَبْ لِي مِنَ الصَّالِحِينَ»، [٧] فأعلم الله عز وجل إبراهيم أن الإمامة لا يرثها من عقد شركًا ولا من بلغ مشركاً وإن آمن وأسلم ولا يرث الإمامة إلا طاهر المنشأ، وكذلك موسى عليه السلام تمّ طهره في ولادته حتى حرم عليه رضاع الفواجر ليتمّ طهره في رضاعه وولادته، وكذلك عيسى عليه السلام في طهر منشأه، وكذلك محمد صلى الله عليه وآله وعلي عليه السلام بعده،

[١] ثلاث عشرة: ثلاث عشر، ه؛ ثلاثة عشر، ل إ.

[٢] القرآن ٦:٧٦.

[٣] ابراهيم: -، ل.

[٤] تعريفهم الايمان: تعريفهم الاسلام، ل؛ يعرفهم الايمان، إ.

[٥] القرآن ٢:١٢٤.

[٦] القرآن ١٤:٣٥.

[٧] القرآن ٣٧:١٠٠.

ومن تمام طهر علي عليه السلام أن جدته وجدة محمد واحدة أم عبد الله أبي محمد وأم[١] أبي طالب واحدة، فهما شقيقان.

قال: يأبى القرآن ما ذكرت، قد قال الله في محمد صلى الله عليه وآله: «وَوَجَدَكَ ضَالاً فَهَدَى»[٢] وقال: «وَإِذْ قَالَ إِبْرَاهِيمُ لِأَبِيهِ وَقَومِهِ إِنَّنِي بَرَاءٌ مِمَّا تَعْبُدُونَ»[٣]، وقال في أم موسى: «لَولاَ أَنْ رَبَطْنَا عَلَى قَلْبِهَا لِتَكُونَ مِنَ المُؤْمِنِينَ»[٤]، و«قَالَ إِبْرَاهِيمُ لِأَبِيهِ آزَرَ أَتَتَّخِذُ أَصْنَامًا آلِهَةً»[٥].

فقلت: الضلال ينقسم على وجوه منها النسيان كما قال الله عز وجل: «أَنْ تَضِلَّ إِحْدَاهُمَا فَتُذَكِّرَ إِحْدَاهُمَا الأُخْرَى»[٦]، وقد يكون ضل في شيء أو في طريق كما قال موسى: «عَسَى رَبِّي أَنْ يَهْدِيَنِي سَوَاءَ السَّبِيلِ»[٧]، وقد يكون الضلال حبًا وشوقًا كما قال ولد يعقوب: «إِنَّكَ لَفِي ضَلالِكَ القَدِيمِ»[٨] يريدون حبه وشوقه إلى يوسف، وكذلك الأبوة منها أبوة التربية وأبوة الرئاسة وأبوة التعليم، و /١٨ كذلك أم

---

[١] وام: ام، ه إ.

[٢] القرآن ٩٣:٧.

[٣] القرآن ٤٣:٢٦.

[٤] القرآن ٢٨:١٠.

[٥] القرآن ٦:٧٤.

[٦] القرآن ٢:٢٨٢.

[٧] القرآن ٢٨:٢٢.

[٨] القرآن ١٢:٩٥.

موسى لما رأت ولدها كادت تدل عليه فثبتها الله تعالى ليزيدها إيمانًا بموسى على إيمانها بشريعة إبراهيم، ولو أبدت حزنها عليه لدلت عليه قوم فرعون فأيّدها الله، وإذا احتمل الشيء[١] وجهين وجب أن يضاف[٢] إلى أولياء الله أحسنهما وينزّهوا[٣] عن أقبح تلك الوجوه.

فأما دلائل العقل والنظر فحاجة الخلق إلى من يسوسهم ويتولى أمرهم ويقيم حجهم وأعيادهم وجُمعهم ويقبض زكاتهم ويقمع[٤] ظالمهم وينصف مظلومهم، وقد أكد الله ذلك فقال: «خُذْ مِن أَمْوَالِهِم صَدَقَةً تُطَهِّرُهُم وَتُزَكِّيهِم بِهَا»[٥]، وقال: «وَلَوْ أَنَّهُم إِذْ ظَلَمُوا أَنْفُسَهُم جَاءُوكَ فَاسْتَغْفَرُوا اللهَ وَاسْتَغْفَرَ لَهُمُ الرَسُولُ لَوَجَدُوا اللهَ تَوَّابًا رَحِيمًا»[٦]، فلما كانت الفرائض دائمة بعد رسول الله صلى الله عليه وآله وجب دوام المستحفظين والموكلين بأمر الأنبياء عن الله تعالى، فبهم تقوم الصلاة وبهم[٧] يقيمون الفرائض والحج، وقال الله عز وجل عن إبراهيم عليه السلام: «رَبَّنَا[٨] إِنِّي أَسْكَنْتُ مِن ذُرِّيَّتِي بِوَادٍ غَيْرِ

---

[١] الشيء: لشيء، ل.

[٢] يضاف: نضيف، ه إ؛ تضيف، ل.

[٣] احسنهما وينزهوا: احسنها ويتنزهوا، ل.

[٤] يقمع: يقنع، ه؛ ينقمع، ل.

[٥] القرآن ٩:١٠٣.

[٦] القرآن ٤:٦٤.

[٧] فبهم ... وبهم: فبهم ... وهم، ل؛ فيهم ... وهم، ه؛ إ غير واضح.

[٨] ربنا: -، ل إ.

ذِي زَرْعٍ عِنْدَ بَيْتِكَ الْمُحَرَّمِ رَبَّنَا لِيُقِيمُوا الصَّلاةَ فَاجْعَلْ أَفْئِدَةً مِنَ النَّاسِ تَهْوِي إِلَيهِم»[١]، فبهم يتمّ الحج فمن عرفهم تمّ حجه. ودليل آخر أن الله عز وجل بدأ الخلق بخليفة[٢] قبل خلق[٣] النوع الذي هم منه[٤] لعلمه بحاجتهم إلى من يسوسهم كما بدأ بخلق اللبن في الضرع قبل خروج الجنين لعلمه بحاجته إلى الغذاء قبل خلقه، وقال الله سبحانه: «كَمَا بَدَأَكُم تَعُودُونَ فَرِيقًا هَدَى / [١٩] وَفَرِيقًا حَقَّ عَلَيهِمُ الضَّلالَةُ إِنَّهُمُ اتَّخَذُوا الشَّيَاطِينَ أَولِيَاءَ مِن دُونِ اللهِ»[٥]. فقد بدأ[٦] الله الخلق بخليفته وأوجب أنه يعيد فيهم مثله حتى يرث الأرض ومن عليها، وقال تعالى: «كَمَا بَدَأْنَا أَوَّلَ خَلْقٍ نُعِيدُهُ وَعْداً عَلَيْنَا إِنَّا كُنَّا فَاعِلِينَ وَلَقَدْ كَتَبْنَا فِي الزَّبُورِ مِن بَعْدِ الذِّكْرِ أَنَّ الأَرْضَ يَرِثُهَا عِبَادِيَ الصَّالِحُونَ»[٧]، فجعل الله الأرض[٨] ميراثاً لأوليائه يعيد فيها بعد كل إمام إماماً، فمن اهتدى إلى أولياء الله فقد فاز ومن اتّخذ

---

[١] القرآن ١٤:٣٧.

[٢] بخليفة: بخليفته، إ.

[٣] خلق: –، ه.

[٤] منه: فيه، ل إ.

[٥] القرآن ٧:٢٩–٣٠.

[٦] بدأ: ابدا، إ.

[٧] القرآن ٢١:١٠٤–١٠٥.

[٨] الارض: –، ل.

«الشَّيْطَانَ وَلِيّاً»[١] «فَسَاءَ قَرِينًا»[٢].

فقال: كل ما ذكرت يدل على الحاجة إلى الإمام، ولكن ما دليلك عليه باسمه وصفته ونسبه ومكانته[٣]؟ ولو كان هكذا لم تقع الشكوك فيه واتّفق الجميع عليه.

فقلت: إن الله تعالى أحب من العباد[٤] أن يكتسبوا المعرفة ويستدلوا ليُؤْجَروا[٥] «وَلَوْ شَاءَ اللهُ لَآمَنَ مَن فِي الأَرْضِ كُلُّهُم جَمِيعًا»[٦] ولكن ليبتليهم ويختبرهم بالامتحان فيميز[٧] الخبيث من الطيب، فالاختبار والاكتساب بالامتحان يبدي جوهر[٨] الإنسان كما تخرج النار خبث الذهب والفضة[٩]، والمحنة إكسير[١٠] الإنسان كالنار التي بها تمتحن المعادن، فالعاقل يستدل بالأصل على الفرع، فلما أجمعنا على النبي صلى الله عليه وآله وجب أن نطلب الإمام بعد

---

[١] القرآن ٤:١١٩.

[٢] القرآن ٤:٣٨: «من يكن الشيطان له قرينا فساء قرينا».

[٣] مكانته: مكانه، ه.

[٤] العباد: العبادات، إ.

[٥] ليؤجروا: ليرجبوا، إ؛ ليوجبوا، ل.

[٦] القرآن ١٠:٩٩.

[٧] فيميز: فميز، إ ه ل.

[٨] جوهر: جواهر، ه.

[٩] والفضة: -، ل.

[١٠] اكسير: كير، ل إ.

النبي في معدن[١] ذلك النبي ونستدل عليه من مكانه وفي نسله وفي ولده وأقرب الناس إليه وأكثرهم فائدة. فلو أراد الخلق الاستدلال لدلهم[٢] الله تعالى، مع أن النبي صلى الله عليه وآله قدم وأشار وضرب / ٢٠ الأمثال ثم أفصح وشرح وأوضح، ولكن الأمة كذّبت الوصي وطعنت على النبي عليهما السلام وأرادت الترؤّس على أهل معدن الوحي، ففرّت من جوار رسول الله صلى الله عليه وآله بعد موته، وثوّروا الطغام والعوام ودخلوا سقيفة بني ساعدة وتركوا بيت[٣] الوحي ومهبط الملائكة ومجمع القرآن، ولو اجتمعوا عند جثة رسول الله وعند قبره واجتمعوا مع عم النبي صلوات الله عليه وابن عمه وصهره وولده وأزواجه وبناته ومع عبّاد الأمة وزهاد[٤] الملة مثل سلمان والمقداد[٥] وأبي ذر وعمار ورغبوا إلى الله تعالى في توفيقهم[٦] لاختيار من يوكلونه[٧] إن كانوا كما زعموا لم يوص رسول الله[٨]،

---

[١] معدن: معادن، ه.

[٢] لدلهم: لديهم، ل.

[٣] بيت: بيوت، إ ه.

[٤] زهاد: زهاده، إ.

[٥] المقداد: مقداد، ل.

[٦] توفيقهم: توقيفهم، ه.

[٧] يوكلونه: يوكلوه، إ ه ل.

[٨] ان كانوا كما زعموا لم يوص رسول الله: -، ل.

وإن كان رسول الله صلى الله عليه وآله قد أوصى أو أشار أو آخى[١] رجلاً منهم فيجب تقليده والتسليم إليه، ولكنهم استفرصوا شغل بني هاشم وحزن علي عليه السلام واهتمامهم[٢] برسول الله، فاجتمعوا طعنًا على رسول الله ودغلاً لأهل بيته، وأكثر العجب شغل الأبعدين من النبي صلى الله عليه دون الاقربين بهذا، فلو كان النبي صلى الله عليه أمرهم بهذا دون أهل بيته لوجب أن يواروا جنازة رسول الله صلى الله عليه وآله ويظهروا الحزن عليه يومًا واحداً ثم يجتمعوا مع أهل بيته في الاختيار، ولكنهم ضلّوا «وَأَضَلُّوا كَثِيراً وَضَلُّوا عَن سَوَاءِ السَّبِيلِ»[٣]، ولو شئنا أن ندعي اسم الإمام بعد محمد صلى الله عليه وآله لجاز.

قال: وكيف ذلك؟

فقلت: قال الله عز وجل: «أَفَمَن كَانَ عَلَى بَيِّنَةٍ مِن رَبِّهِ وَيَتْلُوهُ شَاهِدٌ مِنهُ»[٤]، يريد من أهل بيته، /٢١ وليس من أهل بيته حرّ إلا علي عليه السلام وحده لأن رسول الله صلى الله عليه وآله قال: لا يأم عبد حراً، وقال عليه السلام: الخلافة محرمة على الطلقاء وأبناء الطلقاء، وقال الله عز وجل: «أَنْزَلَ[٥] اللهُ إِلَيكُم ذِكْراً رَسُولاً يَتْلُوا

[١] او آخى: او واخى، ل إ.

[٢] اهتمامهم: اهمامهم، إ.

[٣] القرآن ٥:٧٧.

[٤] القرآن ١١:١٧.

[٥] أنزل: وأنزل، إ ل ه.

عَلَيكُم آيَاتِ اللهِ مُبَيِّنَاتٍ»[1]، فسمى رسوله محمداً صلى الله عليه وآله ذكراً، ثم قال سبحانه: «فَاسْأَلُوا أَهْلَ الذِّكْرِ إِنْ كُنْتُم لاَ تَعْلَمُونَ»[2]، فليس في آل محمد من يسأل غير علي عليه السلام وحده، وقال تعالى: «هَلْ يَسْتَوِي الَّذِينَ يَعْلَمُونَ وَالَّذِينَ لاَ يَعْلَمُونَ»[3]، فأمر أيضًا بسؤال أهل العلم وعلي صلوات الله عليه هو المراد بعد محمد صلى الله عليه وآله، وقال تعالى: «ثُمَّ أَوْرَثْنَا الكِتَابَ الَّذِينَ اصْطَفَيْنَا مِن عِبَادِنَا»،[4] فعلي صلوات الله عليه هو العالم الوارث[5]، وأكثر الدين كناية وأمثال وهذا شرح وإيضاح، ولنا أن نقول: إن علي بن أبي طالب هو المنصوص عليه بالإمامة بعد رسول الله صلى الله عليه وآله بقول الله تعالى: «وَإِنَّهُ فِي أُمِّ الكِتَابِ لَدَينَا لَعَلِيٌّ حَكِيمٌ»[6] وبقوله: «وَجَعَلْنَا لَهُم لِسَانَ صِدْقٍ عَلِيّاً»[7] وقوله: «هَذَا صِرَاطٌ عَلِيٌّ مُسْتَقِيمٌ»[8]، فالإشارة تغني اللبيب عن الإيضاح والتفسير.

---

[1] القرآن ٦٥: ١٠-١١.

[2] القرآن ١٦:٤٣.

[3] القرآن ٣٩:٩.

[4] القرآن ٣٥:٣٢.

[5] الوارث: -، ل.

[6] القرآن ٤٣:٤.

[7] القرآن ١٩: ٥٠.

[8] القرآن ١٥:٤١.

قال: أهل اللغة يمنعونك من هذا ويردّونك عما أردت، ولا يجيز[١] الإعراب ما زعمت في علي عليه السلام أنه عليّاً وأنّه علي حكيم، وقد كان في أهل البيت علماء كملاء منهم عبد الله بن عباس وغيره.

فقلت: أما الطلقاء وأبناؤهم فلا سهم لهم في الإمامة ولا حظ ولا سابقة في الإسلام ولا جهاد في سبيل الله، وكل ذلك ففي علي صلوات الله عليه اجتمع، والإعراب /٢٢ فما أعرب عن الحق، والرفع والخفض ما وضع مواضعه من صواب المعاني في مراد الله عز وجل، فالرفع لأوليائه[٢] والخفض لأعدائه، وهؤلاء أعربوا حروف اللسان بزعمهم وجهلوا مراد الله عز وجل في المعاني والصروف والأمثال، فلله[٣] عز وجل كنايات ورموز وإشارات وما يعقلها إلا العالمون.

فتبسّم وأشار إلى أبي موسى وأبي زاكي، واستأذنه بدر الخادم لأصحابنا الذين دعاهم قبلي وهم المروذي وولده أحمد وإسحاق ابن أبي المنهال وأبو حبيب بن رشيد، فلم يأذن لهم وقال: يصبرون. ثم قال: فمن بعد علي بن أبي طالب؟

قلت: ولده الحسن بن علي.

قال: ثم من؟

قلت: الحسين بن علي.

قال: ثم من؟

---

[١] يجيز: يجيزوا، ل.

[٢] لاوليائه: لاولياء الله، ل.

[٣] فلله: فان لله، ل.

قلت: علي بن الحسين زين العابدين.

قال: ولم أخرجتها عن الإخوة ورددتها إلى ابن الأخ؟

قلت: لأن القربى من رسول الله صلى الله عليه وآله أحد أركان الإمامة، ومحمد بن الحنفية[١] بعيد من رسول الله، وعلي بن الحسين ابن فاطمة بنت رسول الله، وقد ثبت الخبر عن رسول الله أنه أشار إلى الحسين عليه السلام وقال له: من نسلك القائم المهدي، وأخبر جابر[٢] بن عبد الله الأنصاري أنه يدرك رابع الأئمة من ولده وأمره أن يقرأه[٣] منه السلام ويقول له: أنت الباقر الذي يبقر العلم بقراً.

فقال: وقد ثبت عن علي عليه السلام أنه قال: محمد ولدي حقًا، وأعطاه اللواء يوم صِفين ويوم الجمل وغير ذلك من سرائره، وكان يحاليه[٤] ويوعز[٥] إليه ما لا يفعله / [٢٣] بغيره.

فقلت: علي بن الحسين عليه السلام جمع العلم كله والزهد كله وهو لحمة رسول الله، وقد حرم الله على رسوله ما[٦] مسّه[٧] علي بن الحسين من النساء، فرسول الله جده والله يقول وهو أصدق القائلين

---

[١] الحنفية: الحنيفة، ه إ؛ حنيفة، ل.

[٢] جابر: لجابر، ه ل إ.

[٣] يقرأه: يقرأ، ل.

[٤] يحاليه: يخاليه، ه إ ل.

[٥] يوعز: يوزع، ل.

[٦] ما: وما، ل إ(؟).

[٧] مسه: منه، ل إ.

وأحكم الحاكمين: «وَأولُو الأرْحَامِ بَعْضُهُم أولَى بِبَعْضٍ»[١] وقال: «فَأتِ ذَا القُرْبَى حَقَّهُ»[٢] وقد سلّم محمد بن علي إلى علي بن الحسين وبرئ[٣] إليه وكان يأتمر بأمره، وإنما كان محمد بن الحنفية[٤] ستراً لعلي بن الحسين عليه السلام، فلما بلغ سلم إليه.

قال: ثم من؟

قلت: محمد بن علي باقر العلم.

قال: وما بال زيد وهو الأكبر وهو المجاهد في سبيل الله والباذل نفسه وليس من جاهد وظاهر كمن ستر[٥] نفسه وأرخى ستره؟

قلت: زيد برئ بنفسه ولم يدّع شيئًا وكان مقراً لأخيه محمد بن علي عليه السلام، وقد ثبت عن جعفر بن محمد صلوات الله عليه أنه قال: رحم الله عمي زيداً فلو ظفر لسلّم الأمر إلينا، وقد أخبر محمد بن علي عليه السلام لزيد أخيه أنه المقتول بالكوفة المصلوب بالكناسة وقال له يوم ودعه: يا أخي إني لأجد رائحة دم الشهادة عليك، فقال له: قد فرغ الله مما يكون، وإنما رأى زيد رؤيا تكررت عليه وقائل يقول له: يا زيد قم على هشام الأحول فإنه أفضل لك من العبادة، فلما تكرر ذلك عليه قام.

فقال: قد أراك قد ثبت لك له القيام بأمر الله، فهو الإمام.

---

[١] القرآن ٨:٧٥ و ٣٣:٦.

[٢] القرآن ٣٠:٣٨.

[٣] برئ: يرى، ه ل إ.

[٤] الحنفية: الحنيفة، ه إ ل.

[٥] ستر: سر، ه ل إ.

فقلت: ليست[١] الإمامة بالأحلام والأماني وليس من أمر بشيء في منامه يجب له / [٢٤] بذلك كل شيء، وزيد فلم يدع الإمامة بل كان لأخيه مقراً معظمًا.

قال: فلو ادعى أكان[٢] إمامًا؟

فقلت: لو ادعى لبطلت دعواه إن كذبه محمد بن علي صلوات الله عليه لأن الآية مع محمد بن علي عليه السلام ومعه السكينة والعلم.

فقال: وما آية الإمام؟

قلت: لكل إمام آية يبين بها صدقه وكذب غيره من المدعين ولا يعطي الله عز وجل آياته الكاذبين ولا بد من معجز[٣] مع كل إمام، والعلم أفضل المعجزات كما أن القرآن أعجب المعجزات وأعجز الآيات، وكان زيد يقول: مَن أراد الجهاد فإليّ ومن أراد العلم فإلى ابن أخي، يعني جعفر بن محمد الصادق صلوات الله عليه، وقد أطعم النبي صلى الله عليه وآله الجماعة من طعام لا يشبع الواحد ودعا الشجرة إليه فأقبلت إليه وانفجر الماء من بين أنامله وانشقّ القمر له وغير ذلك من المعجزات التي لا يمكن من عند غير الله.

فقال: في هذا كلام يطول، ولكن من بعد محمد؟

قلت: جعفر بن محمد.

قال: ثم من؟

---

[١] ليست: ليس، ه إ.

[٢] اكان: كان، ه.

[٣] معجز: معجزة، ل.

قلت: ههنا وقفت وانتهى لي اليقين والمعرفة، وإنما رغبت عندك في معرفة من بعد جعفر عليه السلام.

قال: فإن أصحابك الذين دعوناهم البارحة قد نصّوا[١] الأئمة بعد جعفر إلى موسى ولده ثم في ولده إلى محمد بن الحسن.

فقلت: نعلم[٢] ذلك وقلتُ بقولهم، ثم فارقتهم منذ أربع سنين وهم يعلمون ذلك.

فقال: ولِمَ اخترت قول الواقفة؟

قلت: رأيت الشيعة اجتمعت بعد اختلافها على جعفر وافترقت / ٢٥ بعد جعفر في ولده، فقالت كل فرقة بأحدهم للذي[٣] ظهر من فضله، فرأيت أن أقف على ما أجمعوا[٤] عليه وأطلب حقيقة ذلك.

فقال: فتكلم في اختلافهم. فقام أبو موسى فاستعفى[٥] لي وسأله قضاء حاجتي، فقال: دعني أكلمه، حاجته مقضية، لي[٦] معك قريب ثماني عشر سنة ما ناظرتُ أحداً وهذا عنده[٧] ما نريد، دعني نناظره، فإنّ هذا إذا ثبت لكم أنقذ الله به خلقًا كثيراً، ثم قال لي:

---

[١] نصوا: نصبوا، ل.

[٢] نعلم: تعلم، إ ه ل.

[٣] للذي: الذي، ه إ.

[٤] اجمعوا: اجتمعوا، ل.

[٥] فاستعفى: فاستغفر، ل.

[٦] لي: -، ل.

[٧] عنده: -، إ.

اذكر اختلافهم.

فقلت: بلا حرج عليّ؟

فقال: ما عليك حرج، تكلم.

قلت: اختلفت الشيعة بعد جعفر صلوات الله عليه على أربع فرق، فمنهم من قال بإمامة عبد الله بن جعفر وقالوا: هو أكبر[١] ولده وبه كني جعفر أبا عبد الله وهو غاسل أبيه عند موته، وهم الفطحية، كان عبد الله أفطح الرأس وكان إخوته يعززونه ويوقرونه ويعظمونه، فلما مات عبد الله ردوها إلى موسى ثم نقلوها من أخ إلى أخ. وقد قالت طائفة بإمامة إسماعيل وهو حي عندهم إلى اليوم. ومنهم من أثبت موته في حياة جعفر. ومنهم من أنكر موته و<قال>: إن جعفراً[٢] أظهر موته ستراً عليه وإنه دفن ساجة[٣] وقال لهم: هذا إسماعيل، وصلى عليه ودفنه. ومنهم من قال: موسى إمام ناطق وإسماعيل إمام صامت وطاعتهما جميعًا فرض. ومنهم من قال: رجعت الإمامة في محمد بن إسماعيل في حياة جعفر وإن جعفراً أشار / ٢٦ إلى[٤] ولد إسماعيل عليه السلام[٥]. ومنهم من قال: لكل إمام واسطة فإذا جهل الإمام فطاعة الواسطة فريضة، فقالت فرقة بإمامة

---

[١] هو اكبر: هو الاكبر اكبر، إ.

[٢] جعفرا: جعفر، ه ل إ.

[٣] ساجة: ساحة، إ؛ شباهته، ل.

[٤] الى: والى، ه ل.

[٥] والى ولد اسماعيل عليهما السلام: والى ولد اسماعيل ع م، ه؛ والى ولده اسماعيل ع م، ل؛ الى ولد اسماعيل، إ.

المبارك بن علي العبدي وكان بابًا لإسماعيل وأن جعفراً أمر المبارك أن يتخذ دار هجرة بخراسان بين كابُل إلى قَندهار، فلما مات المبارك أوصى إلى ابنه محمد بن المبارك، فرجع أكثر الشيعة عن ولد المبارك وقالوا بإمامة إسماعيل وحده وأنه حي. وقالت طائفة: إنه مات وإن الله يحييه ويرده إلى الدنيا فيملأها عدلاً، وقالوا: لا يضرّ المؤمن فقد الإمام إذا عرف حقوق الأئمة ووقف على علم الإمام. ومنهم من قال: محمد بن إسماعيل حي وعبد الله بن ميمون بن مسلم بن عقيل بابه. و‹قال غيرهم›: إن محمداً مات وصارت[١] الإمامة إلى عبد الله بن ميمون من عبد الله بن جعفر وإن عبد الله لم يعقب فسلم[٢] الأمر إلى بابه عبد الله بن ميمون. وجمهور الشيعة أثبتت الإمامة في موسى ثم[٣] في ولده علي بن موسى الرضى وهو الذي قتله المأمون بعد أن صاهره وزوجه[٤] ابنته، ثم في ولده[٥] محمد بن علي ثم في الحسن بن محمد ثم في محمد بن الحسن، وهم الواصلة الاثنا عشرية، وزعموا أن الأئمة[٦] اثنا عشر إمامًا، وإنما تنتقل من والد إلى ولد ولا ترجع[٧] إلى الإخوة، وأن الإمامة لم تقرّ في الإخوة من بعد الحسن والحسين.

---

[١] صارت: دارت، ه إ.

[٢] فسلم: فاسلم، ل إ.

[٣] ثم: –، إ.

[٤] زوجه: ازوجه، إ.

[٥] في ولده: ولده، ه؛ في ولد، إ.

[٦] الائمة: الامامة، ه ل.

[٧] ترجع: يرجع، ه.

ومنهم من ردّها إلى محمد بن جعفر وأنّ محمداً لم يعقب. / ٢٧ ومنهم من زعم أن موسى حي، وهم القطعية (كذا).

فقال: أليس تزعم الموسائية أن الحسن توفي وإنما ترك أمة[١] حُبلَى، فولد[٢] له بعده محمد بن الحسن هذا الذي يزعمون؟

قلت: كذلك يقولون.

فقال: فكيف يخرج الإمام وتبقى الدنيا هملاً[٣] بلا إمام؟

قلت: يقولون بالتفويض إلى[٤] الأبواب حتى يولد الإمام ويبلغ كما كان محمد بن الحنفية بابًا لعلي بن الحسين صلوات الله عليه حتى بلغ، وكذلك كان يوشع بن نون[٥] ستراً لولد هارون.

فقال: لا يشبه الحبل بالولد الغير البالغ لأن الحبل قد يتلاشى ويضمحل أو يموت أو يكون أنثى، وعلي بن الحسين عليه السلام موجود وكذلك ولد هارون[٦]، والحبل معدوم وليس المعدوم كالموجود، وقد يبلغ الغلام ابن إحدى عشرة[٧] سنة كما تبلغ المرأة ابنة عشر

---

[١] امة: امته، ل.

[٢] فولد: فولدت، ل.

[٣] هملا: مهملا، ل.

[٤] الى: في، ه.

[٥] نون: النون، ه.

[٦] وكذلك ولد هارون: وولد هارون كذلك، ل إ.

[٧] احدى عشرة: احد عشر، ل؛ احدى عشر، ه.

سنين[1]، وقد كان علي بن الحسين عليه السلام حينئذ ابن ثلاث عشرة سنة.

قلت: فإنهم قد أثبتوا ولادته ووقفوا على مولده واستدلوا على أن الأئمة اثنا عشر إمامًا، ولم يقل بهذا غيرهم ولا استخرج أحد هذه الدلائل إلا هم.

فقال: وما دلائلهم؟

قلت: قالوا: إنما خلق الله تعالى في الأنفس والآفاق، فخلق في السماء اثني عشر برجًا[2]، والسنة اثنا عشر شهراً[3]، وفي كل يوم اثنتا عشرة[4] ساعة والليل كذلك، والجوارح اثنتا عشرة جارحة تخدم القلب، وجزائر الدنيا اثنتا عشرة[5] جزيرة.

فلما ذكرتُ مثل هذا أراد النزول عن السرير[6]، /٢٨ وقال: فلغيرهم أن يدعي هذا من غير ولد موسى، فقام إليه أبو موسى ومن حضر وقمت إجلالاً له أن ينزل، فثبت مكانه ورجلاه في الأرض.

فقال: فهلا قالوا: ثلاثة عشر، واحتجوا بقول الله تعالى:

---

[1] سنين: -، ل.

[2] برجًا: بروجًا، ه ل إ.

[3] شهرا: شهورا، ل إ.

[4] اثنتا عشرة: اثنا عشر، ه ل إ.

[5] اثنتا عشرة جارحة ... اثنتا عشرة: اثنى عشر جارحة ... اثنى عشر، ل؛ اثنتا عشر جارحة ... اثنتا عشر، ه.

[6] السرير: السريرة، ه.

«إنِّي رَأَيْتُ أحدَ عشَرَ كَوكَبًا وَالشَّمْسَ وَالقَمَرَ رَأَيْتُهُم لِي سَاجِدِينَ»[١]، فذلك ثلاثة عشر وأربعة عشر، وألا احتجوا بقول الله تعالى: «وَالفَجْرِ وَلَيَالٍ عَشْرٍ وَالشَّفْعِ وَالوَتْرِ وَاللَّيلِ إذَا يَسْرِ هَلْ فِي ذَلِكَ قَسَمٌ لِذِي حِجْرٍ»[٢]، وذلك أربعة عشر وخمسة عشر، وألا قالوا: تسعة عشر، واحتجوا بقول الله تعالى: «عَلَيْهَا تِسْعَةَ عَشَرَ»[٣]، وألا قالوا بعشرين واحتجوا بقول الله تعالى: «إنْ يَكُن مِنكُم عِشْرُونَ صَابِرُونَ»[٤]، وألا قالوا: ثلاثين، واحتجوا بقول الله تعالى: «ثَلاثِينَ لَيْلَةً»[٥]، وألا قالوا: أربعين، واحتجوا بقول الله عز وجل: «أرْبَعِينَ لَيْلَةً»[٦]، وألا قالوا: خمسين، واحتجوا بقول رسول الله صلى الله عليه في القسامة: خمسين رجلاً، وبقول الله سبحانه: «خَمْسِينَ ألفَ سَنَةٍ»[٧]، وألا احتجوا في الستين بقول الله عز وجل: «سِتِّينَ مِسْكِينًا»[٨]، وألا قالوا: سبعين، واحتجوا بقول الله عز وجل: «وَاخْتَارَ مُوسَى قَوْمَهُ

---

[١] القرآن ١٢:٤.

[٢] القرآن ٨٩:١–٥.

[٣] القرآن ٧٤:٣٠.

[٤] القرآن ٨:٦٥.

[٥] القرآن ٧:١٤٢.

[٦] القرآن ٢:٥١ و ٧:١٤٢.

[٧] القرآن ٧٠:٤.

[٨] القرآن ٥٨:٤.

سَبْعِينَ رَجُلاً»[١]، وألا قالوا: ثمانين، واحتجوا بقول الله عز وجل: «ثَمَانِينَ جَلْدَةً»[٢]، وألا قالوا: تسعة وتسعين، واحتجوا بقول الله تعالى: «تِسْعَةٌ[٣] وَتِسْعِينَ نَعْجَةً»[٤]، وألا[٥] قالوا: مائة، واحتجوا بقوله عز وجل في الزانية والزاني: «فَاجْلِدُوا كُلَّ وَاحِدٍ مِنهُمَا مِائَةَ جَلْدَةٍ»[٦]. فانبسط في هذا المعنى واتسع فيه وكثر منه وأبانه بيانًا عجيبًا لم أكن أعلمه ولا سمعت به قبل وقتي ذلك، فوالله ما شبهته إلا بنهرٍ جارٍ[٧] أو رجل يقرأ صحيفة[٨] بيده مكتوبة بخطه / [٢٩] قد فهمها ووقف على صحة معانيها وضعف دلائلهم وشواهدهم وأبطل دعواهم وأفسد[٩] عليهم ما ذهبوا إليه من ذلك.

فقلت: يلزم ما ذكرتَ وفي بعض ما أتيت به من فساد قولهم كفاية.

---

[١] القرآن ٧:١٥٥.

[٢] القرآن ٢٤:٤.

[٣] واحتجوا بقول الله تعالى تسعة: واحتجوا بتسعة، ه.

[٤] القرآن ٣٨:٢٣.

[٥] واربعة عشر والا احتجوا ... والا (كذا ثمانية مرات) ... والا قالوا: واربعة عشر ولا احتجوا ... ولا ... ولا قالوا، ل.

[٦] القرآن ٢٤:٢.

[٧] جار: جاري، ه.

[٨] صحيفة: صحيفته، ل.

[٩] افسد: افسدت، ه.

ثم دعـاني على أثر ذلك وأذن لأصحـابنا الذين دعـاهم قـبلي بالدخول إليـه فحضروا الدعوة. فلما أخذ[١] العهد قال: اعلم يرحمك الله أن هذا العـهد سنة من[٢] الله في خلقه وعباده، أخذه على أنبيائه وأخذه كل نبي على أمتـه، والدليل على ذلك من كـتاب الله عز وجل إذ يقـول: «وَإِذْ أَخَذْنَا مِن النَّبِيِّينَ مِيثَاقَهُم وَمِنكَ وَمِن نُوحٍ وَإِبْرَاهِيمَ وَمُوسَى وَعِيسَى ابْنِ مَرْيَمَ وَأَخَذْنَا منهُم مِيثَاقًا غَلِيظًا»[٣]، وقوله: «وَإِذْ أَخَذْنَا مِيثَاقَ بَنِي إِسْرَائِيلَ لاَ تَعْبُدُونَ إِلاَّ اللهَ»[٤]، وقوله: «وَلَقَدْ أَخَذَ اللهُ مِيثَاقَ بَنِي إِسْرَائِيلَ وَبَعَثْنَا مِنهُمُ اثْنَى عَشَرَ نَقِيبًا»[٥]، وقوله: «وَمِنَ الَّذِينَ قَالُوا إِنَّا نَصَارَى أَخَذْنَا مِيثَاقَهُم»[٦]، وقوله: «وَإِذْ أَخَذْنَا مِيثَاقَكُم لاَ تَسْفِكُونَ دِمَاءَكُم»[٧]، وقـال لرسول الله صلى الله عليه وآله: «إِنَّ الَّذِينَ يُبَايِعُونَكَ إِنَّمَا يُبَايِعُونَ اللهَ يَدُ اللهِ فَوقَ أَيْدِيهِم فَمَن نَكَثَ فَإِنَّمَا يَنْكُثُ عَلَى نَفْسِهِ وَمَن أَوْفَى بِمَا عَاهَدَ عَلَيهِ اللهَ فَسَيُؤْتِيهِ[٨] أَجْرًا عَظِيمًا»[٩]، ثم أتى بجميع ما في القرآن من ذكر

---

[١] اخذ: اخذوا، إ.

[٢] من: سن، ل.

[٣] القرآن ٣٣:٧.

[٤] القرآن ٢:٨٣.

[٥] القرآن ٥:١٢.

[٦] القرآن ٥:١٤.

[٧] القرآن ٢:٨٤.

[٨] فسيؤتيه: فسنوتيه، ه إ.

العهد والوفاء به وقال: لا دين إلا بعهد ومن لم يكن لله[١] عليه عهد فلا ولاية له ولا دين يحجزه[٢] وكنتم قبل هذا قومًا بوراً[٣]، وقال: إن الله يقول: «إنَّ اللهَ اشْتَرَى / ٣٠ منَ المُؤْمنينَ أنْفُسَهُم وأَمْوالَهُم بأنَّ لَهُمُ الجَنَّةَ يُقَاتلُونَ في سَبيلِ الله فَيَقْتُلُونَ وَيُقْتَلُونَ وَعْداً عَلَيه حَقّاً في التوْرَاة وَالإنْجيلِ وَالقُرْآنِ وَمَن أَوْفَى بِعَهْده منَ الله فَاسْتَبْشرُوا بِبَيْعِكُمُ الَّذي بَايَعْتُم به وَذَلكَ هُوَ الفَوْزُ العَظِيمُ»[٤]، وقال: «لَقَدْ رَضِيَ اللهُ عَنِ المُؤْمنينَ إذْ يُبَايِعُونَكَ تَحْتَ الشَّجَرَة» الآية[٥]. ثم قال: اليوم بايعتم الله وكنتم عبيده وعرفتم محمداً وبايعتموه، وقال[٦]: قد بين الله أن الأولين لم يرض عبادتهم إلا بالبيعة لمحمد نبيه[٧] صلى الله عليه وآله، فكيف[٨] يرضى عبادتكم بلا بيعة؟

فقلت: والله والله ما سمعت بهذا قط ولقد قرأت جميع ما وصل إلينا من قول الأفراق وكثير مقالات الملحدين والموحدين فما

---

[٩] القرآن ٤٨: ١٠.

[١] لله: الله، ه.

[٢] يحجزه: يحجز، ه؛ بحجزه، ل؛ إ غير واضح.

[٣] قارن القرآن ٤٨: ١٢: «وكنتم قوما بورا».

[٤] القرآن ٩: ١١١.

[٥] القرآن ٤٨: ١٨.

[٦] وقال: فقلت، ل.

[٧] نبيه: -، ل.

[٨] فكيف: قال نعم فكيف، ل.

سمعت بهذا، وإن هذا لظاهر[١] صدقه وبين برهانه وحقه، وكنا نظن ونقول: إن الله أخرج ذرية آدم من ظهره وأخذ عليهم العهد.

فقال: هذا فاسد لا يعضده برهان ولا يصدقه ذو عقل لأن الله تعالى يقول[٢]: «وَاذْكُرُوا نِعْمَةَ اللهِ عَلَيكُم وَمِيثَاقَهُ الَّذِي وَاثَقَكُم بِهِ إِذْ قُلْتُم سَمِعْنَا وَأَطَعْنَا»[٣]، فكيف يُذَكِرهم[٤] ما لم يذكروا ويجيبوه بهذا الجواب المفهوم؟ بل كما نرى كان الذين من قبلكم.

فقلت: لا دين إلا بعهد.

قال: نعم، ألا تسمع إلى قوله: «لاَ يَمْلِكُونَ الشَّفَاعَةَ إِلاَّ مَنِ اتَّخَذَ عِنْدَ الرَحْمَنِ عَهْداً»[٥] و«قَالُوا لَنْ تَمَسَّنَا النَارُ إِلاَّ أَيَّامًا مَعْدُودَةً[٦] قُلْ أَتَّخَذْتُم عِنْدَ اللهِ عَهْداً فَلَنْ يُخْلِفَ اللهُ عَهْدَهُ أَمْ تَقُولُونَ عَلَى اللهِ مَا لاَ تَعْلَمُونَ»[٧]، /٣١ فالعهد[٨] مقدمة للعبد وشفيع له عند الرب، ومن نكث فله عذاب أليم، والعهد هو الوسيلة، قال الله

---

[١] لظاهر: الظاهر، ه ل إ.

[٢] يقول: قال، ل إ.

[٣] القرآن ٥:٧.

[٤] يذكرهم: يذكره، ل.

[٥] القرآن ١٩:٨٧.

[٦] معدودة: معدودات، ل.

[٧] القرآن ٢:٨٠.

[٨] فالعهد: والعهد، ه إ.

تعالى: «يَا أَيُّهَا الَّذِينَ آمَنُوا اتَّقُوا اللهَ وَابْتَغُوا إِلَيهِ الوَسِيلَةَ»[١].

فقلت: الحمد لله آمنا وصدقنا، وما كنا لنهتدي لولا أن هدانا الله، لقد جاءت رسل ربنا بالحق.

فلما أتى عليَّ جميع ذكر العهد، قال: اعلم يرحمك الله أن الأئمة سبعة، وأتى بجميع شواهد الأسابيع من جميع ما خلق الله وذرأه وبرأه ومن الأفلاك والنجوم الدراري وبنات نعش والأقاليم والأيام والسموات والأرضين والجوارح والمشاعر، ثم قسم القرآن أسابيع من البقرة إلى «قُلْ هُوَ اللهُ أَحَدٌ»[٢]، ثم ذكر الحمد وأنها السبع المثاني ودل على ذلك من الحروف والهجاء وجعلها فصولاً فصولاً يعرف[٣] في كل فصل حقيقة مراد الله وغرضه ونهاية أمره. فلما أشبع هذا أيضًا وأبانه ورتبه قال: واعلم أن لكل إمام اثنتي عشرة حجة ظاهرة نهارية واثنتي عشرة[٤] حجة باطنة خفية ليلية، ودل على ذلك من جميع ما ذكرناه من الساعات وجزائر الدنيا والشهور والبروج والجوارح والأمعاء والقلب وأنهم حجب الإمام وألسنته[٥] وأبوابه ونقباؤه والمبلغون عنه إلى الدعاة والدعاة[٦] يبلغون المؤمنين، ودل على ذلك بما لم تحط به الأفهام قبل ذلك ولا عرفته العقول قبل الدلالة عليه والتنبيه إليه.

---

[١] القرآن ٥:٣٥.

[٢] القرآن ١١٢:١.

[٣] فصولا يعرف: فصولا لا يعرف، إ.

[٤] اثنتي عشرة ... اثنتي عشرة: اثنا عشر ... اثنا عشر، ل.

[٥] السنته: السنة، ه إ.

[٦] والدعاة: -، ه إ.

فقلت: لا إله إلا الله، هذا والله بيان وشفاء لما في /٣٢ الصدور وهدى ورحمة للمؤمنين.

ثم رتّب لا إله إلا الله محمد رسول الله، قسمها على الحدود الاثني عشر وعلى السبعة والتسعة عشر وعلى الحدود الأربعة وأنها كلمة واحدة وفيها الوحدانية وجميع الحدود، وفسّر حديث رسول الله صلى الله عليه وآله فيمن قال: لا إله إلا الله، فقد حقن ماله ودمه وأسقط عنه إصر[1] الجزية، ومن قالها مخلصًا دخل الجنة، وذكر أن إخلاصها معرفة حدودها، فعلمتُ حينئذ أنّي لم أكن أقولها[2] مخلصًا قبل، وكنت قبل هذا قد مرّ بي في بعض المقالات أن من شهد له الصامت فهو صاحب الحق، فذكرت له ذلك.

فقال: قد استشهدنا بالصامت والناطق والجبال والشجر والسماء والأرض والحروف والكلام والسور الطوال والقصار.

فقلت: أرأيت إن قال أصحاب الاثني عشر: إن الاثني عشر هم الأئمة والسبعة هم حجج؟

فقال: يفسد ذلك عليهم لأن السبعة مذكرة والاثني عشر مؤنثة والسبعة أرواح والاثنى عشر بيوت ومساكن. قال الله عز وجل: «كَمَثَلِ حَبَّةٍ أَنبَتَتْ سَبْعَ سَنَابِلَ فِي كُلِّ سُنْبُلَةٍ مِائَةُ حَبَّةٍ»[3]. ثم ذكر بسم الله الرحمن الرحيم، ثم أخذ في شرح القرآن وابتدأ بالحمد إلى آخرها، فسمعت ما لم أسمع بمثله. ثم فنن الحمد وما الحمد والتحميد

---

[1] اصر: امر، ل.

[2] اقولها: اقلها، إ ه ل.

[3] القرآن ٢:٢٦١.

والشكر وما الصلاة على محمد وكيف تمام ذلك واتّباع أمر الله في الصلاة[١] على محمد صلى الله عليه وآله وأن / ٣٣ من قال: اللهم صل على محمد[٢]، فقد أمر خالقه أن يفعل ما أمره خالقه أن يفعله هو، ثم احتجّ في هذا وبرهن وأوضح وقال: أرأيت لو أمرك آمر[٣] أن تعطي فلانًا شيئًا فأجبته أنت أن أعطه أنت هل أنفذت أمر الآمر أم لا[٤]؟

قلت: لا.

قال: فكذلك هؤلاء الخلق في الصلاة على محمد صلى الله عليه وآله، ولا يعرف محمداً إلا من عرف الصلاة عليه، ولا يعرف محمداً من لم يعرف كيف بلّغ محمد إلى كافة الخلق وهو لم يزل من حدود الحجاز.

ثم أخذ في شرح البقرة وذكر آلم وأوائل[٥] السور المعجمة والراآت والحواميم واللواميم وطه وطس وطسم ويس وكهيعص وص.

فقلت: الحمد لله ولا إله إلا الله.

فقال: المستمع أشد ملالة من القارىء، وقد تقارب الصبح ولم تكن تعلم[٦] السهر، وأعلم أنه يصعب عليك ثلاث ليال، ثم لم تبال به نحن نحتاج إليك.

---

[١] الصلاة: الصلوات، ه.

[٢] محمد: + وعلى آل محمد، ل.

[٣] آمر: امرء، ه إ.

[٤] ام لا: -، ل إ.

[٥] وذكر آلم واوائل: وذكر اوائل، ل.

[٦] تكن تعلم: نكن نعلم، ل.

فقلت: معاذ الله أن يمل سامع هذا، وهذا علم غض طري لم نسمع[١] بمثله قط.

ثم ذكر الصلاة وحدودها والأذان وعدده والوضوء والطهر والتيمم ورتّبه وبيّنه ودل على أمثاله وفننه، وذكر الصيام والحج والكعبة والحجر وزمزم والصفا والمروة والحرم والجمار والهدي والمناسك والمشاعر والطواف ومِنى وعرَفات والمقام وكسوة البيت وما دل عليه كل ذلك، وقال: من صام ولم يعلم وصلى ولم يعلم وحج ولم يعلم فهو عامل غير عالم، قال الله تعالى: «وَأَنْ تَصُومُوا / ٣٤ خَيْرٌ لَكُم إنْ كُنْتُم تَعْلَمُونَ»[٢]، وقال: «فَوَيْلٌ لِلمُصَلِّينَ الَّذِينَ[٣] هُم عَن صَلاتِهِم سَاهُونَ»[٤]، وقال: «هَلْ أَتَاكَ حَدِيثُ الغَاشِيَةِ وُجُوهٌ يَومَئِذٍ خَاشِعَةٌ عَامِلَةٌ نَاصِبَةٌ تَصْلَى نَاراً حَامِيَةً تُسْقَى مِن عَينٍ آنِيَةٍ»[٥] من ماء يفرغ في إناء وهو علم الرواية والأخبار عمل بلا علم، والعين الجارية ما جرت عيونه وينابيعه[٦] من عند الله إلى أوليائه وحججه، واعلم أنه لا يصح عمل بلا علم ولا يقوم ظاهر إلا بباطن ولا ينتفع جسم لا روح فيه، فالجسم بلا روح ميت، وذكر باطن بدن الإنسان ووجهه وروحه ونفسه وظهره وبطنه وحواسه الظاهرة الخمسة وحواسه الباطنة وفضلها

---

[١] نسمع: نستمع، ل إ؛ تسمع، ه.

[٢] القرآن ٢:١٨٤.

[٣] للمصلين الذين: للذين، ه.

[٤] القرآن ١٠٧:٤-٥.

[٥] القرآن ٨٨:١-٥.

[٦] عيونه وينابيعه: عيون ينابيعه، ه.

وأن هذه الحواس الظاهرة خدم للحواس الباطنة، وسجع في هذا وتمكن وأطال، وذكر حديث النبي: ما من آية في[١] كتاب الله إلا ولها ظهر وبطن ولكل حرف حد ولكل حد مطلع، ومثّل[٢] بظهرها تنزيلها وببطنها[٣] سرّها وتأويلها، فأبدع وأبان وشرح[٤] بالبرهان.

ثم قال: ما تقول في الإمام، يجوز أن يقترف الكبائر ويأثم ويقتل النفس التي حرم الله وغير ذلك؟

فقلت: الإمام الموفق المؤيد بروح القدس لا يمكن أن يوصف بهذا ولا يضاف إليه اقتراف الكبائر ولا شيء من الفواحش والمآثم.

قال: وما روح القدس؟

قلت: قوة أيّد الله بها أنبياءه وأولياءه.

قال: فالأئمة؟

قلت: الفرق بين الإمام والنبي الوسائط التي عنها يأخذون عن الله، فوسائط الأنبياء روحانية ووسائط الأئمة أنبياء بشرية. /٣٥

قال: والنبي يحابي[٥] الإمام ويخصه بما يمنع منه غيره؟

فقلت: جائز للنبي أن يخصّ كما خصه الله تعالى ويصطفي كما اصطفاه الله، فمن علوم الأنبياء ما يعمّ به الكل ويستوي فيها

---

[١]في: من، ه ل؛ -، إ.

[٢]ومثل: ومثله، ه.

[٣]وببطنها: وبطنها، ه إ ل.

[٤]شرح: اشرح، ل.

[٥]يحابي: يناجي، ل؛ إ غير واضح.

الشريف والمشروف[1] ومن علمه ما يخص به من أراه الله تعالى، فما كان من الشرائع وأعمالها والإقرار بالتوحيد فالناس فيه سواء، وما كان من العلم فالناس فيه متفاضلون، وقد يعرّف الإمامُ الجماعةَ فيحفظ الواحد وينسى الآخرون، وقد روي أنه لما أنزل الله عز وجل: «وَتَعِيَهَا أُذُنٌ وَاعِيَةٌ»[2] قال رسول الله: اللهم اجعلها أذن علي بن أبي طالب.

قال: فكيف أدرك[3] النبي صلى الله عليه وآله كلام الملائكة؟

قلت: بالروح الزائدة فيه من شكل الملائكة من روح القدس، وقد يتصور الملك كما ثبت في الرواية أن جبرئيل عليه السلام كان يظهر في صورة دحية الكلبي، فبزيادة القوة اتصلوا بالملائكة.

قال: وكيف جاز أن يضاف إليهم الذنوب وينسب إليهم الخطايا والنسيان والغفلة والسهو؟

قلت: وما هذه الذنوب؟

قال: قال الله تعالى: «وَعَصَى آدَمُ رَبَّهُ فَغَوَى»[4]، وقال في يوسف: «وَلَقَدْ هَمَّتْ بِهِ وَهَمَّ بِهَا»[5]، وموسى وسؤاله ما هلك فيه قومه، وقول الله عز وجل في محمد نبيه صلى الله عليه وآله: «لِيَغْفِرَ

---

[1] المشروف: المشرف، ه.

[2] القرآن ٦٩:١٢.

[3] ادرك: ادراك، ه.

[4] القرآن ٢٠:١٢١.

[5] القرآن ١٢:٢٤.

لَكَ اللهُ مَا تَقَدَّمَ مِن ذَنْبِكَ وَمَا تَأَخَّرَ»[١].

فقلت: جميع ما ذكرتَ / [٣٦] يحتمل الوجوه والتأويل[٢]، ويجب أن نضيف إلى أنبياء الله أحسن تلك الوجوه وننزههم عن أقبحها ونفرق بين ذنوب الأنبياء وذنوب غيرهم.

قال: وما عسى أن تقول[٣] وقد سميتها ذنوبًا؟

فقلت: قد أجمعنا أن الذنوب اسم جامع لصغائر مغفورة والكبائر التي لله فيها المشيئة[٤] والشرك الذي لا يغفر، ومن الذنوب قصد وتعمد، ومنها سهو وغفلة وخطاء ونسيان، ومنها خطرات بغير تعمد ولا شهوة، ومنها اختيار وتلذذ، فذنوب العباد شهوة وتعمد وقصد واختيار ومخالفة لأمر الله متعمدين لخلافه، وذنوب الأنبياء عليهم السلام سهو وغفلة ونسيان وخطرات لا تعمداً ولا تلذذاً ولا هم لله تعالى فيها مخالفون مع احتمالها للتأويل[٥]. فأما آدم عليه السلام فلم يتعمد ولكنه نسي وصدق القائل له وحسن ظنه به حينئذ، فلما أحس بالزلة والخطيئة استعبر واستغفر وقوله: «غوى»، ليس من الغي، ولكنه انقطع عنه أمر الله تعالى كما يقال غوى الفصيل إذا[٦]

---

[١] القرآن ٤٨:٢.

[٢] والتاويل: في التاويل، ه.

[٣] تقول: نقول، ل.

[٤] فيها المشيئة: فيه التشبيه(؟)، إ ه؛ فيها المشيئة + (في الهامش) التشبيه، ل.

[٥] للتاويل: بالتاويل، ه ل إ.

[٦] اذا: اذ، إ.

انقطع عنه اللبن، فاستحيى آدم من ربه وانقطع عنه حياء منه، ثم تاب الله عليه وهداه. وكل ذنب غفره الله تعالى فلا يسمى ذنبًا بعد المغفرة، بل ذلك رحمة كما قال الله تعالى: «فَأولَئِكَ يُبَدِّلُ اللهُ سَيِّئَاتِهِم حَسَنَات»[1]. وأما يوسف فلم يهم بالمعصية، بل نقول[2]: إنها همت بالمعصية وهم بأدبها وموعظتها، وقد قال قوم / ٣٧ بالتقديم والتأخير: لولا أن رأى برهان ربه لهمّ بها، فلما تقدم البرهان زجره عن الذنب، والبرهان هو العصمة، فلما تقدمت العصمة بطلت الهمة. وأما[3] موسى فلم يسأل من حيث سأل قومه ولم يجهل أن الله تعالى لا تدركه الحواس وأن الله تعالى ليس له غاية وما ليس له غاية ليس له شخص وما ليس له شخص ليس له صورة وما ليس له صورة فلا يدرك بالحواس[4]، وإنما سأل معذرة إلى قومه، وموسى أول المؤمنين أن الله تعالى لا تدركه الأبصار. وكذلك ذنوب محمد صلى الله عليه وآله على[5] سبيل السهو كما يجوز عليه أن يسهو في الصلاة وسها في القرآن، لا[6] على سبيل القصد والتعمد.

---

[1] القرآن ٢٥: ٧٠.

[2] نقول: يقول، ل.

[3] اما: امسى، ه.

[4] يدرك بالحواس: تدركه الحواس، ل.

[5] على: -، ل.

[6] لا: الا، ه.

فقال: وكيف سها آدم أو نسي وقد[١] بين الله له؟ فقال تعالى[٢]: «إِنَّ هَذَا عَدُوٌّ لَكَ وَلِزَوجِكَ»[٣]، وهو القائل له «مَا نَهَاكُمَا رَبُّكُمَا عَن هَذِهِ الشَّجَرَةِ» الآية[٤]، وعدوه المنهي عنه يخاطبه، فكيف تنسبه إلى النسيان؟ ثم قال: ارجع إلى المسألة، فقال: إنْ فعل الإمام ما نزّهته عنه وقصد إلى كبيرة فعلها وقتل من لا يحل قتله؟

فقلت: المسألة محال، لا يفعل الإمام شيئًا من هذا.

قال: وإن[٥] فعل؟

قلت: بعد ثبوت آيته وبرهانه أنه الإمام المفترض الطاعة؟

قال: نعم.

قلت: تجب طاعته ولا نتهمه ولا نسيء الظن به ولا نفعل فعله[٦] إلا بإذنه.

فقال كالمنكر علي: تطيع من يقترف الكبائر والعظائم ويقتل النفس التي حرم الله تعالى؟

فأجابه /[٣٨] أصحابنا الذين دعاهم قبلي كالمعتذرين عني[٧]، فقالوا له: جلالتك حملته على أن أجابك بهذا لما ألحت عليه، وما

---

[١]وقد: قد، إ.

[٢] فقال تعالى: -، ه إ.

[٣] القرآن ٢٠:١١٧.

[٤] القرآن ٧:٢٠.

[٥]وان: فان، ل إ.

[٦]فعله: فعلة، ل إ.

[٧]عني: -، ل.

يقول هذا أحد.

فأنكر عليهم قولهم وقال: أمسكوا، ما حملكم على الكلام؟ لقد استؤذن لكم البارحة فكرهت دخولكم علي[١]. ثم عطف علي بلين واسترسال، فقال: فكيف قلتَ؟

قلتُ: يعيد السيد السؤال.

فقال: الإمام يقترف الكبائر ويقتل النفس التي حرم الله تعالى؟

فأحلت[٢] في السؤال وتزيدت من الإنكار[٣]، فألحّ في تحقيق الفعل، قلت: بعد ثبوت آيته وبرهانه؟

قال: نعم.

قلت: تجب طاعته والرضا بفعله ولا ننكر فعله ولا نفعل فعله[٤] إلا بإذنه.

قال: هل تدل على هذا بشيء[٥]؟

قلت: نعم، قرأتُ في بعض الصحف إذا فعل العالم شيئًا فلا تفعل مثله، وما أمرك به فافعله، وفي كتاب الله خبر موسى والعالم العبد الصالح الذي قتل النفس الزكية وخرق السفينة، فأنكر موسى

---

[١] علي: عليه، ه.

[٢] فاحلت: فاجلت، ل إ.

[٣] الانكار: الافكار، ل.

[٤] فعله: فعلة، ل.

[٥] بشيء: الشيء، ل.

فعله ورضي[١] الله من فعله، فإذا أنكر موسى فعلاً هو عند الله رضى فنحن أحرى أن لا ننكر فعل الإمام ولا نخطئه ولا نستعجله ولا نستجهله ولا نستعجزه، وتالله ما[٢] كنت اهتديت إلى هذا الجواب قبل ذلك ولا دريته ولا سمعته، بل وفق الله ذلك حين الحاجة إليه.

فقال لي: أحسنت وأجدت بارك الله فيك، وقال لمن بحضرته، ومنهم إبراهيم اليماني وكان يسمى[٣] السيد الصغير: رأيت ما أحسن مخارجه ومعانيه في كل ما قصد /[٣٩] إليه، ما شبهته إلا بأبي الحسين. ثم قال لي: أبو الحسين هذا الذي شبهتُك به رجل قام إلينا من المشرق ووجه به[٤] الأولياء، فأقام عندي سنين بكتامة، كأنك إياه في صورته وسنه وكلامه.

فقبّلت يده وشكرت ما كان من قوله من المدح والثناء، وحضر طعامه، فأتي إليه بالغسل وأمرني فغسلت وغسل أبو موسى وأبو زاكي، ودخلت مائدة عريانة خلنج[٥]، فنصبت بين يديه ونصبت أخرى بقربها، وقدم إليه أربع ‹صحاف› من الغضار الصيني[٦]، فإذا هي

---

[١] رضي: رضيه، ل إ.

[٢] ما: لما، ه.

[٣] يسمى: سمى، ل.

[٤] ووجه به: ووجهوا به، ل ه؛ وجهرابه (؟)، إ.

[٥] خلنج: حلنح، ه إ.

[٦] الغضار الصيني: الغضار الزيدي، إ؛ الغزار الزيدي، ه؛ الفضار الريدي، ل.

‹...؟› حُجز بلحم الفراريج[١]، وأمرني بالقعود على المائدة، وافترق أصحابنا على تلك[٢] المائدة الأخرى، وأتوا بطعام كثير من ألوان اللحم بأصناف مختلفة. ثم اغتسل وأردت القيام إلى الغسل، فقال لي: مكانك لا تبرح. ثم انصرفت إلى دار أبي موسى.

فلما كان بعد العصر دخلت إليه، فسأل عن الحال فقال: كيف أنت فيما سمعت وهل أنكرت شيئًا؟

قلت: معاذ الله[٣].

فقال: إن أنكرت شيئًا فاسأل عنه[٤] ولا تتركه فيكون جحوداً، واعلم أن الأشياء أربعة: معرفة وإقرار وجحد وإنكار، فأول شواهد الإقرار المعرفة[٥] وأول شواهد الجحد الإنكار، فإذا تقوّت[٦] المعرفة صارت إقراراً.

قلت: يا سيدي، ما اسم الإمام ومن هو وابن من هو؟[٧]

فقال: يكون لهذا وقت آخر.

فقلت: امنن أو أمسك بغير حساب.

---

[١] الفراريج: الفراريخ، ل إ؛ الزاريج، ه.

[٢] تلك: -، ل.

[٣] الله: -، ه.

[٤] فاسأل عنه: فاسأله، ه.

[٥] الاقرار المعرفة: المعرفة الاقرار، ه.

[٦] تقوت: تقويت، ل إ.

[٧] وابن من هو: واين هو، ل.

فقال بعد سكتة: الإمام محمد بن إسماعيل بن جعفر.

فقلت: المدة طويلة، / [٤٠] اليوم لجعفر مائة وأربعون سنة[١] وإسماعيل يقال: إنه مات في حياة أبيه.

فقال: وتنكر أن يعيش ألف سنة؟، قد عاش نوح في قومه ألف سنة.[٢]

فقلت: ما ننكره تقليداً لك وتصديقًا لقولك، ونقر أن هذا ستر على غيره.

فقال: يفعل الله ما يشاء.

فقلت له: إن في الروايات عن النبي صلى الله عليه وآله أنه قال: المهدي اسمه اسمي واسم أبيه اسم أبي.

قال: يريد بأبيه إسماعيل بن إبراهيم جده، فاتخذه أبًا.

وكتب كتابًا إلى أخيه أبي العباس بأطرابُلس يأذن له في القدوم، ووجّه مائتي فارس مع تميم الوسقاني. ودخل إليه حينئذ بهرام الجنان بثلاثة أطباق ورد أحمر منضد وعلى[٣] كل طبق شمامة بديعة الصنعة، قد أدار عليها الورد على سبع. فأعطاني واحدة وأعطى أخرى لشبيب القمودي[٤] والي طبنة، وكان دعاه تلك الليلة الأولى قبلي، فقبلها شبيب وردّها إلي الطبق وانصرف. فلما أردت الانصراف

---

[١] مائة واربعون سنة: اربعون ومائة سنة، ل إ.

[٢] في قومه الف سنة: الف سنة في قومه، ل إ.

[٣] وعلى: على، ه.

[٤] القمودي: القمرذي، ه.

قبّلتها ورددتها، فقال لي: انصرف بها إلى موضعك. فخرجتُ بها في يدي، فوافيت سقيفة قصره وفيها رجال بني الأغلب وغيرهم، فقاموا إليّ وهنأوني وعظموا مني ما لم أكن أعرفه قبل ذلك، فعلمت أنه أراد تنبيلي بذلك الورد وإكرامي. فما أراد إلا ذلك[١] لما أني قد خرجت بها معي، فسترتها وغدوت إليه ومعي قربان، وحسبت خمسي وقومت ضياعي / ٤١ ودفعت[٢] إليه ما تقربت به، فسرّه ذلك، وعرفته بما أملت[٣] من أداء الخمس إليه وتقويم ضياعي وعلى بعضها خراج. فقال: لا تؤدّ[٤] خراجًا، ليس على مثلك خراج، وحطه عني، وأمر أن لا يعرض لي في خراج كان عليّ بنينة وقنشية[٥] في منزلين، وقال: ما حططت عن أحد خراجًا إلا عنك وعن ابن[٦] عمران الطبني بطبنة[٧].

ثم سألني عن الكنية وقال: قد عرفتُ اسمك، أليس جعفراً[٨] تسمى؟

قلت: نعم.

---

[١] الا ذلك: ذلك الا، ه.

[٢] دفعت: رفعت، ل.

[٣] بما املت: بها واملت، ه.

[٤] تؤدّ: تؤدني، ل ه إ.

[٥] علي بنينة وقنشية: على بثينة وقنينة، ل؛ إ غير واضح.

[٦] ابن: ابي، ل.

[٧] بطبنة: لطبنة، ل.

[٨] جعفراً: جعفر، ه ل إ.

قال: الكنية؟

قلت: أبو بكر.

قال: هذا عجب، شيعي ابن شيعي يرضى بأن يكنى بأبي بكر.

فقلت: الأمر إليك.

قال: اسمك جعفر وتكنى[١] من اليوم بأبي عبد الله، فيجتمع لك الاسم الطيب والكنية الطيبة. وكأني والله ما كنيت بأبي بكر قط، وعلم ذلك مَن عرفني ومن لم يعرفني من قريب وبعيد. ثم قال: كان من تقدم لك على مذهبك؟

قلت: كانوا زيدية يتبرؤون عن عثمان ومعاوية ولا يتبرؤون عن أبي بكر وعمر، ويقولون: نمسك عما أمسك عنه علي بن أبي طالب ونبرأ ممن برىء عنه، وكانوا يقولون بفضل علي بن أبي طالب عليه السلام ويجيزون تقديم المفضول.

ثم سألني عن أوائلنا. فقلت: الأوائل من الكوفة ودخل جدي الهيثم بن عبد الرحمن مع يزيد[٢] بن حاتم، وحيّي[٣] من مضر، جد جدي قيس بن عاصم ‹بن سنان› بن خالد بن مِنقر.

قال: فالهيثم الداخِل[٤] جدك؟

/[٤٢]قلت: جد أبي جدي، هو الخامس من أبي، وكنا نسمع أن

---

[١]تكنى: نكنى، ه.

[٢]يزيد: زيد، ه إ ل.

[٣]حيي: يحيى، ه إ ل.

[٤] الداخل: داخل، ه.

الهيثم تعافى من خدمة روح بن حاتم وكان صديقًا له يؤثره على نظرائه، فأهدى له عشرة آلاف دينار وعافاه وأذن له في الرجوع إلى الكوفة، فخرج إليها، ورجع بأموال عظيمة ومعه سجل الهادي أو هارون إلى روح في إكرامه وحفظه وعونه فيما يريد من البناء. وكان اختطّ[1] بثلاث مواضع بالقيروان، بالسماط الأعظم وباب سلم وبموقف التبن[2]. فسكن وبنى وأنشأ ضياعًا بنواحٍ كثيرة وبالساحل، وهي هذه التي حططت عني خراجها، وبالشرقي[3] وبقَرْنَة وبباجة، واتخذ مُنْيَة[4] تعرف بقصر أبي هارون بقرب البرجين[5]، وكل ذلك بأيدينا إلى اليوم خلا باجة، يقال: إنّها تغلب عليها الجند.

فقال: تركتَ مذهب آبائك وتزيدت عليهم، ما سمعته منك أنت تثقب الجواهر.

قلت: توفي أبي وأنا دون البلوغ سنة خمس وثمانين ومائتين، وقد ختمت القرآن مرات، وكان كثير الكتب متفننًا[6] في اللغة والغريب والجدل والفقه، فحبّب إلي الفقه والجدل، فعزلت تلك الكتب وأقبلت على الدراسة والنظر، وكنت آخذ نفسي كل يوم وليلة بحفظ عشرة مسائل من فقه أبي حنيفة وخمسة من الجدل والتوحيد وخلق

---

[1] اختط: احيط، ه إ.

[2] التبن: البتن، ه؛ التين(؟)، ل؛ البين(؟)، إ.

[3] بالشرقي: بالمشرقى، ه.

[4] واتخذ منية: واتخذ مينة، ل إ؛ وباتخذ منيه، ه.

[5] بقرب البرجين: تعرف بالبرجين، إ ل؛ بقرب بالبرجين، ه.

[6] متفننا: متقننا، ه؛ مفننا، ل إ.

القرآن وإنفاء التشبيه والاستطاعة مع الفعل والقول بخلق[١] الفعل والكلام /[٤٣] في المعرفة والإيمان والوعد والوعيد، وحبب إلي النظر في كتب الأوائل، واشتغلت بكتاب المنطق لأرسطاطاليس، وكثير من كتبه عندي وكتب أفلاطون[٢] وغيرهما. وكنت أختلف في سماع الفقه إلى ابن عبدون وإلى ابن معْمر، وأسمع الحديث من أبي جعفر بن أبان ومن زياد اللؤلؤي، وكنت أكثر الاختلاف إلى من ينسب إلى علم الكلام. فاتصل بي يهودي يعرف بيوسف بن يحيى الخراساني وهو مليء بالمنطق، فأغناني عن الاختلاف إلى أحد، وكان يكثر الاختلاف إليّ حتى وصل إلينا رجل يعرف بمحمد الكوفي من صقلية مظعون،[٣] فبلغه خبري فوصلني، فرأيت رجلاً يفهم الكلام والجدل فواسيته ووصلته، فكان يختلف إليّ، فلما قدمت[٤] صحبته رأيت نفسي أكثر علمًا منه، فنقص برّي به وأحس ذلك مني.

فقال لي ذات يوم: نظرتَ في الإمامة؟

قلت: كان أبي يعلمنا القول بفضل علي عليه السلام على غيره وأن الإمامة في ولده، وقللت عنده ذلك وقلت: الإمامة معروفة.

فضحك وحرك رأسه وقال لي: النظر في[٥] الإمامة باب عظيم يفتح أبوابًا عظيمة، ليس في يديك شيء وجميع ما اشتغلتَ به

---

[١] والقول بخلق: والقول يخلق، ل؛ بقول بخلق، ه إ.

[٢] افلاطون: افلاطن، ه.

[٣] صقلية مظعون: صقلية معطون، ه؛ صقلبة معطون، ل إ.

[٤] قدمت: اقدمت، ل إ.

[٥] في: الى، ه ل إ.

من الجدل والنظر والفقه محال عند الإمامة. لو تفتق ذهنك في الإمامة تركت كل علم واشتغلت بها. وإنما العلوم أربع مسائل وهي التوحيد والنبوة والإمامة وإنفاء /٤٤ التشبيه.

فقلت: تكلم فيها. فتكلم ثلاثين يومًا في الأصول والفروع حتى ثبت ذلك وأنها ركن من أركان الدين موصول بالنبوة.

ثم تكلم في البراءة فلم أجبه وقلت: من مات فلا حاجة بنا إلى ذكره بشر ولا بخير.

قال: لا، حتى تعلم فضل من تواليه وشر من تعاديه، فتكلم معي ثلاثين يومًا في البراءة. فآخر ما قال لي: أرأيت من سرق ثوبك هذا أو غصبك هذا الدفتر، هل تجوره وتظلمه وتجرحه[1] ولا تقبل شهادته؟

فقلت: أجل.

فقال: تظلم من سرق لك ثوبًا قيمته ديناران وتتوقف عمن هتك دين الله ونقض سنة رسول الله وتأمّر على ولي الله وهتك ستر فاطمة بنت رسول الله وقطع ميراثها وانتزع ما في يديها من هبة أبيها رسول الله وقتلها وقتل جنينها[2] في بطنها؟ وأكثر[3] من هذا وحرض.

فقلت: الحق والله ما تقول، فواليته وعانقته وعانقني وبكى وبكيت، ثم واظب علي ولازمني، وتركت النظر في كل شيء كنت

---

[1] تجرحه: تحرجه، ه؛ تخرجه، إ.

[2] جنينها: جنينا، ل إ.

[3] واكثر: وكثر، ل؛ وكثير، ه.

أنظر فيه وألهاني، فكنت[١] أقرأ كتب الإمامة لهشام بن الحكم وفضائل علي صلوات الله عليه ومثالب أبي بكر وعمر وعثمان.

ثم جاءني يومًا وأنا أصلي العصر وقت الجماعة، فلما سلمت قال لي: أي صلاة هذه؟

قلت: صلاة العصر[٢].

قال لي: ليس هذا وقت صلاة العصر في رواية الشيعة.

فقلت: ولهم أوقات غير هذه الأوقات؟

فقال: نعم، لنا علوم وفقه / [٤٥] وفرائض وأحكام وأذان وصلاة[٣]، وكل ما عندكم من[٤] قول أبي حنيفة ومالك فباطل وضلال.

فقلت له: أكمل لي فضلك وعرفني مَن[٥] هاهنا من الشيعة.

فجاءني بكتاب يوم وليلة وعليه اسم إبراهيم بن معشر، وهو جاري وملازم لي يجلس عندي، فحفظته ظاهراً كله ،وكنت أقوم به وبجميع ما فيه من الدعاء والفقه، وجاءني بكتاب مجموع فيه الوصايا والحدود والفرائض بخط محمد بن عمر[٦] المروذي، ‹و› هو كثير الجلوس عندنا، وابنه أحمد صاحبي في السماع عند ابن عبدون وغيره.

فقلت له: ويحك، هؤلاء مشايخنا وأصحاب أبي قبلي.

---

[١] فكنت: وكنت، ه.

[٢] صلاة العصر: العصر، ل إ.

[٣] اذان وصلاة: صلاة واذان، ل إ.

[٤] من: في، إ ل ه.

[٥] من: -، ل.

[٦] محمد بن عمر: محمد بن عمرو، ل؛ عمرو بن محمد، ه.

فقال لي: هم يحرضونني عليك.

فانكشفت إليهم وسألتهم الكتب، فأباحوني كتبهم، واتصلت بمحمد بن خلف، وكان من ثقات[١] الشيعة وعبّادهم وزهادهم، فأفدت منه كتبًا كثيرة واشتغلت بفقه آل محمد وتركت النظر في كتب أبي حنيفة، ووالله ما عدت إلى سماع شيء من تلك العلوم[٢]، وتركت أنا وصاحبي أحمد قراءة كتب أبي حنيفة على ابن عبدون، وكنا نختلف إليه ونقرأ عليه شرح أبي عبيد وآثار ابن قتيبة(؟)[٣] وغير ذلك من الآثار وكتب الفقهاء في الأقضية وكتب الإبانة، فكان يؤثرنا ويقدمنا، فإذا جئنا أسكت من كان يقرأ، فنقرأ ما نريده ونقعد[٤] إن أردنا أو ننصرف[٥]، ونحن على ذلك إلى أن دخلت طلعتك الميمونة المباركة.

فقال: وهذا /[٤٦] الرجل حي إلى اليوم؟

فقلت: هو حاضر، وغداً نأتي به إن شاء الله تعالى. فغدوت به إليه فعرفه بشكري لتعليمه[٦]، وقال له: قد كافاك إذ ذكرك وشكرك، وقد كان سببك[٧] لما هو أفضل، فقد كافاك بالتي هي

---

[١] ثقات: ثقاة، ل.

[٢] العلوم: العلم، ه إ.

[٣] اثار ابن قتيبة(؟): اثارا فهذا، إ ه ل.

[٤] ونقعد: + بها، إ.

[٥] او ننصرف: وننصرف، ه.

[٦] بشكري لتعليمه: بشكري لتعلمه، إ؛ شركي لتعليمه، ه ل.

[٧] وقد كان سببك: وقد نسبك، ل.

أحسن، ودعاه بحضرتي[١].

وسأله أبو الحسن المطّلبي وذكر له أن القرويين[٢] سألوه أن يسأله[٣] لهم في قاض يقدمه عليهم، فأشار إليّ فقلت: المروذي شيخنا هو أولى. فأجمع رأينا عليه، فقدمه وقال له: احذر الأحقاد، وكل من كان بينك وبينه دم في الجاهلية فأهدره، ثم عقد له. فبلغ ذلك أبا موسى هارون بن يونس[٤]، فدخل فوجدني في سقيفة القصر مع المروذي، فسلمنا عليه، فأنكر علي ما[٥] بلغه من تعافيّ واجتماع رأينا على المروذي. فقال لي: والله ليكونن فعلك[٦] هذا وبالاً عليك، المدينة لي وعاملها من دعوتي، فتكون أنت إن كان، فسرني ذلك.

ثم دخل وهو كاره لتقديم المروذي، فبدأه أبو عبد الله وقال له: ذكر لي المطلبي حاجة الناس إلى من ينظر في أسواقهم وموازينهم، وقد قدمنا[٧] المعروف بالمروذي. فقال: وما حاجتنا إلى هذا؟ هل كان لرسول الله صلى الله عليه وآله قاض؟ إنما نريد أن نردهم إلى رأينا وسنتنا كما فعلنا في طبنة وغيرها. قال: وما علينا من هذا؟ نجعل لكل مزبلة كنّاسًا.

---

[١] بحضرتي: بحضرته، ه.

[٢] القرويين: القروبيين، ه ل إ.

[٣] ذكر له ... يسأله: ذكره ... يسأله، ه؛ ذكر له ... يسأل، ل إ.

[٤] يونس: يوسف، ه.

[٥] فانكر علي ما: فنكر علي مما، ل.

[٦] فعلك: فعالك، ل إ.

[٧] وقد قدمنا: وقدمنا، ل.

ثم سألني أن نأتيه بكتب / [٤٧] الفرائض والفقه، فأتيته بها. وكان يناظر ابن عبدون وسعيد ين الحدّاد وموسى القطّان[١] والصديني وحماسًا[٢] في الفرائض وإحراز الابنة جميع الميراث وفي الإمامة وغير ذلك. وقال لي: إنّ المؤمن إذا دعي فهو كالمحرم الذي لا يحل له صيد البر ولا يقتل الصيد ولا يقرب النساء والطيب حتى يخرج من إحرامه، وأنت عندي مؤمن تستحق أن نأذن لك في مناظرتهم والاحتجاج عليهم والفتيا بقول آل محمد صلى الله عليه وآله وتمنعهم من قراءة كتب أبي حنيفة ومالك.

فقلت: يا سيدي، شهر رمضان قد تقارب دخوله، وقد كان علي صلوات الله عليه أراد أن يقطع بدعة عمر في صلاة الليل بإمام، فأرجو أن يشفي الله بك الغليل، فتقدم إلى أبي علي في قطع ذلك.

فقال: أي والله نفعل.[٣] فأمر أبا علي بن أبي خنزير[٤] والمروذي بقطع ذلك، وأذن في كنس المساجد وتوفير[٥] الزيت وأن يجتمع الناس لصلاة الفريضة فقط ولا تصلى نافلة بإمام. فلما دخل شهر رمضان أمضى ذلك من رأيه وتمّت عزيمته، وحضرنا لصلاة الفريضة مع المروذي، فقرأ الإمام: «وَالسَّمَاءِ ذَاتِ الْبُرُوجِ وَالْيَوْمِ

---

[١] القطان: العطار، إ ه ل.

[٢] وحماسًا: وحماس، ه ل إ.

[٣] اي والله نفعل: اي والله تفعل، ه؛ الي والله نفعل، ل إ.

[٤] بن ابي خنزير: بن حبرين، ه؛ بن ابي جعفر، ل؛ ابن حبرين، إ.

[٥] توفير: توفر، ه.

المَوْعُودِ» إلى قوله تعالى: «قُتِلَ أَصْحَابُ الأُخْدُودِ»،[١] فغصّ بباقي قراءته وأومى إلى ما منعوا منه من الصلاة والتهجد، ففهّمت المروذي، فقال: صدقتَ، / [٤٨] والله ما أراد إلا هذا، وأراد أن ينزل به في ذلك الوقت وأن يحبسه[٢].

فقلت له: لا تفعل هذا ليلاً، تعزله[٣] غداً.

وعرف السيد بفعله، فقدّم الكوفي صاحبنا على الخطبة يوم الجمعة وعلى الصلوات[٤]، وكان الكوفي قد رأى رؤيا قبل دخول السيد، كأن الشيعي دخل القيروان وهو يحثّ[٥] ركابه حتى دخل المسجد الجامع ونزل عند المنبر وأعطاه كلبًا سلوقيًا، فمسكه[٦] بمِقْوَده عند رجل المنبر. فتأولت ذلك له وقلت له: يدخل الشيعي ويوليك الخطبة، فضحك وقال: كيف هذا؟ قلت: الكلب السلوقي ممدوح والكلب يصيح ويعضّ[٧] وينبه ويدل على الغريب والخطيب يوضح ويدل وينبه. فذكّرت المروذي برؤيا الكوفي وعرفت السيد بذلك،

---

[١] القرآن ٨٥:١ – ٤.

[٢] يحبسه: تحبسه، ل إ.

[٣] ليلا تعزله: لئلا تعزله، ه؛ ليل تعز، إ؛ الليل تعزل، ل.

[٤] الصلوات: الصلاة، ل.

[٥] يحثّ: تحت، ه ل إ.

[٦] فمسكه: فمسكت ه ل إ.

[٧] ويعض: ويعظ، إ ه ل.

فقدمه على الخطبة والصلوات[١]، وأجرى له رزقًا خمسة دنانير في الشهر.

واجتمعتُ مع ابن عبدون والصدينى وابن جيمال[٢] ‹و› الكلاعي ومعهم الحسيني الجزري(؟)[٣]، فأجريت معهم المسألة في إحراز الابنة لجميع[٤] الميراث. فقال ابن عبدون: لها بقول الله النصف، وإن كان على غير ذلك فقولوا ما شئتم. فقلت: لها النصف مع الأبوين، وللأبوين الثلث لكل واحد منهما السدس، ويبقى السدس، فهو مردود عليها لأنه يلزمها النقصان من النصف لو كان معها زوج أو زوجة، ومن لزمه النقصان كان / ٤٩ أحق بالسهم الفاضل، ولكن الله تعالى قد ورّثها الكل في كتابه.

فقال: في أي موضع هذا في كتاب الله؟

قلت: قوله تعالى: «إِنِ امْرُؤٌ هَلَكَ لَيسَ لَهُ وَلَدٌ وَلَهُ أُخْتٌ فَلَهَا نِصفُ مَا تَرَكَ وَهُوَ يَرِثُهَا إِن لَم يَكُنْ لَهَا وَلَدٌ»[٥] فلم يورث الله تعالى الأخ ولا[٦] الأخت مع الولد شيئًا، ولا نورث العصبة شيئًا إذا لم يورث الله الأخ ولا الأخت.

---

[١] الصلوات: الصلاة، ل.

[٢] جيمال: حمالق، ه إ.

[٣] الحسيني الجزري (؟): الحسني الخرزي، ه إ؛ الحسيني الحرزي، ل.

[٤] لجميع: بجميع، ل.

[٥] القرآن ٤:١٧٦.

[٦] لا: –، ل.

فقال ابن جيمال[١]: كأني والله ما سمعتها في كتاب الله.

فقال له ابن عبدون: أمسك، الولد هاهنا الذكر.

فقلت: أبى الله ما ذكرت، قال الله تعالى: «وَلَكُم نِصْفُ مَا تَرَكَ أَزْوَاجُكُم إِنْ لَم يَكُنْ لَهُنَّ وَلَدٌ»[٢]، فالابنة تحجب الزوج عن النصف وتحجب الزوجة عن الربع، فإن حجبته فهي الولد الذي لا يرث[٣] معها أخ ولا أخت ولا عصبة، وقد قال ذلك ابن عباس وابن مسعود.

فقال له الشيخ الحسيني[٤]: قد والله حجّك[٥]، قد والله قطعك. فغضب ابن عبدون وسكت حتى دخلنا على أبي عبد الله فسلموا. فلما خرجوا عرفته ما جرى بيني وبينهم، فقال: ألا ذكرت هذا بحضرته؟ فقلت: أجللته لأنه غضب وعبس في الطريق عندما بين له الشيخ الحسيني[٦] بقيام الحجة عليه، فسره ذلك من قولي.

وكنت ملازمًا لأبي عبد الله ومترددًا إليه، فكان ثابت الأخلاق وواحد المعاني مؤثراً للعدل والصدق والزهد في الدنيا، طعامه واحد ولباسه واحد، غير متكبر ولا متجبر ولا مؤثر / ٥٠ للبطنة، بل

---

[١] جيمال: جمالي، ه.

[٢] القرآن ٤:١٢.

[٣] يرث: يورث، إ.

[٤] الحسيني: الحسني، ه إ.

[٥] حجك: احجك، ل؛ حجبك، ه.

[٦] الحسيني: الحسني، ه إ.

كان كثير الرغبة في دعوة المجيبين والتزيد[١] في خلاص أرواحهم.

ولقد هاج به يومًا دم خاف على نفسه من إفراطه. فقال له زياد: أخرج الدم وطِرْ بِهِ، ففصده بحضرتي، فما زاد طعامًا ولا استكثر من شيء غير ما كان عليه إلا بيضات سوّيناها[٢] له بين يديه، فحسا محّها[٣].

ولقد حضرتُ مناظرته لسعيد بن الحداد وغيره، وسألته يومًا مناظرة[٤] ابن الحداد وقد تأوّل في حديث رسول الله صلى الله عليه وآله قوله لعلي عليه السلام: من كنت مولاه فعلي مولاه. فقال له أبو عبد الله: علي مولاك؟

فقال ابن الحداد: نعم، مولاي بالمعنى الذي أنا[٥] به مولاه.

فابتدأته[٦] أنا وقلت له: فأنت مولى النبي بالمعنى الذي النبي به مولاك، فأنت أولى بالنبي من نفسه كما النبي أولى بك من نفسك، وقد جعل رسول الله ما ولاه الله من أمته لعلي عليه السلام،

---

[١] التزيد: التنزيه، ه.

[٢] سويناها: شويناها، ه إ ل.

[٣] محها: مخها، ل؛ حسامهما (؟)، إ.

[٤] وسألته يوما مناظرة: وسألت يوما مناظرته، ه إ.

[٥] انا: اتا، ل.

[٦] فابتداته: وابتداته، ه؛ وابتداءه، إ.

وفي قوله تعالى: «النَّبِيُّ أَوْلَى بِالْمُؤْمِنِينَ مِن أَنْفُسِهِم»[١]، وقد قال عمر حينئذ لعلي عليه السلام: أصبحت مولاي ومولى كل مؤمن ومؤمنة.

فتعافى من المناظرة وقال: أيها السيد قد دخلتَ مدائن غير مدينتنا هذه وتركت أهلها على ما كانوا عليه.

فقال أبو عبد الله: «لاَ إِكْرَاهَ فِي الدِّينِ»[٢]، ثم قال لي: دعوهم، فسوف[٣] تناظرونهم وتباهرونهم، ولكنني أقول كما قال شعيب: «وَإِنْ كَانَ طَائِفَةٌ مِنكُم آمَنُوا بِالَّذِي أُرْسِلْتُ بِهِ وَطَائِفَةٌ لَم يُؤْمِنُوا فَاصْبِرُوا حَتَّى /٥١ يَحْكُمَ اللهُ بَيْنَنَا وَهُوَ خَيرُ الحَاكِمِينَ»[٤].

وقد ألف سعيد بن الحداد هذا كتابًا لطيفًا ذكر فيه مناظرته لأبي عبد الله وأبي العباس وبثّه في الآفاق، وزاد عليها وكذب في تأليفه، ولقد كنت حاضراً لمجالسه كلها معهما حينئذ، وقد رأيت كتابه ونقضته عليه وتابعته فيه بكلام جامع لإبطال مقالته وما قصد إليه من[٥] إثبات القياس وإمامة المفضول وغير ذلك من معانيه، وقد انتشر عند جماعة من أصحابه.

وحدثتُ أبا عبد الله حديثنا مع ابن الحداد، وقد دخلنا إليه

---

[١] القرآن ٣٣:٦.

[٢] القرآن ٢: ٢٥٦.

[٣] فسوف: سوف، ه إ.

[٤] القرآن ٧:٨٧.

[٥] من: في، ه ل إ.

يومًا ومعي أحمد ابن المروذي وابن حيّون[١] ومعنا يوسف بن دنقس[٢]، فوجدناه في سقيفته جالسًا[٣] وحده، وذلك بعد ما عُزل ابن مسكين وولي القضاء الصديني، وكنا نُدلّ في أيام العراقيين. فقلنا: مسألة، فقال: سلوا. قلنا: أخبرنا عن قول الله عز وجل: «خَالِقُ كُلِّ شَيْءٍ» هو عام أو خاص؟ فسكت قليلاً ثم قال: هذه مسائل أهل البدع، فحَرِجَ عليكم إن كنتم منهم إلا خرجتم عنا. فقلنا له: أنت شيخ أحمق جاهل، من قعد مقعدك هذا وانتصب انتصابك يردّ الجواب ولا يشتم، البدعة فيك والمحال مذهبك والتشبيه اعتقادك وتكثير الأعداد في الله والمعاني في صفاته قولك واعتقادك أن لله مثلاً، والله الذي يقول: «لَيْسَ كَمِثْلِهِ شَيْءٌ»[٤]. فما أنسى جزعه منا وذلته لنا خوفًا أن نبطش به، وخرجنا عنه. / ٥٢ فطالب بعد ذلك ابن دنقس الإسرائيلي[٥] وقال له: من هؤلاء الذين كانوا معك؟ فعرفه بنا، فقال: نعم، كذلك ينبغي[٦].

وذكرت له خبري مع حِماس القاضي، وكنت أخاصم[٧] عنده

---

[١] ابن حيون: ابن حيوية (؟)، ه؛ ابن حبويه، إ.

[٢] دنقس: ذنقش، إ.

[٣] جالسا: خاليا، ه إ.

[٤] القرآن ٤٢:١١.

[٥] الإسرائيلي: الاسرائيل، إ.

[٦] ينبغي: نبتغي، ل ه؛ تبتغي، إ.

[٧] اخاصم: الخاصم، ل.

في وصـيــة والدي. فكلّفني التــزكـيــة، فـمــا توقف عني أحــد من مشايخنا، فماطلني وآذاني خصمي المعروف بابن التستري، وقال له: إنه يبـرأ من السلف، وحمله عليّ واستـعـان على ذلك بقـوم آخرين، فضـغطتـه يومًا إلى الحكم لي[١]. فـقال لي: تصبـر حتى نكتب بهـذه المسألة إلى مصر.[٢] فقلت له: وما الذي عـجـز عنه فقـها ء إفـريقـيـة حتى تحتاج إلى فقهاء مصر؟ المسألة واضحة، رجل أوصى إلى رجل وشرط في وصـيتـه إذا بلغ ابنه فلان كـان هو الوصي وحده على سائر الأطفال من ولده، وخلع الأوصياء ببلوغ ولده هذا، وقد سألتَني التزكية فـشـهـد عندك رجال أكـثـرهم أجللتـه أن يقـعـد بين يديك ورفعـتـهم إلى مجلسك. فضاق ونزق وقال: لك مذاهب ردية، وكررها[٣] علي، بلغني أنك تبـرأ من السلف وتقـول بخلق[٤] القـرآن وترفض أبا بكر وعــمـر ويجالسك[٥] اليـهـود. فقلت له: أنت قاضي إفريقية وفقيـه أهل المدينة ومنهم من يرمـيـك مـذاهب ردية وينسـبـونك[٦] إلى الـشـكـوكـيــة، فـنزق وهاج وأزبد وأمر بحبسي.

فلما جئت إلى الحبس قال لي حاجبه: اصبر لا تصعد، ليس يتمادى عليك، فأبيت إلا الصعود، فجذبني / ٥٣ وخرق ثوبًا كان علي،

[١] لي: -، ل.

[٢] الى مصر: -، ل.

[٣] وكررها: كررها، إ.

[٤] بخلق: يخلف، ل.

[٥] يجالسك: تجالسك، ل.

[٦] ينسبونك: ينصبونك، ه.

وقام إلي ابن زعلان الأعور وأجلسني في مكانه فجلست فيه، والحاجب يسألني ما بي، فما تمت جلوسي حتى صاح بي الصبي حاجبه واستنزلني[١] الوكيل. فنزلت، فقال لي الصبي حاجبه: تشتم القاضي في مجلس قضائه؟ فلو كان غير عارف بك أو جاهل بك وبآبائك أليس كنت تغتم ونغتم بك؟ قلت: وما قلت؟ إنما قلت له هذا على التعظيم إذ كان هو القاضي ويشنع عليه، فأحرى أن يقال فينا ما ليس فينا وينسبونا إلى غير مذهبنا، فوقى الله شره.

ولقد مررت يومًا إلى باب الربيع، فإني لماشٍ إذ وجدت رقعة في زقاق، فأخذتها، وكنت إذا رأيت رقعة أخذتها لأعرف ما فيها. فإذا هي من أخي ومن صهره خصمي مكتوبة إلى القاضي يحرّضونه على تفتيش كتبي، ويقولون: لو تمادى القاضي عليه في حبسه لأخرجنا له من كتب الرافضة وكتب الدهرية. فرجعت من طريقي وتركت حاجتي في باب الربيع، وأخذت كتبي فرفعتها عند نساء كُنَّ حينئذ عماتي وعمات أبي. فلما كان بعد يومين انصرفت عشية من دار أبي سعيد ابن المعمر بن المنصور، وكنا نسمع عنده كتاب أبيه في الفقه، وكان يذهب إلى إبطال طلاق البدعة. فوجدت الصبي وخصمي وأخي يفتشون الكتب، فلم يجدوا إلا كتب أبي من الفقه والمغازي[٢] والغريب والشعر وكتب الجاحظ وكتب أبي عبيد /[٥٤] وابن قتيبة وكتب الموصلي وغير ذلك. فأرعدت وأبرقت وتراميت على صاحب البريد،

---

[١] واستنزلني: والمستوحي، إ ل؛ والسوحي، ه.

[٢] المغازي: المغازين، ه.

وكان من تربية أبي[١]، وعرفته في بطاقة[٢] خبري. فأمر بإدخالي فعرفني وبكى إذ ذكرت أبي[٣]، وكتب فيّ سجلاً[٤] بعثه مع فرانق على لسان زيادة الله ابن الأغلب أن جعفر بن أحمد بن محمد بن الأسود بن الهيثم ذكر أنك قبلت قول خصمائه عليه وفتشت كتبه، فأنكرت هذا أشد الإنكار ونهيتك أن لا تكشف الناس عن[٥] مذاهبهم، وعليك بالألفة واجتماع الكلمة، وغير هذا. فوصل الكتاب إلى حماس، فقرأه وارتعد وتعافى من النظر بيننا وقال لأصحابه: إنّهم ليتخاصمون إلى اليوم من[٦] سنتين ورددتهم لكي يصطلحوا، وأنا لا أنظر بينهم على حال. وكانت[٧] له ضغينة في قلبي حتى أذله الله ووضعه وأعزنا عليه، فوقيناه[٨] وتذلل لنا واستعان علينا وخضع إلينا وكتب إلينا كتابًا يسترحمنا فيه، ووجّه إليّ بولدَيه حمود[٩] وسالم، فخررت لله ساجداً وحمدت الله على ما وهب لنا وأيّدنا وهدانا

---

[١] ابي: الي، ل.

[٢] بطاقة: نطاقة، ل؛ نظافة، ه؛ نطاقه، إ.

[٣] اذا ذكرت ابي: اذ ذكرت، ل.

[٤] سجلا: سجل، ه إ ل.

[٥] لا تكشف الناس عن: لا تكشف عن، ه؛ لا تكشف الناس على، ل.

[٦] من: في، ه ل إ.

[٧] وكانت: فكانت، ل.

[٨] فوقيناه: فوفيناه، ل إ.

[٩] حمود: محمود، ه.

وأرشدنا، فجعلت لهما على نفسي ولأبيهما أن لا يبلغه عني إلا خير، وأهدرنا الضغائن والأحقاد وتوكلنا على الله تعالى نعم المولى ونعم النصير.

فسرّ أبا عبد الله كل ما حدثته وأمر عامله بحفظ ابن زعلان وإقراره على وكالة السجن، وقال: ومن يتوكل على الله فهو حسبه.

ولقد شكوت تمادي ابن / ٥٥ التستري عليّ وإفساده عليّ عماتي حتى حُملنَ على الحيف علي[١] وأمالهن إلى أخي وخصمي وحرضهن. فقال لي: لا تغتم بهذا، ليورثنك[٢] الله هذا وغيره. فوالله لقد رأيت ذلك وزادتني الأيام عزاً وارتفاعًا وزادتهم ذلة[٣] وصغاراً. ولقد دار إليّ جميع ما كان في أملاكهم بالبيع والميراث، وربنا المحمود[٤] على ما أولى وعلى ما أبلى وعلى الشدة والرخاء. ثم صرنا بعد ذلك كله في محنة يقصر[٥] عنها العزاء ويعجز عنها جلد الصبر، ورأينا الدهر كما قال الشاعر:

كَمْ ذُقْتُ فِي الدَّهْرِ مِن عُسْرٍ وَمِن يُسْرٍ
وَفِي[٦] بَنِي الدَّهْرِ مِن رَأسٍ وَمِن ذَنَبِ

---

[١] علي: عني، ه إ ل.

[٢] بهذا ليورثنك : بذلك ليورينك، ه.

[٣] وزادتهم ذلة: وزادت لهم ذلا، ل.

[٤] المحمود: للحمود، ل.

[٥] يقصر: تقصر، ه ل إ.

[٦] وفي: في، إ.

وَحَادِثَاتٍ[١] أعَاجِيبَ خَسًا وَزَكًا[٢]
مَا الدَّهْرُ من فِعْلِهِ إلاّ أبو العَجَبِ

وقال آخر:

كَفَى المَرْءَ فِي الدُّنْيَا وَإنْ كَانَ حَازِمًا   تَغَيُّرُ[٣] أحْوَالٍ وَخَفْضُ مَرَاتِبِ
تَبَدُّلَ هَذَا العِزُّ ذُلاً وَفَاقَةً   وَذَلِكَ صِدْقًا[٤] من عَجِيبِ العَجَائِبِ
فَكُنْ جَلَداً لِلحَادِثَاتِ[٥] مُسْلِمًا   لِصَاحِبِ عَصْرٍ يُرْتَجَى لِلنَّوائِبِ

ولقد كنت كثيراً أسأل أبا عبد الله[٦] عن خلق القرآن وعن الاستطاعة وخلق الفعل والوعد والوعيد وعن قول المرجئة في الأعمال والإيمان. فكان يقول: سوف يجيئك[٧] من يشفيك من هذا وغيره. ثم قال لي: وما تقول المرجئة في الإيمان؟

قلت: يقولون: القول والاعتقاد هو الإيمان، ولا يضرّ ترك العمل ولا تبطل الذنوب /[٥٦] الإيمان كما لا ينفع عمل الصالحات

---

[١]وحادثات: وحادقات، ل.

[٢]خسا وزكا: حسنا وزكى، ه إ ل.

[٣]تغير: بتغيير، ه.

[٤]صدقا: صدق، ه إ ل.

[٥] للحادثات: الحادثات، ل.

[٦] ابا عبد الله: –، ل.

[٧]يجيئك: تجيئك، ل.

الكافر شيئًا، وإن الله يرحم المذنبين حتمًا كما يعذب المشركين[١] حتمًا. والمعتزلة والإباضية يقولون بإنفاذ الوعيد، فإنه كالوعد في الوجوب[٢] والإلزام، والوعيد والوعد خبر والخبر لا ينسخ ولا يحتمل التأويل. ومنهم من يسمي المذنب كافراً بنعمته[٣]، ومنهم من يسميه فاسقًا مشركًا، وكل مشرك فاسق، ومنهم من لا يسميه مشركًا، ولهم في كل هذا تأويلات. فأهل[٤] التفويض يقولون: إن المذنبين من المؤمنين في مشيئة الله، لا يحتم على الله بعذابهم ولا يحتم عليه برحمته[٥]، ولكنهم منصرفون بين فضل وعدل، فإن عذبهم فعادل وإن عفى عنهم فمتفضل[٦]، ولا يقال في ‹ترك› الوعيد: مخلف، ويقال في ترك الوعد: مخلف، لأن الوعد حق من حقوق العباد جعله الله جزاء لهم والوعيد حق الله، وإن تركه فإلى الفضل يتركه[٧]، ومثلوا هذا برجل وعد رجلاً بهبة وتوعّد[٨] غيره بعقوبة وإن ترك عقوبته مدح ولم يذمّ وإن ترك وعده سمي بخيلاً ومخلفًا، ألا ترى أن الله وصف

---

[١] المشركين: الكافرين، ه.

[٢] الوجوب: الوجود، ل.

[٣] بنعمته:: بعينه، ه ل إ.

[٤] فاهل: واهل، ل إ.

[٥] برحمته: برحمتهم، ل.

[٦] فمتفضل: فتفضل، ل.

[٧] يتركه: بتركه، ه إ.

[٨] وتوعد: وتواعد، ه إ ل.

نفسه بالجود والرأفة والعفو والرحمة والإحسان والمغفرة؟ وإنما يرحم الله[١] المذنبين ويعفو عن الخاطئين، وما على المحسنين من سبيل.

فقال: وما يقول الشيعة في الإيمان؟

قلت: يقولون بقول جعفر بن محمد الصادق صلوات الله عليه: الإيمان[٢] عمل كله والقول بعض /٥٧ ذلك العمل لأنه قول باللسان وعمل بالاعتقاد، والنية والصلاة والزكاة[٣] والصوم والحج أعمال على الجوارح.

فاستحسن ذلك وقال: الإيمان علم وعمل، فمن علم ولم يعمل لم ينفعه علمه ولا يدري حقيقته، ومن عمل ولم يعلم لم يدر ما حقيقة عمله ‹و›لا ينفعه[٤]. وإخراج هذا إلى ظاهر وباطن، فمن لم يعلم باطن ظاهره فغير عالم، ومن لم يقم بظاهره انكشف سرُّه[٥] ولم يكمل عقله، ومن انكشف باطنه لم يكمل ولا يكون منه داعٍ[٦] ولا[٧] يطمأن إليه في الوصول إلى ما بقي عليه.

ثم قال: وأما الوعيد فمتى أجزتم فيه الترك والعفو ففرية من عقلك فيمن قتل إمامًا أو نبيًا أو فيمن قتل علي بن أبي طالب عليه

---

[١] الله: -، ه إ.

[٢] الايمان: والايمان، ه.

[٣] والزكاة: -، ه إ.

[٤] لا ينفعه: -، ه إ.

[٥] سره: ستره، ل إ.

[٦] داعٍ: داعيا، ه ل إ.

[٧] لا: لم، ل.

السلام وقتل الحسين بن علي وكذلك فيمن غصب عليًا وظلمه[١] وهتك ستر فاطمة، وقد قال رسول الله صلى الله عليه وآله: فاطمة بضعة من لحمي فمن أسخطها فقد أسخطني فعليه[٢] لعنة الله والملائكة والناس أجمعين.

فقلت: يقولون: إن هؤلاء مشركون لا مؤمنون وكافرون لا مسلمون ومستحلون متعمدون لتحليل محارم الله، ومن أحل محارم الله فهو كافر بالله، وكذلك لو فرضنا[٣] ذنب المؤمن المقرّ بالإمام العارف بربه ورسوله كأبي ذر وغيره لو زل[٤] في كبيرة وجب أن ‹لا› يحتم عليه بالعذاب المبين والخلود مع فرعون وهامان وأشباههما من الظالمين.

فقال: وإنما تجيز المشيئة فيمن جامعك / ٥٨ على إمامك وقولك.

قلت: كذلك نقول.

قال: هذا تحيُّر منك وخروج عن الإجماع، والخبر عن الله عز وجل إنما جاء مجيئ عموم، ليس لك أن تخص بالتأويل.

فقلت: ما نخصّ إلا من جهة الخبر عن الله عز وجل بقوله: «إِنَّ اللهَ لا يَغْفِرُ أَنْ يُشْرَكَ بِهِ وَيَغْفِرُ مَا دُونَ ذٰلِكَ لِمَن يَشَاءُ»[٥]،

---

[١] غصب عليا وظلمه: ظلم عليا وغصبه، ل إ.

[٢] فعليه: وعليه، ل.

[٣] فرضنا: قرنا، ه؛ فرا، إ.

[٤] زل: نزل، ه.

[٥] القرآن ٤:٤٨.

والمستحل لمحارم الله تعالى هو المتعمد المشرك الذي لا يغفر له، وكل ذنب دون الشرك فجائز فيه المشيئة.

قال: فلا بد أن تعمّ المشيئة جميع أهل الملة، ويلزمك في قاتلي علي والحسين عليهما السلام أن تجري المشيئة فيهما.

فما وجدت من قوله[١] مخرجًا إلا أن عكست عليه أيضًا ذنوب الأولياء مثل أبي ذر وغيره وإخوة يوسف ومثلهم. غير أني قلت: قال الله تعالى: «وَجَزَاءُ سَيِّئَةٍ سَيِّئَةٌ مِثْلُهَا»[٢] ‹لا› بعذاب النار والخلود[٣]، ‹وقال›: «كُلَّمَا نَضِجَتْ جُلُودُهُم بَدَّلْنَاهُم جُلُوداً غَيْرَهَا»[٤] «وَلَهُم مَقَامِعُ مِن حَدِيدٍ»[٥] وشرابهم «يُصْهَرُ بِهِ مَا فِي بُطُونِهِم»[٦]، كل هذا ‹لا› يستحقه فاعل الكبيرة، وليس[٧] هذا مثل ‹فعل› من أكل مال اليتيم أو زنى أو سرق.

قال: وكذلك أيضًا إذا أضفت هذه الوجوه من العذاب إلى الشرك[٨] لم يكن مثله.

---

[١] من قوله: لقوله، ل إ؛ في قوله، ه.

[٢] القرآن ٤٢:٤٠.

[٣] والخلود: والجلود، ه إ ل.

[٤] القرآن ٤:٥٦.

[٥] القرآن ٢٢:٢١.

[٦] القرآن ٢٢:٢٠.

[٧] وليس: وكل، ل إ ه.

[٨] الشرك: المشرك، ل إ.

فقلت: مخالفة الله الذي خلق فسوى وقدر فهدى وأخرج من العدم إلى الوجود أكبر[١] من ‹فعل الكبيرة، فيكبر› عذاب الملحد في الله المشرك[٢] به العابد لما صنعته أيدي البشر من الحجارة والصلبان والنصب.

فقال: وكذلك فاعل الكبيرة يخالف[٣] / ٥٩ الله الذي أطعم وأسقى وأمات وأحيى وأغنى وأقنى.

فقلت: فما تعمل[٤] في قول الله تعالى: «وَلاَ[٥] يُظْلَمُونَ فَتِيلاً»[٦]، و«مَن يَعْمَلْ مِثْقَالَ ذَرَّةٍ خَيْراً يَرَهُ»[٧]؟ فإذا عوقب[٨] على الكبيرة فقد بطل الوعد وذهبت الحسنات وأبطلت السيئات الحسنات، فالقرآن قد أكذب ذهاب الحسنات بالسيئات،[٩] فقال تعالى: «أولَئِكَ يُبَدِّلُ اللهُ سَيِّئَاتِهِم حَسَنَاتٍ»[١٠].

---

[١] اكبر: اكثر، ه ل إ.

[٢] المشرك: والمشرك، ه.

[٣] يخالف: مخالف، ل إ.

[٤] تعمل: يعمل، ه ل إ.

[٥] ولا: فلا، ل.

[٦] القرآن ٤:٤٩ و٧٧ و ١٧:٧١.

[٧] القرآن ٩٩:٧. + «ومن يعمل مثقال ذرة شرا يره»، ل.

[٨] عوقب: عوقبت، ه إ.

[٩] الحسنات بالسيئات: السيئات بالحسنات، ه إ ل.

[١٠] القرآن ٢٥:٧٠.

فقال: وقد قال أيضًا: «الأَخْسَرِينَ أعْمَالاً»[١].

فقلت: خسروها بالكفر والنفاق، والإقرار بالتوحيد والنبوة والإمامة يبطل كل ذنب، ويجوز[٢] في قدرة الله غفرانه لمن أقرّ به وبرسله[٣] وبالأئمة، وقد أكد الله في تنزيله، فقال تعالى[٤]: «إنَّهُ مَن يُشْرِكْ بِالله فَقَدْ حَرَّمَ اللهُ عَلَيْهِ الجَنَّةَ»[٥]، ولم يقل كذلك في فاعل الذنب، بل أوجب فيهم المشيئة.

فقال: وكذلك المشيئة تجب لليهود والنصارى حيث يقول: «وَقَالَتِ اليَهُودُ وَالنَّصَارَى نَحْنُ أَبْنَاءُ الله وَأَحِبَّاؤُهُ قُلْ فَلِمَ يُعَذِّبُكُم بِذُنُوبِكُم بَلْ أَنْتُم بَشَرٌ مِمَّن خَلَقَ يَغْفِرُ لِمَن يَشَاءُ وَيُعَذِّبُ مَن يَشَاءُ»[٦].

فقلت: الآية أكدت عذابهم لا المشيئة في غفران ذنوبهم وشركهم.

فقال: وكيف ذلك؟

فقلت: في قوله رداً عليهم أنهم أحباب الله «قُلْ فَلِمَ يُعَذِّبُكُم بِذُنُوبِكُم[٧]»، فالمشيئة بعد ذلك قد تجوز على صحة أبدانهم وعلى أمراضهم وفقرهم واستغنائهم، وقد تكون المشيئة لمن مات في حياة

---

[١] القرآن ١٨:١٠٣.

[٢] ويجوز: يجوز، ل.

[٣] برسله: برسوله، ل.

[٤] فقال تعالى: -، ه إ.

[٥] القرآن ٥:٧٢.

[٦] القرآن ٥:١٨.

[٧] بذنوبكم: -، إ.

موسى من بني أمته وقبل ظهور المسيح، فقد[١] يجوز المشيئة في أولئك لأنهم / ٦٠ لم يلزمهم اسم الكفر إلا بعد كفرهم بالمسيح.

فقال: وكذلك توجب المشيئة في عذاب المنافقين وتجوز عندك[٢] رحمتهم في قوله: «وَيُعَذِّبَ الْمُنَافِقِينَ إِنْ شَاءَ أَوْ يَتُوبَ عَلَيهِمِ»[٣].

فقلت: العذاب هاهنا اسم مشترك لعذاب[٤] الدنيا، كما قال: «قَاتِلُوهُم يُعَذِّبْهُمُ اللهُ بِأَيْدِيكُم»[٥].

قال: فقول الله: «وَقَدْ خَابَ مَن حَمَلَ ظُلْمًا»[٦]، وقوله: «وَلاَ تُجَادِلْ عَنِ الَّذِينَ يَخْتَانُونَ أَنْفُسَهُم إِنَّ اللهَ لاَ يُحِبُّ مَن كَانَ خَوَّانًا أَثِيمًا»[٧]، وكثر من هذا وأطال فيه.

فقلت: ما يتكلم في هذا مجادلة للمذنبين لكن تعظيمًا لله أن يمنعه خلقه ويتأول[٨] عليه عباده ويحكموا عليه، إذ لا مشيئة له ولا مستثنى في تعذيب من يشاء ورحمته لمن يشاء.

---

[١] فقد: قد، ل.

[٢] عندك: عند، إ.

[٣] القرآن ٣٣:٢٤.

[٤] لعذاب: العذاب، ل.

[٥] القرآن ٩:١٤.

[٦] القرآن ٢٠:١١١.

[٧] القرآن ٤:١٠٧.

[٨] يتأول: يتاولوا، ه إ؛ يتولوا، ل.

فقال: هذا سيوف من قصب لا تقطع شيئًا، وإنما برهان هذا كله في باطنه، وأرجوك تناله إن شاء الله تعالى، فتعلم الوعد والوعيد وحقيقة ذلك.

فكنا نشرب عنده من عين الحياة ونسرح في رياض الجنة وجنات وعيون ومقام كريم «وَفَاكِهَةٍ كَثِيرَةٍ لا مَقْطُوعَةٍ وَلا مَمْنُوعَةٍ»[١] حتى خرج في طلب الإمام الكريم والسيد العظيم زين البلاد وشمس العباد وقبة الزمان، فودّعته بسببه[٢].

فقال لي: قد وصيت بك، فظننت أنه يريد أبا زاكي، فأقمت أيامًا، ثم مضيت فوجدت عند أبي زاكي جميع أصحابنا مع المروذي، فأوسع لي عند نفسه. ثم انصرف أصحابنا، وحبسني / [٦١] عنده وأخرج إليّ كتبًا مجلدة مرسومًا[٣] على أحدهما "كتاب المعرفة والإقرار والجحد والإنكار"، وكتابًا مجلداً فيه قصيدة تسمى "ذات الجواهر" فيها علوم وتوحيد ورموز باطنة وحكمة من حكيم. فقرأت منها عليه ما قد كان خفيًا لديه وشرحت له[٤] من معانيها ما كان معتاصًا عليه، فسرّ بذلك وقال: لأجمعن بينك وبين ضيف كريم على الله، فشكرته على قوله وما ابتدأني به[٥] من لفظه، وقلت له: قد كان ابتداء أمري

---

[١] القرآن ٥٦: ٣٢-٣٣.

[٢] بسببه: لسببه، ل إ (؟).

[٣] مرسومًا: مرسوم، ه ل إ.

[٤] وشرحت له: وشرحت عليه وله، ه.

[٥] به: -، ل.

بأبي[1] مـوسى وأرجـو تمامـه بك وعلى يديك[2]. فـقـام وتركني في مكانه، ودخل ناحيـة في القصر قد كانت حجزت بالخشب وسترت بالكن، ثم خرج ودعاني، فدخلت إلى مقصورة في القصر.

تم الجزء الأول من المناظرات والحمد لله رب العالمين وصلى الله على رسوله محمد وعلى آله[3] أبرار عترته الصادقين وسلم.

يتلوه:

---

[1] بابي: ابو، ه إ ل.

[2] وعلى يديك: -، ل.

[3] آله: -، ل إ.

الجزء الثاني من كتاب المناظرات

بسم الله الرحمن الرحيم
وصلى الله على محمد وعلى آل محمد[١].

قال أبو عبد الله جعفر بن أحمد ⟨بن⟩ الأسود: دخلت على أبي العباس في شهر رمضان بعد خروج أبي عبد الله بثلاثة أيام مع أبي زاكي تمام بن معارك، فقام إليّ ومشى إقداماً وعانقني وقبلت يده فقبل يدي وقال لي: أنت ابن الأسود، شيخكم وصاني بك، وقد سألت[٢] عنك أبا زاكي. ثم / ٦٢ جلس مكانه وأدناني منه ورفعني على فرش[٣] كان على يمينه وبسطني للمناظرة، وأخرج كتاباً من أخيه إليه يذكر فيه[٤] عن زياد المتطبب أنه قضى في علة أبي موسى هارون ابن يونس وكان خلفه عليلاً، وأنه إن حدث به أحد ستة[٥] أشياء: إما رُعاف[٦] أو عرق أو إسهال أو قَيْء، فتلك علامة البُرء، وبُحرانُه[٧]

[١]وعلى آل محمد: وآله وبارك وسلم، ل.

[٢]وقد سالت: وسالت، ل.

[٣]فرش: فراش، ل؛ فرس، إ.

[٤]فيه: به، ل.

[٥]وان حدث به احد ستة: انه ان حدث به ستة، ه؛ انه خدث به احد سنة، إ.

[٦]رعاف: عارف، إ.

يكون بالرعاف وبالإسهال[١] بعد ذلك، فاختبر ما ذكره زياد واكتب إلي بما يحدث[٢] به وبحاله، وإن وجد راحة فلا يتخلف عن اللحوق بنا، فإن قلوبنا متعلقة به. ثم قال لي: هؤلاء الأطباء أتاهم هذا العلم من عقولهم أم تجارب أو وحي أو إلهام أو من أثر النبوة، فيوجب[٣] النبوة عليهم ولا نذكرهم[٤]؟

فقلت: أما التجربة في الأصول فمحال لما في ذلك من هلاك خلق[٥] وصلاح خلق وقد تبطل التجربة في قوم وتصح في آخرين، ومتى يصح هذا ويبطل هذا فبقراط[٦] يقول: العمر قصير والتجربة خطر والزمان حديد[٧] والقضاء عسر[٨] والصنعة طويلة، وقد يمكن التجربة في بعض الفروع فيستدل بالشيء[٩] على نظيره ويحكم عليه بمثل الحكم على شكله، وقد كانوا يجربون التشريح ليقفوا على حقيقة

---

[٧] البرء وبحرانه: المبرء وبحر انه، ل؛ البرء وبحران، ه؛ البراءة وبحرانه، إ.

[١] وبالاسهال: والاسهال، ل.

[٢] بما يحدث: بما تحدث، ه إ؛ ما يحدث، ل.

[٣] فيوجب: يوجب، ه ل إ.

[٤] نذكرهم: تذكرهم، ه ل إ.

[٥] هلاك خلق: الهلاك للخلق، ه ل إ.

[٦] فبقراط: وبقراط، ه ل إ.

[٧] خطر ... حديد: خطاء ... جديد، إ ه ل.

[٨] عسر: عسير، ل.

[٩] بالشيء: بشيء، ل.

العروق الضوارب وغيرها. وأما العقول فلا تؤديهم إلى علم الطب واختلاف العقاقير النافعة والقاتلة وتفاوتها في البلدان، فمنها في الهند ومنها بالأنهار / ٦٣ والبحر[١] كبحيرة طبرية والطين المختوم[٢] والطباشير والكهرباء واللؤلؤ، فهذا[٣] ما لا يوجد معرفته في العقل دون منبه عليه عليم حكيم بمنافعه وهم الأنبياء عليهم السلام. قد أطلع الله آدم على كل شيء من[٤] نافع وضار ومعدنه[٥] واسمه، وعلم آدم في الأرض موروث في يدي[٦] أمثاله من أولياء الله من ولده والأنبياء بعده.

قال: فهم أنبياء؟[٧]

قلت: هم أتباع الأنبياء، ويقال: إن إدريس عليه السلام هو الذي أظهر[٨] علم النجامة والحساب وإنه يسمى هرمس بلسان اليونانية، ويمكن أن يكون لهم أسماء عند العجم غير أسمائهم هذه

---

[١] والبحر: والبحرين، ه ل إ.

[٢] المختوم: المحتوم، ه إ.

[٣] فهذا: وهذا، ه ل إ.

[٤] من: –، ه.

[٥] ومعدنه: بمعدنه، ه.

[٦] يدي: ايدي، ه.

[٧] انبياء: الانبياء، ل.

[٨] اظهر: ظهر، ه.

عند العرب. وقد رأيت أفلاطون يذكر سقليوفس[١] صاحب التقديس ويذكر أرسطاطاليس المستجاب ويذكر سقراط واضع[٢] السير، وكانوا يعظمون مرواس[٣] الحكيم، وحكي أن أفلاطون خلّف كرداوس في الهيكل كأنما يعنى نصره.

قال: فإن كتبهم تدل على الطعن على أصحاب الشرائع وتحكيم[٤] العقول.

فقلت: قد قرأت لأبردقليس إثبات المقلّد وحاجة الخلق إليه ليقيمهم سياسة الشريعة، وذكر أن لأهل كل[٥] زمان لساناً[٦] ولكل لسان سيرة يساسون[٧] بها، وكل هؤلاء مجمعون على النسك وذم الفتنة وحضوا على الزهد واعترفوا بالعدل ونهوا عن الزنا والكذب و‹أثبتوا› تحريم القتل ونهوا عن جميع الفواحش، وقالوا: كل ما تكره فعله بك فحرام على / ٦٤ غيرك.

قال: فهل رأيت لهم صلاة؟

---

[١] سقليوفس: سفليوفس، ل؛ سفليونس، ه إ.

[٢] واضع: واضح، ه.

[٣] مرواس: بروآس(؟)، ه.

[٤] وتحكيم: وتحكم، إ.

[٥] لاهل كل: لكل اهل، ل.

[٦] لسانا: لسان، ه إ ل.

[٧] يساسون: يتاسسون، ه.

قلت: بلى، رأيت للحرنانية[١] شريعة وصلاة نسبت إلى مالك بن سنان الحرناني[٢].

فقال: تعرفها؟ إن ذلك من أهل اللسان وليس من الأوائل.

قلت: ورأيت لجالينوس كلامًا يقال فيه: إنّا امتحنا بأكل الفطير سبعة أيام في كل سنة، فدل أنه كان في شريعة موسى. وقال سقراط: من عني بطلب العلم والأدب شغله ذلك عن اكتساب الذنوب وقلّت سيئاته[٣]، وسقراط أبطل الأصنام حتى قتل على ذلك وأسقي السم، وكان قد قيل له: اهرب[٤] إلى رومية، فقال: أنا لا أدع الحق هنا، وبرومية من يكرهني. وكفاك بقول سقراط فى الباري ونفيه التشبيه، فقال إذا سئل عن الباري: ما ليس له غاية فليس له صورة، وما ليس له شخص ولا صورة[٥] فلا يحس. وقيل له: صف لنا الباري، فقال: الكلام فيما لا يدرك جهل والكلام فيما لا يبلغه الرأي خطاء.

فقال: فإنهم يقولون بقدم الهيولى والطبيعة.

فقلت: القدامة[٦] عندهم[٧] تنقسم على خمسة أقسام،

---

[١] للحرنانية: للحرساسة، ه إ.

[٢] الحرناني: الحرساس، إ ل ه، + (في الهامش) الخرساني، ل.

[٣] سيئاته: سيئته، ل.

[٤] اهرب: انه هرب + (فوق السطر) ان هرب ظ، ه.

[٥] شخص ولا صورة : صورة ولا شخص، ه.

[٦] القدامة: القدمة، ه إ ل.

[٧] عندهم: –، ل.

فالباري قديم بذاته لا لعلة غيره، والهيولى ضربان عندهم: فالهيولى الأول[١] قديم بالإضافة إلى قدم باريه وهو فوق عالم العقل وعالم النفس الناطقة وعالم النفس الحيوانية والنفس النامية، ويكون من الهيولى الثاني الاستقسات الأربع. فالهيولى الأول[٢] بعد أفعاله[٣] العقل، والدهر بعد أفعال العقل، والزمان بعد أفعال / ٦٥ الهيولى الثاني، فما بعده الدهر فغير واقع تحت الحواس وما بعده[٤] الزمان فمدرك[٥] بالحواس.

فقال لي: قرأتَ ميامير[٦] بولس؟

قلت: نعم، وهي عندي.

فاندفع في معانيها فكأنها بين يديه وأتى بها فصلاً فصلاً، وذكر أن نصرانيًا قصّها[٧] عليه. ثم ذكر كتاب بلينوس، فشرّفه وسألني عنه.

فقلت: هو عندي.

فسألني أن أريه الكتاب.

---

[١] الاول: الاولى، ه ل إ.

[٢] الاول: الاولى، ل.

[٣] افعاله: افعالها، ه ل إ.

[٤] بعده ... بعده: بعد ... بعد، ل.

[٥] فمدرك: فيدرك، ل؛ فمدروك، ه إ.

[٦] ميامير: مماميز، ه ل؛ ممامير، إ.

[٧] قصّها: نقضها، ه ل إ.

فقلت: يخالف فيه أصحاب التنجيم ويزعم أن زحلاً قام وحده يدبّر كذا وكذا، ثم صار معه المشتري.

فقال: له معان سوف تقف عليها إن شاء الله تعالى. ثم ذكر كتب[١] المنطق، فلم يحفل بها وأنكر قولهم في الممكن، فقال[٢]: كيف يكون بين الضدين معنى غيرهما؟ ومتى وجب ذلك وجب أن يكون بين الثلج والنار معنى لا نار ولا ثلج وبين الصدق والكذب وبين الحق والباطل.

فقلت له: إنما أراد بقوله: إن الأصول ثلاثة واجب كونه وممتنع كونه وممكن كونه، كالكتابة في شخص الإنسان الواحد فقد يكتب ولا يكتب، أو كالشجرة[٣] يمكن حرقها بالنار ويمكن قطعها بالحديد ويمكن قلعها بالريح، وقد يمكن إطفاء النار بالماء ويمكن بالتراب، ويمكن إيقاف النار عن طبعها آية من الله، وليس ذلك في كل زمان ولا يجري على يدي كل الناس.

فقال: ويمكن قلب الطبع[٤]؟

قلت: نعم، ولكن ليس كل ما أمكنت القدرة فيه وجب كونه. قد رأينا حوادث تحدث تحيل الطبائع عن حدها كاستحالة الدم / ٦٦ صفراء واحتراقه سوداء، وتحيل البلغم عن طبيعته أيضًا[٥] وتحيل الماء

---

[١] كتب: كتاب، + (فوق السطر) كتب، ه.

[٢] فقال: وقال، ل إ.

[٣] او كالشجرة: وكالشجر، ل.

[٤] الطبع: الطباع، ل إ.

[٥] ايضا: -، ل.

هواء، والهواء يستحيل ناراً، فوجب أن نقول بإثبات القدرة لله تعالى في قلب الطبائع وقلب الواجب إلى غيره والممتنع إلى ضده كما جاز استحالة العناصر.

قال: أفليس إذا أمكن كون الممكن قد[١] صار واجبًا، فالممكن هو الواجب أو هو[٢] الممتنع؟

فقلت: هذا إذا كان إنما يكون خاصًا[٣] في شيء بعينه لا عامًا في كل شيء، فليس كل ممكن واجبًا ولا ممتنعًا[٤] إذ ليس في الذات كون الواجب ممتنعًا أو الممتنع واجبًا والممكن واجبًا أو ممتنعًا، وهذا كان إنما يكون بمعنى من الله عز وجل.

قال: فيمكن كون الإنسان حماراً؟

قلت: يمكن، وقد مسخ الله قومًا قردة وخنازير.

فقال: ويمكن كون الحمار إنسانًا والقرد والخنزير[٥] إنسانًا؟

فقلت: إن شاء فعل، ولكن إذا مسخ الله الإنسان خنزيراً فذلك عقوبة من الله وسخط عليه، وردّه إنسانًا رحمة وفضل[٦] ورضى

---

[١] قد: فقد، ه ل إ.

[٢] او هو: وهو، ه إ ل.

[٣] خاصا: خاصة، ه إ ل.

[٤] واجبا ولا ممتنعا: واجب ولا ممتنع، ه ل إ.

[٥] القرد والخنزير: القردة والخنازير، ل.

[٦] فضل: فضلا، ل.

عنه، ويستحيل رضى الله عمن يسخط[١] عليه، وجائز أن يرده إلى أشر من الخنزير وإلى هوامّ الأرض وحشرات[٢] السباخ وهوام البحر.

فتبسم وقال لي: قرأت كتاب التناسخ للشيعة؟

فقلت: بل قرأت ذلك لهم ولغيرهم ممن يقول بالتناسخ والمسخ[٣]، والنسخ غير المسخ، والنسخ[٤] بعد الإنسانية والمسخ بعد النسخ[٥].

فقال: كيف هذا؟

فقلت: النسخ رجوع الإنسان في الإنسانية والمسخ خروجه من /٦٧ الإنسانية إلى البهيميات.

قال: ولهذا علة؟

قلت: لهم في هذا علة، يقولون: إذا كان فيه خير غالبًا على الشر عاد إنسانًا بقدرة الله تعالى، وإذا لم يكن فيه خير يرجح[٦] مسخه الله في البهائم وهو يتردد في لعنة الله وعذابه.

ثم أخذ في كتب[٧] المنطق وانهمر[٨] فيها ولعن ابن قتيبة

---

[١] يسخط: سخط، ه.

[٢] حشرات: حرشات، إ ه ل.

[٣] المسخ: النسخ، ه؛ الفسخ، إ ل.

[٤] والنسخ: والمسخ، إ.

[٥] والمسخ بعد النسخ: والنسخ بعد المسخ، ه إ.

[٦] يرجح: يرجى، ه إ ل.

[٧] كتب: كتاب، ه ل إ.

وذكر طعنه على كتب المنطق.

فقلت: ابن قتيبة من العوام وسفل الأنام، قد طعن على الشيعة، وقال: لو كانوا من الطير لكانوا رخمًا ولو كانوا من البهائم لكانوا حمراً؛ وذكر عن الشعبي أنه قال: لو أردت أن أملأ بيتي ذهبًا وفضة منهم حدّثتهم عن علي بن أبي طالب.

فقال: على ابن قتيبة لعنة الله، ما أعابهم بهذا بل مدحهم، وكفى بالعبد فضيلة إذا انقاد إلى أهل الفضل وصدق بفضائلهم وأنفق ماله عليهم، وهل على من صدق بفضل الله وأوليائه من عيب؟

ثم قلت: لو لم يحمد[١] لصاحب المنطق إلا ما ذكره من هذه الأصول الثلاثة وقضاياها وما يؤول إليه من المهمل والمحصور والمخصوص والصدق والكذب والموجب[٢] والسالب وكيف يكون اختلاف المتناقض وكيف يوضع الإبطال تلقاء الإثبات في الكلام المؤلف من اسم وحرف، فالمهمل ما لم يُبِنْ عن كل ولا بعض، والمحصور ما أبان عن الكل والبعض، والمخصوص ما خص واحداً، نقول:[٣] فلان كاتب، والمهمل: الإنسان كاتب، والمحصور: كل الناس كاتب، وما يتبع هذا من السلب والإيجاب[٤]، وما / ٦٨ يتبع ذلك من الأزمان

---

[٨] وانهمر: وانهم، ه ل.

[١] يحمد: تحمد، ه ل إ.

[٢] والموجب: والواجب، ه إ.

[٣] نقول: فنقول، ل.

[٤] وما يتبع هذا من السلب والايجاب: –، ه.

الثلاثة الماضي والمقيم والآتي، والأسوار[١] للكلام أربعة: كل ولا كل وبعض ولا واحد، وما يتولد من هذا من القضايا البسيطة والقضايا المتغيرة والقضايا المحصورة ‹والمهملة› والقضايا الاثنينية والثلاثية والرباعية ونقائضها وأضدادها[٢] وصدقها وكذبها، وقوله: إن كل مطلوب يفحص عنه بأربعة أشياء: إما هل هو موجود أو غير موجود، ثم ما هو ذلك الموجود محدوداً[٣] أو غير محدود، ثم كيف هو، ثم لِمَا هو، فهل هو من كيف هو كمثل ما هو من لِمَ هو، فهل هو وما هو بسيطان فاعلان والكيفية واللمية مركبان منفعلان، فتركيب الكيف بهل هو وتراكيب[٤] البسيط الثاني من المركب بلِمَ هو[٥]، فهل هو وكيف هو ناعتان وما هو ولِمَ هو منعوتان يفحص عنهما بالحد والجنس ‹و›يجيب عنهما المجيب من الحد والجنس كيف أحب، وتلك الأولى محصورة بنعم أو لا. وأيضاً من فضل المنطق والحاجة إليه تقاسيمه الكلام على أربعة أوجه: أمر وسؤال ومسألة وخبر، فالثلاثة ما ليس[٦] فيها صدق ولا كذب، والخبر وحده فيه الصدق والكذب.

فقال لي: المترجم غلط، إنما هو أمر وسؤال وجواب وخبر.

فاستحسنت ذلك من قوله، ثم قلت: وكفى بقوله: إن الأربعة

---

[١] والاسوار: والاصول، ل ه إ.

[٢] والقضايا الاثنينية ... واضدادها: -، إ.

[٣] محدودا: محدود، ه ل إ.

[٤] تراكيب: تركيب، ل إ.

[٥] هو: -، ه.

[٦] ليس: لهم، ل ه إ.

فيـها وجـود العشـرة التي جعلها الله أجناسًا لكل شيء، وذلك مـثل قولنا: واحد ثم اثنين ثم ثلاثة ثم أربعة، فإذا نظمت العدد على تتاليه كان / [٦٩] عشرة، فالعشرة مضمونة في عدد الأربعة، وكل شيء موجود في العشرة، وكل جوهر وعرض موجود فيـها. فالجوهر والكم والكيف والمضاف وأين ومتى ونصبة وجدة وفاعل ومفعول فـهذه العشـرة لهـا[١] أنواع وحدود، فمتى فـهـمـها المتكلم لا يخلط كلامه كـما يخلط أهل الجدل كلامهم بالمهمل والمحصور والخصوص والعموم.

فـقـال: ومـا عـيب أهل الجدل إذا فعلوا ذلك وكانت حجـتـهم حجة حق، والحجج[٢] تتصرف كتصرف اللغات؟

فـقلت: أرأيت لو أن متكلمًا ذكر حروف الرفع، هل ينبغي أن يدخل حروف الخفض معها أو يحتج بها من 〈دون〉 حروف الرفع؟

فـقـال: لا ينبـغي هذا، وربما رجعت الحروف إذا لقيـهـا[٣] ما يردّها، مثل الهاء الراجعة والزوائد الأربعة.

قلت: فكذلك معاني الكم في الكيف لأن الكم ذو عدد وهو ينقسم قسمين متصل ومنفصل، والمتصل خمسة أقسام تشترك[٤] وهي الخط والسطح والجرم والزمان والمكان، والمنفصل قسمان العدد والكلام وهمـا متـصرفـان أولاً أولاً كـمـا يوجَدان شيـئًا بعـد شيء، ولا تبـقى[٥]

[١] لها: لهم، ه.

[٢] الحجج: الحجة، ه.

[٣] لقيها: لقيتها، ه إ؛ القيتها، ل.

[٤] تشترك: مشرك، ل؛ مشترك، إ.

[٥] تبقى: يبقى، إ ل.

أجزاؤهما إلى حصور كلياتها، بل يحصره السمع ويعيه القلب ويفصله[١] اللسان، والكيف ما وجد بكليته كالبياض والسواد والقوة والضعف، والمضاف ما أضيف إلى غيره كالابن والأب والسيد والعبد، وقد يكون أحد ذاتَي المضافَين الآخر إلا أنه لا يسمى ابنًا إلا بوجود الأب ولا[٢] يقال له أب[٣] إلا بوجود الابن، وكذلك / ٧٠ السيد والعبد، والمضاف أيضًا ما دار بعضه على بعض كما يقال سيد العبد وعبد السيد، والضد لا يدور بعضه على بعض، لا يقال حار البارد ولا بارد الحار، والوجود والعدم يدور العدم على الوجود ولا يدور الوجود على العدم كما يقال أعمى البصر ولا يقال بصر الأعمى، ويقال موت الحياة ولا يقال حياة الموت، والعدم ما حل موضع الوجود كالعمى حل موضع البصر.

فقال: الظلمة والنور أضدان[٤] أم من العدم والوجود؟

فقلت: الظلمة عدم النور لأن الظلمة والنور لا يوجدان معًا كما لا يوجد الأضداد من السواد والبياض والحار والبارد، وكذلك العمى والبصر لا يوجدان معًا.

قال: فقد ترى في المكان ظلمة ونوراً.

فقلت: ظلمة ذلك عدم وصول النور إليه، ألا ترى أنّا نأخذ نور النار فندفع به الظلام، ولا نجد من يأخذ ظلمة فيدفع بها النور؟

---

[١] يفصله: يفضله، إ.

[٢] ولا: فلا، ل.

[٣] اب: ابا، إ ل ه.

[٤] أضدان: اضداد، ه ل إ.

قال: فإن الجسم ظلمة والبصر نور قد اجتمعا في مكان.

فقلت: أرأيت[1] لو كنا في ظلمة الليل، هل يرى البصر شيئًا؟ فهذا يدل على أن الجسم كله ظلمة وأن البصر موضع لقبول الشمس وغيرها من الأنوار.

قال: فقد أثبتَّ أن الظلمة موجودة والنور موجود وهما ضدان، لا عدم ووجود، فكذلك الظلمة اسم لشيء والنور اسم لشيء[2]، وما وجد اسماهما معًا فهما ضدان.

فقلت: النور اسم لذاته، إنما هو عدم لغيره.

فقال: فالأين والمتى وباقي النعوت؟ ارجع إليها.

فقلت: هذه الستة باقي النعوت، / ٧١ فالأين تركيب جوهر مع مكان، ومتى تركيب جوهر مع الزمان، والجدة تركيب جوهر مع جوهر، والنصبة تركيب جوهر مع جوهر[3]، والفاعل تركيب جوهر مع كيف، والمفعول تركيب جوهر مع كيف أيضًا.

قال: فما معنى قوله: الجوهر والعرض والجرم والجسم، ولِمَ يسمى العرض عرضًا والجسم جسمًا والجوهر جوهراً، ولم يسمى الشيء شيئًا؟

فقلت له: الجسم سمي جسمًا لما فيه من التأليف والاجتماع الطول والعرض والعمق، فالجسم هو المؤلف المركب من جوهر وعرض،

---

[1] ارايت: لو رايت، ل إ.

[2] والنور اسم لشيء: وان النور اسم لشيء، ل إ؛ -، ه

[3] والنصبة تركيب جوهر مع جوهر: -، ه.

وكل محسوس فجسم مركب من هذين، والجوهر هو القائم[١] بذاته والحامل لغيره، والعرض ما عرض في الجوهر وعرض في الجسم من الأعراض الزائلة كالخضرة والصفرة والزرقة، والله عز وجل هو المحدِث للعرض[٢] في الجوهر للذي[٣] أراد من حدوث الجسم المحسوس.

فقال: إذا حددت[٤] الجوهر أنه القائم بذاته والله قائم بذاته فقد اشتبها.

فقلت: الفرق بينهما أنه لا يقال في الله حامل ولا متأثر[٥]، ويقال في الجوهر حامل قابل للتأثير قابل للمتضادات.

قال: فما يسمى به الله؟

فقلت: جائز أن نسميه شيئًا كما سمى نفسه، ولا نسميه جسمًا لأن الجسم هو القابل للتأليف والفاعل لا يشبه فعله، ففاعل الجوهر لا يسمى جوهراً[٦] ولا عرضًا ولا جسمًا.

قال: أوَليس الشيء أيضًا فعله وخلقه؟ وقد قال: «خَالِقُ كُلِّ شَيْءٍ»[٧]، فيجب على قياسك أن لا تسميه شيئًا كما لا تسميه جوهراً.

---

[١] القائم: قائم، ه ل إ.

[٢] للعرض: العرض، ه إ ل.

[٣] للذي: الذي، ه ل إ.

[٤] حددت: حدوث، ل.

[٥] ولا متاثر: -، ه.

[٦] جوهرا: جوهر، ه.

[٧] القرآن ٦:١٠٢ و١٣:١٦ و٣٩:٦٢ و ٤٠:٦٢.

قلت: إن الشيء إثبات لذاته واسم لعينه[١]، والجسم / ٧٢ اسم لغيره في[٢] التأليف، وسمى نفسه شيئًا كما سمى نفسه حيًا وعالمًا، وإذا قلنا: لا شيء، أبطلنا الحقيقة، وكذلك إذا قلنا: لا حي ولا عالم. ألا ترى أنه من قال: لا أعبد شيئًا، فقد نفى العبادة، ومن قال: لا أعبد جسمًا ولا أعبد صنمًا، فلم ينف المعبود الحق خالق كل[٣] شيء؟ وكذلك إذا قال: لا أعلم شيئًا ولا أقدر على شيء، فقد نفى القدرة والعلم، ومن قال: لا أعلم جسمًا ولا أقدر على عتق رقبة، فلم ينف كل شيء، والشيء اسم يعم كل معلوم وكل مذكور، والجسم مخصوص للأجسام فقط.

ثم رجع إلى ذكر المنطق، فذكر الأسماء المتواطئة والأسماء المترادفة والأسماء المتشابهة والمشتقة والمتباينة وحدود ذلك كله، فتكلم عليها. وتكلم في اشتراط[٤] ‹كتاب› أنولوطيقا وتقاسيم فصوله وقضاياه، فأبدع وأجاد وسألني عن النقيض[٥] والضد والقضايا المتغايرة.

فقلت: أما القضايا المتغايرة فهي التي تتغير[٦] عن حدها

---

[١] لعينه: بعينه، ه ل إ.

[٢] في: من، ه إ ل.

[٣] كل: –، ل.

[٤] اشتراط: اشتراك، ل إ.

[٥] النقيض: المتبعض، إ.

[٦] تتغير: تستغير، ل.

الأول، فبينما هي محدودة إذ تصير لا محدودة بزيادة حروف السلب فيها، وذلك قولنا: الإنسان كاتب، قضية مهملة ممكنة ليست[١] واجبة في كل الناس، والمهمل ما لم يحصره أحد الأسوار[٢] الأربعة التي هي[٣] كل ولا كل وبعض ولا واحد، فما لم يحط به أحد هذه الأربعة فهو مهمل غير محصور. ولهذه القضية المتغيرة حدان: حد موضوع، وهو قولك: الإنسان، وحد محمول، وهو[٤] قولك: كاتب، لأنه حمل على الإنسان. فإذا ضممنا / ٧٣ إلى حدها المحمول الذي هو: كاتب، حرف لا، فقلنا: الإنسان لا كاتب، فقد تغيرت[٥] القضية عن وضعها الأول. فلذلك سميت متغايرة لتغيرها[٦] عن الوضع[٧] الأول، ومن هذه القضايا المتغيرة موجبة ومنها سالبة، فالموجبة[٨] قولنا: الإنسان ‹لا› كاتب، والسالبة: الإنسان ‹لا› لا كاتب.

قال: وقد يكون فيها سالبة جزئية وموجبة جزئية، والمتغيرة تنقسم قسمين إما موجبة وإما سالبة، والجزئية تنقسم أيضًا. فأبدع

---

[١] ليست: ليس، ه ل إ.

[٢] الاسوار: الاصول، إ ه ل.

[٣] هي: -، ه.

[٤] وهو: -، ه ل.

[٥] فقد تغيرت: هو تغيير، ه؛ هو تغيرت، ل إ.

[٦] متغايرة لتغيرها: متغيرة لتغيره، ه ل إ.

[٧] الوضع: الموضع، ه.

[٨] فالموجبة: الموجبة، ه.

وتمادى في ذكر القضايا البسيطة والمتغيرة. ثم قال: أيهما أشد تباينًا، النقيض أم الضد؟

فقلت: ما خالف القضية بالكم والكيف فهو أشد تباينًا مما يخالف بالكيف فقط، فالنقيض أشد مباينة لأنه يخالف القضية[١] من جهتين: من الكم ‹من جهة الكل والبعض› والكيف من[٢] جهة الإيجاب والسلب.

ثم صلى الظهر وأمرني بالمقام عنده، وصلينا، ثم خرج فدعاني وما قال ولا استراح، وأخذ في شرح باطن ما ذكرناه من الثلاثة والأربعة والعشرة والواجب والممكن والممتنع والعناصر[٣] وخلق الإنسان وتركيبه وعدد أوصاله وعروقه ومفاصله حتى لقد قلتَ: إنه ليعلم عدد شعره[٤]. ثم ذكر ما فيه من تشابه الأجزاء[٥] وغير متشابه[٦] الأجزاء، وذكر الأنهار وأمثالها في الإنسان، وهي العروق والجبال والسباخ، فأضاف كل شيء في الإنسان إلى ما شاكله وماثله، وذكر أنه العالم الصغير. فلم يزل يصف / [٧٤] ذلك حتى رأيت جميع ما في السماء والأرض في الإنسان. ثم ذكر الكبد والقلب والمعدة والمعاء

[١] القضية: الضد، ه ل إ.

[٢] من : ومن، ه.

[٣] والعناصر: بالعناصر، ل ه إ.

[٤] شعره: شفره، ل.

[٥] الاجزاء: الأعضاء + (فوق السطر) الأجزاء، ه.

[٦] متشابه: المتشابه، إ.

والرئتين والدماغ والقوى الطبيعية والآلية وجميع الأدوات، فوالله لو أنه بقراط واضع الطب ما زاد. ثم أشرك بين الطب وبين النجوم وبين الحساب وعلم الفلسفة الربوبيات والرياضيات[١] حتى جعلها دائرة جامعة لا يستغني بعض ذلك عن بعض[٢]. ثم ذكر العقاقير ومنابتها وأشجارها وأسماءها وصفاتها، وكأن بين يديه كتاب أسقوريدس.

ثم أبان الشريعة وفضل ما أتى به النبي[٣] محمد صلى الله عليه وآله وأن كل ما ذكره المتقدمون وحكاه الأولون وأطالوا فيه وأغمضوا[٤] من ذكر النقطة والسطح والجرم جمعه الله عز وجل لرسوله في حرف الألف، وذكر حروف المعجم، وذكر الباء والياء والكاف ولِمَ كان خط العرب مستقيمًا والخط الأول حروفًا مفردة ومقلوبًا. ثم أخذ في ذكر الشرائع وابتدأ بقول: لا إله إلا الله محمد رسول الله، فذكر ابتداءها بحرف السلب ثم الإيجاب بعد السلب وما جمع الله عز وجل لمحمد صلى الله عليه وآله في هذه الكلمة من حدود الحق وبيان الحكمة وترتيب منازل الموعظة. فرأيت رجلاً كاملاً قد جمع علومًا شتى كثيرة جمة عظيمة مع لين واسترسال وكرم معاشرة غير بخيل ولا حسود ولا مخف لمعانيه ولا ساتر لجواهر ألفاظه، إشارته بيان و بيانه إفهام. ثم

---

[١] والرياضيات: لعل الصحيح والسياسيات.

[٢] يستغنى بعض ذلك عن بعض: يستفى بعض ذلك، ل؛ يستغنى بعض ذلك، إ.

[٣] النبي: –، ه.

[٤] واغمضوا: واغمضوه، ه إ.

/٧٥ قرأ «وَلَقَدْ خَلَقْنَا الإنْسَانَ مِن سُلاَلَةٍ مِن طِينٍ» الآية[١]، وشرحها وبين معانيها ورتّبها وثبّتها وقرنها بشاهد من كتاب الله مثلها، فقرأ «أنَّا صَبَبْنَا المَاءَ صَبّاً، ثُمَّ شَقَقْنَا الأرْضَ شَقّاً فَأنْبَتْنَا فِيهَا حَبّاً وَعِنَبًا وَقَضْبًا وَزَيتُونًا وَنَخْلاً وَحَدائِقَ غُلْبًا وَفَاكِهَةً وَأبّاً»[٢]، فكانت في الترتيب كأختها، ثم أكدها وحققها بأمثالها أيضًا، قوله تعالى: «وَلَقَدْ خَلَقْنَا فَوقَكُم سَبْعَ طَرَائِقَ وَمَا كُنَّا عَنِ الخَلْقِ غَافِلِينَ»[٣] وسبعًا طباقًا وسبعًا شداداً، وكثر وأنار وأبان وسهل العسير وقرب البعيد وأتى بجوامع مراد الله في فصل الخطاب. ثم ذكر الشيطان الممدوح والشيطان المذموم والإنسان المتمرد[٤] والشياطين[٥] والإنس والجن.

وسمعت[٦] ما لم أسمع، وقلت: هذا علم يفتح علومًا وباب يفتح أبوابًا كثيرة، فقلت: الحمد لله. فقال: وما الحمد الذي لله في قيامكم وقعودكم وسرائكم وضرائكم؟ ثم قال: لا نحمل عليك ولا[٧] نكلفك الجواب إلا بعد أن تفهم، ثم أبانها، فعلمت أني لم أعقلها[٨]

---

[١] القرآن ٢٣:١٢.

[٢] القرآن ٨٠:٢٥-٣١.

[٣] القرآن ٢٣:١٧.

[٤] المتمرد: المفرد، ل ه؛ المفرود، إ.

[٥] والشياطين: والشيطان، إ.

[٦] وسمعت: فسمعت، ل.

[٧] لا: -، ه إ.

[٨] اعقلها: اقلها، ل ه إ.

بمعناها قبل ساعتى تلك، فقلت: الحمد لله حقًا، كما قلت لا إله إلا الله مخلصًا. ثم ترجحت للقيام.[١]

فقال: لا تبرح، تبيت عندنا الليلة فتؤنسنا.

فقلت: معي دابة وغلام.

فقال لأبي زاكي: مُرْ مَن يحوط الدابة والغلام، وقال لي: تمكن، فإني أرجو أن تكون الإنسان الممدوح، أنت تكون حجة / ٧٦ لله[٢]. فقبلت يده وقبل يدي، ولم يزل يتكلم في القرآن ومعانيه بنية صادقة وقلب زكي لا يلهيه شيء حتى اشتبكت النجوم، فقال: قد جاء وقت الصلاة.

قلت في نفسي: رجل شيعي تعلّم مذاهب الشيعة، وقلت: الشيعة لا تفطر حتى ترى النجوم.

فذكر كتاب يوم وليلة وأتى بجوامعه ومعانيه، وصلاة جعفر الطيار عليه السلام وما يصلّى في ليالي شهر رمضان من النوافل وأن مبلغ جميعها ألف ركعة. فجلّ في قلبي وعظم في عيني وما رأيت قبله مثله وما ظننت أني ألاقي[٣] نظيره، قد جمع كل العلوم وقرأ جميع المذاهب ونظر في مقالات المختلفين وفهم قول المؤالف والمخالف. وقام إلى بيت في المكان، فصلى، ثم دعى سليمان الخادم، فأمره بدخولي مع أبي زاكي، فدخلت، فأمر سليمان بنزع خفي فخرجت لأنزعه.

---

[١] للقيام: + لا اله الا الله محمد رسول الله علي وليّ الله، ه.

[٢] لله: الله، ه.

[٣] اني الاقي: ان للاقي، ل.

قال: اجلس مكانك، إدناء منه وكرامة وبراً. فخلع سليمان الخف وطوى الطيلسان والعمامة وأحضر الغسل في آنية الفضة. ثم قدم سفرة جديدة مذهبة، وحضرت مائدة يحملها خادمان وعليها مِكَبّ[١] خيزران قد ستر جميعها، فنزع الخادم المكب عن مآكل مختلفة بسكارج[٢] مذهبة صينية. ثم تواترت الأطعمة الحارة العجيبة الصنعة، فلم يزل الطعام يختلف إليّ بعد الروّاء[٣]، وأكثر من الحلوة[٤] الرطبة مثل اللوزنج وفالوذج[٥] السكر. ولقد كان يناولني بيده ويقول: ليس هذا أكل صائم. ثم /٧٧ تكلم على أصناف الطعام والأرايح وأصناف الطير وألوان الحيوان البري والبحري ظاهراً وباطنًا والممدوح منه والمذموم.

ثم رفعت المائدة وقدم إلينا الغسل، فغسل، ثم أردت أن أغسل ناحية، فقال لي: مكانك، فغسلت مكاني. ثم قدم سفرة جديدة غير تلك ووضع عليها أطباق كثيرة بعضها على بعض بأصناف الفواكه الرطبة، التفاح والكمثرى والعنب واللوز الطري مقشراً وسكر الطبرزذ. فذكر الفواكه واختلافها وتفاوت طعومها وهي تسقى بماء واحد، وذكر أن منها ما يؤكل ظاهره ويرمى باطنه، ومنها ما يؤكل باطنه ويرمى ظاهره، ومنها ما يؤكل ظاهره وباطنه، وعلة كل شيء من

---

[١] مكب: سكب، إ.

[٢] بسكارج: سكارج، ل إ ه.

[٣] الرواء: الزورة، ل؛ الروة، إ؛ الرواة، ه.

[٤] الحلوة: الحلو، ه إ.

[٥] اللوزنج وفالوذج: اللوزنج وغالوذج، ل؛ الزبيج وفالوذج، ه.

ذلك ومثله وباطنه. وذكر الحيوان أنه مقلوب، أيدينا رجلاه وأرجلنا يداه. وذكر الإنسان أنه كالشجر[١]، مقلوب رأسه، أصله وعروقه رأسه ورجلاه فروعه، يسقى من رأسه، والنخلة[٢] شبيهة[٣] به، إذا قطع رأسها هلكت. ثم ذكر النحل واختلاف عسلها وألوانه ومعرفتها بالرياح المؤذية لها ومعرفة النمل بإقبال الأنواء وزوالها، وذكر كثيراً من منافع الحيوان، فعلمت أنه قرأ كتاب الحيوان لأرسطاطاليس. ثم أخذ في ذكر المعادن وصفة الزجاج وأصله وأبيضه وأحمره وأصفره[٤] وقطعه وخرطه، فكأنه مع الزجاجين نشأ وفي صنائعهم كبر.

ثم رفعت المائدة وغسل يده وغسلنا. ثم أخذنا وأخذ في شرح سورة /[٧٨] يوسف عليه السلام، فسمعت ما لم أسمع ولا خطر على بال بشر، فحمدت الله تعالى على ما رزقناه من فضله ووهب لنا من إحسانه ونعمه. ثم تلا ذكر الرآت واللواميم والحواميم والتسابيح بنسق بديع وقول عجيب وأمر غريب وعبارة تزيد على الكمال والتمام. ثم قال كقول أخيه: نخشى عليك الملل، إن المستمع أشد ملالة من القارىء، فقلت: هذا غض طري لا يمل، كما قال الله تعالى: ولهم «فِيهَا مَا تَشْتَهِيهِ الأنْفُسُ وَتَلَذُّ الأعْيُنُ»[٥]، هذا «لُؤْلُؤٌ مَكْنُونٌ»[٦]،

---

[١] كالشجر: كالشجرة، ه إ.

[٢] النخلة: النخل، ل.

[٣] شبيهة: شبهة، ل.

[٤] واصفره: -، ه إ.

[٥] القرآن ٤٣: ٧١.

[٦] القرآن ٥٢: ٢٤.

فسرّه ما سمع مني ورآه من اغتباطي ونشاطي، وتزيد في كلامه إلى الساعة التاسعة من الليل.

ثم قال: لا تعلم السهر، كما قال أخوه، فإنا نحتاج إليك. ثم أمر أبا زاكي ⟨أن⟩ يرقدني في مكانه نهاراً، وأتاني برداء جديد وكساء بركان جديد، ورقد أبو زاكي قدامي فلم يلبث إلا ساعة حتى سمعته يدعو سليمان. فقام إليه أبو زاكي وسليمان، فقال لسليمان: اجعل من يجيئنا بدابة سهلة لينة نركبها، نفتقد أبا موسى ما دام غلسًا. فأحضرت الدابة وقدمت[1] إليه، وقمت إليه[2] فصبحته بالسلامة ودوام السرور، فقال: أسهرناك.

فقلت: خير ما سهرت فيه وأكثر فائدة وأحسن عاقبة. فلما ركب تخلفت به الدابة فسقط عنها، فتلقاه أبو زاكي والخدم فأخذوه، فقال: ويحكم نحن لا نركب، وعهدنا بالركوب مدة، أليس عند هؤلاء القوم حمار مصري؟ قالوا: بلى، فأتي بحمار فاره شدوا عليه وركبه، ومضى معه أبو زاكي وخادمان، / ٧٩ وبقي سليمان معي. فهجعت قليلاً، فرجع في الغلس، فصلى ورقد إلى ضاحية النهار، ثم خرج وجلس مكانه بالأمس نهاراً ورجع إلى ذكر القرآن والعلم والحكمة[3] والموعظة الحسنة. فأقمت يومي ذلك أيضًا عنده وحبسني فبت عنده، وأفطرنا معه الليلة الثانية على مثل تلك الحال وكثرة الفواكه والطعام ودوام الإقبال والبر والإكرام.

---

[1] وقدمت: تقدمت، ل.

[2] وقمت اليه: –، ه.

[3] والحكمة: –، ه.

فقلت: هذا رجل أعظم من أخيه مرتبة وإنه في الرتبة[١] بحالة في الزيادة من العلم على أخيه، ولقد كان في حسن معاشرته وكريم أخلاقه وأدبه أزيد وأكثر إكرامًا[٢] من أمسه. ولقد أحس بي فتوراً آخر النهار من اليوم[٣] الثاني، فأمر لي بشراب ورد ممرود[٤] أفطرت عليه دونه.

وقال لي: هذا فما[٥] استعددناه من المرق[٦] يقوي المعدة ويشهّي[٧] الطعام ويذيب حدة الصفراء، فانتفعت به وطعمت منه تلك الليلة أكثر مما[٨] طعمت منه قبل ذلك. فلما أصبحنا اليوم الثالث وجلس دخل[٩] إليه أبو زاكي فقال له: المروذى القاضى وأبو الحسن المطلبي وأبو الحسن الجعفري. فقال: لا[١٠]، ما يدخل إليّ أحد ولا يظهر حتى يقدم السيد والشيخ، اصرفهم، فخرجت مع أبي زاكي

---

[١] الرتبة: حال الرتبة، إ ه ل.

[٢] اكراما: اكرامه، ل.

[٣] اليوم: يوم، ل.

[٤] ممرود: مردد، ه؛ مرددا، إ ل، + (في الهامش) مورود، إ.

[٥] فما: ما، ل.

[٦] المرق: المشرق، إ ه.

[٧] ويشهي: ويشتهى، ل.

[٨] مما: ما، ه ل إ.

[٩] دخل: ودخل، ل إ.

[١٠] فقال لا: فقال لا لا، ل.

إليهم.

فقال المروذى: سألنا عنك وافتقدناك، وأعلمنا[١] أنك هاهنا، وعرفنا أنك وجدت فائدة استوحدت بها.

فقلت: تصل إن شاء الله تعالى إليها[٢] وتشركنا فيها، وتحدثت معهم قليلاً، وانصرفوا، وقلت للمطلبي: ارجع، نحتال لك في الدخول، / [٨٠] ها أنذا منتظرك[٣] في السقيفة. فأظهر المطلبي دخوله[٤] إلى حجرة قد كان أمر لنا بها أبو عبد الله فكنا نقيل فيها، فلما عاد إليّ[٥] المطلبي إلى السقيفة دخلت إلى أبي العباس، فأخرجت حديث المطلبي وإكرام السيد له وأنه إذا أتاه قام عن مكانه وأجلسه مع نفسه، وإذا دخل إليه الجعفري قعد ناحية ورمى إليه مخدة.

فقال: ولِمَ فعل هذا والجعفري أقرب إلينا؟

فقلت: بينه وبين الإمام بسجلماسة معرفة، وشمله عهده.

فأنكر ذلك.

فقلت: ما عرفتك إلا بما وقفت عليه، وقرأت كتبه إليه فيما أراد من حوائجه.

---

[١] واعلمنا: واعلمناك، ل.

[٢] اليها: -، ل.

[٣] منتظرك: ننتظرك، ل؛ انتظرك، إ.

[٤] دخوله: الدخول، ل إ.

[٥] الي: اتي، ل.

فكذب ذلك[١].

فقلت له: هو في السقيفة وحده.

فقال: قد صرفناهم، وبيننا وبين الجعفري صحبة بأطرابلس.

ثم قال لي: كأنك تحب دخوله.

فقلت: رأيك.

فقال: يدخل.

فخرجت إليه فعرفته ما جرى من ذكره.

فقال: الكتب معي حاضرة.

فدخل عليه وقام إليه، فأجلسه ناحية ورمى إليه مخدة وخرجت عنه، فدار بينهما كلام كثير إلى أن قال له: شيخ مثلك يكذب، وضاق عليه. فقال له: هذه كتبه معي، وأخرج إليه كتابين. فلما رأى الطوابع قام إليه أبو العباس مسرعًا، فعانقه وبكى بكاء شديداً وأجلسه معه في فرشه، فتحادثا إلى بعد الزوال. ثم دخلت إليه فقال لي: قد صدق وصدقت، وقد أفدتنا بفائدة، وأذن له في المجيء معي وقت ما أراد، وانصرف وانصرفت معه إلى القيروان. ودعاني أبو العباس، / [٨١] فأخرج[٢] إليّ الفياشة[٣] التي فيها شراب الورد المرود[٤] وقدحين محفورتين محكمة الصنعة. فقال: هذا ورد زيت السقمونيا وهذا بنفسج زيت السقمونيا، وأخذ قوة السقمونيا، وليس

---

[١] ذلك: -، ل.

[٢] فاخرج: واخرج، ه.

[٣] الفياشة: الغياسة، ه.

[٤] الممرود: المردود، إ ل ه.

فيه من جرم السقمونيا شيء[1] ينتفع به. فشكرته على ذلك، وأمر الخادم بحملها حتى أوصلها إلى الغلام مع الرداء الذي بت فيه والكساء البركان، وانصرفنا إلى القيروان، وكنت أتردد إليه.

فلما[2] كانت ليلة الفطر أجمع عليه أبو زاكي وسهل بن بركاس وابن القديم على أن يقعد[3] للناس يوم العيد ويدخلوا إليه، فكره ذلك وامتنع منه، فقالوا له: قعودك مما تجدد به[4] الدولة وتنفي الشناعات، قد شنع على العسكر بأخبار سمجة كرهنا أن نخبرك[5] بها، وقعودك مما يبطلها، فأجابهم إلى ذلك وأمر بإصلاح الأطعمة وشراء الغنم، فلما صلى الناس انصرفوا ودخلوا مسلمين عليه، ثم أمر لهم بالطعام فطعموا، ووعظهم وأسمعهم ووعدهم بكل فائدة من عاجل الدنيا وثواب الآخرة، وانصرف الناس حامدين ولله شاكرين على ما وهب لهم وجدده فيهم من المواعظ والخيرات والبركات. ثم انتصب للدعوة وسارع إليه وجوه الناس، وشدد شكيمة المروذي وأمره بإظهار قول آل محمد صلى الله عليه وسلام وأن لا يظهر أحد من كتب مالك

---

[1] شيء: بشيء، ه.

[2] فلما: من هنا نقل النص في عيون الأخبار، تحقيق اليعلاوي، ص ١٥٧–١٥٨؛ قارن Stern, pp. 100-01 (#1).

[3] اجمع عليه ... على ان يقعد: دخل ... الى ابي عباس اخي ابي عبد الله فسألوه ان يقعد، عيون الأخبار.

[4] به: له، ه.

[5] نخبرك: يختبرك، ه.

وأبي حنيفة شيئًا، وأمر بالفتيا حسب ما أمرني به أخوه، وقال: اجمعوا / ^٨٢ أمركم وشملكم وأصلحوا ذات بينكم تسعدوا وتفلحوا ويعل أمركم على غيركم، فسارع إليه الناس وأجابوا دعوته[١]، منهم أبو سعيد ‹بن› المعمر[٢] بن منصور الفقيه وبنو أبي المنهال والكلاعي وبنو أبي محرز القاضي وعمران بن أبي خالد[٣] وجماعة من قرابتي وإخوتي وبنو خلاد[٤] وبنو الشواذكي[٥] وبنو العراقي، وما بقي متكلم ولا ذو جدل وفقه ولا تاجر ولا راغب إلا أجاب دعوته ورغب في قربه والاتصال به، ودخل إليه وجوه البلد وفقهاء أهل الكوفة والمدينة وأصحاب الحديث. وكان يكرم ابن عبدون ويؤثره[٦] على غيره لفقهه وفهمه وعلمه بالحديث والغريب والترسيل واللغة والوثائق، ودارت بينه وبين سعيد بن الحداد وموسى القطان مجالس في الإمامة وتقديم المفضول وفي السنة ما هي وفي الصيام والإحصان. وكان يكثر ذكري معهم ويقول في غيبتي وحضوري: ما رأيت عندكم[٧] غير هذا الفتى، ما عندكم أحد مثله، فكان ابن عبدون وابن ظفر وأصحابنا ومشايخنا من العراقيين يسرهم ذلك ويقولون له: هو من أولادنا ولقد كنا نتوسم

---

[١] دعوته:انتهى هاهنا مقتبس عيون الأخبار.

[٢] المعمر: المعتمر، ل.

[٣] خالد: خلد، ه إ؛ الخلد، ل.

[٤] خلاد: اخلاد، ه إ.

[٥] الشواذكي: الشوازكي، ل.

[٦] يوثره: يوثر، ل.

[٧] عندكم: عنكم، ه.

هذه البركة ونراه بعين الزيادة والإقبال، وهذا منه تقريب لي وتنبيه عليّ وتثبيت وسياسة لغيري. وكان يحبسني كل يوم للغداء معه وكثيراً[١] كنت أبايته في الليل، فانتفعنا[٢] بعلمه وآدابه / ٨٣ منفعة[٣] لا يبيد خيرها ولا يضمحل فضلها.

ثم قدم عليه الشيخ أبو جعفر أحمد بن محمد الخزري، وكان الخزري يعظم أبا العباس ويعززه[٤] ويوقره ويقول[٥] في حين احتفال الناس عنده: هذا فيكم عصى موسى، تلقف ما يأفكون.

ولقد سألته في قرابة لنا أخذهم عقبة الرابطي بناحية قمودة. فقال لي الخزري: اقطع قريبك الرديء كما تقطع الأكلة، فإنك إن تركت الأكلة ولم تقطعها رعت وزادت حتى تقطع ما هو أجل عضو من مكانها، فقال له أبو العباس: سبحان الله، وكيف يعرف الناس فضله عندنا ومكانه منا، بل يُخلَوا له، وأمر بإطلاقهم. فشكرته على جميل قوله وفعله، وشكره كل من حضر المكان. وكان يكرم أهل دعوته ويفتقد عليهم ويأمر بحفظهم وتقريبهم ويوصي العمال والقضاة بهم، وأمرني بحفظهم وتقريبهم، فكانوا يجتمعون عندي ويختلفون إليّ، وأسمعهم كتب الفقه وفضائل آل محمد صلى الله عليه وآله، وانتسخ ذلك من عندي جماعة، وسألني نسخها لأبي دجانة قاضي أطرابلس،

---

[١] وكثيرا: وكثير ما، ل.

[٢] فانتفعنا: وانتفعنا، ل.

[٣] منفعة: منفوعا، ه.

[٤] يعززه: يعذره، ل.

[٥] ويقول: يقول، ه.

وسألني نسخها لمفرج الأطرابلسي[١] ضيف كان عنده من أطرابلس، وكان يكرمه وأنزله في حجرة القصر عنده.

وقد كنت[٢] يومًا عنده حتى دخل إليه رجلان من دعوته شكوا المروذي أنه ضربهما وشق بهما الأسواق، فضجر وضاق، واستخفه ما هاج به من الغم والاهتمام من أجلهما، ثم قال لي: /٨٤ ألا تكفيني أمر هذا، وأخذ القرطاس وكتب بعد التسمية لله عز وجل: فاء الله بك إلى طاعته، قد وقعنا معك في عجائب من هذا الأمر، أبحت ظهور المؤمنين وهتكت حرمتهم وزعمت أنهما رديئان مؤذيان، فقد قلت كما قال الأولون لنوح عليه السلام: «وَمَا نَرَاكَ اتَّبَعَكَ إِلاَّ الَّذِينَ هُم أَرَاذِلُنَا بَادِيَ الرَّأْيِ»[٣] و«قَالُوا أَنُؤْمِنُ لَكَ وَاتَّبَعَكَ الأَرْذَلُونَ»[٤]، وقد أخبر الله عز وجل عن قول أعدائه وشغلهم بأوليائه وهم في عذابه، والنار تلفح وجوههم: «وَقَالُوا مَا لَنَا لاَ نَرَى رِجَالاً كُنَّا نَعُدُّهُم مِنَ الأَشْرَارِ»[٥]. وسواء عندنا من يقطع صلاة وصيامًا ثم زنى البارحة وأصبح تائبًا، فلا تغترن بالدنيا، فكثير ممن عرف فضل هذا البيت ثم صدف[٦] عنهم وعاد إلى غير الواجب «وَمَا اللهُ بِغَافِلٍ عَمَّا

[١] لمفرج الاطرابلسي: المفرج الاطرابلسي، ه؛ لمفرح الاطرابلس، ل.

[٢] عنده وقد كنت: عند وكنت، إ.

[٣] القرآن ١١:٢٧.

[٤] القرآن ٢٦:١١١.

[٥] القرآن ٣٨:٦٢.

[٦] صدف: صرف، ل.

تَعْمَلُونَ»[١]، وقد قيل لعيسى عليه السلام لِمَ دعوت الجبّائين والخطّائين[٢] ولم تدع الفقهاء والعلماء؟ فقال: إذا كان الفقهاء لا يجيبوننا والجبّاؤون والخطّاؤون[٣] يجيبوننا لا ندعوهم،[٤] فمن ندعو؟ وإنما نحن مؤدبون ومعلمون، فمن استقام لتعليمنا رفعناه وأحييناه ومن لم يستقم لتعليمنا رفضناه، نبلغ بمن دعوناه غاية الأدب لنا، ونحن نأمرك من اليوم أن لا تنظر في أحد صار معنا إلا بعد أن تطالعنا فيه، فقد تركنا النظر في ما أقلقنا من فعلك في هؤلاء والسلام.

فأوصلت الكتاب إليه وأخذته عندي، وكان في كتبي مضمونًا حتى ذهب[٥] / ٨٥ فيما ذهب لنا في أيام الدجال عليه غضب الله.

وكان الشمل مجتمعًا والصدع ملتئمًا والفضل واسعًا والعلم مطلوبًا والراغب كثيراً وكلمة الحق عالية وقول المؤمنين مقبولاً ونصيحة المؤمن معجولاً بها، فكم من[٦] مال وصل بأسبابهم من نهب رقّادة

---

[١] القرآن ٢:٧٤، ٨٥، ١٤٠، ١٤٩ و ٣:٩٩. تعملون: يعملون، ه.

[٢] الجبائين والخطائين: الجنانين والحطابين، ه ل؛ الجنانين والخطائين، إ.

[٣] الجباؤون والخطاؤون: الجنانون والحطابون، ه ل؛ الجنانون والخطابون، إ.

[٤] ندعوهم: ندعهم، إ.

[٥] ذهب: + لنا، ه.

[٦] من: –، إ.

وغير ذلك، وكم من[١] منافق ظهروا عليه وأظهروا من استتر من آل الأغلب، فكم ‹من› قتيل وأسير، وما كنا نسمع للنساء[٢] حينئذ صيتًا وللجبابرة والساسة[٣] ذكراً ولا فخراً ولا لمالك[٤] وأصحابه رجاء ولا لغيره معنى، قد استعلى الحق وظهر وانكتم الباطل وحقر، فبين مضروب ومهتوك ومخاف ومهجور ومحقور[٥].

فلما نفذت أخبار السيد المرفوض وهمزوا وتنفسوا ثبت على رجلين أنهما أظهرا بعض ما يخفيانه من الغل والحسد نطقًا بفضل معاوية على سيد البشر وأن عليًا صلوات الله عليه خرج إلى حرب معاوية وطلب الإمامة وأن طالب الإمارة لا حَقّ له على المطلوب. فأمر بقتلهما فربْطهما إلى ذنبي بغلين يجرّان بالقيروان، فقتلا وفعل بهما ذلك ونودي عليهما. ولقد عارض الجعفري في أحدهما، وهو المعروف بابن الهذيل، وسأل فيه قبل قتله، فزجره الخزري وأسمعه كلامًا يقبح إعادته، فارتدع كل من طمح واكتتم كل من ظهر ورجعوا أذلة خاسئين. ولقد كانت كتب مالك وأبي حنيفة تباع من الأطباء والصيادلة والعطارين يربطون / ٨٦ فيها استخفافًا بها واستحقاراً لها وإياسًا من الانتفاع بشيء منها، وأرسل منها شيء إلى الأندلس وإلى المشرق.

---

[١] من: –، ه.

[٢] للنساء: بالنساء، ه.

[٣] الساسة: السياسة، إ.

[٤] فخرا ولا لمالك: فخر ولا مالك، إ.

[٥] ومهجور ومحقور: ومقهور ومهجور، ل؛ وبجهور وبحقور، إ.

فلم نزل في مثل ذلك من النعيم والمقام الكريم حتى ورد[١] كتاب أخيه بوصول مولانا عليه السلام إلى إيكجان بكتامة موطن[٢] الدين ومعدن الإيمان، فتجهز للخروج إليه، فانفلق الإصباح وظهر الفجر وجاء النهار وذهب الليل وابتهجت النفوس وأنارت القلوب لورود خبره، فيا لها من[٣] فرحة لا تُنسى[٤] وضياءٍ لا يطفأ ونور لا يخفى، ذلك الذي لم يخف فضله و«جَاءَ الحَقُّ وَزَهَقَ البَاطِلُ»[٥]، وغارت النجوم فظهر[٦] الحي القيوم. فخرج وخرجنا معه، فلقيه بفج سبيبة، فلا أنسى طلعته السعيدة وبهجة نوره وضياء وجهه وعلو قدره وكمال خلقه وبهائه في فجره[٧]، فلو قلتُ: إن الأنوار المضيئة خلقت من فضل نوره، لقلتُ حقًا يقينًا وصدقًا مبينًا، فنزل إليه صلوات الله عليه وقبل الأرض وتمعّك بين يديه، ونزل إليه أخوه أبو عبد الله وجميع الأولياء من كتامة وغيرهم من أتباعهم، ولم يبق راكب إلا أمير المؤمنين صلوات الله عليه الشمس المنيرة، والقمر الزاهر والنور الباهر

---

[١] ورد: من هنا نقل النص في عيون الأخبار، تحقيق اليعلاوي، ١٦٩-١٧٠؛ قارن Stern, pp., 101-02 (#2).

[٢] موطن: موضع، عيون الاخبار.

[٣] من: -، ه إ وعيون الاخبار.

[٤] تنسى: يتناهى، إ.

[٥] القرآن ١٧: ٨١.

[٦] فظهر: وظهر، إ ل وعيون الاخبار.

[٧] فجره: فخره، ل وعيون الاخبار.

أبو القاسم، فهما صلوات الله عليهما كانا نور الدنيا، ومولانا أبو القاسم خلف المهدي صلوات الله عليه. فسلم أبو عبد الله على أخيه وقربني أبو عبد الله إلى مولانا عليه السلام وقال له: يا مولانا، هذا الذي عرفتك بخبره بسجلماسة، وتكلم أبو العباس وشكر / [٨٧] وأثنى. فلا أنسى قول مولانا صلوات الله عليه: أحسن الله إليك وبارك لنا فيك وشكر سعيك، أنتم شيعتنا حقًا وأهل ولايتنا ومن أحبنا قديمًا. ثم ركب الناس ومشى أمير المؤمنين عليه السلام[١]، وقرب أبا العباس إلى نفسه وأمرني بمسايرته، فأشرقت الأرض بنوره، وشرقت[٢] الدنيا بحلوله، وفضل المغرب بكونه فيه وملكه إياه.[٣]

فكنا في نعم تترى محمودة الأوائل مغبوطة الأواخر في عز عزيز وقرار مكين مع عليم حكيم وملك حليم ورؤف بالمؤمنين رحيم «فِي ظِلٍ مَمْدُودٍ وَمَاءٍ مَسْكُوبٍ وَفَاكِهَةٍ كَثِيرَةٍ لا مَقْطُوعَةٍ وَلا مَمْنُوعَةٍ»[٤]، وكنا مع مشايخ كتامة ودعاتهم وعلمائهم وأهل الديانة[٥] من رجالهم على «فُرُشٍ مَرْفُوعَةٍ»[٦] «وَأَكْوَابٌ مَوْضُوعَةٌ

---

[١]ومشى امير المؤمنين عليه السلام: حرك امير المؤمنين عليه السلام دابته للمسير، عيون الأخبار.

[٢]شرقت: اشرقت، ل.

[٣] إياه: هاهنا انتهى مقتبس عيون الأخبار.

[٤] القرآن ٥٦: ٣٠-٣٣.

[٥] الديانة: الديانات، ه.

[٦] القرآن ٥٦:٣٤.

وَنَمَارِقُ مَصْفُوفَةٌ[١] وَزَرَابِيُّ مَبْثُوثَةٌ» [٢] «فِي سِدْرٍ مَخْضُودٍ وَطَلْحٍ مَنْضُودٍ وَظِلٍّ مَمْدُودٍ وَمَاءٍ مَسْكُوبٍ» [٣]، نشرب عندهم «بِكَأْسٍ مِن مَعِينٍ بَيْضَاءَ لَذَّةٍ لِلشَّارِبِينَ» [٤] لا لغو فيها ولا تأثيم بين «سُنْدُسٍ وَإِسْتَبْرَقٍ مُتَّكِئِينَ» [٥] نجني من ثمار فكرهم ونتنسم من روائح زهرهم ما عظمت عندي منفعته وجلت عائدته، فرحمة الله على جميع المؤمنين الموقنين الموفين بعهدهم[٦] الصابرين، والله رؤوف رحيم[٧] بنا وبهم أجمعين.

فما منهم داع مطلق إلا وقد سمعت منه بإذن الشيخ أبي موسى، واجتنيت من ثمارهم ظاهرة وباطنة، وما منهم أحد إلا وقد نزل عندي ودخل داري، وما[٨] أنسيت فلا أنسى / ٨٨ داعي ملوسة وشيخ الجماعة وفقيهها أفلح بن هارون العباني[٩]، فقد كان جمع مع الدعوة

---

[١] ونمارق مصفوفة: -، ه إ.

[٢] القرآن ٨٨:١٤-١٦.

[٣] القرآن ٥٦:٢٨-٣١.

[٤] القرآن ٣٧:٤٥-٤٦.

[٥] القرآن ١٨:٣١.

[٦] بعهدهم: يعهدهم، ل.

[٧] رحيم: -، ل.

[٨] وما: من هنا نقل النص في عيون الأخبار، تحقيق اليعلاوي، ٢١١-٢١٣؛ قارن Stern, pp., 102-04 (#3).

[٩] العباني: العبادتي، إ؛ العباسي، عيون الأخبار.

علوم الفقه وأدرك أبا معشر والحلواني[١]، وكان يحدث عنهما عن الحلبي، وكنت كثير الاجتماع معه والدخول إليه، ونزل عندي مراراً كثيرة ونسخ كثيراً[٢] من كتب الفقه والآثار والفضائل وخطب مولانا وسيدنا أمير المؤمنين علي بن أبي طالب صلوات الله عليه وعلى الأئمة من ولده[٣]، وسمعت عنده دعوة النساء وما يخاطبهن به من الدلائل التي تقبلها عقولهن ويحفظنها. وكان يقول: «فَلِلَّهِ الحُجَّةُ البَالِغَةُ»[٤]، قال: هي الحجة التي يخاطب بها[٥] العالم من علمه ويخاطب به الجاهل من حيث يعقل. ولقد كان يخاطب المرأة ويقيم لها الدليل[٦] من حليها وخاتمها وقرطها وتاجها وخناقها وخلخالها وسوارها وثوبها وعجارها، ثم من المغزل والمنسج واللباس والشعر وغيره مما هو من خلقة[٧] النساء. وكان يخاطب الصانع من صناعته ويخاطب الخياط من إبرته وخيطه وخِلْقته ومِقَصّه، ويخاطب الراعي من عصاه وكسائه وقرنه وكُرْزيته[٨]. فما أعرف اليوم من يفي بهذا

---

[١] والحلواني: الحلواني، ه.

[٢] كثيرا: كتبا كثيرا، ل.

[٣] وعلى الائمة من ولده: -، ل.

[٤] القرآن ٦:١٤٩.

[٥] بها: به، إ ل.

[٦] الدليل: الدلائل، ل.

[٧] خلقة: حلية، عيون الأخبار.

[٨] قرنه وكرزيته: فرقه وكرزيته، ه؛ قِرقه وكرزه، عيون الأخبار.

ولا من يقوم به قيامي ولا من يحفظه حفظي، كل ذلك بتوفيق ربي وخالقي والمنعم عليّ ورازقي. فرحمة الله عليه، فلقد كان في كلامه إذا تكلم خاشعًا لله مريداً ما عند الله رقيق القلب غزير الدمعة رطب اللسان، يذكر / ٨٩ الله خشوعًا ومتذللاً عطوفًا، وإني لأحفظ من أمثاله ووصاياه لي[١] أنه قال: إياك واحذر أن تثق بأحد حتى يتمكن، فإذا تمكن ظهر منه ما يسر وما يعلن[٢].

ولقد بلغني أن أمير المؤمنين المهدي بالله صلوات الله عليه بلغه عن أفلح حسن صوت وجودة قراءة وصدق نية، وكان قد كلفه النظر[٣] في القضاء بالمهدية وبرقادة وغيرها من جميع عمله، وكان تقيًا نقيًا زكيًا ورعًا عفيفًا، فوجه في طلبه اشتياقًا إليه، وأمر البوابين بدخوله راكبًا إليه، وكان أمير المؤمنين عليه السلام حينئذ متخلفًا في بعض علله،[٤] فدخل عليه حتى نزل على باب الحرمة في القصر الكبير، فأدخل إليه، وقربه ورحب به واستدعاه للكلام، فأجله، وعظم ذلك عليه، فأذن له في الكلام فتكلم. ثم قال له[٥] أمير المؤمنين صلوات الله عليه: اسكت، فسكت وتكلم أمير المؤمنين عليه السلام وأفلح يشهق بالبكاء حتى علاه النحيب، وسمع من المهدي صلوات الله عليه ما جل موقعه وكبر في مسامعه، فمعك خديه بين يديه ورغب

---

[١] وصاياه لي: وصاياه، ل؛ وقضاياه، عيون الأخبار.

[٢] ما يسر وما يعلن: السر في العلن، عيون الأخبار.

[٣] كلفه النظر: كفلة لنظر، ل.

[٤] متخلفا ... علله: مختلفا ... علله، ل؛ متخلفا ... عمله، عيون الأخبار.

[٥] له: -، ل.

إليه أن يدعو له بالموت.

فقال: ويحك ولِمَ؟

قال: يا مولاي، أحللتني[1] منك محلاً جليلاً، وهذا مقام كريم، وكلام مكنون «لا يَمَسُّهُ إلاَّ المُطَهَّرُونَ»[2]، وأخاف الزلل على نفسي، فموتي بهذه الطهارة أزكى موضعًا وأجل مقامًا، فسألتك يا مولاي بالعظمة إلا دعوت لي.

فقال المهدى: يا أفلح، لا تفجعني بنفسك.

فقال: يا مولاي، عند[3] الله الملتقى.

فبكى المهدي عليه السلام وقال له: خار الله لك. / ٩٠

وخرج أفلح ذلك اليوم وقعد وهنأناه بما بلغنا من هذا، وذكر لنا بعض ذلك. وتوفي ذلك الشهر، رحمة الله عليه ورضوانه.[4]

فبينما[5] نحن في تلك الأحوال الرضية والمقامات الزكية إذ نعق فينا ناعق البين ومزعج الأقدار، فاختلفت علينا طوارق الليل والنهار، فتشتّتت الكلمة وكثرت الأهواء، واختلفت الآراء وتدابرت الأمور، ووقع الخوف المحذور، فاضمحلت العزائم ومازج الضلال الهدى والشك اليقين إلا من عصم الله من المخلصين، وعلت الفتن، فوصل بقايا رجال بني الأغلب إلى محبوبهم من الشتات والفرقة والتهريب

---

[1] احللتني: حللتني، ه.

[2] القرآن ٥٦:٧٩.

[3] عند: اعند، ل.

[4] رضوانه: انتهى هاهنا مقتبس عيون الأخبار.

[5] فبينما: فبينا، ه.

وإلى مرادهم من الخبال[١] والفتنة. فانقطعت تلك المشارب، وتوقدت نيران الحرب، وتواترت تلك المكاره، وعطلت العشار، «وَهُدِّمَت صَوَامِعُ وَبِيَعٌ وَصَلَوَاتٌ[٢] وَمَسَاجِدُ يُذْكَرُ فِيهَا اسْمُ اللهِ كَثِيراً»[٣]، وغاضت الأنهار، وانكدرت النجوم ،وانقطع[٤] الغيث، وتغيرت شمس النهار، وكثر الغمام وتكاثُفُ السحاب وحلول الزلازل والإظلام، وتواترت الصواعق والبروق والرعود. وأخر الله مدتي حتى رأيت من الزمان عجائب، ولقد أحسن الذي يقول:

قَدْ كُنْتُ آمُلُ أنْ أمُوتَ ولا أرَى فَوْقَ المَنَابِرِ من أمَيَّةَ خَاطِبا
فَاللهُ أخَّرَ مُدَّتِي وَتَطَاوَلَتْ حَتَّى رَأَيْتُ مِن الزمَانِ عَجَائِبا

وأقول كما قال الأول:

أبَتْ هِمَّتِي إلاّ سُمُوّاً إلَى العُلَى وَإنْ طَأطَأتْ رَأسِي صُرُوفُ الحَوَادِثِ
/ ٩١

فركبنا الأهوال، وذقنا بعد مولانا المهدي صلوات الله عليه حلو الدهر ومره، وتصرفنا في شطريه، وكنا كما قال ابن دريد:

---

[١] الخبال: الخيال، ل إ.

[٢] وصلوات: -، ه.

[٣] القرآن ٢٢: ٤٠.

[٤] انقطع: انقطعت، ه إ ل.

لَوْ كَانَتْ[1] الأحْلامُ نَاجَتْني بما ... أَلْقاهُ يَقْظانَ لأصمَانِي الرَّدَى
إنْ يَحْمِ عَن عَيني البُكَا تَجَلُّدِي ... فَالْقَلْبُ مَوْقُوفٌ عَلى سُبْلِ البُكَا
فَإنْ أَمُتْ فَقَدْ تَناهَتْ مُدَّتِي ... وكُلُّ شَيْءٍ بَالِغِ الحَدِّ انْتَهَى
ما كُنْتُ أدْرِي وَالزَّمانُ مُولَعٌ ... بِشَتِّ مَلْمُومٍ وتَنْكِيثِ[2] قُوَى
رَضِيْتُ قَسْراً وَعَلَى القَسْرِ[3] رِضىَ ... مَنْ كَانَ ذَا سُخْطٍ عَلَى صَرْفِ القَضَا
إنِّي حَلَبْتُ[4] الدَهْرَ شَطْرَيْه فَقَدْ ... أَمَرَّ لي حِينًا وَأَحْيانًا حَلا
لَوْ لامَسَ الصَّخْرَ الأصَمَّ بَعْضُ[5] ما ... يَلْقاهُ قَلْبِي فَضَّ أصْلادَ الصَّفَا

وأما اليوم فنحن نقول كما قال الأولون:

زَمَانٌ يَمُرُّ وَعَيشٌ يَضُرْ ... وَدَهْرٌ يَكُرُّ بِمَا لا يَسُرْ
وَوَجْدٌ مُقِيمٌ وَهَمٌّ مَقِيتٌ ... وَدُنيَا تُنَادِيكَ أَنْ لَيسَ حُرْ
وَأَحْسَنُ مَا اسْتَعْمَلَ المؤمنو ... نَ عِنْدَ النَّوائِبِ حِلْمُ الصُّبُرْ[6]

---

[1] كانت: كان، ل.

[2] تنكيث: تنقيص، ه.

[3] قسرا وعلى القسر: قصرا وعلى القصر، ه.

[4] حلبت: جليت، إ؛ حليت، ه ل.

[5] بعض: ببعض، ه.

[6] الصبر: وصبر، إ ه ل.

وأقـــول: يا ليت شـــعـــري، وهل في ليت من طمع،[١] هل يسعدني من الأيام ما فيها، توكلت على الله عز وجل، وأيقنت أن أعلى المراتب تعود[٢] والخيرات تزيد بالاعتصام بأئمة الهدى صلوات الله وسلامه عليهم والتسليم إليهم والرضى بأمرهم في السراء والضراء وفي الشدة والرخاء، فبهم تتم النجاة في اليوم الموعود عند الديان / ٩٢ مع الشاهد والمشهود. فنحن على ذلك حتى خرج ابن الإمام وزين الأنام[٣] وزينة الأيام لصلاح ما قد فسد وكشف ما استتر وإنارة ما أظلم وعمارة ما خرب، فقطع ما سول وحصد ما أنبت حتى أزهر[٤] الحق، وأضاء الفجر[٥]، وانكشفت تلك الظلمة، ولم يزل الله عز وجل يبتلي عباده بالسراء والضراء محنة واختباراً وللذي[٦] أراده وعلمه، فاظهره الله على الدين حتى رفع مناره وشدد أركانه وثبت مراسيه[٧] ووطد[٨] دعائمه وأوهن قوى من حادّه[٩] وهدم أركانهم وأطفأ نيرانهم

[١] من طمع: نطمع، إ.

[٢] تعود: قعود، إ ه.

[٣] وزين الانام: -، إ.

[٤] ازهر: اظهر، ه.

[٥] الفجر: الحق، ه.

[٦] للذي: الذي، ه ل إ.

[٧] مراسيه: مراسمه، ل إ.

[٨] ووطد: وركد ووطد، إ ل ه.

[٩] حاده: جاده، ل.

وجاهد من ضل بمن اهتدى حتى أعز الله الدين، وفلح[١] بأولياء الله، فرجعوا بعد القهقرى وأقبلوا بعد الإدبار ودانوا بقوله وأذعنوا بعد الامتناع، وأيد الله بهم الدين وهدم بنيان المنافقين وأصلح لوليه بهم الفساد وأحيى بهم العباد، وظهرت سبل الحق للمؤمنين، وأنار الهدى للمهتدين والمسترشدين. والحمد لله رب العالمين ولعنة الله على الظالمين من الأولين والآخرين، وصلى الله على محمد النبي وعلى الأئمة من آله الطاهرين الأخيار المنتجبين صلاة دائمة متصلة[٢] إلى يوم الدين.

كمل كتاب المناظرات والحمد لله رب العالمين وصلى الله على محمد خاتم النبيين وسيد المرسلين وعلى أخيه ووصيه علي بن أبي طالب أشرف الوصيين وعلى الأئمة من ذريتهما الطيبين الطاهرين وعلى سيدنا ومولانا ومالكنا[٣] ومالك أمورنا[٤] والحبل الممدود الذي /٩٣ أمرنا بالتمسك به الإمام من ذرية الإمام[٥] الطيب أبي القاسم أمير المؤمنين صلوات الله عليه وعلى آبائه الطاهرين وأبنائه الأكرمين المنتظرين إلى يوم الدين وسلم عليهم أجمعين وحسبنا الله ونعم الوكيل.

---

[١] وفلح : وفلج، ه إ.

[٢] متصلة: متصلا، ه إ.

[٣] ومالكنا: -، ه إ.

[٤] امورنا: امرنا، ه إ.

[٥] من ذرية الامام: -، ل إ.

الفهارس

١ - الاعلام

٢ - الجمعات والفرق

٣ - الاماكن

٤ - الكتب